RAJESH KADIAN is an Indian-born medical specialist in practice in the United States. He has followed the evolution of relations between the countries of South Asia and the United States from close quarters for a number of years.

His previous books on the Indian Army, the experiences of the Indian Peacekeeping Force in Sri Lanka, an analysis of the Kashmir dispute, and about Indian interests in Tibet were all critically acclaimed. In addition, Dr. Kadian has written for a number of other books and encyclopedias.

Five years of extensive research has gone into the making of this book. It is a unique work with a holistic approach towards American ties to the countries of the South Asia.

Concise Encyclopedia of United States South Asia Relations

Rajesh Kadian

VISION BOOKS
(Incorporating Orient Paperbacks)
New Delhi • Mumbai • Hyderabad

www.visionbooksindia.com

ISBN 10: 81-7094-740-5
ISBN 13: 987-81-7094-740-0

First Published in 2009 by
Vision Books Pvt. Ltd.
(Incorporating Orient Paperbacks and CARING Imprints)
24 Feroze Gandhi Road, Lajpat Nagar-III
New Delhi-110024, India.
Phone: (+91-11) 2983 6470: 2983 6480
Fax: (+91-11) 2983 6490
e-mail: visionbk@vsnl.com

Printed at
Rashtra Rachna Printers
C-88, Ganesh Nagar, Pandav Nagar Complex
Delhi-1100092, India.

Contents

Preface 7

Introduction 9

Encyclopedia Entries 19

Bibliography 289

Appendices:

Appendix I: Major Political Parties and Regional Institutions in South Asia 330

Appendix II: Systems of Governance in South Asia 334

Appendix III: Significant Economic Entities and Terms 339

Glossary 343

Index 347

Preface

For the United States, the most traumatic event in the new millennium was the terrorist bombings of the twin towers of the World Trade Center in New York City and of the Pentagon building in the Washington metropolitan region on 11 September 2001. In the United States the date and the event are widely referred to as 9/11. Accordingly, the numerals are used in that context throughout the book.

Afghanistan has played a very large role in the shaping of American relations with South Asia since the Soviet military intervention in that country in 1979; more so after 9/11. Hence, the number of entries pertaining to Afghanistan is relatively large.

The author is deeply indebted to Dr. Stephen Cohen and Dr. Harold Gould for their inputs; to Dr. Surjit Mansingh and Dr. Jon Woronoff, who suggested the project and gave it direction, to Kapil Malhotra and staff at Vision Books for their consistent professionalism and good humor. In closing, I must mention the unstinted support and understanding from my wife, Preeti, who coped with the long hours that inevitably go into the writing of any book.

RAJESH KADIAN

Introduction

The year 2007 marked the 400th anniversary of the first permanent British settlement in North America at Jamestown in Virginia. Less than a year later, in 1608, on the other side of the globe, the first ship to establish the British presence in India reached the port of Surat in the northwest of the subcontinent. The two regions were thus tenuously linked for the first time. However the two regions were later linked a bit more substantively through a third entity, England. Since then, direct relations have evolved slowly and often as a consequence of developments elsewhere on the globe. In the early phases, the ties were not just trilateral for aggressive British mercantilism had created a quadrilateral involving Britain, North America, Africa, and India. It was based on slavery and textiles. Slaves from Africa, bound for the Americas were clad in cheap, comfortable, and sturdy Indian cotton instead of the more expensive and coarse English wool. In addition, a substantial demand had developed for fine Coromandel textiles ranging from handkerchiefs to bed-linens for both planters in the south and merchants in the north in the British colonial settlements along the eastern seaboard of the North American continent. Inevitably, spices and gemstones were also imported by the increasingly prosperous and cosmopolitan European colonies along the new world's eastern coast.

A hundred years later, around 1707, the character of quadrilateralism changed. The union between England and Scotland greatly strengthened the small island in the North Sea. The same year, the last great Mughal emperor of India, Aurengzeb Alamgir, died. His death was followed by the precipitous decline and slow disintegration of the Mughal Empire. Two years later, much further north the Russians dealt a crushing blow to the Swedes at the battle of Poltava in the snows of the Ukraine. As a result the great Eurasian giant, Tsarist Russia, emerged as an expansionist new power. Though the tsars sought close ties with Western Europe, the expansion of the Russian empire was eastwards with the focus being on Great Plains of Central Asia and the wealth in the wilderness of Siberia. In a reversal of fortunes, the former vassals in Moscow now threatened bonds long steeped in time, trade, kinship, and war between the Khanates of Central Asia and the Indian subcontinent. Meanwhile, a distinct American cultural identity was evolving. Accordingly, new institutions of higher learning were emerging in the new world. A striking example was in the small town of New Haven, Connecticut where the American-born retired English Governor of Madras, ELIHU YALE, among the first of the new rich from the Eastern trade, bequeathed Indian textiles including muslins, calico, poplins, and silk crepe for the institution. The sale of these items raised enough funds that the institution honoured Yale by naming itself after him. Hence, Yale University was born. For the next 150 years, quadrilateralism was marked by the rise of Britain and Russia as great powers; the subjugation of the Indian subcontinent by London, and by increased awareness of the religious, philosophical, and cultural traditions of the subcontinent by Americans, a people, only marginally tainted by the arrogance of the conqueror. The increased sensitivity was to inspire a great deal of useful missionary work by Americans across the sub-continent. During the 171 years of British rule in India and the comparable years of American independence (1776-1947) there were thirty-two British Governors-general and viceroys in India. The United States had just as many Presidents.

A pivotal year in the relationship was 1917. That year the United States shed its remaining constraints of isolationism and joined World War I on the side of Britain. India, though a dependency, too, was an active participant in the conflict. President Woodrow Wilson's landmark Fourteen Points speech was the only explicit statement about war aims made by any of the major combatants. Wilson's speech included references to other foreign policy objectives like free trade, open agreements, democracy and self-determination for subject peoples. Britain, too, faintly supported some of Wilsonian aspirations when Edwin Montagu, the Secretary of State for India, declared that August:

> "The policy of His Majesty's Government, with which the Government of India are in complete accord, is that of the increasing association of Indians in every branch of the administration and the gradual development of self-governing institutions, with a view to the progressive realisation of responsible government in India as an integral part of the British Empire. I would add that progress in this policy can only be achieved by successive stages. The British government and the government of India, on whom the responsibility lies for the welfare and advancement of the Indian peoples, must be the judges of the time and measure of each advance, and they must be guided by the co-operation received from those upon whom new opportunities of service will thus be conferred and by the extent to which it is found that confidence can be reposed in their sense of responsibility."

This vaguely couched and reluctantly made commitment in 1917 set the stage for Indian independence. The other monumental event in 1917 was the Communist revolution in Tsarist Russia. The Bolshevik revolution introduced a new paradigm: A European power that was actively anti-colonial and replaced the credo of innately superior white race with the doctrine of the equality of all races, some more oppressed than others. In the aftermath of World War I, agents from the Comintern (the international Communist organization founded in Moscow in 1919 to further the spread of communism. It was dissolved in 1943) were active in pro-independence movements in India. Other Indians were more influenced by the idealism of Wilson's vision of the post-war world for the U.S. President's speech reflected the attractive reality of American soft power. Joseph Nye who coined the term much later, defined soft power as "the ability to get what you want through attraction rather than coercion or payments." This concept slowly dominated both the Indian subcontinent as well as Britain, the fading imperial power. American soft power was characterized by the glamor of Hollywood, the vitality of America's universities, the widely shared taste for the country's fast-foods and fizzy drinks, the availability of the automobile for the masses, the

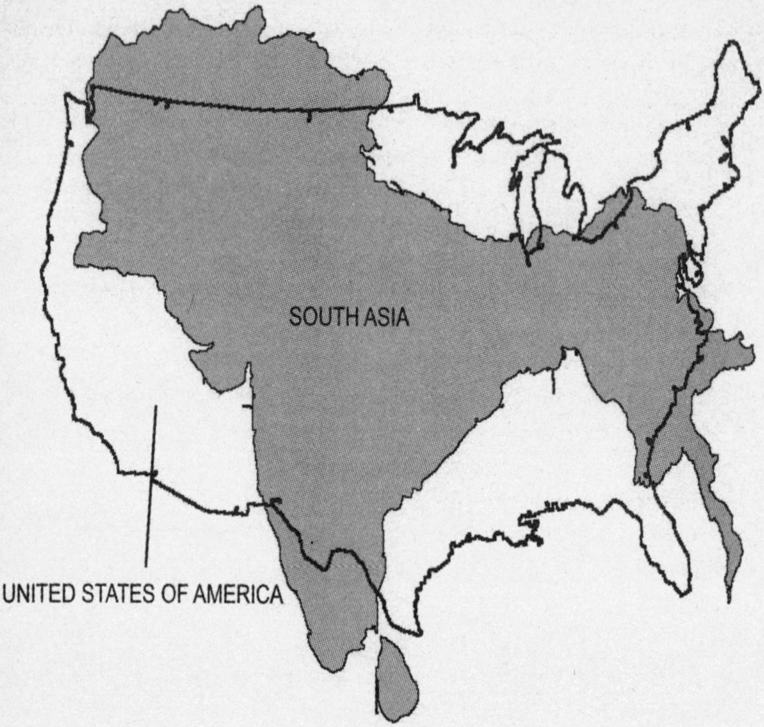

Relative Sizes of the United States (48 Contiguous States) and South Asia

egalitarian can-do spirit of the citizenry, etc. In addition, unlike the heavy-handed colonial regimes in South Asia, Americans clearly were notunder the yoke of a big and intrusive government (prohibition being a sad and notable exception). Hence soft power contributed greatly to its own credibility, dynamism, innovation, and a distinctly American personality. The great depression of the 1930s and the rise of competing totalitarian states like Germany did little to dampen it. World War II further coalesced the social and cultural phenomena with political and strategic functions as the U.S. became "the leader of the free world" and the "arsenal of democracy."

By the late 1940s, a new quadrilateral was predominant in international ties with South Asia. Both the new cold war super-powers, the U.S. and the Soviet Union, independently and collectively impacted the region. There were two other parts of the quadrilateral. One was the big, recently divided, secular, predominantly Hindu, poverty-stricken, and unconfident India with its own reservoir of soft power manifested by its well-defined cuisine, culture, entertainment, pluralism, political philosophy of non-violence, spiritualism, tolerance, and the commitment to democracy and constitutionalism. Paradoxically, Indian soft power was the source of much envy and nervousness in most of the countries that constituted the fourth vector of the quadrilateral. These countries were India's neighbors. All were much smaller and most were contiguous with India. Afghanistan, an Islamic kingdom was a British protectorate till 1919, Buddhist Bhutan was a British protectorate and after Indian independence, an Indian one, Buddhist Burma was hived off from British India in 1937 and became fiercely independent in 1948, the Maldives, a self-proclaimed Islamic country, was a British protectorate till 1965, the feudal Hindu kingdom in the Himalayas, Nepal, was reluctantly recognized as an independent country by Britain in 1934, the two wings of Pakistan were the notional homeland for the Muslims of British India that had constitutionally seceded from the British Indian Empire on 14 August 1947, and Buddhist Sri Lanka was granted independence in 1948 without much of a struggle to achieve it. In order to assert the fullness of their independence and their distinctive confident identity, the smaller neighbors, would often join with each other against a perceived obstreperous India Hence, though South Asia was a well-defined geographical entity; it was politically a much fractured region. Accordingly, both super-powers tried to tailor country-specific policies but did little to promote regional cooperation.

The thorniest relations among the newly independent countries of South Asia were between the youngest, Pakistan, and the largest, India. The former, in its quest for security and for the maintenance of a regional balance of power, sought alliances with stronger countries, especially the United States. The latter, however, little knowledge of or vital interests in South Asia. Accordingly, Washington's policies were marked by abrupt swings in strategy as it was a reflection of other American global priorities. This U.S. attitude took many a toll in regional sensibilities. Despite the obvious hurdles, a small degree of tacit Indo-U.S. cooperation developed. It was timely, for by 1952, the Korean War was dangerously stalemated. NEHRU then stepped in to propose a neutral commission to oversee the sensitive issue of the handling of prisoners-of-war. The issue was ultimately resolved, somewhat to India's credit.

Four years later, an unusual but abortive bilateral cooperation between the United States and India was briefly mooted in the wake of the 1956 Suez crisis that pitted Britain, France, and Israel against Egypt. The then U.S. President EISENHOWER suggested the possibility of setting up of an "elder statesman board of appeals" composed of Nehru and himself to "develop a solution to the Middle East dispute." A joint Indo-U.S. peace brokering effort was contemplated in Washington as one "commanding the respect of the world."

Despite such rhetoric and vision, it was Washington's relationship with the newly created country of Pakistan that effectively defined the limits of Indo-American ties. Described as late as 1982 by General ZIA UL-HAQ, U.S.-Pakistani ties were a "union of unequals" because of the underlying incompatibility of the culture, geography and national power of the two countries. This "union of unequals" also belied Pakistan's early expectations of being treated at par with the much bigger India. Nevertheless, the economic, military, and political cooperation between the two countries proved to be unexpectedly durable. During the first decade of the new country's existence, its economic policies were a major factor in doing so. The economy in Pakistan was then largely controlled by an urbanized elite that had migrated from India. This elite favored industry over agriculture and private entrepreneurship backed by easy credit, tax incentives, a liberal import policy and privatization of state-owned assets. This economic model, though much favored by Washington was not enough to create truly binding ties as Washington viewed Pakistan as a minor military ally and regarded India as the most important nation in the region. Therefore, India, not Pakistan was targeted for substantial economic aid. During the same decade, the U.S.-Pakistan military alliance, formalized in 1954, aroused hostility and suspicion in India. Despite generous military aid, there was a great deal of frustration in Pakistan because of the perceived American unwillingness to apply enough economic pressure on India to settle the Kashmir dispute in its favor. Indeed, the variability of the U.S. position on the Kashmir issue would continue to queer the pitch. Therefore, Pakistan unable to wrest the Kashmir region from India, faced numerous national humiliations in trying to do so unilaterally or militarily. These humiliations were often underestimated in Washington. In addition there were little publicized but significant policy differences between the two counties for Pakistan, like the vocal India, too, quietly backed decolonization, opposed apartheid in South Africa, and supported the Arab position in Palestine. Not unexpectedly, many Pakistanis were privately opposed to the American policies and considered the United States as an anti-Islamic country.

India, unlike Pakistan, was vociferous in its support for decolonization, championed the position of the Arab countries on Palestine, and was a leading advocate against apartheid in South Africa. In addition, India clearly aspired to lead a Third World movement that was separate from both superpowers. Such a movement was intrinsically anti-American and generally adopted the economic policies espoused by the Soviet Union and Communist China. In turn, both the Communist giants strongly supported non-aligned movements for their anti-imperialist and pro-socialist stance. As a leading member of this enlarging, anti-West group, India, with close ties to the Soviet Union, was perceived as being aggressively anti-Western. However, most Indians including many who publicly railed against Washington were privately drawn towards the United States, its prosperity and liberalism, and for the opportunities it afforded their family and children.

Quadrilateralism began to wane around 1979. The overthrow of the pro-western Shah of Iran by a theocratic revolutionary movement led by an elderly exiled Ayatollah fuelled the rise of militant Islam in Iran and elsewhere. Furthermore, that fateful year was marked by massive Soviet military intervention in land-locked Afghanistan. Consequently, for the first time there was a convergence of hearts and minds between the two notional allies, Washington and Islamabad. Hence, the state-wide "Islamization" orchestrated by Pakistan's then leader, General Zia Ul-Haq was buttressed by Washington's parallel support of the anti-Soviet MUJAHIDEEN movements. In the over-riding national interest, another significant faction in Washington, the U.S.-led nuclear non-proliferation lobby targeted India for its independent nuclear program. Whereas this lobby widened the gap between the governments in Islamabad, New Delhi, and Washington, the increased immigration of peoples from South Asia to the U.S. brought a closer understanding and interaction between the peoples of the two regions.

The other, much smaller countries in South Asia did not figure much in super-power equations or in the policies of either India or Pakistan. Accordingly, the regional grouping, SAARC, was slow to develop and even slower in acquiring substantive functions. Both super-powers provided some military, economic, and political aid to these small countries. After the end of the cold war and the dissolution of the Soviet Union, the smaller countries of the subcontinent had greater interaction with the U.S. as these nations made substantial contributions to U.N. peacekeeping operations and attracted American attention in the "global war against terror."

After a short spell of obvious unilateralism by the sole superpower, the U.S. and countries of the Indian subcontinent have matured towards bilateralism and multilateralism in an increasingly connected world despite the profound schisms, antagonisms, violence, and differences in the handling of resources, climate change, the disposal of waste, etc. By the 1990s, the Indian embrace of free markets resulted in the rapid growth of the country's economy. The Indian economic surge brought the belated recognition that India and the U.S. could be "natural allies" as observed by the then Indian Prime Minister, Atal Bihari Vajpayee. The Vajpayee government also formalized India as a state with nuclear weapons. Pakistan swiftly followed suit. Intense Indo-American dialogue was initiated shortly afterwards. The two countries developed a new understanding of each other's positions on numerous issues for the first time. In addition, New Delhi's measured response to Pakistan's incursion into the Kargil region of Kashmir in 1999 created a perception that India was a mature and responsible power. Another key impetus for the growing bilateral cooperation was the U.S.-led Global War on Terrorism as it increased military-to-military ties between the United States and many of the countries of South Asia. Other challenges, like the rise of China and instability in Pakistan may lead to greater Indo-U.S. cooperation.

Ties between the United States and South Asia will evolve as both the global world order and the nature of power changes in the coming decades. The latter is not limited to economic, military, or political strength. It is also civilizational.

A

Adam, William (1796-1881)

Scottish missionary. Adam, a Baptist missionary arrived at Serampore, north of Kolkata, in March 1818. Profoundly influenced by the great Bengali intellectual, Raja Rammohun Roy, Adam became a Unitarian five years later. However, his enthusiasm was soon dampened by the lukewarm support he received from the two parent British and American Unitarian churches. Nevertheless, Adam and Roy along with a few other Indians and Europeans formed the Calcutta Unitarian Society. The society remained fitfully active for seven years till it was invigorated in 1828 by its Hindu supporters who created a new Unitarian form of Hinduism called *Brahmo Somaj*. The *Somaj* nurtured and propagated a school of thought, which flowered into the famous Bengal Renaissance of the nineteenth century. It was characterized by a modern, yet distinctively Indian political theory, idealism, art, and poetry.

After twenty eventful years in India, in 1838 Adam took up the professorship of Oriental Literature at Harvard University in the United States. After the tumult and vitality of the Bengali movement, Adam was stifled and bored by the academic atmosphere in Boston. Therefore, he resigned from Harvard after just twelve months. Several years of further frustration followed. Finally, he returned to England to die in obscurity in Hampshire in 1881. Adam was among the first few to form a triangular intellectual relationship between India, England and the United States.

(*See also:* DALL, CHARLES (1816-1886); MISSIONARIES, UNITARIANISM, UNITARIANS OF KHASI HILLS)

Afghanistan-U.S. Relations

Afghanistan was the last battlefield of the Cold War (1949-1989) and because the first field of battle in the vaguely defined U.S.-led global struggle against terrorism (started in 2001). Diplomatic relations between United States and Afghanistan were first established in 1934 but interaction between the two countries was negligible. American developmental aid to Afghanistan began in 1949 with a $21 million loan made through the Export-Import Bank for Helmand Valley Development Project. Little other aid was offered as a study that year for the U.S. Department of Defense had concluded, "Afghanistan is of little or no strategic importance to the United States . . . its geographic location coupled with the realization by Afghan leaders of Soviet capabilities presages Soviet control of the country whenever the international situation so dictates."

Despite this analysis, Washington tried to include Afghanistan in the proposed northern tier of countries to hem in the U.S.S.R. However, the close ties between Kabul and Moscow dating back to 1880, and Afghanistan's inimical relationship with its neighbor and usually, Pakistan, precluded such an alliance. Hence, Washington paid little attention to the country till the Marxist coup in 1978, though in 1959 DWIGHT D. EISENHOWER became the first U.S. President to visit the country.

By 1979 the Soviet Union had provided to Afghanistan $1,265 million in economic assistance compared to less than half as much ($533 million) from the U.S. Similarly, 3,725 Afghan military personnel were trained in the Soviet Union while only 20 were enrolled in American military institutions in 1978. The few projects undertaken by Washington included the construction of Qandahar International Airport, the Kabul-Qandahar Highway, and a few of the new buildings at the Kabul University campus. During the mid-1950s, the newly established Ariana Afghan Airlines received technical support from Pan American Airways. During the Eisenhower years, U.S. Afghan relations were also strained because Washington publicly recognized Durand Line, which London had established as the frontier between Afghanistan and British India in 1893. Kabul only reluctantly and intermittently accepted the validity of the Line but always remained committed to the reunification of all Pashtuns living on either side of the Durand Line under the banner of Afghanistan. American military aid to Pakistan added further friction between the two countries.

The situation changed dramatically after the first communist coup in Afghanistan in late April 1979. In response on 3 July 1979 the then U.S. President CARTER signed the first directive for secret aid to the opponents of the pro-Soviet regime in Kabul. On that very day Zbigniew Brzezinski, the National Security Adviser wrote a note to the president explaining to him that in his considered opinion such aid was going to induce a Soviet military intervention in the country. And so it came to pass that 29 December 1979 the Soviet military entered Afghanistan to support the increasingly beleaguered communist regime in Kabul. The ensuing ten-year undeclared war in Afghanistan was waged by anti-communist guerrillas supported by the United States and its allies against the Soviets and the Kabul Government. In February 1989 the proxy war between the Washington and Moscow ended with the withdrawal of the Soviet forces from the country. The cost to Afghanistan was 1.5 million dead, 4.6 million refugees, and more than 100,000 crippled children. The rugged country was further scarred by high-explosives and despoiled by an estimated ten million mines still in the ground. Even in the relative safety of Kabul, 41 percent of children aged between eight and eighteen had lost one or both parents. American disengagement at the end of the war was swift leaving behind brutal internecine conflicts that paved the way, in 1996, for a sullen peace imposed by the Pakistan sponsored young Islamic fundamentalists, the TALIBAN. Washington mindful of the prospect of pipelines transiting through Afghanistan discreetly sought to accommodate the impoverished Taliban regime in Kabul. However, Afghanistan-based Saudi fundamentalist, OSAMA BIN LADEN, attacked prominent targets on U.S. soil on 11 September 2001. The twin towers of the World Trade Center in New York City were struck by hijacked American commercial airliners. Both towers collapsed. A third hijacked airliner struck the Pentagon near Washington DC while the fourth aircraft, presumably aimed at a high-value target in the American capital, crashed in rural Pennsylvania during a struggle between the hijackers and the passengers and crew of the ill-fated airplane. American retribution followed six weeks later. A deal was struck with the anti-Taliban warlords known as the Northern Alliance. Supported by the United States and NATO, the Alliance routed the Taliban and AL-QAEDA forces and by the end of the year the country was notionally controlled by U.S. supported Afghan groups. However, most of the leadership of the Taliban or the al-Qaeda was neither killed nor captured. The rank and file of the Taliban militia either returned to their homes and villages or joined the al-Qaeda cadres and escaped to Pakistan. In late December 2001 picked Afghan leaders then met in Bonn, Germany to reach an agreement for a broad-based government in the country. About $30 billion in humanitarian aid and reconstruction assistance to Afghanistan was also mooted. Progress in governance and the flow of aid have been slow under the American supported government of President HAMID KARZAI. However, the power of the Kabul government is very limited, corruption and warlordism is rampant and Afghanistan has become the greatest producer of opium in the world. Ironically, one of the main regions for the cultivation of opium was Helmand, the province where developmental U.S. aid was first given in 1949. Consequently, there are deep divisions between the Americans and other NATO allies over the counter narcotics policy. The Americans favor widespread spraying of the poppy fields while the Europeans oppose it as it would further antagonize farmers who have little recourse to alternative crops.

In addition, since 2006, violence has again soared in Afghanistan as the al-Qaeda and Taliban fighters having regrouped in safe havens along the rugged Afghan-Pakistan border have attacked NATO forces and the allied Afghans in the east and south of the country. Most Americans consider that Pakistan lacks the will and the ability to combat militants operating from its soil. Hence, in July 2008, President Bush secretly cleared U.S. Special Forces to carry out ground assaults inside Pakistan without approval from thc government in Islamabad. In addition, the U.S. is inducting more troops to Afghanistan and reportedly supports an Afghan government proposal to double the size of the country's army by creating an active-duty force of 122,000 troops by 2014. By late 2008 American allies like the British were stepping up pressure for a political and diplomatic settlement in the country that could talks with the Taliban.

(*See* also: ANTI-SOVIET RESISTANCE GROUPS, ARAB AFGHANS, BAGRAM, BHUTO BENAZIR, BHUTTO ZULFIKAR ALI,, CARTER JAMES EARL, CENTER FOR AFGHANISTAN STUDIES, DAUD SARDAR MUHAMMED, DOSTUM ABDUL RASHID, GENEVA ACCORDS, HEKMATYAR GULBUDDIN, INTER-SERVICES INTELLIGENCE, KARMAL BABRAK, KHAN AKHTAR RAHMAN, KHOST, KHYBER PASS, MADRASSAS, MASSOUD AHMAD SHAH, MAZARI ABDUL ALI, NAJIBULLAH MOHAMMED, MUJHAHIDEEN, MULES, OIL AND GAS PIPELINES, OPIUM PRODUCTION, OJHRI CAMP EXPLOSION, PEOPLES' DEMOCRATIC PARTY OF AFGHANITAN, PROVINCIAL ECONSTRUCTION TEAMS, RABBANI BURHANUDDIN, U.S. MILITARY AID IN SOUTH ASIA AFTER 9/11, ZAHIR SHAH, ZIA UL-HAQ MOHAMMED)

Aids/HIV in South Asia

When infection by the Human Immunodeficiency Virus (HIV) becomes advanced it is clinically manifested by the Acquired Immuno-Deficiency Syndrome (AIDS). The syndrome is characterized by the development of opportunistic infections, tumors, and other debilitating diseases as a result of the host's weakened immune system. HIV is a Retrovirus consisting of Ribonucleic Acid (RNA, the template for translation of genes into proteins). A special enzyme, Reverse Transcriptase, allows the virus to convert its own RNA to DNA (Deoxyribonucleic Acid, the double-stranded chemical instruction manual for everything a plant or animal does: grow, divide, and die). When infection occurs the virus takes over the host cell's genetic material and the new cell — now infected with HIV — begins to produce new HIV retroviruses. The replicates kill helper T cells, the body's main defense against such infections. The incidence of AIDS and HIV positivity in South Asia has been made needlessly difficult to estimate as most patients are diagnosed with AIDS because of their clinical symptoms and not by confirmatory tests that measure antibodies against HIV virus or an RNA test which detects the virus itself. The ostensible reason is that local laboratories are unreliable. Therefore, patients who have the clinical presentation should be treated for the viral infection regardless of whether laboratory tests are positive or not.

The first of case HIV/AIDS in South Asia was reported in India in 1986. Twenty years later, supposedly more than six million HIV-positive people live in South Asia. The increase is attributed primarily to various high-risk behaviors, e.g. unprotected sexual intercourse with sex workers, males having sex with men [MSM], injection-drug users [IDUs]. The other usual societal maladies of poverty, exploitation of women, etc., too, contribute to the spread of the infection. In addition, inadequate screening of blood and related products for transfusions and the high number of professional donors have contributed to the spread of the disease.

Reliable data on the prevalence of HIV/AIDS in Afghanistan is sparse. In 2006 international agencies like UNAIDS and WHO estimated the number of people living with HIV could be a thousand or twice as many. The spread is likely to hinge on the usually suspect populations of IDUs, unsafe paid sex-workers, and MSMs. The latter are particularly common in Afghanistan. According to a 2006 study four percent of IDUs in Kabul were HIV positive and 32 percent had sex with men or boys, and 69 percent had paid for it. In 2006, four deaths due to AIDS were registered in Afghanistan.

Bangladesh with a population of about 150 million, too, is a low-prevalence country for HIV/AIDS despite being contiguous with two countries with high populations with HIV positive citizens (India and Burma). The first HIV positive case in the country was detected in 1989. According to government sources, at the end of 2005 an estimated 11,000 Bangladeshis were HIV positive. A local epidemic among IDUs in a neighborhood in Dhaka with an HIV prevalence of 7.1 percent was reported in 2006. This epidemic among IDUs could lead to further spread of the infection through their sexual partners and their clients into the general population.

In Burma the first HIV positive case was reported in 1988 and the first AIDS patient in 1991. HIV in the country is mostly spread by IDUs and unprotected sex, both heterosexual and MSM. Prevalence among IDUs in the old capital, Rangoon had reached 74.3 percent by 1993 among the sex workers in the city and in Mandalay it had increased from four percent in 1992 to twenty-six percent in 1997. Among military recruits the prevalence of HIV infection was at 1.6 percent in early 2004. The country may be on the verge of one of the most serious HIV epidemics in the region.

Though India is a low prevalence country (rate of positivity of less than one percent of the population is defined as a low prevalence country), the sheer number may be enormous. However, reliability of information is in considerable doubt as the incidence is based on estimates, clinical circumstances, and extrapolated data. Approximately 80 percent of infections in India are acquired heterosexually. Other data is much more controversial for in 2005, an estimated 5.7 million Indians were infected with the HIV virus their number was expected to reach 25 million by 2010. However, in 2006 the estimates released by the National AIDS Control Organization (NACO) were strikingly different as they indicated that the adult HIV prevalence in the country was between 2.0 to 3.1 million. These drastically revised figures were also supported by the major international agencies like UNAIDS and WHO. Similarly, the estimate of annual deaths range wildly from a low of 270,000 to a high of 680,000. Nevertheless relatively reliable information from four Indian states showed a substantial decline in HIV prevalence among pregnant women aged 15-24 years, from 1.7 percent in 2000 to 1.1 percent in 2004.

A comprehensive AIDS Control Program was launched in the Maldives in 1987, even before a single case of HIV positive patient was detected. A National AIDS Council, a multi-disciplinary body with high ranking officials from the government and from NGOs was created. The program focused on building awareness in the general public, and raised both ethical and moral issues about the cause, prevention, and treatment of the disease. Up to 2005, the incidence remained low — only 13 cases involving Maldivians and another 168 among expatriate workers. However, there was an unexpected flare up in cases among IDUs in the capital Male and on Addu atoll. A government survey in 2006 concluded that the country was highly vulnerable to an HIV/AIDS epidemic because of the sharp rise in IDUs.

Nepal had, by the end of 2005, an estimated 75,000 HIV positive individuals (0.5 percent of the population in the 15-49 age groups) with estimated death toll of 5,100. Earlier, in Kathmandu, HIV rates among IDUs skyrocketed, from under two percent to about 50 percent between 1991 and 1997 before declining steadily.

HIV positive cases in Pakistan were estimated at 70,000-80,000 (0.1 percent of the adult population). The limited available figures suggest that HIV prevalence is 1-2 percent in vulnerable populations such as female sex workers and long-distance truck drivers. In 2004, an outbreak was detected among IDUs in Karachi, where more than twenty percent of those tested were found to be HIV positive and an incidence of four percent was detected among MSMs in the city.

In Sri Lanka the incidence is reportedly low. Only 1,000 cases were estimated in 2006. However, there is little public education about AIDS and surveillance is trivial.

There is probable underreporting by most countries mainly due to the social stigma attached to the infection and the limited availability of surveillance and testing systems. The future spread of HIV/AIDS in South Asia's is likely to depend on three obvious determinants: The scope and effectiveness of HIV prevention programs for sex workers and their clients, IDUs, and MSMs; on addressing the underlying socio-economic determinants of the epidemic, and on the availability of treatment.

The largest U.S. government initiative to control the spread of the disease was launched in 2003 under President GEORGE W. BUSH. He announced the President's Emergency Plan for AIDS Relief (PEPFAR). The plan was a five-year, $15 billion, multifaceted approach to combating HIV/AIDS in more than 120 countries. In reality, the funds were clearly targeted towards countries considered politically important by Washington. Hence, thirteen sub-Saharan African countries, Guyana, and Vietnam received most of the funding.

In South Asia the Washington was most directly involved through the U.S. Agency for International Development (USAID). It provides condoms and HIV-related educational materials throughout the region. Multilateral support through international agencies and NGOs is also a significant part of American assistance. In Afghanistan around 50 international NGOs and another 100 or so national NGOs provide approximately 80 percent of health facilities in the country. U.S. financial support gives medications, other medical supplies, affords general supervision, training, and other incentives. In Burma, the situation is very different. Political and economic isolation, limited resources, and the regime's unwillingness to collaborate openly with international organizations or with the indigenous NGOs may lead to a severe epidemic of the disease. In India, in November 2003 former President CLINTON launched a major initiative to make treatment more affordable. Along the same lines, the Bill and Melinda Gates Foundation, pledged 200 million dollars to control the spread of HIV/AIDS. In Nepal, even during the active insurgency, national programs with international support dispensed some anti-retroviral treatment to patients. The stigma and discrimination against people living with HIV is a major problem in Pakistan. Patients are reluctant to disclose their HIV positive status to their immediate family or health care providers. This results in an informal and unstructured treatment of patients. Nevertheless, at least 54 NGOs are involved in HIV/AIDS public awareness and in the care and support of patients living with HIV/AIDS. Like elsewhere, although NGOs are active in prevention activities and reach less than five percent of the vulnerable populations. In addition, the availability and acceptability of anti retro-virals (ARVs) is small and patients generally have to buy their medications. New Light, funded by the U.S.-based Catholic Relief Services is the only NGO in West Punjab (Pakistan) with an outreach program dedicated to actually providing treatment to patients.

Al-Qaeda

Islamic fundamentalist international terrorist organization. In the aftermath of the Soviet withdrawal from Afghanistan in 1989, a Saudi national, OSAMA BIN LADEN, a multi-millionaire building contractor who worked with the CIA in Afghanistan (1985-1989), returned to his native land and set up an informal establishment to assist in the resettlement of the Arab veterans of the Afghan war. Later, he publicly became hostile to the U.S. and the Saudi government for allowing American troops to be stationed in Saudi Arabia, the birthplace of Islam. It is unclear which other factors were involved in his focused opposition to the Saudi establishment and the United States and Western countries. The Saudi response is equally mystifying. Riyadh did not arrest or restrict him. Instead, in 1991 he was expelled from Saudi Arabia to Khartoum, Sudan, where the al-Qaeda was born.

Within two years, the organization was implicated in the bombing of World Trade Center, New York (February 1993) and in the killing of U.S. servicemen at Khobar Barracks in Saudi Arabia in October that year. By May 1996 the changing domestic politics in Sudan, and the quiet but firm pressure from Egypt, Saudi Arabia, and the U.S. forced him to leave the country. Bin Laden, assisted by the Afghan warlord ABDUL RASOOL SAYYAF then returned to Afghanistan where the ruling TALIBAN initially received him with some reluctance. Once established in Qandahar bin Laden issued a "Declaration of War" against the U.S. in August that year. Al-Qaeda then assiduously forged alliances with other radical groups and in February 1998, bin Laden announced the formation of an alliance of terrorist organizations labeled as the "International Islamic Front for Jihad Against the Jews and Crusaders." The Front included the Egyptian al-Gama'at al-Islamiyya, the Egyptian Islamic Jihad, the Harakat ul-Ansar, and others. Al-Qaeda's theological leader was Ayman al-Zawahiri, an Egyptian surgeon who joined the country's Islamist movement in the late 1970s and was imprisoned for three years for a minor connection with the assassination of President Anwar Sadaat.

The leadership oversees a loosely organized network of cells. It can recruit members from thousands of ARAB AFGHAN veterans and radicals around the world. Its infrastructure is small, mobile, and decentralized — each cell operates independently with members not knowing about the identity of other cells.

Al-Qaeda differs from other traditional terrorist organizations as it does not depend on the sponsorship of a political state, and, unlike the PLO or the IRA, it is not denitrified with a particular conflict or territory. Instead, al-Qaeda operates as a franchise. It provides financial and logistical support, as well as its name recognition, to terrorist groups operating in such diverse regions as Afghanistan, Algeria, Chechnya, Eritrea, Kashmir, the Philippines, Somalia, Tajikistan, and Yemen. Furthermore, local groups may act in the name of al-Qaeda in order to bolster their own reputations — even if they are not receiving support from the organization.

The principal aims of al-Qaeda are to drive Americans and American influence out of all Muslim nations, especially Saudi Arabia; destroy Israel; and topple pro-Western dictatorships around the Middle East. Bin Laden has also stated that he wishes to unite all Muslims under a single political entity and forge, if necessary by force, a pan-Islamic nation adhering to the rules of governance established by the first four Caliphs. Under bin Laden's 1998 *fatwa* (religious decree), it is the duty of Muslims around the world to wage holy war against the U.S., American citizens, and Jews. Muslims who do not heed this call should be considered apostates. Therefore, they should be culled. This willingness to kill fellow Muslims as apostates has its roots in the works of two modern Sunni Islamic thinkers, Mohammad ibn Abd al-Wahhab and Sayyid Qutb. Al-Wahhab was an eighteenth-century reformer who considered Islam to have been corrupted within a generation after the death of the Prophet Mohammed. He denounced any theology or customs developed after that period as non-Islamic. His followers conquered most of the Arabian peninsula by the 1930s and constituted the present Kingdom of Saudi Arabia, where Wahhabism remains the dominant creed. Sayyid Qutb, a radical Egyptian scholar of the mid-twentieth century, declared Western civilization as the enemy of Islam and denounced leaders of Muslim nations for not closely following the teachings of the prophet. Furthermore he taught that *jihad* should be undertaken not just to defend Islam, but to purify it as well. In response to the 11 September 2001 attacks on the World Trade Center in New York City and the Pentagon in the Washington DC area, the U.S. invaded Afghanistan in October that year.

The mission was to destroy al-Qaeda and to replace the Taliban regime with a pro-Western one in Afghanistan. The operation was a partial success as the al-Qaeda's infrastructure was substantially damaged and its reported military commander, Mohammed Ateh, was killed; the Taliban was ousted from Kabul, and a pro-Western regime installed in Afghanistan. However, both bin Laden and al-Zawahiri escaped as did the leadership and cadres of the Taliban. In March 2003 the U.S. widened the war by invading Iraq. Some of the most ferocious and well-directed resistance to U.S. occupation forces in Iraq was mounted by the late Abu Musab al-Zarqawi, a Jordanian radical. The case of al-Zarqawi was instructive as to how al-Qaeda had morphed since 9/11. In the beginning of the insurgency in Iraq al-Zarqawi positioned himself as a rival to bin Laden, but in October 2004 he declared his allegiance to al-Qaeda, and changed the name of his group from "Unification and Jihad in Iraq" to "al-Qaeda in Iraq." Despite some American successes, al-Qaeda based along the Afghan-Pakistan border with slender and flexible lines of control and communication remains a major terrorist threat in many parts of the globe as evidenced by the dozen or so major attacks world-wide by the terrorist group and its associated fundamentalists since 9/11.

(*See also:* ANTI-SOVIET RESISTANCE GROUPS IN AFGHANISTAN,)

Ambedkar, Bhim Rao (1891-1956)

Indian politician and constitutionalist. Ambedkar was born in the low-caste Mahar community in the cantonment town of Mhow, Madhya Pradesh, India. He was educated at Elphinstone High School in Bombay, where he was not allowed to learn Sanskrit because of his low caste. Nonetheless, his brilliance brought him to the notice of the Maharaja of Baroda. Caste considerations notwithstanding, the Maharaja paid for a scholarship for him to attend Columbia University, New York. Ambedkar arrived in the United States in July 1930 and took up a huge academic load consisting of subjects including political science, moral philosophy, anthropology, sociology, and economics. He was awarded a Ph.D. in the latter. Ambedkar was much impressed with the U.S. Constitution, especially the 14th Amendment granting emancipation to African-American slaves. Hw was also awed by the life of the great African-American activist. Booker T. Washington. As Chairman of the Indian Constituent Assembly, Ambedkar greatly influenced the framing of the new constitution with its emphasis on equality, freedoms, and fundamental rights. Late in life, disillusioned at the slow integration of untouchables (Dalits) into mainstream Hindu society, he embraced Buddhism. Many of his supporters followed suit and are commonly known as neo-Buddhists.

Amin, Hafizullah (1929-1979)

Second President, "Democratic Republic of Afghanistan," (September 1979-December 1979). A Ghilzai Pashtun, educated in Afghanistan and at the Teachers College, Columbia University, New York, he was an avowed PASHTUN nationalist till he converted to Marxism while studying in the U.S. He returned to Afghanistan in 1965 and eventually became Principal of the Ibn Sina Teachers Training School in Kabul. During the republican period in Afghanistan (1973-78), he covertly recruited officers and men serving in the military into the *Khalq* faction of the communist part in Afghanistan. After the SAUR REVOLUTION, he became the Deputy Prime Minister and Minister for Foreign Affairs. Following the purge of the *Parcham* faction, Amin took over as Prime Minister in April 1979, and ousted President Taraki in September that year. As president, Amin pledged greater religious freedom. He also repaired some mosques, and presented copies of the Holy *Quran* to various religious groups. He invoked the name of Allah in his speeches and declared that the Saur Revolution was based on Islamic principles. Nevertheless, his short rule was noted for its brutality (15,000-45,000 were executed) and his inimical relationship with the Soviet Union, possibly because Moscow was inherently suspicious of American-educated leaders. With rising insurgency against the communists in Afghanistan, the Soviets intervened militarily in December 1979. *Spetsnaz* (Soviet Special Forces) troops assassinated him on 27 December 1979. He was replaced by an exiled rival, BABRAK KARMAL.

(*See also*: ANTI-SOVIET RESISTANCE GROUPS IN AFGHANISTAN, PEOPLE'S DEMOCRATIC PARTY OF AFGHANISTAN)

Anti-Soviet Resistance Groups of Afghanistan

During 1973-79 many dissidents fled from Afghanistan to Pakistan and Iran because of repression under the Daud and the early Communist regimes. Altogether, perhaps five million, or one-quarter of the country's population, left. The dissidents fell into three broad categories: monarchists, secularists or nationalists, and Islamists. The monarchists and secularists were the smaller and weaker groups. Furthermore, both the host countries, Pakistan and Iran deliberately sidelined them.

After the Soviet intervention in Afghanistan in 1979, the Islamist groups, collectively known as the MUJAHIDEEN were often romanticized as fiercely independent under-dogs, the struggle was not as unequal as reported in the western press. The guerrillas had the enormous advantage of safe havens and firm bases in both Iran and Pakistan. The latter not only provided the fighters with sanctuary, training and arms but also professional military personnel who went into Afghanistan as advisors on military operations. The two factors, namely, ample financial and material support, and the presence of secure bases, especially on foreign soil, are the key prerequisites for waging asymmetric war against an invading conventional army. The Mujahideen were also described as "freedom fighters" with an implied commitment to Western style democratic ideals. However, their goal was not to institute representative democracy in Afghanistan but to defeat the Soviets and establish a theocracy in the country.

The amount of resources committed by Iran is unclear but the U.S. assistance during 1979-89 amounted to $5-6 billion to the Pakistan based guerrillas. An equal amount was reportedly contributed by Britain, China, Egypt, Israel, and Saudi Arabia, with the latter providing the bulk of the funds. Most Islamist groups in Pakistan were headquartered in Peshawar, whereas others including the royalists were based in Quetta.

Not all anti-Soviet resistance was in exile in Pakistan or Iran. Unlike most men-folk, the female leadership stayed in the country. The most prominent women's' opposition group, RAWA (the Revolutionary Association of the Women of Afghanistan) was established in Kabul, in 1977. It was an independent politico-social organization under the leadership of Meena Keshwar Kamal. RAWA promoted human rights, social justice, secular democracy, and the emancipation of women. In addition, it opposed religious fundamentalism and all foreign intervention in Afghanistan. Hence, Meena made many enemies. Two adversaries apparently cooperated in silencing her. In 1987 she was assassinated in Quetta, Pakistan, reportedly by KGB agents in connivance with GULBUDDIN HEKMATYAR. Under ABDUL ALI MAZARI, the Iranians set up *Hizb-I Wahdat*, a coalition of nine Shia factions. The major factions based in Pakistan were either "fundamentalists" or "traditionalists."

The fundamentalists based their organizing principle around mass politics within the confines of an Islamized society and included several splinter groups of *Jam'iat-i-Islami*.

The leader of the parent branch, BURHANUDDIN RABBANI, began devising a mass based organization in Kabul before SARDAR MUHAMMAD DAUD's repression of religious conservatives in 1974 forced him to flee to Pakistan.

Another refugee from that era was Hekmatyar, who soon broke with Rabbani to form another resistance group, *Hizb-e-Islami*. The *Hizb* was particularly favored by Pakistani authorities. An estimated 70 percent of all Pakistani directed assistance was given to him.

Another split, engineered by one of Hekmatyar's colleagues, Yunus Khales, resulted in a second group also using the name *Hizb-e-Islami*. Khales was slightly more moderate than Hekmatyar.

A fourth fundamentalist group was *Ittihad-i-Islami* led by ABDUL RASOOL SAYYAF. Rabbani's group received its greatest support from northern Afghanistan where the best known resistance commander in Afghanistan, AHMAD SHAH MASSOUD, a Tajik, like Rabbani, operated with considerable success against the Soviets. The traditionalist groups focused on governance of the country on the basis of sharia (Islamic law) and its interpretation by the *ulema* (elders and scholars). The most important of the three main groups was *Jebh-e-Nejat-e-Milli* led by Sibghatullah Mojadeddi. Some traditionalists were willing to accept the restoration of the monarchy. Others had links within *Sufi* orders, such as the *Mahaz-e-Milli Islami*, and the Gilani *Sufi* order led by Pir Sayyid Gilani.

(*See also:* ARAB-AFGHANS)

Arab-Afghans

The total number of Arabs who served in Afghanistan during the Soviet occupation is not established. However, it is commonly believed that about 5,000 Saudis, 3,000 Yemenis, 3,000 Egyptians, 2,800 Algerians, 400 Tunisians, 370 Iraqis, 200 Libyans and scores of Jordanians fought with MUJAHIDEEN in Afghanistan between 1979 and 1991. They were collectively known as Arab-Afghans. Their presence in the region was informally regulated and at any given time during the war no more than 3,000 Arab Afghans were present in Afghanistan. Most worked alongside the three particularly fundamentalist Pashtun groups led by ABDUL RASOOL SAYYAF, Mohammad Yunus Khales, and GULBUDDIN HEKMATYAR. Many Arab-Afghans were considered as either misfits in society in their own homelands or were Islamic fundamentalists with a death wish who went to Afghanistan with the avowed purpose of even dying for the cause. Their military experience and training was little. In general, the Afghans felt that they did not have the toughness or the discipline for the tedium of guerrilla warfare in a distant and alien land and tried to keep most of them out of combat zones though the Mujahideen readily accepted their money and resources. Nevertheless, many Arab-Afghans acquired some battlefield experience, bonded with like-minded Muslims from other lands, who, too, were alienated from the reactionary and Godless regimes of their home countries. Their presence was tolerated for it was an impetus for private and unregulated funding from wealthy middle-eastern donors. OSAMA BIN LADEN's group was one of the few exceptions. His men did participate in some military actions but their effectiveness was mixed. Bin Laden was also able to retain their loyalty despite the overwhelming presence of Egyptian fundamentalists in his personal entourage. Following the Soviet withdrawal from Afghanistan the Arab-Afghans, many with the support and direction from bin Laden, fanned out to countries including China, India, the Philippines, and Tajikistan, as well as middle-eastern states like Algeria, Egypt, Iraq, Jordan, Saudi Arabia, Sudan, Tunisia and Yemen.

(*See also:* AL-QAEDA, ANTI-SOVIET RESISTANCE GROUPS IN AFGHANISTAN, BIN LADEN, OSAMA)

Asian-American Hotel Owners Association (AAHOA)

Founded 1989. By 2007, the association represented more than 8,000 members and was one of the leading influences in the hospitality industry in the United States. Its members owned more than 22,000 hotels with one million rooms accounting for more than 50 percent of the economy lodgings and nearly 37 percent of all hotels in the U.S. Approximately 13,000 properties were franchised while 9,000 were independently operated. The total market value of the assets was estimated at $29.9 billion in franchised properties and $8.1 billion in independently run hotels, motels, and resorts. The industry was dominated by the Gujarati-American community.

Like many other newer businesses run by immigrants, AAHOA faced alleged discrimination from city and state governments. In response, at the turn of the millennium the association contested a number of such disputes in court, particularly in San Francisco, California. Public confidence and acceptance was gained after surveys conducted by a number of public relations firms revealed that services in AAHOA-run hotels were not inferior to those run by other companies or individuals. In addition, members developed working relationships with the major franchisors as the latter normally provide marketing and reservations support; expertise with operating skills; training facilities both on and off the premises, and technological assistance.

Like many South Asian organizations, AAHOA, too, attempted to become a public advocacy group with mixed results. In March 2005 the controversial Chief Minister of Gujarat, Narendra Modi, was invited to speak at the AAHOA meeting in Fort Lauderdale, Florida. However, the U.S. Department of State refused to issue him a visa for his alleged role in exacerbating Hindu-Muslim riots in the state. In addition, a prominent talk show host cancelled a speech to the conference after coming under pressure from Muslim organizations and human-rights group. On the other hand, AAHOA strongly supported the "Border Security and Immigration Reform Act of 2007," a conservative bill backed by the White House.

Some Indian American hoteliers are investing in India as well. Most plans envisage tie-ins with local partners for mixed land use development projects that would include hotels, multiplexes, restaurants and educational institutions. Most members expect to begin with small investments. Others seek to establish AAHOA as its own brand name.

B

Bagram

Key airbase in Afghanistan. Bagram is reputed to be the site of the city of Alexandria ad Caucasum (Alexandria by the Caucasus), built by Alexander the Great around 330-329 B.C. Perhaps it is the location of an even earlier city, Kapisa, which was destroyed by the Persians. The town is 47 kilometers (30 miles) north of Kabul near the confluence of the Panjshir and Ghorand Rivers. The Soviets selected this strategic spot to build a large modern airbase in the 1950s. It was the staging point for intervening Soviet forces in Afghanistan in 1979 and elite Soviet formations were deployed at the airbase throughout Moscow's intervention (1979-89) in the country for both the defense of Kabul and of the Salang Pass on the main highway from Afghanistan to the Soviet Union. After the Soviet withdrawal, Ahmed Shah Massoud seized it in collaboration with Abdul Rashid Dostum. The latter, lost control of the base to the Taliban who were ousted by U.S.-backed Northern Alliance in 2001. The chickened history of the airbase did not end there. In 2002, torture and homicide were allegedly carried out by U.S. forces and other U.S. agencies at the detention center known as the Bagram Collection Point (BCP). In October 2004, the U.S. Army's Criminal Investigation Command charged 27 officers and men with offences ranging from dereliction of duty to involuntary manslaughter. In 2006 the air base was converted into an exclusive U.S. Air National Guard facility. It was expected to be the only Air National Guard base in the Middle East.

Bains, Didar Singh (1940-)

Indian American, largest peach farmer in the world. In 1958, Bains came to the United States to join his father (immigrated, 1948) and grandfather (immigrated in 1890 to Canada and thence to the U.S. in 1920). He had eight dollars in his pocket and the belief that money grows on trees. He was right. After driving tractors and irrigating orchards at a wage of 75 cents an hour in Sutter County, California, for three years without taking a single day off, he had saved enough to buy a 25 acre peach orchard. He then bought another, and another. By 1980, he owned 12,000 acres in California and Canada and had become the largest peach grower in California. By then Bains also learnt that money grows on land. He became a developer of both commercial and residential real estate. In the early 1980s Bains became enmeshed in Sikh politics both in India and abroad. He donned a turban and grew a long open beard. He joined the Punjab based political party, the *Shrimoni Akali Dal* led by the veteran Sikh politician, Parkash Singh Badal. Bains also founded the secessionist *Vishva Sikh Council*. By the new millennium he had moderated his politics and increased his philanthropic activities.

Baltimore Clipper

Merchant ship. The American built 250-350 ton three-masted sailing ship with a crew of 25-45 challenged the supremacy of the British merchant marine in the early nineteenth century. After the abolition of the East India Company's commercial monopoly in 1813, for the next forty years the speedy Baltimore Clippers outran the slower, larger, and clumsier East Indiamen built by the British. Accordingly, the Clippers captured much of the market in transporting Indian opium to China. A New England family to make a fortune in this trade was the Delanos. One of the Delano women, Sara, was the mother of FRANKLIN DELANO ROOSEVELT, the great American President (1933-1945).

Bangladesh-U.S. Relations

Bangladesh, formerly East Pakistan, came into being in 1971 after a bloody Civil war. Pakistan, as the country founded in 1947, was strongly supported by the U.S. in the civil war. Accordingly, Bangladesh's independence made for a troubled start in ties between Washington and Dhaka which, then developed rapidly. Emergency relief, economic and food aid were initiated shortly after independence. Since then, U.S. assistance concentrated on long-term development projects included ones to stabilize the growth in the country's population, meet its health-care needs, and support broad-based economic growth. By 2007, the U.S. had about $4.3 billion in food and development assistance to first country. Since 1986, with the exception of 1988-89, the balance of trade between the two nations has been in favor of Bangladesh due to growing imports of ready made garments into the U.S. from the South Asian country. Jute carpet-backing is the other major product from Bangladesh. Imports from Bangladesh to the U.S. were about $2.2 billion (excluding services) in 2006.

Relations between the two countries were substantially strengthened by the participation of Bangladesh troops in the 1991 Gulf war and their presence, alongside U.S. forces, in a number of U.N. peacekeeping operations since 1994. Furthermore, U.S. military assistance in providing disaster relief has further brought the two countries into a closer working relationship. These ties were further boosted in March 2000 when President WILLIAM J. CLINTON visited Bangladesh, the first visit ever by a serving U.S. President. The presidential stopover was followed by trips by Secretary of State Colin Powell in June 2003 and Secretary of Defense Donald Rumsfeld a year later. Washington maintained a discreet silence during the prolonged constitutional crisis that has gripped the country since late 2006 and the dominant role played in it by the notionally apolitical military.

Since 9/11, the country has been touted as a valuable asset in the Global War on Terrorism. The reality may be different for though Bangladesh has cooperated in curbing money laundering, and the monitoring of the movement and activities of some suspected Islamic fundamentalists in the country. However, it is considered as a safe-haven by many such militants. Hence, despite the rhetoric and some tangible action, Islamic fundamentalism and anti-Americanism is reportedly on the rise in Bangladesh, especially in the countryside.

Bhattarai, Baburam (1954-)

Communist ideologue, and political leader in Nepal. Born in the historic Gorkha district, Bhattarai went to a missionary high school in rural Nepal. In 1977, Bhattarai under a Colombo Plan Scholarship, obtained an honors baccalaureate from the prestigious Chandigarh College of Architecture (India) where he founded the All India Nepalese Students Association. He left India in1986 after receiving his PhD in architecture from Jawaharlal Nehru University, New Delhi.

On returning home, he joined the Communist Party of Nepal (Masal) and became the spokesperson of the United National People's Movement during the 1990 uprising. During the subsequent Communist splits in 1991 and 1994 Bhattarai sided with the hardliners in the party and became the leader of the parallel the Samyukta Janamorcha Nepal (United People's Front Nepal, SJN) — the political front of the Communist Party of Nepal (Maoist His Anti-Indian and anti-Americanism may be more inflexible than that of other Maoist leaders though in June 2007, only he and the undisputed party leader, PRACHANDA, met the former U.S. President JIMMY CARTER during the latter's four day fact-finding trip to Nepal. It is widely believed that Bhattarai was the principal author of the Election Manifesto of the Maoists before the Constituent Assembly polls were finally held in April 2008. The Maoists emerged as the largest party in the Constituent Assembly and formed the government headed by Prachanda. Bhattarai was given the finance portfolio but his position as the deputy leader of the party was not formalized.

(*See also*: NEPAL CIVIL WAR)

Bhopal Gas Leak, 3 December 1984

Industrial Disaster. Forty tons of poisonous gases, most being Methyl Isocyanate, escaped from a pesticide plant owned by the American company, Union Carbide Corporation (U.C.C), in the central Indian city of Bhopal. The exact composition of the killer gas remained unknown for the company claimed it to be a trade secret. This lack of exact information prevented effective research into remedies and treatment of patients. About 8,000 people died soon after the leak and another 15,000-33,000 succumbed to complications in the next 20 years. The number of maimed and chronically injured is estimated to range between 500,000-800,000. U.C.C paid $470 million to settle the civil suits in an out-of-court arrangement devised by the Government of India in 1989. It was a far cry from the Indian government's initial claim of $3.3 billion. In addition, under the settlement U.C.C was not held criminally liable. Much of the money was tied up in bureaucratic and legal issues and survivors received only $500 each. This perceived miscarriage of justice, the issue of cleaning up the site, the lack of provisions for medical treatment, and the absence of economic rehabilitation, sparked widespread public campaigns by activists and survivors' associations. In 1991 the criminal liability case were revived. In 1994 U.C.C sold its stake to Union Carbide India Ltd. This local subsidiary was renamed Eveready Industries. In 2001, U.C.C was bought out by Dow Chemical. Dow assumed all assets and liabilities of U.C.C but denied any responsibility for the Bhopal disaster. Nevertheless, the Bhopal courts directed India's Central Bureau of Investigation to include Dow as a defendant in its criminal case. In 2000, the survivors' organizations filed a class action suit in the Southern District Federal Court of New York. It was summarily rejected. However, the Second Circuit Court of Appeals later reinstated parts of the suit dealing with matters of contamination and cleanup of the site, but the judge again denied certification for a class action suit. Nevertheless, litigants filed suit again, and the case was pending in court in 2006. Apart from the question of criminal culpability for the disaster, contamination at the leak site is a serious concern. After the accident, U.C.C. simply abandoned the factory. Vats and tanks containing highly toxic chemicals leaked and contaminated the soil and groundwater and no surveillance of the long-term effects of the gases on the victims was undertaken. In most cases, the absence of alternative accommodation forced the survivors to live in blighted areas around the site despite the hazards. Allegations about diseases effecting the lungs, eyes, and joints are commonplace as are instances of high rates of cancer and miscarriage among these unfortunate victims.

Bhutto, Benazir (1953-2007)

Pakistani political leader. Bhutto, the eldest child of ZULFIKAR ALI BHUTTO, (Pakistan's ruler, 1971-7) she was educated at Oxford and Harvard Universities. At Oxford, she was elected as the president of Students' Union. As a step in grooming her for future leadership of the country, her father took her with him to India in 1972. The trip culminated in the Simla Agreement. Seven years later, she took-over as co-chair-person of her father's party, the Pakistan Peoples Party (PPP). By then Z. A. Bhutto had been overthrown and hanged and both she and her mother were incarcerated for several months before being exiled from the country. In April 1986, in an act of calculated audacity, Benazir returned to Pakistan to a rapturous welcome. Two years later, the military dictator, ZIA UL-HAQ, was killed in an air crash. She swiftly launched a vigorous campaign across the country and the PPP emerged as the single largest party in the National Assembly. She became the county's prime minister in December 1986 but it was apparent that the president, Gulam Ishaq Khan, a retired civil servant, and the Army Chief, General Mirza Aslam Beg, retained control over issues pertaining to national security, foreign policy, Kashmir, and nuclear weapons development. In addition, two retired generals held the two key ministries, foreign affairs and the interior, in her cabinet. She remained popular in the United States but at home, she and husband ASIF ALI ZARDARI, were increasingly regarded as venal, corrupt, and incompetent. The situation was further complicated by a power struggle with the president resulting in the dismissal of her government in August 1990. She was back in power, however, after elections in October 1993. Further deterioration of the economy, increased graft and corruption, allegedly spearheaded by her husband, followed. Her government was again dismissed in November 1996 after a controversy regarding her right to appoint judges to the country's Supreme Court. She went into exile while legal proceedings were instituted against her husband and herself. She was a frequent visitor to United States where she enjoyed considerable goodwill and support. In Washington and elsewhere it was generally believed that she had the widest popular appeal in Pakistan and she was expected to remain a major factor in the country. As the public standing of the Pakistani military dictator, President PERVEZ MUSHARRAF declined; Washington reportedly brokered an improbable deal. Despite their obvious mutual antagonism, Benazir would return to take over as the Prime Minister whereas Musharraf would shed his uniform and continue as the President, albeit as a civilian. She was expected to deal more firmly with the Islamic fundamentalists in the country than the President and she had stated as much in her public appearances. However, the arrangement further weakened the public standing of both of them. Nevertheless, she returned to Pakistan in October 2007. A crowd of 1.5 million was on hand to receive her. So were at least two suicide bombers. Two explosions shook her convoy as it slowly made its way from the airport to the tomb of the father of the county, Mohammed Ali Jinnah. About 140 were killed and at least three times as many were seriously injured. However, she narrowly escaped unhurt. Despite her complaints about the lax security arrangements for her personal protection, it was only marginally improved after the attack. The increased protection did not prevent her assassination on 27 December 2007 in Rawalpindi by a gunman and a suicide bomber. Perhaps it was a single individual.

Bhutto, Zulfikar Ali (1928-1979)

Pakistani leader. His father, Sir Shah Nawaz Bhutto, was one of the richest landlords in Sindh and was the prime minister of the Princely State of Junagarh at Partition. Zulfikar was schooled in Bombay (Mumbai) and further educated at the University of California, Berkeley and at Oxford. He was called to the bar in 1953 and set up a legal practice at the Sindh High Court. In 1958 he was inducted into an unelected cabinet by General AYUB KHAN. On the sudden death of Foreign Minister Mohammed Ali Bogra in 1963, Bhutto persuaded Ayub to reassign him as the foreign minister. There was open displeasure in Washington as Bhutto was considered as being too pro-Chinese and a leftist. In 1965, he played a critical role in precipitating the India-Pakistan war by reassuring the hesitant Ayub that the U.S. would support Pakistan and India would not enlarge the war beyond the confines of Kashmir. He was wrong on both counts. Washington cut off aid to both the belligerents and India extended the war into Punjab and into the Thar Desert. Pakistan much more dependent on U.S. assistance, suffered more under the embargo than India did. Bhutto, despite his wrong advice, accompanied Ayub to Tashkent to sign the eponymous agreement restoring the status quo ante between the two countries. On returning home, Bhutto soon turned on his mentor, Ayub, and joined the increasing clamor of opposition to the Tashkent Declaration and left the government in 1966 to form his own political party, the Pakistan Peoples Party (PPP) in late 1967. The party's manifesto was to transform the country into a socialist society. After the discredited Ayub's ouster, the elections of March 1970 gave the PPP a majority in the western wing of the country whereas the Bengali dominated Awami League swept the polls in the east and acquired an absolute majority in the whole of Pakistan. Bhutto, as the leader of the largest party from the western wing was firmly opposed to a constituent assembly that would be controlled by the avowedly secessionist Awami League. Civil war followed. India intervened, Pakistan lost the war, and Bangladesh was born. Bhutto took office as the President of a truncated Pakistan in December 1971. During 1971-74 Bhutto pursued his stated policy goals of socialism through nationalization and increased the government's control over market forces within the country. Widespread disruption of trade and economic activity followed. The result was increased poverty, accompanied by fiscal and monetary indiscipline. He also nationalized the educational institutions causing a decline in academic standards. Bhutto realigned Pakistan's foreign policy away from its close dependence on the U.S. Instead, the unvarying factor in his foreign policy was friendship with China, a country he pointedly visited shortly after coming to power. Washington, ever more distrustful, built up the Shah of Iran as the main regional ally and military power. On 14 August 1973, the twenty-sixth anniversary of the country's independence, Bhutto bestowed a new Constitution upon Pakistan. Under the new charter, he stepped down from the presidency and became the prime minister. In January 1977 the increasingly imperious Bhutto held the constitutionally scheduled elections. He was widely expected to win. However, the victory was so marked by flagrant rigging and intimidation that protests led by organized labor and students further assisted by the military's intelligence service, the ISI, swept across the country. The stage was thus set for a coup and the military deposed him in July 1977. He was sentenced to death on the egregious charge of conspiracy to commit murder of a political opponent. By March 1978, public indifference was so marked that the citizens of Lahore paid greater attention to a cricket match being played in the city than to the judgment delivered by the Lahore High Court sentencing Bhutto to death. Despite the dubious verdict and widespread pleas for clemency, the sentence was carried out on 4 April 1979. However, his party remained the most significant political force in Pakistan and is estimated to have the largest grass-roots organization in the country.

(*See* also: ZIA UL-HAQ MOHAMMED)

Bin Laden, Osama (1954-)

Terrorist and Islamic fundamentalist and founder of al-Qaeda. Bin Laden, the only son from the tenth wife of the Saudi-based construction magnate and billionaire, Mohammed Awad bin Laden, has an estimated 54 half-siblings and at least 24 children of his own. In 1979, Osama earned a degree in civil engineering from King Abdul Aziz University, Jeddah. In 1984, he helped fund the *Maktab al Khadamat* (MAK, Office of Service) established by his mentor, the Egyptian cleric Abdullah Azzam, a close associate of the well-known fundamentalist and fellow Egyptian, Mohammed Qutb. The MAK was the means to funnel arms, money, and recruits to the MUJAHIDEEN in Afghanistan. In 1988 he split from MAK, became more radical and personally supervised construction of defenses in Afghanistan. After the Soviet withdrawal in 1989, Osama was lauded as a hero on his return to Saudi Arabia. He then founded an organization to help Afghanistan veterans who fought against the Soviets, commonly known as the AFGHAN-ARABS. His assistance was particularly directed towards those who went off to fight in other war-zones involving Muslims like Bosnia and Chechnya. This outfit was later to become AL QAEDA (Arabic: foundation or basis). It is widely held that the presence of Western forces on the holy soil of Saudi Arabia during the 1991 Gulf War transformed him into a strident critic of the Saudi royal family and the West. Therefore, he was expelled from Saudi Arabia and sought haven under the Islamized government in Khartoum, Sudan. Where he built roads, planted crops, and trained Islamic militants in the use of firearms and explosives. He also formally established al Qaeda and forged alliances with other radical groups. He publicly opposed the September 1993 Oslo Peace Accords between Israel and the Palestinians. Seven months earlier (February 1993), al-Qaeda had launched its first strike against the World Trade Center in New York City killing six, injuring 1042, and consuming 1,500 pounds of a complex variety of explosives. About a month after the Oslo Accords, in October 1993, al Qaeda masterminded the massacre of elite U.S. soldiers in Somalia. In 1996, the leadership in Sudan changed and, bowing to pressure from the United States, Saudi Arabia, and Egypt, expelled him. He then flew to Afghanistan where the newly victorious TALIBAN warily welcomed him. Thanks to warm ties with Mullah Omar, the *Amir* (leader) of the Taliban, he moved with his huge entourage to Qandahar. In 1998 he along with six others issued a *fatwa* (edict) waging war against Jews and crusaders in general and Americans in particular. A series of highly provocative attacks against U.S. targets followed. The first one was on 7 August 1998, when al Qaeda operatives bombed U.S. embassies in Tanzania and Kenya which claimed 300 lives. Two years later a couple of suicide bombers severely damaged the American warship the *U.S.S. Cole* in Aden harbor in October 2000. Washington retaliated with air strikes using cruise missiles against a number of al Qaeda camps in Afghanistan and by announcing a $25 million reward for bin Laden's capture. The leadership, including bin Laden, possibly tipped off by Pakistan, escaped unhurt. On the morning of 11 September 2001, four American civilian airliners were hijacked along the east coast of the United States by nineteen members of al Qaeda. Two aircraft struck and destroyed the 110 storey twin towers of the World Trade Center in New York City. Another hit the headquarters of the U.S. military, the Pentagon, near Washington DC. The fourth, too, was apparently targeted for a high-value objective in the Washington area. However, passengers and crew fought off the hijackers and the aircraft crashed in rural Pennsylvania. The U.S. invaded Afghanistan in October 2001. Despite the swift and successful occupation of the country a majority of the Taliban leaders, Bin Laden and most of the leadership of al Qaeda escaped death or capture. Subsequent release of videos implies that most of them are alive, well, and active, presumably in safe havens along the Pakistan-Afghan border.

(*See also:* ANTI-SOVIET RESISTANCE GROUPS IN AFGHANISTAN)

Bonn Agreement

The United States and its coalition partners overthrew the Taliban Government in Afghanistan in late 2001. Thereafter, representatives of various Afghan factions met in Bonn, Germany under the aegis of the Special Representative of the U.N. Secretary-General for Afghanistan to draw plans for the future of the country. Various warlords, leaders of different ethnic groups, expatriate Afghans, and representatives of the exiled monarch reached an agreement on interim power sharing, the creation of a new constitution, and a commitment to hold elections in the country in 2004. The Bonn Agreement was signed on 5 December 2001.

Borlaug, Norman Ernest (1914-)

Agronomist, Nobel laureate (Peace, 1970). Borlaug developed new high yielding strains of cereals thereby ushering in the GREEN REVOLUTION in the parts of South Asia. On finishing his doctorate in plant pathology at the University of Minnesota in 1942, Borlaug did further research for two years on industrial and agricultural bactericides, fungicides, and preservatives at the Du Pont de Nemours Foundation before becoming the director of the Cooperative Wheat Research and Production Program in Mexico. The program, a joint undertaking by the Mexican government and the ROCKEFELLER FOUNDATION, undertook the study of genetics, breeding, and pathology of plants life. Entomology, agronomy, soil science, and cereal technology were researched as well. Dr. Borlaug then became the director of the International Wheat Improvement Program at the newly established International Maize and Wheat Improvement Center (CIMMYT) set up by the Rockefeller and FORD FOUNDATIONs in cooperation with the Mexican government. At CIMMYT Borlaug trained young scientists from numerous countries in research and production methods. Within twenty years he developed high-yielding short-strawed, disease-resistant wheat. The new cereal strains were put into extensive production in Latin America, the Near and Middle East, Africa and most spectacularly in India and Pakistan. The first Green Revolution was born.

Into his nineties Borlaug was experimenting with triticale, a man-made species of grain derived from a cross between wheat and rye that showed promise of being superior to either grain in productivity and nutritional quality.

Bose, Amar Gopal (1929-)

Electrical engineer, legendary acoustics technologist. Born in Philadelphia, PA, the son of an Indian father (Noni) and a white American mother (Charlotte), Bose founded the eponymous Bose Corporation.

He owns most of the shares in the $1.7 billion company and reinvests almost all its earnings in research and development.

At MIT, in 1956, while working on his doctorate, Bose bought the then best available hi-fi system and discovered that the output of sound was not accurate (he played the violin and had a good ear for music). Therefore, he experimented at MIT acoustics laboratory to device the means to improve the production of sound from speaker systems. After nine years of experimentation, Bose launched his product on the market. The sphere-shaped speakers evolved into the 901 system (1968), the company's most successful product. Like in a live performance, the 901 blended both direct and reflected sound.

In the early 1980s Bose faced a major financial crisis as interest rates rose to more than 20 percent on the $14 million bank loan he had secured for developing an audio system for use in GM cars. Following a single meeting with the CFO of the automobile giant, GM took over the loan and provided him with an additional $700,000 worth of new production equipment. The rest is history. The company has diversified into automobile suspension systems. Bose continues to teach at MIT.

Bowles, Chester (1901-1986)

Governor of Connecticut, American Ambassador to India and Nepal, 1951-1953 and to India, 1963-1969.

Of all the American Ambassadors to serve in Delhi, Chester Bowles is undoubtedly the most fondly remembered. During his first tenure, the first significant capital loan grant for $54 million was made to India. Fearing the impact of the Chinese revolution on India, Bowles aggressively sought the participation of American NGOs and Foundations in the country. During his second tenure, he was responsible for President JOHN F. KENNEDY's commitment to $1 billion in annual aid to the first two years of India's Third Five Year Plan. Despite the Sino-Indian War of 1962, Bowles views on China changed. He regarded Chinese communism as being more nationalistic than revolutionary or expansionist.

British Raj

The period of British colonial rule (1858-1947) over India, including those parts of British India those were later to become Burma (1937), Pakistan (1947) and Bangladesh (1971). The period began with both the dissolution of the Mughal Empire and the end of the rule of the East India Company. The Raj came to an end with the independence of India and Pakistan. During the Raj, the British crown was represented in India by a viceroy.

Burma (Myanmar)-U.S. Relations

A devastating cyclone in April 2008 briefly brought the country into the global spotlight. In contrast, Burma with its high, rugged mountains, dense jungles, and large rivers discouraged had trade and travel. This lack of contact shaped it into a distinctly different, xenophobic, and proud country. The sea brought European missionaries, merchants and the military in the early nineteenth century. The penultimate king, Mindon (ruled 1853-1878), attempted to develop closer ties with the U.S. in order to balance the rising power of British colonialism. He failed. The British completed the piece-meal conquest of the country in 1885.

The U.S. had little interest in the country till October 1940, when the Burma Road became the sole lifeline to China. The 712-mile road was built by the Chinese at the start of the Sino-Japanese War (1937-45). It was used to transport U.S. lend-lease war supplies to China from the Burmese railhead at Lashio to the town of Kunming in the Yunnan province of China. Traffic increased greatly after the Japanese took control of Chinese ports and French Indochina. After Burma fell to the Japanese in 1942, this vital land route was cut. Most of Burma had to be recaptured by the allies to re-establish the road link to China via the newly built Ledo Road (later called the Stilwell Road) from Ledo, in Assam, India to Bhamo in Burma. This road constructed in 1942-44 with American assistance and supervision re-established the road link to China via the Burma Road. Hence, the first Americans, other than missionaries and academics, to work with the Burmese were logistics and maintenance personal who handled the cargo bound for China from Rangoon harbor by rail and road to Kunming, China. After the Japanese conquest of Burma, about 700

American prisoners of war worked alongside an estimated 200,000 Burmese used as slave labor for the construction and maintenance of the 258-mile Burma-Siam railway built to supply the Japanese Army in Burma. Neither the road nor the railway, however, established any substantive contact between Americans and Burmese.

After Burmese independence in 1948, relations between the two countries were strained, as in the early 1950s the U.S. Central Intelligence Agency (CIA) trained and aided Kuomintang (KMT) troops who fled to the Shan State in Burma after the communist victory in China. In Shan State the KMT forces formed a virtually autonomous and hostile zone within the country. This situation sparked anti-American riots and the Burmese Premier U Nu urged the then U.S. Secretary of State Dean Rusk to press KMT President Chiang Kai-shek to resettle the Chinese forces in Taiwan. In March 1962, General Ne Win overthrew U Nu and the new military regime declared that Chinese irregulars were no longer a problem. Instead, Ne Win raised concerns about alleged CIA support for the separatist movements among the Shan and Karen minorities in the country and for the introduction of opium cultivation in the two regions. Suspicion and hostility against the U.S. persisted while the country moved towards an indigenous "Burmese Road to Socialism" and minimized contacts with the West.

Washington re-emerged as a factor when the U.S. sought to isolate Burma after the military junta called the State Law and Order Restoration Council (SLORC) ousted Ne Win in 1988. Further sanctions followed after the military refused to transfer power to the democratically elected National League for Democracy (NLD) led by AUNG SAN SUU KYI in 1990. The junta abolished SLORC in November 1997 and replaced it with the equally sinister and repressive organization called State Peace and Development Council (SPDC). The U.S. also refused to recognize the government's legitimate authority to change of the name of the country from Burma to Myanmar. Accordingly, Washington maintained limited diplomatic and economic ties, including in counter-narcotics operations as Burma was the world's second largest grower of opium. In 1990, after the NLD was prevented from taking power, the U.S. withdrew its ambassador from the country and opposed Burma's membership in various multilateral financial institutions. In addition, Washington imposed limited economic sanctions and suspended Burma from the U.S. Generalized System of Preferences.

One of the most prominent U.S. investors in Burma was UNOCAL CORPORATION. The company helped develop offshore gas fields in the Andaman Sea and built, as a joint venture, a $1.2 billion, 254-mile pipeline to transport natural gas to Thailand. However, in the late 1990s Unocal, like most other U.S. companies left Burma because of worsening business climate and increasing criticism from human rights groups and shareholders arising from the government's abuse of human rights and the lack of progress towards democracy in the country. In May 1997, Washington applied increased pressure on the junta by proscribing new investment by Americans and U.S. entities in Burma and imposed countermeasures due to Rangoon's noncompliance with recommendations of the Financial Action Task Force on Money Laundering. In 2003, the U.S. Congress passed the Burma Freedom and Democracy Act (BFDA), which prohibited imports from the country, banned the export of financial services to Burma, froze assets of certain Burmese financial institutions, and imposed visa restrictions on travel by Burmese officials. Congress renewed the BFDA in July 2004. Despite the despotic posturing, the military, mindful of the rising economic prosperity in neighboring countries like the military dominated Thailand, and the public demonstrations by monks and others, quietly but slowly liberalized trade, commerce, travel, education, and low level political activity. A new capital city, called Naypyidaw (Abode of Kings), was officially inaugurated in March 2007 though after two years of construction, only huge buildings belonging to various ministries, some hotels, and a handful of pastel-colored apartment blocks for government employees, were completed. Most impressive was the military's own fortress-like complex where the country's frail leader, General Than Shwe, resided. Later, in September that year the junta resurrected a patently unrepresentative and undemocratic constitutional convention that drafted the guidelines for a new constitution. The next stage was supposedly a seven-step road map to the creation of a new constitution that would formalize the military's grip over the country. In 2007 widespread protests and demonstrations followed after a steep rise in the price of commodities, especially oil and gas, and the perceived wastefulness in the construction of a new capital. The demonstrators included members of the widely respected Buddhist clergy. The regime brutally suppressed the protestors but did resume talks with Suu Kyi. Nevertheless, Burma's relations with the U.S. remained low-key as the U.S. Secretary of State CONDOLEEZZA RICE labeled the country as an "outpost of tyranny," along with North Korea, Cuba and Iran.

Burton, Danny Lee (Dan) (1938-)

Republican U.S. Congressman from Indiana, well-known for his bias against both India and China. After thirteen years in state politics, Burton was elected to the U.S. House of Representatives in 1982. He reportedly received strong support from separatist Kashmiri and Sikh communities during his election campaigns then and since. In turn, he sought legislative censure and the cut-off in foreign aid to India for alleged human rights abuses, especially in Kashmir, Nagaland, and Punjab. For sixteen years the Burton Amendment to the Foreign Operations Appropriations Bill (FOAB) was routinely defeated, sometimes after bruising battles in the U.S. Congress between pro-India and anti-India legislators. In addition, these debates served as a platform for Burton and others to showcase vicious anti-India allegations. 1997 was a watershed year, for the Burton Amendment mustered less than 100 votes in the House and was the first clear indication of the warming Indo-U.S. ties and the increased effectiveness of political lobbying by the Indian-American community. Thereafter his position on India slightly changed and he led a congressional delegation to both India and Pakistan in 2005. Furthermore, he gave his conditional support to the Indo-U.S. nuclear deal proposed by President Bush that year. Along with Congresswoman Sheila Jackson Lee, a Democrat from Texas, Burton founded the Congressional Pakistan Caucus in September 2004. However, his chairmanship of the caucus was not been free from controversy.

Because of his strident politics, his fellow law-makers reportedly prevented him from becoming the chairman of the coveted Committee on Foreign Affairs. Instead, he chaired the House Government Reform

Committee (1997-2002). As chairman, he headed an investigation into possible Democratic Party campaign finance abuse, especially in the 1996 presidential election. Shortly after the investigation began in March 1997 Burton was accused of demanding a $5,000 contribution from an American lobbyist working for the Pakistan government. As the lobbyist was unable to raise the funds, Burton complained about him to the Pakistani ambassador. Burton also cast himself as a moral watchdog in Washington but was forced to confess to an adulterous affair which resulted in the birth of a child out of wedlock.

Typical of his unusual career in Congress, Burton missed the beginning of the year's legislative session in 2007 for he was playing golf in California. Upon his return, embarrassed lawmakers passed a measure banning the acceptance of gifts and free or discounted trips from lobbyists by members of the house by a margin of 430-1 votes. Burrton's was the sole dissenting vote against the bill.

Bush, George Herbert Walker (1924-)

U.S. President (1988-92). In South Asia the Bush administration produced no major policy breakthroughs. Instead, the strategy was to circumvent the myriad non-proliferation strictures in order to sustain an increasingly unstable Pakistan, and to develop a normal and smooth relationship with a politically and economically assertive India. Both objectives were achieved by resorting to presidential waivers, a peculiarly U.S. foreign policy ploy that gives the president wide-ranging discretionary powers, usually by invoking the national interest as the pretext. Though India and Pakistan were under aid embargos of varying degrees, U.S. interests in both countries intensified as a result of the growing strategic relevance to militant Islam, and the resurgence of the two Asian giants, China and India. Accordingly, the Bush administration was the first to comprehend that the U.S. nuclear policy towards the region required greater political flexibility and pragmatism, but did little.

Bush, George Walker (1946-)

U.S. President (2001-8) Bush won office as the 43rd president of the United States, after a bruising, disputed election. Few imagined that his administration was destined to have a greater impact on U.S. —

South Asian relations than any President since Eisenhower's first term (1953-57). Among the early signs of change was when Bush the candidate stated that as president he would favour the immediate lifting of all sanctions, and would not pressure India to sign the CTBT. In addition, CONDOLEEZZA RICE, slated as National Security Advisor, declared that U.S. foreign policy toward India had been "wasted years" due to Washington's obsessions with nuclear non-proliferation, Pakistan, and Kashmir rather than to focus on broader issues like India's potential role as the stabilizing force in South Asia. When President Bush and Prime Minister MANMOHAN SINGH signed the agreement on nuclear cooperation in New Delhi on 2 March 2006, the U.S. administration brought to fruition the initiatives undertaken by his immediate predecessor, President CLINTON. Bush in cooperation with the U.S. Congress lifted post-Pokhran (the site of the Indian nuclear tests in 1998) sanctions against both India and Pakistan in the wake of 9/11 and to developed new strategic relationships with the two countries. However, the imperatives were different: Pakistan, because it was contiguous with both Afghanistan and Kashmir and was deeply involved in Jihads insurgencies in both regions; India for its spectacular entry into the global economy, its demographics, and its vibrant democracy. Under such circumstances it was natural to co-opt the latter as a chaotic and prickly ally. In the fine tradition of both change and continuity, the BJP's Jaswant Singh's long-drawn dialogue with the preceding Clinton Administration's Strobe Talbott had preserved the space within which the Bush administration's diplomacy could operate. A terrorist attack on the Indian parliament directed from Pakistan on 13 December, 2001, followed by mobilization of the Indian armed forces and an unrelated outbreak of communal strife in Godhra, Gujarat, in February 2002, did not disrupt the larger strategic picture. Similarly, Secretary of State Colin Powell's abrupt designation of Pakistan as a Major Non-NATO Ally in March 2004 did little to disrupt the wary U.S.-Indian reconciliation or to reassure Islamabad.

(*See also:* INDO-U.S. NUCLEAR COOPERATION, OIL AND GAS PIPELINES, PEACE CORPS, U.S.MILITARY AID IN SOUTH ASIA AFTER 9/11, U.S.-INDIA KNOWLEDGE INITIATIVE ON AGRICULTURE).

Business Process Outsourcing (BPO) And Information Technology (IT) In India

The trend towards contracting of specific business tasks, such as payroll and data entry, to a third-party service provider began in the 1980s. When firms contracted with companies outside their own country, this service was often called offshore outsourcing. Within ten years, India, catering mainly to MNCs (Multi National Corporations), emerged as a leader in the field. The key factor was the excess capacity of the installed bandwidth (the data rate or the frequency range of the communication systems) leading to much lowering in the cost of telecommunications for leased fiber-optic lines laid across the globe. In addition, the availability of an English speaking workforce on the other side of the globe ensured that 24 hour service was available as Indians were at work during the sleep and leisure hours of their counterparts in the west. Once the trend started, the number of different functions outsourced grew steadily and included purchasing and disbursement, order entry, billing and collection, human resources administration, cash and investment management, tax compliance, internal audit, etc.

The BPOs further benefited from the increasing need to outsource business processes by western companies who were under increasing pressure from the changing and challenging business environment and the technological and legislative demands placed on them at home. In the new millennium Information Technology (IT)-enabled services and Knowledge Process Outsourcing (KPO), which are considered as the higher levels of the BPOs, were steadily developing in India. According to a NASSCOM-McKinsey report, annual revenue projections for India's IT industry in 2008 were $ 87 billion. IT Exports account for thirty-five percent of the total exports from the country. Software and Services contribute over 7.5 percent of the overall GDP growth in India's GDP and has created 2.2 million jobs. Foreign Direct Investment (FDI) is around $ 4-5 billion and Market capitalization of IT companies is estimated at $ 225 billion. Market openings are emerging across the four broad sectors of IT services, software products, IT- enabled services, and e-businesses. In addition to the export market, all of these segments have a domestic market component as well.

American companies are rated by their effectiveness in performing functions and solutions by the U.S. Department of Defense's Software Engineering Institute (SEI). The highest such a rating is Level 5. In addition the Capability Maturity Model (CMM) is used as a tool for objectively assessing the ability of contractors' *processes* to perform a contracted software project. Though it comes from the area of software development, it is often applied as a generally applicable model to assist in understanding the process capability maturity of an organization in diverse areas. A large number of SEI-CMM Level 5 companies are operating in India.

India, with a large pool of skilled manpower like chartered accountants, doctors, MBAs, lawyers, and research analysts, may be able to add further value to the global KPO businesses and its high-end processes like valuation and investment research, patent filing, legal and insurance claims processing, online teaching, and developing media content. By 2002 all major Indian software firms were in the BPO business as well. Included were companies like Infosys (Progeon), HCL, Satyam (Nipuna) and Patni. By 2003 international third party BPO giants like Convergys and Sitel, too, set up subsidiaries in India, as did the service arms of corporations like Accenture, IBM, Hewlett Packard, and Dell.

In the early 1990s, BPO activity burgeoned after a meeting between the iconic head of General Electric (GE), Jack Welch, and K.P Singh, of the multi-billion dollar DLF Group, who were the legendary developers of land in and around Delhi. Singh suggested the sleepy, arid region of Gurgaon in Haryana, a part of the National Capital Region (NCR) as a particularly suitable site for back office operations. Accordingly, Pramod Bhasin, the then head of GE in India hired Raman Roy and several members of his management team then working for American Express to start-up GECIS (GE Capital International Services). Roy went a step further and tried out voice operations out of India for the first time. In 2004 GECIS was spun off as a separate entity called Genpact.

However, the undisputed IT/BPO capital of India is not suburban Delhi but the south Indian city of Bangalore, officially Bengaluru. The city contributes a whopping 36 percent of the country's software exports and became India's third largest city in 2007 (population 5.1 million). The IT industry is located in three main clusters — Software Technology Parks of India, Bangalore (STPI); International Technology Park Bangalore (ITBP) formerly known as International Technology Park Limited (IPL), and Electronics City (EC)With an economic growth of 10.3 percent per annum , it is the fastest growing metropolis in India. It also has the highest number of biotechnology companies in the country. Around 47 percent of the 265 such companies in India were located there and include Biocon, India's largest biotechnology company. Infosys and Wipro, India's second and third largest software companies are headquartered in Bangalore as are many of the global SEI-CMM Level 5 Companies.

The growth of Information Technology has presented the city with unique challenges. Ideological clashes sometimes occur between the city's IT moguls, who demand an improvement in the city's infrastructure and the state government, whose electoral base is primarily the people in rural Karnataka. Currently, Bangalore has the largest number of broadband internet connections in India.

Another garrison town like Bangalore, Pune, 120 miles (185 kms) west of Mumbai, is another emerging IT center in the country. It has the highest PC penetration among households and is home to the usual well known giants of the Indian software industry like Wipro, Infosys, Satyam, Tata Technologies, TCS, Veritas, Cognizant, PCS and Mahindra British Telecom. The town, long known as a center of learning, is establishing the Indian Institute of Software Engineering in association with the Carnegie-Mellon University, of Pittsburgh, Pennsylvania, U.S.A. competitor to Bangalore for the top spot is the city of Hyderabad located a mere 308 miles (495 km) away. Here on a sprawling 54 acre campus the Microsoft India Development Center (MSIDC) was established in 1998. That November "Cyber Towers" as the first phase of the Hyderabad Information Technology Engineering Consultancy City (HITEC City) were inaugurated as well. The HITECH city situated in the Madhapur area of Hyderabad attracted multinational software giants like IBM, Microsoft, GE Capital, Toshiba, and Oracle and Indian companies like Satyam Computers Not unexpectedly, Hyderabad's IT export revenue grew to $1.6 billion in 2007, an increase of 62% from fiscal 2004. Hence, the city is sometimes referred to as Cyberabad. A major investment in digital infrastructure has been crucial to the growth of the IT and BPO industry in the city. However, other infrastructural shortcomings, communal tensions in the region, and the indifferent law and order situation in the area are obvious constraints to future growth. Other cities like Kolkata, Mumbai, and Chennai, too, are important centers as well.

Another key impact of the global sourcing was the reversal of the brain drain, as an estimated 60,000 people of Indian origin returned home to India to launch new projects or simply to work in the comfort and familiarity of their native soil. Besides the direct positive impact on national income and the creation of jobs, the sector spawned several ancillary industries and services ranging from security guards to fast-food delivery businesses. It also triggered a rise in the collection of direct taxes and propelled an increase in consumer spending. In 2007 Indian revenues were estimated at $13.8 billion of the $24 billion global offshore BPO market. Hence, its share had declined from a peak of about 70 percent to 58 percent in three years despite the industry growing at the rate of 38 percent per year. Eastern European countries, Ireland, the Philippines, and South Africa had cut into the Indian share of the market. Nevertheless, India's share of the BPO industry is expected to maintain its pre-eminent position and continued growth.

Call centers are another aspect of out-sourcing. The setting up of infrastructure can be complex and expensive. Typically, the consumer uses a toll-free telephone connection to a call center. The operator responds to the consumer's queries by accessing a database. Hence, call centers assist sales support staff, complete airline and hotel reservations, answer technical queries, perform tele-marketing research, and provide various financial services ranging bank statements to accounts receivables.

Indian IT companies notably Satyam, Wipro and HCL employ about 17.000 Americans in their U.S. based operations. Tata employs another 19,000 Americans in its sixteen businesses in the United States. Not all sixteen are in the IT field.

Other South Asian countries, too, have benefited from the Outsourcing boom. For instance, Pakistan, a distant second, has an IT industry valued at approximately $2 billion in 2008. It exports were around $1 billion and the industry employed around 90,000 professionals.

(*See also:* SILICON VALLEY, Y2K PROBLEM)

C

Carter, James (Jimmy) Earl (1924-)

U.S. President (1976-80), Nobel laureate (Peace, 2002). President Carter tried to replace the realpolitik of his Republican predecessors with the politics of morality with a strong focus on nuclear non-proliferation and the furtherance of human rights. His stance was more pronounced during the presidential campaign, when Carter condemned the failure of the incumbent, Republican GERALD FORD, to denounce a recent nuclear test by India, and his muted response to a French deal to sell Pakistan a reprocessing plant that could be used for the development of nuclear weapons. However, following the Soviet invasion of Afghanistan in late 1979, the Carter administration turned a blind eye to Pakistan's nuclear ambitions but tensions over the supply of enriched uranium for the India's Tarapore nuclear reactor persisted. In addition, the new administration examined the whole concept of aid to South Asia. Economic aid, once conceived as a lever to entice India, among others, into the American camp, was downgraded to a policy of "meeting basic needs" of developing countries. The new initiative was conceptualized as a part of the "Carter-Brzezinski policy" of cultivating regionally influential countries as a means of devolving some of the excessive responsibilities that the U.S. had assumed in the post-War decades. On the whole South Asia received little attention as the administration felt that the Simla agreement negotiated between ZULFIKAR ALI BHUTTO and INDIRA GANDHI had resolved many perplexing issues and had markedly reduced tensions between India and Pakistan. The agreement signed in July 1972 in the eponymous town of Simla, laid down the principles that should normalize future relations between India and Pakistan. It also committed both countries "to settle their differences by peaceful means through bilateral negotiations." In addition, the agreement redesignated the "Ceasefire Line" as the "Line of Control" in Jammu and Kashmir thereby giving it the implied sanctity of a permanent border

border between the two countries. Furthermore, when the equally moralistic but more austere and distinctly quirky Morarji Desai became Prime Minister of India under Janata Party rule (1977-79), Carter considered him as an Indian politician well suited for the new dispensation for Desai was more centrist than Indira Gandhi and pursued an even-handed policy of Non-Alignment. However, the honeymoon did not last long as four disruptive events impacted South Asia in the last two years of the Carter Administration: The Soviet military intervention in Afghanistan in December 1979, and the attendant U.S. support to Pakistan and its clients in Afghanistan; Mrs. Gandhi's return to power in January 1980; the U.S. Senate's refusal to approve the second shipment of enriched uranium for Tarapore nuclear plant, and the seizure of the U. S. embassy staff as hostages in Iran. The latter dominated U.S. news and thought during the last fourteen months of his presidency and still has global repercussions.

As an ex-president, Carter has done much humanitarian work and peace-making. Among the former is the Habitat for Humanity project begun in 1984. Both the former President and Paul Leonard, Habitat for Humanity International's chief executive officer, traveled to India in October 2006 to join volunteers from around the world to help build houses for needy families during the 23rd annual project named in honor of the former president. Selecting India was a natural for Carter for various personal reasons. For instance, his mother, LILLIAN, had worked as PEACE CORPS volunteer in India at the age of 67. In addition, on 3 January 1978, President Carter visited a small village, Daulatpur-Nasirabad, in Haryana State in India. The villagers felt so honored by the trip that they renamed the village as Carterpuri and celebrate the occasion on 3 January every year. Furthermore, in 1997 Carter received the Indira Gandhi Prize for Peace, Disarmament and Development.

President Carter interest in Nepal was considerable but understated. In 1977 he pressured King Birendra to release the respected political leader BP Koirala and let him come to the U.S. for medical treatment. Not unexpectedly, as early as 2003 the former president gave his attention to the Maoist insurgency in Nepal. Consequently, in June 2007, he met with the undisputed Maoist leader, Prachanda, and his deputy Baburam Bhattarai during a four day trip to Nepal. Carter concluded that Washington should establish lines of communication with the Maoists because it was obvious that the people of Nepal had accepted the erstwhile insurgents as a factor in shaping the future of their country. His involvement in Nepal eased relations between the Bush Administration and the incoming democratically elected Maoist government in the post-monarchist republic of Nepal.

Casinos in South Asia

Increasingly in South Asia, it is the American or an Indian presence that competes and/or collaborates on various ventures. Casinos are no different. The first such gaming establishment, Casino Nepal, was set up in 1968 by an uncle of the king at an Indian-owned hotel, the Oberoi Soaltee. In 1976, a former American soldier, Richard D. Tuttle, took over its management. Later he founded the Nepal Recreation Center (NRC), a joint venture that ran a total of seven casinos in the capital and one in the resort town of Pokhara. Tuttle brought in Rakesh Wadhwa, an author and a chartered accountant from New Delhi, to help him manage the enlarging enterprise. The two then established casinos in Sri Lanka and Kyrgyzstan as well. However, in 2007, Tuttle and Wadhwa fell out over a dispute about the control of the casinos in Nepal. The quarrel was probably a reflection of the decline in the monarchy's power in the Himalayan kingdom for prior to the Maoist insurgency, the palace had a finger in most of Nepal's moneymaking ventures, even more so in the gaming industry for the royals had established it as a monopoly. With the abolition of the country's monarchy in 2008, other entrepreneurs are likely to step into a field where the unlikely duo of a septuagenarian American and his erstwhile Indian associate, who was still in his 50s, were wrangling to retain enough of the assets for themselves.

The casino industry was one of the prime tourist attractions in the Himalayan nation. It employed over 9,000 workers and was one of the major sources of the payment of royalties and taxes to the government of Nepal. In a further sub-continental twist, the Nepalese rivalry spilled over in India for Wadhwa took a stake in two floating casinos in India's tourist friendly Goa, the only Indian state where offshore gambling was allowed. Not to be outdone, Tuttle reportedly tied up with an Indian partner in Mumbai to launch another gambling ship in Goa. Meanwhile, in another Himalayan Indian State, Sikkim, the South Africa-based businessman Vivian Reddy and the former cricketer Kapil Dev, along with other investors launched their first casino in 2008.

Center for Afghanistan Studies (CAS), University of Nebraska at Omaha

The university started a modest program in Afghan studies in 1972. Two years later it was strengthened by the donation of the Arthur and Daisy Paul Afghanistan Collection of about 1,000 artifacts and other items to the Center. The following year the Center established an institutional linkage with Kabul University. Four years later (1979) the Soviets militarily intervened in Afghanistan and the university suddenly became a major resource for the American effort against U.S.S.R in the Pakistan-Afghanistan region. Since then, the CAS staff provided consulting services for various federal agencies, the media, the private sector, and citizen initiative groups. The Center received nearly $60 million in grants and contracts to support technical assistance programs, training, and educational exchanges. More than 100 members of the faculty and staff were involved in projects related to Afghanistan. The United Nations sent over 500 Afghans in exchange programs and other assignments to the Center and the university continued to maintain a Field Office in Kabul. For about twenty years following the Soviet invasion the Center received millions of dollars for producing the Holy *Quran,* anti-communist propaganda, and schoolbooks glorifying *Jihad* for distribution to the Afghan children. Reportedly the U.S. government continued to ship these textbooks even after the fundamentalist, xenophobic TALIBAN came to power in Kabul. The Taliban continued the use of the American-produced books, though the radical movement scratched out human faces in keeping with its strict fundamentalist codes. The Taliban also demanded that the American oil company, UNOCAL, provided the Center with $900,000 as a part of the deal to lay pipelines through Afghanistan. After the overthrow of the Taliban, the university again cranked up the presses in neighboring Pakistan to churn out new schoolbooks funded by a $6.5 million grant from the U.S. Agency for International

Development (AID). The Agency's Central Asia Task Force arrived in Peshawar, where the textbooks were printed, to oversee hasty revisions to the printing plates. Ten Afghan educators labored night and day, replacing rough drawings of weapons with sketches of pomegranates and oranges. After thirty year, on a break from a war-scarred past, children in Afghanistan opened traditional textbooks written by scholars based at CAS and other universities in the U.S.

Central Treaty Organization (CENTO), 1955-1979

An alliance created in 1955 by Iraq, Turkey, Pakistan, Iran and Britain, with the strategic goal of containing the Soviet Union by instituting a line of strong stable states along the U.S.S.R.'s south-western frontier. Its original name was Middle East Treaty Organization (METO). As it was headquartered in the Iraqi capital, it was also known as the Baghdad Pact. To avoid alienating Arab states friendly to the West, the U.S. did not join it till 1958 although it was widely known that American military and economic aid was essential for the alliance to function. Modeled after NATO, the treaty committed member countries to mutual cooperation, protection, and non-intervention in each other's affairs. In 1959 a coup toppled the monarchy in Iraq and the new republican regime withdrew from the Pact. Thereafter, its name was changed to CENTO. The U.S.-Pakistani defense arrangements led to an increase in the number of U.S. military and intelligence personnel in Pakistan from less than 50 in 1953 to about 1,000 by 1960. In addition to radar scans and signals intercepts, U.S. aircraft flew reconnaissance missions over the Soviet Union from Pakistan. However, few Pakistanis considered these flights as a potential liability till a Lockheed U-2 spy plane was shot down deep in Soviet territory in 1960. The aircraft had taken off from an airbase near Peshawar. In the wake of the U-2 incident Moscow warned Pakistan that it had become a target for a possible Soviet nuclear attack. Thereafter, the presence of U.S. intelligence personnel declined greatly. The CENTO region was extremely volatile during the 1960s with the ongoing Arab-Israeli Conflict and the Indo-Pakistani wars. With the U.S., preoccupied in Vietnam and with other CENTO members unwilling to get involved in either dispute, the value of the alliance to member states declined. Importantly, the alliance could not prevent the expansion of Soviet influence to non-member countries in the region, such as Egypt, Syria, and the Iraqi republic. It nominally lasted till the Iranian Revolution (1979), although it was already defunct in 1974, when a member of CENTO, Turkey, invaded Cyprus. Because of the invasion, a fellow member of the pact and NATO, Britain, withdrew its commitment of forces to CENTO. It was one of the least successful of the Cold War alliances.

China-Burma-India Theatre of Operations (CBI)

This little remembered theater of World War II was established in December 1941 with a divided headquarters: The British in New Delhi and the Chinese in Chunking. Of the 12.3 million Americans under arms during the World War II, only 250,000 served in CBI and few saw combat in this theater of operations. America's major contribution was to provide materials and manpower to build the Ledo Road, a land-route from India to China and to fly supplies over the Himalayas to that country. The road-building faced formidable challenges from the dense jungle, the craggy mountain ranges, tropical heat, drenching monsoons, leeches, mosquitoes, intestinal parasites, unheard of skin diseases, and from the Japanese forces occupying Burma whose major strategic goal was to prevent supplies from reaching the Chinese from the allied powers. Despite these odds, the road was completed in March 1945. Within six months of its completion, the war was over and its relevance precipitously declined. In disuse, portions of the road were reclaimed by the surrounding Burmese jungle and form a part of a wildlife preserve.

The CBI was not an operational headquarters. It was merely an administrative set up for American formations deployed in China, Burma and India. From March 1942, it operated under the headquarters of the South-East Asia Command based in Ceylon (now Sri Lanka). Just as the headquarters were divided so were the war aims of the two allies. The British aim was the re-conquest of Singapore and not the retaking of Burma. The American mission was to secure enough territory to build a road to supply China through northern Burma. Since neither country fully supported the war aims of the other, the theater received little attention. Furthermore, in 1942 the Indian National Congress launched the Quit India Movement against continued British occupation of the country. Hence, the Americans got little cooperation from Indians. Politically and socially, the situation was worsened in 1943 by the Great Bengal Famine. From the Indian perspective, the many causes of the famine included wartime inflation, the reallocation of transportation systems (especially boats) to sustain the war effort, and diversion of foodstuffs to foreign troops that included thousands of Chinese, West African, British, and American soldiers. Indians were also shocked by the racial segregation between American black and white troops. None of these factors were conducive to a pleasant Indo-American interaction or to happy memories of the servicemen's stay in the CBI Theater. Even Dean Rusk (1909-1994) who served as a colonel in this theater from 1942-45 and developed life-long interest in Asia paid little personal attention to South Asia as the U.S. Secretary of State, (1961-69). Only yarns about General "Vinegar Joe" Stilwell and Colonel Merrill's Marauders are remembered by some Americans.

Clinton, William Jefferson (1946-)

U.S. President (1992-2001). The Clinton Administration, more by fortuitous circumstance than by purposeful design, initiated the transition in the U.S. South Asian policy from the militarized grand strategy promulgated by DULLES and the Cold War hawks in the 1950s to one of more nuanced diplomacy.

Under Clinton, New Delhi came to be considered as a strategic partner, whereas other South Asian countries, including Pakistan, were deemed as fragile political entities in need of multifaceted support, but, without direct Indian participation. This process started slowly during Clinton's first term (1992-1996) as the Administration was centered on managing the drastically altered international situation following the collapse of the Soviet Union and the resurgence of Asia. As Clinton's second term (1997-2000) unfolded, however, a host of new issues surfaced including some outside South Asia that were to impact the region as well. The major extra-regional issues included the war in the Balkans, and the various acts of terrorism against the U.S. carried out by Islamic fundamentalists. In South Asia concerns over overt nuclear proliferation were predominant as Pakistani operatives were detected peddling in nuclear technology and relevant hardware from Texas to Pyongyang while resumption of nuclear testing by India could not be ruled out. Deeply committed to non-proliferation, the Clinton Administration used a combination of inducements and intimidation to stall further nuclear proliferation. Washington urged both countries to sign the NPT and the CTBT, by offering them relief from sanctions imposed by the Glenn and PRESSLER AMENDMENTS. To Pakistan it offered the resumption of sales of the multi-role F-16 fighter-bombers along with other conventional weaponry. These incentives outraged India. Nonetheless, Prime Minister P. V. NARASIMHA RAO agreed to abort nuclear tests that were already in the final stages of preparation, when he made his official visit to the U.S. in May 1994. Clinton and his Deputy Secretary of State Strobe Talbott used Rao's presence in Washington to persuade him to do so in order to avoid sanctions and other obstacles that would inhibit his plans and those of his finance minister MANMOHAN SINGH to liberalize the Indian economy and open it to market forces. When the Democrats lost control of both houses of Congress in 1994, Clinton's latitude for maneuver on persuading India and Pakistan to forego nuclear weaponization by signing the CTBT was severely undermined as the Republican majority refused to ratify the treaty. This obviously emboldened the BJP government in India, and the India-phobic Pakistani regime, to be far more resistant to doing so.

In South Asia there was mounting terrorism in a number of countries, increasing political turmoil especially in Pakistan and the rise of the more stridently nationalist BJP in India. Two years into Clinton's second term (1998), the BJP led by ATAL BIHARI VAJPAYEE as Prime Minister, came to power. Nuclear tests swiftly followed, taking Washington by surprise and outrage. These reactions gave way to a long dialogue that then commenced between Vajpayee's Finance Minister, Jaswant Singh, and Clinton's representative, Strobe Talbott, that continued for more than two years and embraced fourteen formal and numerous informal encounters for the purpose of trying to resolve the pattern of estrangement that had dogged U.S.-Indian relations. Parallel talks were also held with a Pakistani team led by Shamshad Ahmed, the foreign secretary. As Talbott himself states, the meetings with Indians constituted a dialogue whereas the ones with Pakistanis could not be classified as such. The talks with the latter were often more querulous, conducted at a lower level and the officials concentrated on blaming India for the tests and the need for American intervention to solve KASHMIR once and for all. Meanwhile, Pakistani incursions in the remote heights of Kargil, the informal U.S. acceptance of Islamabad's continued support of terrorism in Indian Kashmir, the overthrow of Pakistan Prime Minister NAWAZ SHARIF by General MUSHARRAF and the resurgence of military dictatorship in that country, finally led Washington to tailor U.S. policy to the reality of a failing Pakistan in contrast to the much larger, stronger, and politically viable India. Henceforth, the primary stress was on the burgeoning relationship between India and the United States and the shift was marked by the Clinton's trip to South Asia in March 2000. His impact was stunning in India and dismaying in Pakistan. His condemnation of a recent terrorist massacre in a Sikh village in Kashmir won him much favor in India and his speech before the Indian parliament was a rhetorical triumph. Clinton accurately sensed the mood of the approximately 700 Indian parliamentarians and redrafted parts of the speech as he talked. En route home, the President somberly stopped in Pakistan, symbolizing thereby the moral distinction he made between the two states. Nevertheless, Pakistanis felt that a presidential visit regardless of its duration and its icy cordiality was a triumph for the country in general and for Musharraf in particular. Clinton briefly met the Pakistani dictator, and gave a fifteen minute address, televised live and in full so that Islamabad would not be able to selectively censor or highlight parts of his speech. During his South Asia trip, Clinton also made a little remembered one-day trip to Bangladesh. The side-trip was constrained by concerns about the president's security and talks were limited to mundane discussions on tariffs, immigration procedures, the possibility of the write off of debts, and the finalization of some agreements on energy. A new course in South Asian policy had been set which the succeeding Bush administration would carry forward.

Cooke, Hope (1940-)

A U.S. citizen who became queen of Sikkim, then an Indian protectorate. Born in San Francisco, California, orphaned in childhood,

Cooke was a ward of her uncle, Seldon Chapin, a former U.S. ambassador to Iran. In 1959, she was a New York City debutante and traveled the world as a teenaged socialite. While in India, she met Palden Thondup Namgyal, the crown prince of Sikkim at the bar in the Windermere Hotel in Darjeeling, India. He was a widower nearly twice her age. Nevertheless, in March 1963, they were married in a Buddhist monastery in Sikkim. Neither imagined that the vivid ceremony accompanied by the drone of long Tibetan horns, the clang of cymbals and the chants of lamas would be the last of its kind. In 1965, he became the twelfth *chogyal* (ruler) of the Indian protectorate of Sikkim and she became "The Grace Kelly of the East." The Government of India, with its long-held misgivings about marriages between foreigners and the rulers of Princely States was increasingly concerned about the royal couple's intensified contacts with foreign nationals, many of whom advocated full sovereignty for the small, strategically located Himalayan fiefdom. In April 1973, Sikkim erupted with demands for full democracy and closer ties with India. The unrest, mostly among the Nepali settlers in the princely state, was presumably aided and abetted by New Delhi. Unable to control the disturbances, the *chogyal* was forced to seek India's protection. Thereafter, he was guarded by Indian army units and though he retained his throne he was reduced to a powerless figurehead. The marriage swiftly soured. In August 1973 Cooke left with their two children, Hope Leezum and Palden Gyurmed for New York. In a referendum in 1975, the Sikkimese people overwhelmingly voted to join India. Hope divorced her husband in 1979. She has since remarried and works as a tour guide in New York City.

Coomaraswamy, Ananda (1877-1947)

Curator and historian. Ananda was the son of Sir Muthu Coomaraswamy, a Sri Lankan, and an Englishwoman, Elizabeth Clay Beebe. He was born in Colombo, Sri Lanka, shortly before the death of his father in 1879. The young widow never returned to Sri Lanka and never remarried. In 1906, Coomaraswamy became the first Sri Lankan to obtain Doctorate in mineralogy from the University of London. Like his father, he married an English girl, but unlike him, he returned to Sri Lanka. On returning to the island, Coomaraswamy shifted his attention to Buddhism, nationalism, art and philosophy. His first book, *Medieval Singhalese Art*, was published in 1908 and was favorably reviewed by critics. More books and articles followed. Two of them were published in *Vanity Fair* in 1916 and established his reputation in the United States. He thereafter joined the Boston Museum of Fine Arts where the oriental collection had grown haphazardly during the past thirty years. Coomaraswamy organized and catalogued most of the collection and greatly enlarged it as well. He was also caught up by the high tide of Indian nationalism and became the leader of the Foundation for the Appreciation of Indian Aesthetics and Spirituality. He had planned to go to India on his 70th birthday, but that was not to be. On 9 September, 1947, within a few days of Indian independence, he died of a massive heart attack.

Cornwallis, Lord Charles (1738-1805)

British soldier and administrator Cornwallis typified the triangular relationship between North America, the British Isles, and the Indian subcontinent. Success or failure on one continent was sometimes balanced by the opposite result elsewhere. In the United States Cornwallis was the general who surrendered British forces at Yorktown in October 1781, thereby effectively ending the British imperial presence in the U.S. Hence, Americans view him as the losing general of the war. In Ireland he suppressed a rebellion thus enabling the Act of Union between Britain and Ireland in 1800. This act created the United Kingdom of Great Britain and Ireland and was widely detested by the Irish. Accordingly, in Ireland he was "not a favorite." In India, as the Governor-General of British-controlled territories (1786-93) he reformed the administration of the East India Company and defeated the formidable Tipu Sultan in the battle of Srirangapatnam, Karnataka. The general personally took the responsibility of looking after the welfare of the sons and family of the dead sultan. In addition, he gave his prize money, almost £50,000 to the army. Therefore, he was regarded as an able administrator and a humane, popular, and victorious military commander. In England, he reinforced the notion of the innate superiority of the aristocracy for he was the first nobleman to govern India and the first governor-general to return home with an unblemished reputation. He was also a nobleman committed to the service of his country: In 1805 he was again asked to return to India again to reform the Company and restore order in the territories under its control. Aged and weary, he dutifully returned to India and promptly died. He was buried at the small town of Ghazipur on the banks of the Ganges, where his grave is maintained by the Government of India.

Correa, Charles (1930-)

Indian architect and designer. Charles Correa studied architecture at the University of Michigan and at the Massachusetts Institute of Technology (MIT), Boston. In private practice in Bombay since 1955, his work laid special emphasis on the use of prevailing resources, and on harmonizing it with regional cultural and climatic conditions. Guided by these principles, he developed specific patterns of housing for the poor in India. Correa has also designed numerous townships and residential projects across India. His alma mater honored him with an Honorary Doctorate and he continues to maintain his affiliation with MIT.

Cotton

Both India and the American South were major producers of cotton in the nineteenth century. At the onset of the American Civil War (1861-65), the breakaway Confederate States of America considered cotton as its key export commodity which could compel Britain to recognize the confederacy as an independent country. The South supplied 78 percent of the cotton used in Britain's 3,000 mills. However, this dependence on southern cotton was offset by the rapid rise in the production of Indian cotton from 987,000 bales in 1861 to 1,798,000 bales by 1863. This growth in India saved the cotton industry in the United Kingdom and contributed to the collapse of the Confederacy in America. The impact of Indian production was reflected in cotton prices for they were twice as high in New York as compared to Liverpool. During the course of the Civil War the price of cotton in New York soared by more than 800 percent. In contrast, the rise in Liverpool was little more than four-fold. The growth of cotton production in Egypt and in Tsarist Russia's Central Asian possessions was also related to the American Civil War. An unforeseen consequence of the civil war was the further conquest of Central Asia by Russia, perhaps to prevent the British from securing the cotton-fields of the region. By 2007 India was the third largest cotton producer in the world with 3.2 million people working in the industry. However, yields began to decline in the 1990s as cotton was more vulnerable to pests than wheat or rice, and farmers were forced to invest heavily in pesticides and fertilizers. In addition, the price of cotton on the New York Board of Trade steadily dropped by more than 50 percent during the twenty-five years since the 1980. Accordingly, an estimated 95 percent of the farmers were believed to be heavily indebted in India's Vidharbha region stretching across central India and the eastern part of the state of Maharashtra. The next major culprit was the genetically modified cotton seed, introduced into India by the St. Louis, Missouri, based American agrochemical company, Monsanto, and enthusiastically endorsed by the local government. The new seed was supposedly resistant to boll weevil, the main cotton pest. It also required just two sprays of insecticide per year instead of the usual eight. The modified seed was priced at 450 percent more than that of normal seeds. Yet many farmers bought it because of its supposed indestructibility and higher yield. However, the higher production was heavily dependent on availability of water and to the new seed was not as resistant to Indian pests as anticipated. Accordingly, in the arid Vidharbha, plants died and took many of the farmers with them. Altogether, about 3,500 cotton farmers have killed themselves in the first seven years of the new millennium. The saga had come its full cycle. The American Civil War brought cotton to the region and an American agricultural company and the New York Board of Trade may end up playing a major role in its decline 150 years later.

D

Dall, Charles (1816-1886)

Unitarian Missionary. The Harvard-educated Dall was the first ever foreign missionary of the Unitarian Church of America. On arrival in Calcutta in 1855, it was clear to him that India needed the spirit and not the form of Christianity. Hence, Dall made wide-ranging social contacts with Bengalis and wrote more than a hundred pamphlets. He was also the key supporter of the Unitarian lay preacher, Hajom Kissor Singh in the Khasi Hills. Within a year of his arrival following his speech at the University Metropolitan College, he met the 18-year-old Keshub Chandra Sen (1838-1884). Dall was instrumental in converting Sen to Unitarianism. Under his influence, Sen founded the Goodwill Fraternity, a Unitarian Society for students and joined the reformist monotheistic Vedantic movement, the Brahmo Somaj. Sen soon became the central figure of Brahmo Somaj.

(*See also:* ADAM WILLIAM; MISSIONARIES)

Daud, Sardar Muhammad (1909-1978)

First President, Republic of Afghanistan (1973-78). Born in Kabul, educated there and in France, Daud, like most of the Afghan elite of his generation, joined the army. As a cousin of the king, he became a governor and a General Officer commanding an entire province at the age of 25. Other military and provincial commands followed. In September 1953 he became the Prime Minister in a quiet intra-family transfer of power following a prolonged political crisis precipitated by an uncle who was then the premier. Considered modern and progressive, Daud proved as much. He initiated two Five Year Plans (1956-61 and 1962-67) for modernizing the country. After seizing power, he embarked on a more ambitious and comprehensive Seven Year Plan (1976), mostly with Soviet aid, but it was overtaken by Daud's assassination in 1978.

In 1955 Daud announced a ten year extension of the Soviet-Afghan Treaty of Neutrality and Non-Aggression, first signed in 1931. Afghan-Soviet ties grew throughout his prime-ministership as did Afghan relations with East European countries, especially Poland and Czechoslovakia. Despite close ties with the giant neighbor to the north, Daud tried to maintain good relations with the U.S. Washington's initial interest in Kabul was more strategic as the EISENHOWER administration had planned to create an alliance in the "Northern Tier" (Turkey, Iraq, Iran, Afghanistan, and Pakistan) of Asia bordering the Soviet Union. Daud refused. Accordingly, the U.S. continued with small amounts of aid to Afghanistan. The U.S.-aided projects during the Daud years included construction of the Qandahar International Airport, development of Ariana Afghan Airlines, and continuation of the Helmand Valley Project. However, the U.S. was averse to providing military assistance because of its potential use against an American ally, Pakistan. Daud, therefore, turned to the Soviet Union and its satellites. Military aid begun in 1955 was to continue till the collapse of the Soviet Union.

Daud also undertook a number of social reforms, including the 1959 laws enabling women to abandon the veil. However, Daud obsessively supported the reunification of all Pashtuns under the central tenet that his country was their natural home. As the envisioned Pashtunistan would embrace considerable territory from the new nation of Pakistan, recurrent crises between the two neighbors followed. The Afghan economy suffered greatly because the remote rugged landlocked country was heavily dependent on Pakistan for access to much of the world. Daud was, therefore, forced to resign in 1963. Ten years later, he staged a coup while his cousin, King ZAHIR SHAH, was out of the country. Departing from tradition, the new ruler did not proclaim himself as king. Instead, Daud established a republic with himself as the president. He also inducted a number of communists into his cabinet but reneged on his pledge of making progressive reforms. Instead, his was an increasingly repressive regime with widespread arrests and political executions, especially of Islamists. Most of the latter fled to Pakistan where they received support from Prime Minister ZULFIKAR BHUTTO. These men, including HEKMATYAR, MASSOUD, and RABBANI would later become leaders of the MUJAHIDEEN. On 19 April 1978, the funeral of a prominent left-wing ideologue, murdered by the government, served as the rallying point for the communists. Surprised by this demonstration, Daud ordered the arrest of the communist leaders, but acted too slowly. It took a week to arrest Taraki. By then KARMAL had escaped to the U.S.S.R. Meanwhile, AMIN though under house arrest, sent out members of his family with plans and orders for staging a coup. Units of the army, already infiltrated by communists, joined the revolt. On 28 April 1978 Daud and most of his family were shot in the presidential palace. Afghanistan's nightmare of unprecedented and prolonged violence and intrigue had begun.

(*See also:* PEOPLE'S DEMOCRATIC PARTY OF AFGHANISTAN, SAUR REVOLTION)

Defense Related U.S. Export Controls

A MYRIAD system of export controls handled by various departments and evolved in the United States. The Export Administration Regulations (EAR) of the United States contains an Entity List that imposes license requirements for transactions involving certain "listed" entities. The Entity List was first established in February 1997 to inform American companies of entities whose activities imposed a risk of diverting exported and re-exported items for use in the development of Weapons of Mass Destruction (WMDs). The List was supervised by the Bureau of Industry and Security (BIS) in the U.S. Department of Commerce. In accordance with this sub-chapter of EAR, U.S. exporters are required to report all export information using the Automated Export System (AES) for exports to the Entities on the List. In addition, BIS enforces export controls under the Export Administration Act of 1979 (EAA) on dual-use technology. Broadly, the term, dual-use, serves to distinguish items that can have both military and strategic (e.g., nuclear) functions and commercial applications.

Since the late 1960s, the State Department has informally regulated exports through a practice called the Commodity Jurisdiction Process. Later it was formalized as the U.S. Munitions List (USML) as a part of the International Traffic in Arms Regulations (ITAR) under the Office of Defense Trade Controls. The Commerce Department usually consults the State Department on whether certain export items need a license under the USML. If the licensing officer at the Department of State feels the need for greater technical expertise, the application is forwarded to the Defense Technology Security Administration (DTSA) at the Department of Defense (DOD). The export of militarily sensitive technology, technical data, and defense related services, too, are under the purview of the State Department. The Directorate of Defense Trade Controls (DDTC), in the Bureau of Political-Military Affairs, handles the export and temporary import of defense articles and defense services covered by USML the DDTC also adjudicates on license applications for exports of defense articles and services, on compliance of defense trade, and provides the relevant reports to Congress. Both Defense and State Departments can veto any item on USML; the former on grounds of national security and the latter based on foreign policy considerations. "Major Defense Equipment" is defined as items on the USML whose production costs exceed $200 million, or when the expenditure on research and development is more than $ 50 million. These items require Congressional notification.

The U.S. also participates in four related multilateral control regimes.

The Wassenaar Arrangement. Twenty-eight countries met in Wassenaar, the Netherlands, in December 1995 to create the first multilateral institution covering both conventional weapons and sensitive dual-use technologies. Consequently the Vienna based forty country group was established at the end of the Cold War. Its members included former East European communist countries and members of COCOM (Coordinating Committee for Multilateral Export Controls, an American led export control system against the Soviet Union and its allies).

Nuclear Suppliers Group (NSG), The NSG is a 45 nation informal arrangement that has no Secretariat but is based in Vienna. It was founded in 1974 in response to an Indian nuclear test earlier in that year. The test demonstrated that certain non-weapons specific nuclear technology could be used for the development of nuclear weapons. The members of the NSG are all signatories of the Nuclear Non-

Proliferation Treaty (NPT) who have voluntarily agreed to coordinate their export controls on the transfer of civilian nuclear material and nuclear-related equipment and technology to non-nuclear-weapon states. It was earlier referred to as London Club or the London Suppliers Group due to the series of meetings held in the British capital.

Australia Group (AG) is another informal forum of countries which, through the harmonization of export controls, seeks to ensure that exports do not contribute to the development of chemical or biological weapons. The number of countries participating in the Australia Group has grown from fifteen in 1985 to forty and the European Commission in 2008. Several other countries, notably China, India, and, Russia have national export controls for some, but not all, of the items on the group's lists.

Missile Technology Control Regime. It was established in 1987. The MTCR partners hold an annual Plenary Meeting chaired on a rotational basis as an informal and voluntary association of countries with the shared goals of non-proliferation of unmanned missile systems capable of delivering weapons of mass destruction, and coordinating various national export licenses to prevent the proliferation of such systems. The number of MTCR partners is 34 countries. The greatest restraint is applied to Category I items. These items include complete rocket systems (including ballistic missiles, space launch vehicles and sounding rockets) and unmanned air vehicle systems (including cruise missiles systems, target and reconnaissance drones) with capabilities exceeding a range of 300km (about 500 miles) and a payload of 500kg (1,100 lbs). Category II included a wide range of equipment, material, and technologies, which may have dual uses, i.e., both civilian and military applications. The Guidelines sanctimoniously declare that the Regime is "not designed to impede national space programs or international cooperation in such programs."

Most members belong to all four control systems. None of the South Asian countries is a member of any of these cartels. Both Indian and Pakistani institutions are impacted by these controls. The NSG became an exception in September 2008 when it issued an India-specific waiver.

Dostum, Abdul Rashid (1954-)

Uzbek warlord. He is the de facto governor of Mazar-e-Sharif province and perhaps the six Northern provinces of Afghanistan. Dostum is archetypal of the select few in countries like Afghanistan whose power was based on tribal, racial, and regional bonds. Such leaders but were quick to switch loyalties depending on changed circumstances.

After training as a paratrooper in the 1970s Dostum was a union leader in the oil and gas fields around Shiberghan. Shortly after the SAUR REVOLUTION, as a known member of the *Parcham* faction of the communist party, he was inducted by the Ministry of National Security as the commander of a small detachment of a locally raised militia. By 1988, the unit was recruiting men throughout Jowzjan province but the core remained of troops and commanders from Dostum's own village, Kahoka Duke. Their fanatical loyalty to him and their ferocity in battle made Dostum into a powerful warlord His success as a ruthless military commander propelled him to the Defense Ministership in the communist regime. In early 1992, recognizing the inevitability of the fall of NAJIBULLAH, he changed sides and joined MASSOUD. Together, the two captured Kabul but when the newly installed President RABBANI refused to legitimize Dostum's position by giving him a cabinet post because of his communist background. The latter then defected and joined HEKMATYAR. The two failed in their joint bid to capture Kabul. However, in 1996, following the rise of TALIBAN and their capture of Herat and Kabul, Dostum realigned himself with RABBANI against the new threat. Along with the Tajik General Fahim and the Herati strongman Ismail Khan Dostum was one of three factional military commanders of the Northern Alliance. While much of the rest of Afghanistan lay in ruins, his stronghold of Mazar-e-Sharif (population, two million) thrived, supposedly on profits from the opium trade. In 1997, it was Dostum's turn to be betrayed by a deputy. Consequently, he fled to Uzbekistan allowing the Taliban to capture both BAGRAM and Mazar-e-Sharif. At Massoud's behest Dostum returned and rejoined the Northern Alliance in early 2001. After 9/11, as the leader of the second largest party in the Alliance, he recaptured and consolidated his hold on an area which covered six provinces with a population of around five million. The U.S. backed interim President HAMID KARZAI formalized his power by appointing him as a deputy defense minister and special adviser on security and military affairs in the northern Afghan provinces. There he ruled through his own political party, *Junbishi Melli*. Women work and move freely in his domains. Music, sports, and alcohol are permitted, and religious freedoms prevail. He continued to jockey for more power and clashed with other warlords but once again divining the impending U.S. — enforced changes, he surprised his many enemies by agreeing to disarm his powerful militia in 2004. He then he morphed into a populist politician and ran against Karzai in the presidential elections of 2004. He received ten percent of the votes that established his democratic credentials in the five provinces he already controlled. In March 2005 Karzai acknowledged Dostum's power base and conferred on him the honorific title of Chief of Staff of the Afghan armed forces. In early 2008 he was removed from his position in the army because of his role in the kidnapping of a rival Uzbek leader. However, the political and security situation in the country made it difficult to prosecute him for he was the most powerful Uzbek warlord in Afghanistan.

Dot Busters

Hate crimes against India-Americans in New Jersey, U.S.A. In the 1980s the Indian immigrant community numbered around 15,000 in the Jersey City area. A group mainly of local teenagers calling itself as "Dot Busters" began targeting the community with low-level harassment. The "dot" referred to the decorative dot-like *bindi* that married Hindu women wear on their foreheads. In August 1987, events took a dramatic turn for the worse when a thirty-year-old Indian immigrant was beaten to death by a gang chanting, "Hindu, Hindu!" A month before the killing, a local newspaper called attention to the rising number of racial incidents in the region. In response, the newspaper received a letter, signed by "Jersey City Dot Busters." The authors threatened more attacks and claimed to have made plans to drive the Indian community out of Jersey City. The writers also professed shock at the large number of Patels listed in the local phone book (Patel is a common last name in Western India). A few weeks later another Indian was assaulted by three young men with baseball bats. One of them yelled, "There's a dot head! Let's get him!" He was severely beaten and left unconscious with a fractured skull and permanent neurological damage. These incidents were a severe blow to the Indian immigrant community and jarred it into taking action. A group called Indian Youth Against Racism (IYAR) from Columbia University helped implement a series of educational programs on South Asian cultures for students and faculty at a Jersey City high school. The group also assisted in the passage of a bill in the New Jersey legislature that increased the mandatory penalties for "bias crimes" in 1990. Sporadic incidents continued to occur.

Dulles, John Foster (1888-1959)

U.S. Secretary of State (1953-59) during the EISENHOWER Administration. Dulles had a long-lasting impact on U.S. relations with India and Pakistan. On his maternal side there were two Secretaries of State, another ancestor was a pioneering woman in Sri Lanka, and his grandfather, the Rev. John Welsh Dulles, was a missionary in British India. The latter wrote a book, *Life in India,* which was full of praise for British colonial rule. Dulles first attracted public attention in 1918, when President Wilson appointed him as legal counsel to the U.S. delegation at the Versailles Peace conference. The delegation was headed by his uncle, Robert Lansing, the then Secretary of State. By the early 1950s Dulles had developed a reputation as being aggressively anti-communist and profoundly religious. He infused American foreign policy with an ideological passion that matched the intensity of Marxist-Leninist dogma that powered both the Soviet and Communist China's foreign policy. Accordingly, Dulles considered NEHRU's non-alignment, socialist belief, and agnostic views as immoral and repugnant. His ire against India was already stirred before he became the Secretary of State for in 1951 he had crafted the peace treaty with Japan which New Delhi refused to sign for it included provisions for war reparations. He visited the Indian subcontinent in May 1953 and like many U.S. officials then and since, was chilled by his reception in New Delhi and charmed by the welcome he received in the then capital of Pakistan, Karachi. His subsequent support for

Pakistan and his anti-Indianism were to shape U.S. relations with these two main countries in South Asia, for many decades.

(*See also*: U.S.-India Relations)

E

Eisenhower, Dwight David (1890-1969)

Army General, U.S. President (1953-60). Born in Texas, brought up in Abilene, Kansas, Eisenhower graduated from the U.S. Military Academy, West Point in 1915. After the Japanese attack on Pearl Harbor (December 1941), Eisenhower was posted to Washington DC as the Assistant Chief of the U.S. Army's War Plans Division. Eisenhower, then a highly respected but little-known Brigadier General, concluded, "We've got to keep Russia in the war — and hold India. Then we can get ready to crack Germany through England."

Ten years later, as the newly elected U.S. President, the General was no longer that sanguine about the subcontinent. Under his hawkish Secretary of State, JOHN FOSTER DULLES, U.S. policy towards South Asia turned away from the earlier emphasis on nurturing democratic institutions and providing assistance for economic development. Instead, Dulles refused to accept the legitimacy of the Indian doctrine of non-alignment and recruited Pakistan into the mosaic of containment alliances along the perimeter of the Soviet Union and China.

The impact of Dulles and the Cold War left little memory of Eisenhower's enormous contributions to South Asia. The large scale economic and food aid to India, a relatively stable, though militarized Pakistan, the settlement of the Indus waters dispute, technical and educational assistance, including the Atoms for Peace Program, are enduring, little appreciated legacies of the Eisenhower Administration.

Eliot, Thomas Stearns (1888-1965)

Poet, critic, dramatist, Nobel laureate (Literature, 1948). Early in life, Eliot read Edwin Arnold's *The Light of Asia* and developed an abiding admiration for Indic philosophy and religions. At Harvard he took courses in Sanskrit and Pali under Irving Babbitt and George Santayana. He then concluded that the subtleties of Indian thinkers "make most of the great European philosophers look like schoolboys."(*After Strange Gods*) Among his famous poems, "The Waste Land," "Four Quartets," "Ash Wednesday" and "Murder in the Cathedral," were clearly influenced by Buddhist and Hindu philosophy and mysticism. In 2001, Professor Shyamal Bagchee from India fittingly became the first non-American President of the T.S. Eliot Society.

Ellis and Angel Islands

Opened on 1 January 1892, Ellis Island was the premier immigration station for the U.S. Government. In operation until 1954, the station processed over twelve million immigrants who came to the U.S. by ship. The buildings were restored after thirty years of neglect and opened as a museum in September 1990. Over forty percent of America's population can trace their ancestry through Ellis Island. Across the continent, in San Francisco Bay, between 1910 and 1940, more than one million immigrants were admitted into the country through Angel Island. The two largest groups were the Chinese (175,000) and the Japanese (60,000). While the vast majority of immigrants at Ellis Island spent only a few hours in the processing center, Asians were subjected to humiliating medical examinations and detailed interrogations, often lasting days and weeks. Twenty years after renovations began at Ellis Island, restorations were started at Angel Island. However, unlike Ellis, no detailed records of immigrants are available at Angel. Few records would have been from South Asia, as most of those immigrants entered the U.S. long after the two islands had ceased to function.

(*See also:* IMMIGRATION FROM SOUTH ASIA)

Emerson, Ralph Waldo (1803-82)

AMERICAN philosopher and poet. His transcendentalism earned him the appellation of "The Boston Brahmin," a term coined in 1858 by Dr. Oliver Wendell Holmes (1809-94) to describe blue-blooded New-Englanders. Emerson drew a great deal of inspiration from the philosophy of the *Bhagavad-Gita*, the *Upanishads*, and Buddhist and Zoroastrian texts.

Who found "wonderful power of abstraction" in India's ancient texts. Emerson concluded that whereas Christianity considered man to be a born sinner; Hinduism regarded all humans as potentially divine. In his influential essay, "Nature," Emerson described the principle of transcendentalism as the "mystical unity of nature." He wrote three major poems, *Brahma*, *Maya,* and *Hamatreya*. The latter is a free rendering of a passage *Vishnu Purana (Book IV)*. By 1856 Emerson had read the *Kathopanisad* and his ideas increasingly reflected Indian influences. He was concerned with illusion (*maya*). He wrote, in his essay "Illusions", "I find men victims of illusion in all parts of life. Children, youths, adults and old . . . are led by one bauble or another. *Yoganidra,* the goddess of illusion, is stronger than the Titans, stronger than Apollo." Understandably, his evocative little poem, "Maya", begins with: "Illusion works impenetrable Weaving webs innumerable." (Maya is the Hindu Goddess who keeps mankind bound by spells of illusions). His most famous and controversial piece of poetry, "Brahma," is an example of Vedantic ecstasy. The opening stanza is typical: "If the red slayer thinks he slays, Or if the slain thinks he is slain, They know not well the subtle ways. I keep, and pass, and turn again."

Emerson's great granddaughter, Gertrude, married a Bengali.

(*See also*: THOREAU, HENRY DAVID; WALDEN POND)

Energy Overview of South Asia

The South Asian region is notable for its large and growing population and rapid economic growth during the 1990s. This growth was partly sustained by billions of dollars from the International Monetary Fund (IMF) and the World Bank. In return, the IMF stipulated certain measures including cuts in energy subsidies and increased privatization of that sector. The economic growth resulted in markedly increased demand for energy. The Energy Information Administration (EIA) of the United States estimated that primary energy consumption rose by nearly 64 per cent between 1992 and 2002 (EIA's energy statistics include only "commercial" sources and not animal waste, wood, or other biomass, which then accounted for more than half of South Asia's total final energy consumption).

The predominant source of power generation varied greatly from one country to another. Bangladesh used natural gas (66.4 percent), India relied on coal (54.5 percent), Sri Lanka and the Maldives were overwhelmingly dependent on petroleum (82 percent and 100 percent respectively), and Pakistan was diversified between petroleum (42.7 percent) and natural gas (42.2 percent). Hydropower supplied 38.5 percent of Myanmar's electricity, with gas turbines producing another 48.44 percent. The Himalayan countries, Bhutan and Nepal used hydroelectric power for generating 80 percent and 31 percent of their electricity. Despite growth and apparent diversification, the region consumed only 4.1 percent of the world's commercial energy and accounted for 4.8 percent of the global carbon emissions.

India produces 80 percent of the electricity generated in South Asia. Similarly, India is likely to consume 75 percent of the region's expected doubling of oil imports by 2020. South Asia contains coal reserves of 95.5 billion short tons or approximately nine percent of the world total. Although coal generates 43 percent of South Asia's energy nearly all of it is produced and consumed by India. The coal is generally of poor quality for it is low in calorific content and high in ash. South Asia continues to rely heavily on biomass (animal waste, wood, etc.) for residential energy consumption, particularly in rural areas. Because the primary end uses of biomass are cooking and heating, increased access to electric power is expected to be used primarily for lighting. Hence, no significant change in the use of biomass is anticipated. Clean, efficient, and reliable sources of energy for economic growth are clearly oil, gas, nuclear power, and hydro-energy. India faces the most serious shortage of power supply as the current capacity is at least thirty percent below minimal demand. As a result, although 80 percent of India's population has access to electricity, power outages and brownouts are common. Bhutan's hydropower potential, estimated at 30,000 MW is one source of commercial energy that may meet some of the Indian demand. As early as 2001, the sale of hydroelectricity to India provided 45 percent of Bhutan's revenue and constituted 11.6 percent of the country's GDP. For India, other regional sources are both limited and unreliable as South Asia contains only 5.7 billion barrels of oil, around 0.5 per cent of world reserves with India's offshore Bombay High field accounting for approximately one-third of total Indian oil output. Likewise, South Asia's proven natural gas reserves were estimated at 67.5 trillion cubic feet (Tcf), approximately one percent of the world total. Indian and Pakistani reserves were roughly equal at 30.14 Tcf and 26.83 Tcf, respectively. Bangladesh contains 32.1 Tcf and has additional undiscovered and unquantified reserves. Recent natural gas finds in Burma may also be a potential source of supply for India.

American support for cross-border projects, especially for pipelines, power-grids and river basin resource sharing is likely to be critical. The 2005 proposed Indo-U.S. nuclear deal offers an important mechanism to address the country's burgeoning energy requirements. Regardless of increased production of nuclear energy, India and others are likely to join the rivalry for energy from the Middle East and Central Asia. Such competition may be inimical to U.S. interests in the region and beyond.

(*See also:* ENRON POWER PLANT, INDO-U.S. NUCLEAR COOPERATION, OIL AND GAS PIPELINES)

Enron Power Plant

Multifaceted disastrous American investment project in India. Begun in 1992, the $3 billion Dabhol power plant near India's financial capital, Mumbai (Bombay) in Maharashtra state, was to supply about 2,200 megawatts of electricity by 1997. The project was awarded to Enron, a Houston based energy conglomerate founded as recently as 1985, but already ranked at number seven in the Fortune 500 list of companies. Under the agreement, the state-owned Maharashtra State Electricity Board (MSEB) was to buy electric power from Enron's Indian subsidiary, the Dabhol Power Company (DPC). The DPC was a joint venture between Enron and two other major American corporations, General Electric and Bechtel. It was the largest developmental project undertaken in India and was one of eight fast track projects that New Delhi had swiftly approved to showcase the country's new investment climate for the expansion of the power sector through foreign participation. However, the enterprise quickly came under considerable criticism as the agreement was negotiated exclusively between Enron and the state government with no competitive bidding and the contract was drawn up in just a few days for what was the largest investment project in the history of the country. In addition, there was lack of transparency in the deal as no information was divulged about the breakdown of the project costs, its operational and maintenance expenses, or of the financial parameters used for the calculation of the payment for the electricity. Furthermore, there was no clear description of DPC's project capitalization, capital recovery charges, depreciation, interest capitalization, debt servicing, or return on equity. Other critics were concerned about the safety of Liquefied Natural Gas (LNG) vapors and their long term impact on local farms and fisheries. Nevertheless, construction at the site was initiated.

The project was in two phases, with the state of Maharashtra retaining the right to cancel the second phase. The first phase was to produce 740 megawatts of electricity. The second phase, if agreed upon, would generate another 1,624 Megawatts of power. As MSEB, like most state electricity boards in India, was in poor financial condition, counter-guarantees were given by both the state and central (federal) governments in case of default of payment by the electricity board. By providing such guarantees for the first time in its history, the Indian government agreed to underwrite the liabilities of a private company. To import LNG for the project, Enron lobbied New Delhi to change its tariff system, which was specifically designed to discourage such energy imports. Nevertheless, India slashed its duty on imports of LNG from 105 percent to 15 percent. The conglomerate then brokered a deal with Qatar to provide 2.5 million tons of LNG per year for 25 years, starting in 1997. Despite this huge tariff cut by India, the country's Central Electricity Authority (CEA) concluded in August 1993 that the price of power charged by Enron was approximately twice the acceptable amount and was more expensive than other gas projects and only slightly cheaper than coal-fired plants. In fact, as it was a much larger plant, the cost per unit should have fallen further. Another concern about the tariff was that it was negotiated in U.S. Dollars without regard to currency fluctuations at a time when the Indian Rupee was steadily depreciating against the dollar. As political opposition mounted, in July 1994, Washington prompted the Overseas Private Investment Corporation (OPIC), an independent agency established by U.S. government to provide $160 million loan guarantees to support the project. Despite Washington's intervention, a year later, in the state elections in Maharashtra the main campaign issue of the BJP-Shiv Sena alliance were concerns about the Dabhol project. In March 1995, the BJP and allies won the elections. The new Chief Minister, Manohar Joshi, set up a committee under Deputy Chief Minister Munde to review Dabhol. In August 1995, the Munde Committee recommended that the deal be scrapped. Thereupon, Enron sought $600 million from the state government in order to recoup its alleged investment. Then the CLINTON Administration again stepped in and increased the loan guarantees to $360 million. In addition, Treasury Secretary Robert Rubin, Energy Secretary Hazel O'Leary, and the U.S. Ambassador to India, Frank Wisner, all urged the two parties to renegotiate the deal. Both countries were anxious for the project to succeed as Washington was apparently convinced that India offered U.S. companies the best opportunity to beat Japan in a big emerging market in Asia, whereas New Delhi wanted Dabhol to showcase the new business-friendly India. Under these circumstances, in January 1996, the state government renegotiated the contract and announced that under the new agreement, the Enron had agreed to reduce the rate for purchase of power by about fifteen percent. The fine print revealed that the savings would be in Phase II of the project. Hence, the second phase was made mandatory with MSEB committed to pay an estimated $1.3 billion annually to Enron for the next twenty years. Indian experts calculated that the return on equity for Enron was at least thirty percent per annum. This return on investment was almost twice as much as the permitted rate in power projects by Indian laws and statutes. In June 2001 the project, though 90 percent complete, went into limbo after MSEB declared its inability to pay for such expensive electricity. By the end of the year, Enron's corporate house of cards collapsed. Investors lost billions of dollars and some retirees were financially wiped out. Enron's accounting tricks with off-shore entities and massive pay-offs to politicians at home and abroad also discredited the respected accounting firm, Arthur Andersen LLP, which, too, closed down. The Enron saga was a great setback for both the U.S. and India. In India, it typified the powerful heavy-handed U.S. corporation, expert at manipulating the media, local experts and political leaders across the globe. New Delhi became more cautious and slower in clearing other projects involving foreign participants thereby reinforcing the international business perception that India was still slow, corrupt, and inefficient.

Ethnic Medical Associations in the United States

Following the Hart-Celler Act of 1965 and with the physician shortage in the U.S., partly because of the on-going war in Vietnam, there was a large influx of foreign medical doctors into the country. South Asians were among the largest number to come. By 2006, Indian physicians accounted for approximately five percent of all medical doctors in the United States and numbered around 40,000. Their number exceeded the combined total of physicians and medical students from the rest of the region. In the 1970s and 1980s numerous difficulties with licensure and residency (clinical) training were faced by Foreign Medical Graduates (FMGs). In response, various ethnic, regional, and international organizations were established. The first one from South Asia was the Association of Physicians of Pakistani Descent in North America (APPNA) in 1976. It was soon followed by others: the Bangladesh Medical Association of North America (BMANA) in 1980, American Association of Physicians of Indian Origin (AAPI) in 1982, the Afghan Physicians Association of America (APAA) in 1989, Burmese Medical Association of North America (BMA-NA) in 1991, and Sri Lanka Medical Association of America (SLAMA) in 1996. In general these organizations operated individually and collectively with varying degrees of success to address professional issues faced by their members in the U.S. They were perhaps more successful as social organizations for ethnic gatherings. In addition, they have tried to provide support and assistance in various ways to their countries of origin. SLAMA was particularly active after the devastation caused by the 2004 TSUNAMI. Despite considerable difficulties, BMA-NA has shipped text-books, journals and medical equipment to Burma and to refugee camps in Thailand. APAA has instituted collaborations with U.S. medical institutions to revive their counterparts in war-ravaged Afghanistan. AAPI initiated a number of health-related studies of diseases with a high incidence in the Indian-American community and took steps to develop specialized centers for the management trauma, burns, emergency care, etc., in India. AAPNA was the first to create its own distinct Political Action Committee (PAC) called PAKPAC. The latter has stirred some controversy from time to time because of its perceived closeness to various political leaders in Pakistan.

F

Ford Foundation

The Ford Foundation was incorporated in 1936. Its activities were limited to the state of Michigan till 1950, when under pressure from Washington and with the assistance from the CIA, the foundation joined in the battle against communism. Accordingly it went national and international. Its collaboration with the CIA was greatest when John McCloy (1958-65) headed the foundation. He reportedly created a special administrative unit just to liaise with the CIA and personally headed a consultation committee to facilitate the use of the foundation as a cover and a conduit for funds from the CIA.

In New Delhi, U.S. Ambassador CHESTER BOWLES, worried about the impact on India of the 1949 Communist take-over of China, stressed to Paul Hoffman, the then President of the Ford Foundation, to concentrate on India. So he did, first meeting with VIJAYALAXMI PANDIT, the Indian ambassador in Washington DC, who duly invited him to visit India and discuss with her brother, Prime Minister NEHRU, the possibility of assistance from the foundation for furthering of democracy in India. After his meeting with Nehru, the New Delhi office of the foundation, the very first one outside the United States, was set up in 1952. The report of the Hoffman Mission led to widespread activities and grant-making in the rural sector, agriculture, village development, educational and vocational training, industrial and business management, public administration, economic and social research and support for legal training and research. The foundation helped train 35,000 village workers for one of Nehru's pet projects, the Community Development Program (CDP). A sociologist, Dr. Douglas N. Ensminger was the chief representative of the foundation in New Delhi for nearly two decades and was responsible for establishing its goals and widely respected reputation. The Indian government with support from the foundation also launched the Intensive Agricultural Development Program (IADP) in seven selected districts. By 1959, with its accumulated experience, the foundation recommended that much greater focus should be on food sufficiency. Thus, the Ford's recommendations were a precursor to the GREEN REVOLUTION of the 1960s. In the meantime, it made an effort to improve education and research in a number of the newly established Agricultural Universities and Technical Institutes in India. The New Delhi office remains the largest of the foundation's thirteen overseas offices. It also covers activities in Nepal and Sri Lanka. As a part of its golden jubilee celebrations in India (1952-2002), the foundation's annual grants were doubled to $45 million. Despite the earlier CIA connection, the foundation categorically stated that it has an endowment of $13 billion and receives no funds from governments or from other outside sources. The foundation also supported various other ventures such as the Ahmedabad based self-employed women's assistance organization (Sewa), the Professional Assistance for Development Actions (Pradan); the Manipal Industrial Trust, the Anand Niketan Ashram Trust, the Indian Institute of Management, Bangalore, and the Institute of Rural Management in Anand, Gujarat. Since the 1990s China, India, Nepal, Pakistan, Bhutan, and Bangladesh have participated with the foundation in multinational projects especially in the management of natural resources, biodiversity, water harvesting, and hydropower development in the mountains.

Ford, Gerald Rudolph (1913-2006)

U.S. President (1974-77). Ford succeeded the disgraced Richard NIXON as the thirty-eighth President of the United States on 9 August 1974. He retained HENRY KISSINGER as his Secretary of State despite his controversial role in the Vietnam War and in the 1971 Indo-Pakistan conflict. Though South Asia was low on the new administration's priorities, the May 1974 nuclear test by India had provoked great concern about global nuclear proliferation. For Washington, the nuclear issue was particularly galling as the 1963 Indo-U.S. agreement for building and refueling two nuclear reactors at Tarapore included an understanding that India would refrain from weaponizing its nuclear capability. In Pakistan the ascent of ZULFIKAR ALI BHUTTO was accompanied by the attenuation of Islamabad's participation in SEATO and CENTO and increased ties with Islamic countries, China, and North Korea. Bangladesh still bristled at U.S. hostility during its secession from Pakistan and Afghanistan under DAUD was increasingly repressive towards both the Communists and the Islamists in the country. In response, Kissinger undertook a trip to all four countries (October-November, 1974) but achieved little. The repercussions of the inconsequential trip and presidential neglect of the same were to be felt many years later.

Perhaps the enduring positive legacy of the Ford years was its handling of Mrs. GANDHI's suspension of democracy in India in June 1975. There was little public denunciation or pressure. Instead, the American liberal establishment was encouraged to quietly persuade Mrs. Gandhi to restore democracy. So she did and in 1977 Mrs. Gandhi and her Congress Party were resoundingly defeated at the polls. Consequently, both Indian democracy and Indo-U.S. ties were strengthened.

Fulbright Program

The program was conceived by Senator J William Fulbright (1905-95) of Arkansas in the aftermath of World War II to promote peace and understanding through educational exchanges between the United States and other countries. Consequently, the Fulbright Act was passed in 1946. It is sponsored by the United States Department of State, Bureau of Educational and Cultural Affairs and is considered one of the most prestigious award programs in the world. It operates in 144 countries and has 37 Nobel Prize winners among its alumni. There are two basic types of grants: Full grants and Teaching Assistantships. In 1961, the Fulbright-Hays Act updated and expanded the original program. The latter provided opportunities for short-term overseas travel for American educators and administrators in the humanities, languages and area studies. The entire process grew further by the incorporation of other legislative, academic, and cultural initiatives. Hence, a number of distinct activities come under the umbrella of "the Fulbright." The grants program is the best known as approximately 5,000 Fulbright grants are awarded each year for foreign national students, teachers, professors, and professionals to study, teach, lecture, and conduct research in the United States and for U.S. nationals to do likewise outside of the country. The related Fulbright Scholars Program sends 800 academics and professionals each year to over 140 countries, where they lecture or conduct research in a wide variety of academic and professional fields. An equal number of foreign scholars come to the United States to do the same. The Visiting Fulbright Scholar Program provides another 800 pre-Doctoral Fellowships to U.S. and foreign graduate students and graduating seniors annually. The Fulbright Teacher Exchange Program provides opportunities for one-for-one exchanges between American and foreign elementary, secondary and post secondary teachers. The Fulbright also includes the Hubert Humphrey Fellowship Program, established in 1979, to bring accomplished mid-career professionals from developing countries to the United States at a mid-point in their careers for a year of study and related professional experiences. The College and Universities Affiliation Program seeks to establish linkages between U.S. universities and institutions overseas through the exchange of faculty and staff.

The primary source of funding for the Fulbright Program is an annual appropriation made by the United States Congress to the Department of State. It is administered in about 50 countries by Bi-national Commissions and in the remaining nations by the U.S. Department of State's overseas staff. Since its inception, more than 280,000 participants have been chosen as Fulbright scholars. The countries of the South Asian region have participated in varying degrees in the Fulbright Program.

In Afghanistan, after an absence of twenty-four years, the Fulbright was revived in 2003. About forty Afghans per year were recipients of the awards since then. In contrast only a dozen or so Bangladeshi and American scholars participate in the program each year. The Burma Refugee Scholarship Program (BRSP), established by the U.S. Congress in 1992 was to provide annual grants to five Burmese students and professionals whose educations were interrupted by the closure of educational institutions in Burma in the aftermath of 1988 democracy uprising. The BRSP was discontinued in 2008.

The Fulbright U.S. Student Program in India is the pre-dominant one in South Asia. A typical year like the 2006-2007 competition, India ranked sixth worldwide in terms of most applications received for the Program. While India attracted 161 applications in 2006, the rest of the South Asia combined received a total of just 48 applications. Since its inception in 1950, the United States Education Foundation in India (USEFI) has awarded over 5,000 Fulbright grants to Indians in almost every field of academic endeavor. At the same time about 3,000 Fulbright grants were awarded to U.S. citizens in three main sectors: research; lectures to promote mutual understanding in area studies (both American and Indian), and specialized study in areas of contemporary relevance to the U.S. and India. As a reflection of the growing ties between the two countries, on 4 July 2008, a new agreement established both India and the United States as full partners in the scholarship program and doubled the number of scholarships awarded each year. Under the new agreement for the first time direct financial contributions by the Government of India were accepted and an official from the Indian Government would co-chair the Board of Directors of the Foundation and participate in the policy and decision-making process on the exchange of Indian and U.S. scholars. The Foundation was renamed as the "U.S.-India Educational Foundation" (USIEF) and the awards were designated as the "Fulbright-Jawaharlal Nehru Scholarships and Grants". Under the new arrangement approximately 100 to 120 grants are available to U.S. nationals and an equal number to Indians.

The Fulbright Program was started in the Maldives in 2005. The Program offers opportunities for students to study in the U.S. to obtain Master's and Ph.D. degrees at American universities. Each year up to two lecturing, research or combined awards are given to American scholars to go to the Maldives. In Nepal, there is bi-national commission to administer the program. In 1952, the first two Nepali Fulbrighters were selected. Both went to the U.S. to study public administration. Since then, some 260 students, 47 post-doctorate scholars and 46 travel grantees have been to the United States under the Fulbright to study, teach and to conduct research. In return, 122 American students and 133 senior scholars have come to Nepal. Many Nepali Fulbrighters joined the civil service and rose to senior positions in the bureaucracy but very few entered politics.

The United States Educational Foundation in Pakistan (USEFP) was established in 1950. It was guided by a bi-national commission composed of an equal number of Pakistani and American citizens. The chairmanship of the commission alternates each year between a Pakistani and an American national. In 1951 first group of Pakistani grantees arrived in the United States. The following year the first of the American Fulbrighters visited Pakistan. About a thousand Pakistanis had participated in the Program by 9/11. In the wake of the terrorist attacks Washington stepped up its developmental activities in the country. Accordingly, in 2005 the U.S. Agency for International Development (USAID) and Pakistan's Higher Education Commission (HEC) announced plans to greatly expand the Fulbright Program in the country. USAID was to provide $15 million per year to the program making it the best supported Fulbright degree program in the world.

The U.S. Educational Foundation of Sri Lanka (U.S.-SLFC) was established as an autonomous bi-national commission by the governments of the United States and Sri Lanka to administer the Fulbright in the country. Initially a short-term program was agreed upon by the two countries by an executive agreement signed in November 1952. It was given a permanent status in 1964 with the institution of the present bi-national Commission. The U.S.-SLFC is the only independent commission of its kind in the field of academic exchange in Sri Lanka and the only such entity that functions under a bi-national Board of Directors. The Program provides students and scholars who are registered for a Ph.D. course in a Sri Lankan university to study for one year in an American university or academic institution. Professionals working in fields that have no recourse to further training in Sri Lanka can also avail of the opportunities offered by the Fulbright. Over a thousand Sri Lankan and American scholars have participated in the various academic programs monitored by the Fulbright Scholarship Board.

G

Galbraith, John Kenneth (1908-2006)

Economist, ambassador to India (1961-63). Born in the rural Ontario, Canada, he as an economist was greatly influenced by a British colleague, John Maynard Keynes. The latter believed that government should protect its citizens by actively intervening in the economic affairs of the country. In addition, Galbraith, unlike most economists, did not emphasize numbers, formulas, and abstract models but concentrated on politics, power dynamics, and human nature. A social thinker, an economic historian, and a keen observer of the affluent society, Galbraith was on the faculty of Harvard University and advised Democratic presidents and candidates from FRANKLIN D. ROOSEVELT to WILLIAM J. CLINTON.

In recognition of his work during the 1960 Presidential campaign, Galbraith was appointed as the U.S. envoy to India. He later summed up the assignment as, "The job of an American ambassador is to maintain civil communication with the government to which he is accredited and, to the extent that personality allows, to personify the majesty and dignity of the United States. No one should suppose that this is either intellectually or physically taxing." Therefore, during his two years in India, he managed to write four books. He was also the only American envoy who enjoyed the confidence of Prime Minister NEHRU. Hence, his detractors and some canny observers likened him to another white viceroy tending the brown-skinned prime minister of India. This characterization was most apparent during the Indian reverses in the border war with China in 1962. Galbraith summed up his role in the crisis as, "My general line is to give quiet sympathy and encouragement to the Indians, let them know who are their true friends, be receptive to requests for aid." Sympathy and encouragement included the demand for the removal of the America-baiting V.K. KRISHNA MENON, from the Ministry of Defense before military aid could flow. Menon was duly sacked and the first shipment of American equipment and light artillery arrived from Frankfurt, Germany. Galbraith's impact on the Indian economy was less clear. He appears to have provided Nehru with the stimulus to further increase the economic clout of the public sector by the nationalization of more private sector undertakings.

At the age of 92, Galbraith received India's second highest civilian award, the *Padma Vibhushan*, comparable to the U.S. Congressional Medal of Freedom. No other American Ambassador to India, before or since, was as influential as he, both in New Delhi and in Washington DC.

Gandhi, Indira Priyadarshini, née Nehru (1917-1984)

Prime Minister of India (1966-1977; 1980-1984). Born in ALLAHABAD (U.P.), she was the only child of Jawaharlal and Kamala NEHRU. Her early years were tumultuous as her father was often away in the struggle for Indian independence and her mother who was frail and sickly. Hence, Indira shuttled between Allahabad and Switzerland, where her mother convalesced from her periodic illnesses. At twenty-one, in 1938, she, too, joined Indian National Congress. Four years later, in 1942, she married Feroze Gandhi, a journalist, and bore two sons, RAJIV the older and a future prime minister, and the politically active, Sanjay, the younger.

As her marriage was not close, and her mother had died in 1936, Indira became the hostess and confidante of her father, the prime minister of newly independent India. NEHRU. He did not induct her into his cabinet, though she did become the president of the Indian National Congress 1959. She was then elected to the *Lok Sabha* in 1964. Nehru died that year and Indira joined the cabinet formed by the new Prime Minister Lal Bahadur Shastri. On his untimely demise in 1966, Indira was picked as prime minister as a compromise candidate by the top leaders of the party, informally known as the Syndicate. The syndicate considered her as inexperienced, unsure and malleable. She soon proved them wrong. With extraordinary political dexterity and tenacity she outmaneuvered them and secured complete control of the Congress Party. Her greatest triumph soon followed: The liberation of Bangladesh in the 1971 Indo-Pakistan war despite overt Sino-American hostility and insipid support from the Soviet bloc. The Sino-American axis was a key factor in her decision to develop and test a nuclear device in 1974. The heady years gave way to a general malaise that climaxed in June 1975, when the High Court of Allahabad found her guilty of technical and minor irregularities during the previous election campaign. In response to mounting public clamor for her resignation, Indira declared a state of emergency. Meanwhile, the younger of her two sons, Sanjay Gandhi, imposed forced sterilization as the means of birth control,

In 1977 she unexpectedly called for a general election partly as a result of informal U.S. pressure that coincided with the re-emergence of some American influence in New Delhi. Only six years earlier, the international situation had pushed India-U.S. relations to their lowest ebb. Then President RICHARD NIXON had abruptly terminated $82 million in economic assistance while India terminated the large U.S. Agency for International Development (USAID) program and restricted the presence of American scholars and students in the country. In addition, Indian criticism of U.S. policies in Vietnam and Cambodia increased, and Delhi upgraded its diplomatic mission in Hanoi. Meanwhile, despite vocal Indian objections, the U.S. had expanded its naval base on the British-owned Indian Ocean island of Diego Garcia and participated in joint naval exercises with Pakistan in 1974.

However, both governments tempered brinkmanship with other acts and gestures to limit the damage to bilateral relations. A 1973 agreement defused a dispute over the American rupee holdings by writing off more than 50 percent of the debt and directing the remaining funds towards mutually acceptable programs. In 1974 the Indo-United States Joint Commission was established to provide mechanisms for regular exchanges at high levels of public life and promote bilateral dealings in education and culture, economics, and science and technology.

Indira's return to power in 1981 coincided with the election of RONALD REAGAN as the new U.S. president. Unexpected personal rapport between the two leaders developed during a series of meetings in the early 1980s, and enabled the two countries to gradually improve bilateral relations. The Reagan administration expanded the areas of cooperation, especially in economics and the sciences, partly to counteract the perceived notion of considerable Soviet influence in India, particularly in the defense, trade, and scientific fields. In addition, Washington tacitly accepted the obvious: New Delhi as the major regional power in South Asia. For her part, Indira, too, came to appreciate that India was not in a position to significantly influence U.S. sales of military equipment to Pakistan. Under these altered and favorable circumstances Mrs. Gandhi made a highly successful state visit to the U.S. in 1982. The trip was followed by a series of high-level exchanges, including the visits of Vice President George Bush and Secretary of State George Shultz to India. In addition, that year the two countries partially resolved their dispute concerning supplies of fuel and spare parts for the nuclear power plant at Tarapore.

In June 1984, Indira attempted to crush a secessionist movement by Sikh militants led by Jarnail Singh Bindranwale. She ordered an army attack on the Golden Temple in Amritsar, the holiest of the Sikh shrines, where Bindranwale and his heavily armed followers were ensconced. The assault led to the death of Bindranwale, and considerable damage to certain important structures in the Golden Temple Complex. In vengeance, in October that year, Mrs. Gandhi was assassinated, at her residence, by two of her own Sikh bodyguards.

Her tumultuous years in and out of power did not alter the basic contours of the ties between the two countries. Her decision to hold elections in 1977, partly as a gesture of shared democratic values with the United States, left the two estranged democracies on the path to better relations.

(*See also*: KISSINGER HENRY ALFRED)

Gandhi, Mohandas Karamchand (1869-1948)

Indian political leader and humanitarian. He was born in Porbandar in coastal Gujarat and educated in India and England. Gandhi, a practicing lawyer, became a political and social activist during his twenty years in South Africa. His activism started in earnest in 1894 when he founded the Natal Indian Congress to agitate for rights for the Indians in South Africa. In 1896, Gandhi began to teach a policy of passive resistance to, and non-cooperation with, the South African authorities.

These concepts were influenced by the writings of HENRY DAVID THOREAU that Gandhi received from the British pacifist and fellow vegetarian Henry Stephen Salt (1851-1939). In later years the Eton-educated Salt like Gandhi was probably celibate for he was married to a lesbian. However, the Mahatma considered the phrases, passive resistance and civil disobedience inadequate, and coined another term, *Satyagraha* (Sanskrit, "truth and firmness"). His philosophy profoundly altered the political and social landscape of India.

During his two year imprisonment after a 1922 conviction for promoting civil disobedience, Indians added the honorific Mahatma ("Great Soul") to his name. The suffix "Ji" after his name also became commonplace as another mark of respect. His impact in the U.S. was mixed. He enjoyed widespread following among the pacifist and liberal Americans including members of the Jewish community. Other Jewish-Americans were less supportive largely because of his nuanced views on the Palestine question. In a widely circulated editorial published in his Journal, the *Harijan*, on 26 November 1938, he stated:

> "My sympathies are all with the Jews. I have known them intimately in South Africa. Some of them became life-long companions. Through these friends I came to learn much of their age-long persecution. They have been the untouchables of Christianity. The parallel between their treatment by Christians and the treatment of untouchables by Hindus is very close. Religious sanction has been invoked in both cases for the justification of the inhuman treatment meted out to them. Apart from the friendships, therefore, there is the more common universal reason for my sympathy for the Jews But my sympathy does not blind me to the requirements of justice. The cry for the national home for the Jews does not make much appeal to me. The sanction for it is sought in the Bible and in the tenacity with which the Jews have hankered after their return to Palestine. Why should they not, like other peoples of the earth, make that country their home where they are born and where they earn their livelihood?
>
> Palestine belongs to the Arabs in the same sense that England belongs to the English or France to the French."

Then in a remarkable critique of Hitler's Germany, he wrote:

> "The German persecution of the Jews seems to have no parallel in history. The tyrants of old never went so mad as Hitler seems to have gone. If there ever could be a justifiable war in the name of and for humanity, a war against Germany, to prevent the wanton persecution of a whole race, would be completely justified. If they must look to the Palestine of geography as their national home, it is wrong to enter it under the shadow of the British gun. They should seek to convert the Arab heart (into accepting Jewish migration into Palestine)."

It was a rare and reluctant sanction to wage war on any issue by the Mahatma.

The controversy would linger beyond his lifetime. In January 2008, a South African-born grandson, Arun Gandhi was forced to resign as the President of the MK Gandhi Institute for Nonviolence which he had founded. His resignation was precipitated by the uproar that followed his remarks in a *Washington Post* blog where he wrote that the Jewish identity was locked in the holocaust experience and it was time to move on. He also deplored the frequent use by force by the state of Israel. Americans in general found the Mahatma a mystifying figure draped in a white sheet who asked, "Who is Charles Chaplin?" just before his meeting with the British-born American icon, the actor Charles ("Charlie") Chaplin. Nevertheless, as early as 1930 the leading U.S. newsmagazine *Time* presciently named him as the "Man of the Year." A network of pro-Gandhi "Friends of India" associations was also established in Europe and the U.S. His following was eclectic. The religious admired him for his piety whereas political radicals supported his philosophy of non-violence and opposition to imperialism and totalitarianism. In 1937 a member of the Norwegian *Storting* (Parliament), nominated him for the Nobel Peace Prize for the first time. The next ten years were dominated by three mutually related major events: the struggle between Indians and Britain; the question of India's participation in World War II; and, the conflict between the Hindu and Muslim communities of the subcontinent. Despite the mixed reviews he received in the U.S. for his pacifism during World War II. By then, he was truly a universal figure and he was nominated by the 1947 Nobel Peace laureates, the American Friends Service Committee, for the Peace Prize in 1948. However, the committee declined to award the prize to anyone that year.

Almost ten years later the leaders of the civil rights movement in the United States, especially MARTIN LUTHER KING, JR. used Gandhi's theories to develop his own brand of non-violent political activism. Later, more books and movies about the man, his times and his philosophy appeared. Statues, too, were erected. Among the better known ones in the U.S. were Union Square Park in New York City at the Martin Luther King, Jr. National Historic Site in Atlanta, Georgia, and on Massachusetts Avenue in Washington DC. *Time* magazine named Gandhiji as the runner-up to Albert Einstein as the "Person of the Century" at the end of 1999, and labeled the Dalai Lama, Lech Walesa, Martin Luther King, Jr., Cesar Chavez, AUNG SAN SUU KYI, Benigno Aquino, Jr., Desmond Tutu, and Nelson Mandela as "Children of Gandhi" and his spiritual heirs to nonviolence.

Gandhi, Rajiv (1944-1991)

Indian prime minister (1984-89). He was the General Secretary of the Congress Party when his mother INDIRA GANDHI was assassinated in October 1984. He quietly and quickly succeeded her as the Prime Minister of India at the age of 40.In the 1980s, India and United States held differing positions on a wide range of international issues, including Afghanistan, Cambodia, Central America, the Middle East, nuclear proliferation, and Pakistan. Nevertheless, relations were beginning to thaw between the two countries towards the end of MRS. GANDHI's rule. The process was furthered by Rajiv's two official visits to the U.S. in 1985 and 1987. He developed an unexpectedly warm personal relationship with President REAGAN. Accordingly, the U.S. understanding of India's role as a factor for stability in South Asia grew and Washington tacitly supported Rajiv's military intervention in Sri Lanka (1987-90) and in the Maldives (1988). Military cooperation, too, increased as the U.S. cleared the supply of GE's F-404 jet engines for the Indian Light Combat aircraft (LCA) though Washington refused to the sell the Cray XMP-24 supercomputer sought by New Delhi, ostensibly for improved weather forecasting. Instead, India was allowed to purchase the less sophisticated XMP-14 version. Obviously, there was still a long way to go for the true warming of ties between the two countries.

Geneva Accords

The accords were the culmination of initiatives undertaken by Moscow and Kabul in 1981. Both governments maintained that Soviet forces had entered Afghanistan to protect the country from rebels backed by Pakistan and its allies. Accordingly, if the foreign threat to Afghanistan was removed, then the forces of its ally, the U.S.S.R., would leave the country. In July 1982 under mediation by the U.N. Secretary General's special representative, Diego Cordovez, indirect negotiations between the Communist regime in Afghanistan and Pakistan were started. Both Washington and Moscow committed themselves to guaranteeing the implementation of the resultant agreement that would lead to Soviet withdrawal. The consequent 'proximity talks' between Afghanistan and Pakistan led to the Geneva Accords concluded on 14 April 1988. The settlement consisted of four documents and an annex. Three of the agreements were between Afghanistan and Pakistan. In pedantic detail, both countries agreed to stop acts that could even remotely impact upon the sovereignty or security of the other. The agreement also prohibited expatriates and refugees from issuing statements that the other government could interpret as contributing to unrest in the country. The remaining fourth document obliged the U.S.S.R. and the U.S. to 'refrain from any form of interference and intervention.' An annex with a Memorandum of Understanding was to provide assistance to the U.N. in the implementing the agreements. However, the agreements, overloaded with too many details and impracticable limitations did not hold either in letter or in spirit. Hence, foreign interference did not end nor was peace restored. In addition, as MUJAHIDEEN were not bound by the accords, the war continued. Its intensity increased in anticipation of the swift disintegration of the Kabul regime after the Soviet withdrawal. On the contrary, the communists energized by NAJIBULLAH and abundantly equipped and supplied by the departing Soviets under the Treaty of Friendship (December 1978) inflicted some humiliating defeats on the rebels such as the battle for Jalalabad. In the wake of such set-backs, the two super-powers haggled over 'symmetry' and 'negative symmetry' of arms supplies to their respective clients. Eventually, the Soviets and the U.S. informally agreed on 'positive symmetry', i.e., the two super- powers reserved the right to send arms in response to shipments by the other. The war continued till the collapse of both the Soviet Union and the Marxist government in Kabul. More wars in Afghanistan followed. The Geneva Accords only provided a fig leaf to cover the ignominious withdrawal of Soviet forces from its hapless neighbor Afghanistan.

Green Revolution

The Green Revolution swept through the Indian subcontinent in 1967-68 and lasted for a decade. Its basic elements were the expansion of cultivable land; double cropping in existing farmland; the use of genetically improved high-yield seeds, especially for the two staple crops, rice and wheat. In addition, and improved irrigation accompanied by increased use of petrochemical fertilizers, pesticides, herbicides, etc., contributed to the growth. The introduction of high-yield seeds and the intensified utilization of chemicals were largely as a result of research performed at two institutions supported by American money and skills. In 1944, under the aegis of ROCKEFELLER FOUNDATION research in higher yielding strains of wheat was initiated as the Cooperative Wheat Research and Production Program at Sonora, Mexico. Eighteen years later, in 1962, the other major staple, rice, was subjected to similar scrutiny at the International Rice Research Institute (IRRI), Los Banos, in the Philippines with funds from both the Rockefeller and FORD FOUNDATIONS. The two foundations also collaborated with the Mexican government to establish the International Maize and Wheat Improvement Center (CIMMYT), an autonomous international training institute near Mexico City.

The results were the introduction of semi-dwarf strains of wheat, the Sonora 64 and Lerma Rojo 64 and of the rice strain, IR8. Altogether, wheat production increased by 300 percent and rice by about 200 percent. This growth was followed by further commercialization of agriculture with the planting of cash crops such as cotton, sugarcane, fruits, vegetables, and tobacco. Mechanized farming, agro-industries, fertilizer factories, cold storage facilities, etc., were greatly expanded. The American agronomist, Norman BORLAUG, was clearly the key figure in the Green Revolution and his enormous contribution was suitably acknowledged by the world community by the award of the Nobel Peace Prize to him in 1970. His most prominent Indian associates were Dr. K. Rammiah and Dr. M.S. Swaminathan. The former worked specifically on rice and the latter concentrated on the white dwarf wheat. They developed strains like Sharbati Sonora which grows well in arid conditions and Norin 10 characterized by longevity in storage. Further collaboration by entities such as the Rice-Wheat Consortium for the Indo-Gangetic Plains (RWC), the Indian Council for Agricultural Research (ICAR), the Agricultural Biotechnology Support Project, and the International Crops Research Institute in Semi Arid Tropics (ICRISAT) with American and other multilateral institutions sought to further raise productivity and reduce some of the problems associated with the Green Revolution.

The negative impacts were characterized by the loss of biodiversity, dependence on fossil fuels and increased salinity of the soil. Despite further research and success, after about ten years of spectacular growth, the per capita agricultural output stagnated or fell. The high levels of mechanization and reduced dependence on low-skilled workers led to their greater migration into the cities with resultant massive slums. In addition, 80 percent of pesticide related deaths occurred in the third world because the farmer was unprotected while using chemical fertilizers, herbicides, and insecticides. Furthermore, many hybrid seeds were sterile. Hence the farmer and the country were dependent on corporations to provide seeds from year to year. Since the turn of the century, a new revolution may be underway. Low-till farming across South Asia reduced water consumption by 30-50 percent and a 50 percent decline in the use of herbicides. In addition, the emerging Gene Revolution and the newer technologies may have an impact as great as the Green Revolution of the 1970s. A striking example was the introduction of biotechnological cash crops like cotton (production soared by 160 percent) that were being more easily accepted in the third world (23 percent compared to only 5 percent usage in developed countries). The long-tern consequences of the farming of biotech crops are not well determined and there are increasing concerns about its impact on the soil and on animal feeds. In 2005, India and the U.S. announced the establishment of a Knowledge Initiative Board drawn from academia, government, and the private sector to develop new viable technologies in agriculture. Private sector seed companies from Bangladesh and the Philippines, too, joined the initiative.

Towards the end of the first decade of the twenty-first century including the decline in food-stocks and the increased allocation of land and resources for the production of biofuels led to a spiraling rise in the cost of cereals and agro-commodities. These changes may usher in a new revolution that may not be entirely technological.

H

Harlan, Josiah (1799-1871)

American adventurer. Harlan supposedly left the United States for India after being jilted by a woman. On reaching the subcontinent, he served as a surgeon in the Anglo-Burmese War of 1824. After spending a few years in the eastern parts of British India, he moved north and met Shah Shuja-ul-Mulk, the exiled Amir (King) of Afghanistan, then living in Ludhiana in the Punjab. The desperate and friendless Shah Shuja, distrustful of the British, sent the American as his spy to Kabul. On reaching Kabul, however, Harlan befriended Jabber Khan, the head of powerful Qizilbash Shia community. The latter, a half-brother of Dost Mohammed Khan, the Amir (King) of Kabul owned large estates near Kafiristan. The Shia leader introduced Harlan to French officers in the service of the Lahore-based Sikh Maharaja, Ranjit Singh. The French officers recommended Harlan to the Maharaja as a resourceful intriguer who hated the British. In Maharaja Ranjit Singh's court, Harlan established his credentials by his honest handling of the gold used in various intrigues that preceded the Sikh conquest of Peshawar in 1836. Satisfied by his conduct, the Sikhs used the American as one of the two emissaries at the court of Amir Dost Mohammed Khan in Kabul. The latter, though unsure of Harlan, found him to be an efficient and loyal military commander. Therefore, he bestowed him with the title of Prince of Ghor: an ironic choice as 645 years earlier, a ruler from the same principality was the first Muslim conqueror of Delhi and Pakistan was to name a missile as Ghori in the 1990s. After the humiliation of the first Anglo-Afghan war, the British forced the shadowy American to leave the subcontinent. Harlan then returned to Philadelphia in August 1841 and promptly published a book, *A Memoir of India and Avfghanistan*. It was sharply critical of the British whom he described as systematic looters of the country. The American was the model for Rudyard Kipling's 1888 short story set in Kafiristan, "The Man who would be

King." In 1975, the story was made into a film bearing the same title and starred two well-known British actors, Sean Connery and Michael Caine.

Hekmatyar, Gulbuddin (1948-)

Afghan warlord, Prime Minister (1993-4, 1996), head and founder of HEZB I ISLAMI. Hekmatyar (HIM), AKA HEZB I ISLAMI Gulbuddin (HIG). Born in northern Kunduz province, a Kharoty Pashtun, Hekmatyar first enrolled at the military academy; then switched to the engineering department of Kabul University in 1968. Hence, he is sometimes referred to as "Engineer Hekmatyar." He started his political career as a member of the communist party in the country before entering into Islamic politics. Violence, tribal intrigue, and shifting loyalties were the predominant features of the Islamic, secular, communist, and royalist factions with each vying for power in the turbulent 1970s in Afghanistan. Emblematic was Hekmatyar, a communist of four year standing, who then switched to the Hizb i-Islami, was implicated in the murder of a Maoist student and imprisoned but escaped to neighboring Pakistan in 1975 along with other activists like RABBANI and MASSOUD. The Soviet invasion in 1979 brought Afghanistan onto the world stage. Hekmatyar became one of the factions organized with U.S.-Saudi-Pakistani aid to fight against the Soviets. He was widely feared and distrusted, for he was considered as brutally power hungry, cunning, and a ruthless Sunni fanatic who was an erratic puppet of U.S. and Pakistani intelligence services.

When the Communist regime fell in Kabul the Islamic government, led by Rabbani, invited him to join the regime. Hekmatyar's ambition, however, was to head the government. Accordingly, he formed an alliance with his former enemies, DOSTUM (another former communist) and Hezb i Wahdat (Shias) to topple the Kabul government. Rockets rained on the Afghan capital, causing greater destruction than the ten years of the preceding civil war. In early 1993, Hekmatyar was again offered the Prime Ministership. He accepted (March 1993-January 1994) but his personal avarice and ambition brought on an end to the uneasy partnership. DOSTUM and he tried to oust RABBANI. Again they failed. Finally, the faltering RABBANI government invited him as the prime minister in June 1996. By then, it was too late. Another Pakistani-backed militia, the Taliban, was on its way to power in the country Some analysts contend that the Hekmatyar-Dostum combine had so weakened the Kabul government that it was in no position to challenge the rise of the Taliban. In late 1996, the Taliban, a militia suspected of being created, manned, and funded by the Pakistanis, overran Kabul and forced both RABBANI and Hekmatyar to flee north. Thereafter most of Hekmatyar's men defected to the Taliban.

The warlord then turned to Iran for support. It was long rumored that Hekmatyar had sold most of his share of stingers to Iran. The hand-held anti-aircraft missiles were given to him during the Soviet-Afghan War by the CIA. Tehran now returned the favor by giving him asylum. After 9/11, Hekmatyar claimed that his men had helped bin Laden, Ayman al-Zawahiri, and key leaders of the al Qaeda escape through the U.S. dragnet in the mountains of eastern Afghanistan. The United States, too, had its suspicions for the Department of State classified him as a "Specially Designated Global Terrorist" and "has participated in and supported terrorist acts committed by al-Qa'ida and the Taliban." The 9/11 Commission report, too, indicated a connection with BIN LADEN by stating, "BIN LADEN apparently kept his option open, maintaining contacts with Gulbuddin Hekmatyar, who, though an Islamic extremist, was also one of the Taliban's most militant opponents." By 2007 Hekmatyar had reportedly regained considerable following among the Islamic fundamentalists opposed to the U.S.- backed government in Afghanistan for the paunchy middle-aged warlord reputedly had some support in the Arab sheikhdoms, and in the Pakistani and Afghan bureaucracy.

Hindustan Ghadr Party

U.S. based revolutionary organization committed to achieving Indian independence from the British. As many of the early immigrants were former soldiers the members called "Ghabrites" favored an armed revolt as the means for achieving Indian independence. The Hindustan *Ghadr* (Hindustani: "mutiny/revolt") Party was founded in November 1913 with Sohan Singh Bhakna, a lumberjack from Oregon, as its first president and the well-known Indian revolutionary, Lala Har Dayal, as the secretary. Though headquartered at Yuganter Ashram (named after the eponymous Bengali revolutionary newspaper) most of the correspondence and records were kept by Agnes Smedley, a white American school teacher and self-proclaimed revolutionary. Some funds were provided to the party by the German government, as a means of embarrassing British imperialism in the U.S.. The party also established ties with Irish revolutionary groups. Under British pressure, the U.S. government arrested Har Dayal and forced him to leave for Switzerland. He went to Germany thereafter. He was succeeded by Ramchandra Bhardwaj as the secretary of the party. Following the outbreak of World War I in 1914, with German assistance, the Ghadrites chartered two ships loaded with arms from Mexico. However, as the movement was heavily infiltrated by British agents, London successfully intercepted both ships. Meanwhile, about 4,000 Indians left North America and returned to India to join in an uprising planned in Punjab for February 1915. Other terrorist and revolutionary groups, too, were expected to join the revolt. Like the Ghadrites, the majority of the India based insurgent groups, too, were penetrated by British intelligence agents. Hence, most revolutionaries were swiftly rounded up and a few hanged thereby effectively destroying the party in India. In the U.S. 56 Indians, twenty-six Germans and thirteen Americans were indicted for violating American Neutrality Laws. Only thirty-five were brought to trial. Dr. Tarak Nath Das, the publisher of a newspaper, *Free Hindustan*, received the heaviest sentence of twenty-two months in prison. The party weekly, *Hindustan Ghadr*, was published into the 1940s. Har Dayal was drowned under suspicious circumstances while sailing back to India in 1947. In the same year, the party was disbanded following Indian independence and its assets were turned over to the government of independent India. Plans to repurchase the original site, 5 Wood Street, were initiated in 1955 and the foundation stone of the new building was laid in November 1959 by a Ghadr veteran, Amar Singh Sandhwan. The new building was completed in 1975 to house the documents and literature of the Ghadr Party. Fittingly, it was inaugurated by the then Indian Minister of External Affairs, Swaran Singh, himself a Sikh.

I

Ice

Ice was an unusual American export to the Indian subcontinent in the 1830s. A New Englander, Fredric Tudor, devised a technique of insulating ships so that ice cut from the deeply frozen lakes around Boston could be transported from New England to tropical ports like Calcutta, Colombo, and Bombay. Ice was wrapped in felt and sweet-smelling pine-dust. By the end of the four-month journey about two-thirds of the cargo was still intact. Ice was such a precious commodity in the tropical summer heat of Calcutta that the captain of the first ice-ship, William C. Rogers, was presented with an inscribed silver cup by the Governor General, Lord William Bentinck. Distinctively shaped ice houses were erected in Calcutta, Colombo, Madras and Bombay. The ice trade lasted for about 30 years before being overtaken by modern technologies.

Immigration from South Asia

The United States is a land of immigrants. The saga of the South Asian immigration to the new world was as unique and different as the experience of many other communities. A colonial diary from 1670 mentions an Indian from Madras who accompanied a sea captain and settled in Salem, then a town in the British colony of Massachusetts. He was perhaps the first Indian immigrant to North America. More substantial immigration followed much later. The Punjab, now divided between India and Pakistan, was the first great source of Indian immigration to the United States and Canada. The first immigrants arrived in Vancouver, British Columbia, at the end of the nineteenth century on their way back from England to Malaya and Hong Kong after participating in Queen Victoria's Diamond Jubilee celebrations. The majority of them were illiterate or semi literate soldiers from the British Indian Army, Malay State Guides, and the Hong Kong and Singapore Royal Artillery. Others were laborers who had served under the British in Malaya, Singapore, and China. The soldiers were mainly peasant Sikhs and some Muslims from the Doaba and Malwa regions of the Punjab. Between 1903 and 1908, the Punjabis primarily worked on the Western Pacific Railway in Northern California. Though largely Sikh and Muslim these laborers were collectively known as "Hindu crews," especially in the Sacramento Valley. Two thousand Punjabis also labored on the 700-mile road between Oakland, California and Salt Lake City, Utah. The highway later became a part of Interstate 80. Other South Asians worked in the lumber mills and logging camps in Oregon, Washington, and California. Several hundred Punjabis moved across the border to Bellingham, Washington State, because of rising anti-Asian sentiment among the Canadians. The mill-owners of Bellingham, already familiar with the work ethic of the few Asians in their service, hired more Punjabis from Canada as the new labor was dependable, hardworking, and prepared to work for less pay than their white counterparts. Trouble followed. Rioting and arson engulfed the little town of Bellingham on the night of 5 September 1907. A mob of 600 lumberjacks of European ancestry raided the living quarters of the 153 Indians who worked in five different mills. Thereafter, most left Washington State for British Columbia or California. On the other hand, Punjabis also served as strike-breakers in some situations along the west coast of the United States. However, the Asiatic Exclusion League, established in 1908, successfully lobbied for restrictions on further immigration from the Indian subcontinent. Altogether, an estimated 7,348 Indians migrated to the United States and Canada between 1899 and 1920. Barred from owning land under the anti-Asian laws, about 80 percent of the Punjabis married Hispanic women. Washington then passed the Cable Act (1922). The new act stripped women who married Asians of their U.S. citizenship and made them ineligible for land rights as well. Under such stresses marital conflicts multiplied in the small "Mexican-Hindu" community. At least 20 percent of marriages ended in divorce (almost twice the U.S. rate for the times) and the women received custody of the children. Most of these children married among other Anglo-Hispanics and became a part of the American melting pot although a fusion culture was forged in California's Yuba City and Imperial Valley.

Nevertheless, as early as 1909, the Khalsa Diwan Society was established and the first Sikh Gurudwara in the United States was built in Stockton, California in 1912. It became the center of most social activity among the South Asian immigrants primarily because 85 percent of them were Sikhs. At the Gurudwara Sikhs, Hindus, Mexicans, Catholics, and Muslims met, worshipped, and socialized. Here, too, they dreamed of independent India and the HINDUSTAN GHADR PARTY used the Gurudwara for many of its meetings. After working as laborers, mill-hands, and lumberjacks, some moved into farming jobs in the Fresno area and in the Sacramento, San Joaquin, and Imperial Valleys of California. By 1919, about 60 percent of Imperial Valley was owned by these non-residents. Following the Cable Act, most were reduced to tenant farmers. Nevertheless, as tenant farmers, Punjabis ran 88 percent of all ranches in the region by 1924. These enterprising and gritty pioneers from South Asia also started to pool their savings and lease lands. It took several more years before loans were sought and received from financial institutions.

In 1965, immigration laws were radically modified under the Hart-Cellar Act. Quotas based national origins that were in place since 1882 were abolished. The Act allowed 170,000 immigrants from the Eastern hemisphere with a limit of 20,000 per country. From the Western hemisphere immigration was pegged at 120,000 with no consideration for national boundaries. This was an enormous change from the earlier European quota of 149,667 and an Asian quota of only 2,990. Under the Act, "Employment based immigration" admitted those with specific skills and professions that were needed in the country. "Family based immigration" was enacted for the unification of families. Following the Hart-Cellar Act, immigration from the Indian subcontinent greatly increased. Accordingly the 2000 U.S. census, there were approximately 1.7 million American citizens of Indian origin representing the various languages, religions and regions of India. By 2007, their number was estimated at 2.3 million.

Within fifteen years of the passage of the act, immigration from south Asia took a different turn: it was dominated by the illegal, the technocrat, and the political refugee. Afghanistan, India, and Sri Lanka constituted the largest such groups.

The first Afghans to reach the U.S. shores probably arrived in the 1920s. Most of them were probably residents of British India and were from the elite of society. As such, they were highly educated, and had trained in the learned professions. Some were married to Europeans. The destinations of choice were Washington, DC and other metropolitan cities. Immigration remained a trickle between 1953 and 1973. During that period only 230 Afghans immigrated to the United States and became American citizens. Due to subsequent political uncertainty in the country, the numbers actually fell with only 110 Afghans being naturalized during the next four years (1973-1977). Large numbers of Afghan refugees began arriving in the United States in 1980 in the wake of the Soviet intervention. Some were officially designated as refugees. Estimates of the total number of varied greatly ranging from 45,000 to 75,000. Approximately 35,000 were officially resettled in the country. Others were granted political asylum. Some arrived through the family reunification program and others by illegal means of entry.

With the creation of Bangladesh in 1971, official records of immigration from that country, separate from that of Indians and Bengalis, were created. In the 1960s, many East Bengalis fled to the United States to avoid political persecution, or, in the case of religious minorities, to avoid religious discrimination. This first wave of immigrants was generally composed of professionals who were well educated and affluent. After a slow rise in their numbers throughout the 1970s, the next decade saw much greater immigration. Between 1982 and 1992, the U.S. Immigration and Naturalization service legally admitted 28,850 Bangladeshi. From 1988 to 1993, some 6,000 Bangladeshis also won visas through a lottery. There were also a large number of undocumented Bangladeshis living in the United States. Some estimates were as high as 150,000, with more than 50,000 living in the metropolitan New York area alone. Other large enclaves of Bangladeshis were in Los Angeles, California, Miami, Florida, and Atlanta, Georgia. In Los Angeles, the Bangladeshi community is centered in the downtown area, where shops and restaurant signs were often in Bengali.

By 2007, about 500,000 Pakistanis had also settled in the U.S. Like other South Asians, the initial immigrants were technocrats and professionals. However, since the late 1980s, many Pakistanis took blue-collar jobs such as taxi drivers or shopkeepers. Through hard work and canny business practices, the majority were financially well off. Hence, their annual household income was approximately $70,000 compared to the national average of $40,000 in 2002. Both incomes and rates of immigration appeared to have declined since 9/11. Most were still clustered in the metropolitan areas around New York City, Chicago, Illinois, the states California and Texas, and in Washington, DC.

The fractured polity in Sri Lanka was reflected in how Sri Lankan Americans identified themselves in the U.S. census forms. Most mark themselves as Tamil, Singhalese, or Dutch Burgher rather than as Sri Lankans. Most settled in large cities such as Chicago, Illinois, Los Angeles, California, New York City, Newark, New Jersey, and Miami, Florida that already had Sri Lankan and Indian communities. Sri Lankan Americans who practice Hinduism are likely to live near an established Hindu community. The same is true for Sri Lankan Buddhists. For example, when the prominent Buddhist monk, the Venerable Wipulasara, arrived in the U.S. in 1993, he joined the Buddhist Asian-American community of 30,000 in Tampa Bay, Florida, where only a tiny Sri Lankan community was present. The Sri Lankan Tamils from the embattled Jaffna region are scattered across the globe. Surprisingly, their population was estimated at only 35,000 in the U.S. whereas there were ten times as many in Canada and the United Kingdom.

Indian American Forum for Political Education (IAFPE)

On 11 October 1981, on the 489th anniversary of Christopher Columbus's arrival to the Americas (though he thought he had reached India), some Indian Americans met in the Washington suburb of Wheaton, Maryland to discuss means of developing political awareness among Indian Americans and to encourage them to participate in civic and political activities in the country. Accordingly. IAFPE was formed. Numerous other Indian-American organizations soon emerged but most were marked by internecine rivalries and splits. On the other hand, IAFPE tried to complement and supplement them rather than compete with them. It was partly successful in doing so. Its greatest achievement was in the early 1980s when it successfully lobbied against several legislative proposals in U.S. Congress to restrict the immigration of close relatives of U.S. citizens and permanent residents. The most notorious of these proposals was the Simpson-Mazzoli Bill passed by the Senate in May 1983 but the House restrained most of its provisions in June that year. The IAFPE chose another symbolic date, 1 August 1975 the day that the thirty-five nation Helsinki Human Rights Convention had facilitated the immigration of relatives of U.S. citizens from Soviet Union and eastern European countries for a massive rally. The newer immigrants to the United States on 1 August 1983 observed the family unification day across the country. As a result of these and other efforts, U.S. Senator Edward Kennedy and Representative Peter Rodino came forward in support of preserving the rights of family re-unification for immigrants. The IAFPE also served as an Advocate for the rights of small businessmen and in 1986, one of IAFPE's leaders, Dr. Joy Cherian, was appointed to the Sub-Cabinet position of Commissioner of the U.S. Equal Employment Opportunity Commission (EEOC). Since 1984, IAFPE has become a regular feature in Washington for organizing a well-attended and widely publicized annual congregational luncheon in the U.S. Capitol building. However, its effectiveness as an organization to promote political awareness and empowerment in the Indian-American community appears to be no different than that of the myriad ethnic associations that have subsequently sprung up.

Indian Institutes of Management (IIM)

Premier Indian business schools set up on the lines of those in the United States. Soon after India became independent, the requirement for trained managers to run the many enterprises in the country became obvious. Hence, the country looked towards the United States and towards the end of 1959 contacted George W. Robbins an Associate Dean at the Graduate School of Business Administration, University of California, Los Angeles (UCLA). In collaboration with UCLA, The Indian Institute of Management (IIM), Ahmedabad in Gujarat State was established in 1965. The FORD FOUNDATION provided the foreign exchange for recruiting the faculty, developing the library and other academic facilities. A five year academic collaboration with Harvard University Graduate School of Administration was established. Since then, six other IIMs were subsequently launched in different parts of the country. All seven are regarded as the leading business schools in India and are completely autonomous though owned and financed by the Central Government of India. Though autonomous, the IIMs, presumably under some encouragement by the government devote considerable attention to the non-corporate and under-managed sectors like agriculture, rural development, public systems management, energy, and health education.

Indian Institutes of Technology (IIT)

Premier Indian engineering colleges. Five such Institutes were initially set up, starting in 1955. The institute at Kanpur was established in collaboration with the Massachusetts Institute of Technology (MIT). A three member team came to India in 1961 and enlisted the support of other leading technical universities in America like the California Institute of Technology, the Carnegie Institute of Technology, Ohio State University, Princeton University, University of California at Berkeley, and the University of Michigan. The Kanpur Indo-American Program was started in 1962 and completed 10 years later. Large numbers of IIT graduates, many now based in the United States, have made major contributions to their country of adoption and to their alma mater.

Indo-U.S. Nuclear Cooperation

In the United States, at the dawn of the nuclear age in 1945 the Acheson-Lilienthal Report concluded that, "Development of atomic energy for peaceful purposes and the development of atomic energy for bombs are in much of their course interchangeable and interdependent." Accordingly, no country could be trusted to develop atomic power because even a primarily peaceful program might provide fissionable materials to build bombs. Accordingly, in August 1946 the

Atomic Energy Act was passed. The act made the entire nuclear program secret and created an independent Atomic Energy Commission under civilian control to oversee nuclear research and to maintain physical control over U.S. nuclear weapons until their release to the military. The policy first changed under the incoming Republican administration. On 8 December 1953, President EISENHOWER proclaimed the Atoms for Peace Program at the General Assembly of the United Nat ions. This proposal to share nuclear secrets for the betterment of humankind was probably a concession to the worldwide calls for banning nuclear tests after the U.S. had exploded the first ever Hydrogen bomb earlier that year. Within a month of the Eisenhower speech, Dr. S. S. Bhatnagar, the Director-General of India's Council for Scientific and Industrial Research (CSIR), inquired whether the U.S. would establish a "joint enterprise with the Indian AEC analogous to the U.S.-U.K. arrangement with South Africa" and collaborate in the development of Indian uranium resources. New Delhi received its first rebuff. Nevertheless, heavily dependent on the mediocre quality Indian coal and imports of costly and insecure foreign oil for its energy needs, New Delhi declared that nuclear plants would provide 8,000 Megawatts of electricity by 1980-81. This optimistic forecast was partly based on the U.S. Atomic Energy Commissions commitment to sell to India ten tons of heavy water in February 1955 for use in the Canadian supplied Cirus research reactor four years before its completion. Thereafter Washington provided India with about $93 million in Atoms for Peace loans and grants between 1954 and 1974, three-quarters of which subsidized the construction of the country's first power reactor at Tarapore, near Mumbai. The confidence was further buttressed in late 1955, when the U.S. Agency for International Development put on a large exhibit at a New Delhi Trade Fair featuring a 30-foot-high diagram of a reactor diagram, "hot" laboratories, and numerous working models. It was also common knowledge that Washington's promotion of nuclear technology was a particularly high priority in South Asia for it supported two of the administration's major policy directives: NSC 5409 ("U.S. Policy toward South Asia"), under which the U.S. President approved the support for "strong, stable and responsible governments" in a region that was "a major battleground in the Cold War," and NSC 5507/2 ("Peaceful Uses of Atomic Energy"), which approved the transfer of nuclear technology to promote American international and regional interests.

However, by 1970 despite U.S. assurances and Indian expectations, only 420 megawatts of electricity was being generated from the two U.S.-supplied plants at Tarapore. Accordingly, the following year Vikram Sarabhai, the Chairman of India's Atomic Energy Commission (AEC) sadly concluded that by the projected years of 1980-81, his country was likely to produce only 2,700 megawatts of electricity from nuclear plants. About thirty-five years later, in 2005 Indian reactors were still generating about 2,500-3,000 megawatts of electricity and the country was running out of nuclear fuel for its existing reactors and plants as imported fuel was not available to India under the existing non-proliferation rules.

In this context the India-U.S. nuclear deal signed by President GEORGE W. BUSH and Prime Minister MANMOHAN SINGH in July 2005 was important to New Delhi for it secured both nuclear fuel and access to modern technology that would be a major source of energy for the country. It was also a defining moment between the two countries for it was a major shift in U.S. foreign policy as Washington first having led the initiative to create a nuclear non-proliferation regime specifically targeted against India, now took the lead in exempting New Delhi from the draconian sanctions imposed by various agreements since the 1974 Indian nuclear test. For India it also meant a broader economic and political partnership with the U.S., and acceptance of the country as an important and responsible member of the comity of nations. For Washington the agreement was a combination of the furthering of U.S. commercial interests and the utilization of India's other assets (size, stability, strategic location, democratic ethos, etc.) to develop a useful strategic balance in the changing world order.

In the wake of the Bush-Singh agreement, in December 2006 the U.S. House of Representatives in an adroit bipartisan move passed a frame-work accord called the Henry J. Hyde U.S.-India Atomic Energy Act of 2006 named after the Chairman of the Committee on International Relations. Under U.S. legislative tradition such accords create the framework that can then consummate a companion implementation pact. In the context of the Indo-U.S. nuclear deal the companion implementation pact was the 123 Agreement, a section of the U.S. Atomic Energy Act.

Under the Hyde Act India would place fourteen out of it twenty-two nuclear reactors under permanent safeguards, negotiate an additional protocol with the International Atomic Energy Agency (IAEA), harmonize its export controls, and seek a waiver from the Nuclear Suppliers Group (NSG). On 1 August 2008, the Board of Governors of the IAEA approved by consensus a Nuclear Safeguards Agreement with India. Termed as an "umbrella" arrangement, it would allow India to add facilities over time to be placed under IAEA safeguards. Five weeks later, the 45 member NSG agreed to adjust its guidelines to enable full civil nuclear cooperation with India. Meanwhile, the agreement, visionary in its perspective, but low on specifics had withstood a number of challenges in the two signatory countries.

In the United States the committed non-proliferationists considered the deal as the first critical step in the dismantling of the edifice of nuclear controls painstakingly created over four decades. In addition, U.S. legislators were skeptical about the wording in the 123 Agreement for it appeared to contradict the language contained in the Hyde Act particularly where it related to the supply of nuclear fuel and the possibility of nuclear testing by India in the future. The Bush Administration tried to mollify the U.S. Congress by declaring the fuel supply assurances contained in the 123 Agreement were not legally binding on the United States. Furthermore, in September2008 a confidential letter from the Bush Administration to the House Foreign Affairs Committee Chairman Howard Berman, a California Democrat and an opponent of the deal, was released. The letter reassured him that the U.S. would not sell sensitive nuclear technologies to India and would immediately terminate nuclear trade if New Delhi conducted a nuclear test. It created a firestorm in India, with political opponents portraying the letter as proof of American attempts to restrict India's strategic options. In the U.S. Congress, the impact of the letter was quite different for it demonstrated to the lawmakers that the administration was fully aware of the serious implications of a future Indian nuclear test, and was well-prepared to deal with it.

In India, the regionally entrenched leftist parties, disciplined and intellectually committed to hostility towards the United States were capable of toppling the Congress Party coalition in New Delhi. These parties were vociferous in their opposition to the deal and withdrew their support for the government. A motion of no-confidence in the government was then introduced in parliament. It was soundly beaten presumably because both the main parties, the Congress and the BJP, were unwilling to face the electorate at a time of global economic instability On the other hand the Indian scientific establishment and the bureaucracy, with long and shared collective memory of previous U.S. undependability was not convinced that Washington would fully honor its commitments to India. In addition, the Gandhian legacy of swadeshi ("indigenous effort") was deeply embedded in the Indian psyche and was nursed by occasional reports of technological breakthroughs achieved by the country's scientific institutions. These claims, readily accepted with great pride by most Indians, were hard to evaluate as the country's nuclear program was not transparent enough and demands for clarity were muted by perceived national security considerations.

A little recognized perspective was the impact of the deal on other developing countries. None of them denounced the American intention to supply nuclear fuel and technology to India. Their silence suggested that the divide between the technological "haves" and "have-nots" was being slowly bridged, by two key countries: India, long a leader of the have-nots; and the U.S., the leader of the haves. In the twilight of the Bush administration, as the day dawned in India on Gandhiji's birth anniversary on 2 October 2008 the U.S. Senate ratified the United States-India Nuclear Cooperation Agreement and Nonproliferation Enhancement Act thereby giving the deal its final passage. American business estimated that India may be a $175 billion market over the next twenty-five years in the field nuclear energy and companies like General Electric and Bechtel would be the major beneficiaries. In contrast, others argued that the French and the Russians were more likely to profit from the deal. Perhaps, India's greatest economic gain may be export of the indigenously developed 220 Megawatt Pressurized Heavy Water Reactor (PHWR) to smaller developing countries who have been steady though tacit supporters of the deal.

(*See also:* DEFENSE RELATED U.S. EXPORT CONTROLS, NUCLEAR NON-PROLIFERATION TREATY [NPT], SANCTIONS AS A STRATEGEM IN U.S. FOREIGN POLICY).

Indo-U.S. Relations

The relationship had a promising beginning. Under the ROOSEVELT administration, the United States supported India's struggle for independence from the British, especially during the World War II when the concept of freedom from Japanese and German occupation was extended to British imperial possessions, including India. India became free in 1947 and the newly independent country's foreign policy was heavily influenced by the Jeffersonian principles of "peace, commerce, and honest friendship with all nations, entangling alliances with none." Ironically, the Jeffersonian aspects of U.S. foreign policy were long obsolete by the 1940s. Instead, most countries were entangled in alliances because of the Cold War. India was the only major democracy that did not join the U.S. against the communists. The early American response to Indian non-alignment was one of development and condemnation. One of the most articulate and self-righteous critics was President EISENHOWER's Secretary of State, JOHN FOSTER DULLES, who described it as 'immoral,' 'short-sighted,' and perhaps illegal because he claimed that nonalignment in the face of communism was inconsistent the United Nations Charter. As colonialism declined, successive U.S. administrations, committed to the containment of communism, too, took a similar though less abrasive view of India's leadership of the NON-ALIGNED MOVEMENT. Hence, multi-lateral diplomacy was the major arena of Indo-U.S. interaction. Here, too, the record was mixed. India initially supported the U.S. when North Korea invaded the South in June 1950. New Delhi voted for the U.N. Security Council's resolutions condemning the invasion and supporting military action to drive back the North Koreans who were then about to occupy the whole of the Korean peninsula. Both countries tacitly agreed that this aggression was a test of U.N. credibility and decisive action was critical. However, as U.S.-led U.N. forces crossed the Thirty-eighth parallel that divided the two Koreas, India counseled Washington that further advance was likely to provoke a Chinese military response. When China did intervene and pushed back U.N. forces, India played an important diplomatic role both at the U.N. and as a direct mediator between the United States and China to end the Korean War.

Even after NEHRU, who was the architect of India's non-aligned policy, ties between the world's two largest democracies remained lukewarm. Natural affinities between the two characterized by pluralistic and open societies, a common language used by their elites, democracy, and commitment to the rule of law and basic freedoms, were not enough. India opposed the American war effort in Vietnam (1964-1974). Frequent public and private criticism by Indian officials and the media was a source of irritation in the U.S. especially as India was receiving substantial American economic aid during those years. Both nations were alarmed by the Soviet intervention in Afghanistan in December 1979. Whereas American concerns were publicly aired, India, the recipient of much Soviet military aid, expressed its disquiet in private. Neither country was silent when Pakistan-backed Islamic zealots, the TALIBAN, seized Afghanistan in 1994 following the Soviet withdrawal in 1989. Nevertheless, India again differed with the U.S. in its use of force in Yugoslavia in 1999, in Afghanistan in 2001, and in Iraq in 2003. The unrestrained use of force by the American-led Western alliance was one of the post-hoc justifications for Indian nuclear weapons tests in May 1998.

Another major cause of friction throughout the period was American military aid to Pakistan. Nehru complained that Pakistan had not joined the American-led pacts "because it expected some imminent or distant invasion or aggression from the Soviet Union. Statements of responsible people in Pakistan make it perfectly clear that they have joined this Pact because of India." American arms supplies to Pakistan ushered in a sub-continental arms race. Perhaps its most serious repercussion was the neglect by India of its Himalayan borders although Sino-Indian relations were tense because of disputed borders. Consequently, India suffered a humiliating reverse in the 1962 Sino-

Indian border war. Less than ten years later a perceived new triangular alliance between Pakistan, the United States and China, prompted India to sign a "Treaty of Peace and Friendship" with the Soviet Union in August 1971. Nehru's carefully crafted policy of nonalignment lay in ruins. This reality was further underlined when India used force to resolve the East Pakistan issue and the United States sent its only nuclear carrier, the *U.S.S. Enterprise*, into the Bay of Bengal, in a show of gunboat diplomacy.

On economics and development, too, the two countries differed. India did not embrace the American system of free markets and unlimited private sector capitalism. Instead, the country embarked on economic socialism at home in a series of Five Year Plans. The U.S. considered the dominance of the state sector in the economy as inefficient, wasteful, and detrimental to India's own interests. Nevertheless, American aid flowed and India benefited considerably from U.S. food assistance (under PL-480), economic, scientific, and technological assistance that, among others, made possible the GREEN REVOLUTION of the mid-1960s. The United States provided the largest economic aid to India in the 1950s and 1960s, and yet India pursued closer ties with China (until the Sino-Indian war of 1962), and with the Soviet Union. This perception of Indian ingratitude was another source of dissatisfaction among members of the U.S. Congress, intelligentsia, and the media. The succession of RAJIV GANDHI as prime minister in 1984 following the assassination of his mother produced a brief upswing in Indo-U.S. relations during the REAGAN administration.

The end of the Cold War coincided with the liberalization of the Indian economy and improvement in Indo-American ties. The CLINTON Administration responded to the new realities by identifying India as one of the ten Big Emerging Markets (BEMs). High-level exchanges and the commencement of a "strategic dialogue" were expected to culminate in a U.S. Presidential visit to India in 1998. The nuclear tests of May 1998 were a setback as the U.S. imposed wide-ranging economic sanctions under the 1994 Nuclear Proliferation Prevention Act (Glenn Amendment). Sanctions also terminated all forms of defense cooperation, including the International Military

Education and Training (IMET) program. Nonetheless, both nations recognized the need to remain engaged. Soon after the tests (June 1998), talks were initiated between Indian Minister of External Affairs Jaswant Singh and the U.S. Deputy Secretary of State Strobe Talbott. After thirteen meetings, some normalcy was restored though major issues remained unresolved.

India's rapid economic growth since 1992 a shift in American priorities in Asia and demands of the war on terrorism, have led to further convergence of interests between the two countries. Significant problems remained, such as Washington's complaints about alleged Indian violations of American pharmaceutical patents and Indian concerns about U.S. agricultural subsidies. Certain Indian sensibilities, too, persisted as demonstrated by India's President K.R. Narayanan who broke protocol during President CLINTON's visit to India (1999), to publicly complain about U.S. nuclear policy and continued American support for Pakistan. With the election of President GEORGE W. BUSH in 2000, relations moved forward with more vigor. Bush's criticism of CLINTON for failing to recognize that China was "a competitor, not a strategic partner" was also well received in India. In an article in the influential journal *Foreign Affairs* in early 2000, CONDOLEEZZA RICE, the National Security Adviser and later Secretary of State in the Bush Administration, put the candidate's anti-China sentiments into a pro-Indian context. She wrote,

> "China's success in controlling the balance of power depends in large part on America's reaction to the challenge. The United States should pay closer attention to India's role in the regional balance. There is a strong tendency conceptually to connect India with Pakistan and to think only of Kashmir or the nuclear competition between the two states. India is an element in China's calculation, and it should be in America's too."

Nevertheless, India was not an issue in the presidential campaign of 2000 and Bush's foreign policy speech contained only a brief mention of the region. After 9/11, Indian support and its acceptance by the U.S. remained variable. On the other hand, India accepted active but quiet U.S. engagement in resolving Indo-Pakistani disputes. Trade and commerce benefited greatly by the improved relationship. Although India's share of American overseas trade is about one percent of the total volume, it is a significant proportion of India's external trade. Till 2007, the United States was India's largest trading partner accounting for nine percent of Indian imports and twenty-one percent of Indian exports. In 2005, total Indian exports to the U.S. were about $18.8 billion of which about $6 billion was from the software industry. Merchandise exports included diamonds, gold Jewellery, woven and knit apparel, textiles, fish and seafood, machinery, carpets, iron and steel, and pharmaceuticals. Indian imports from the United States included machinery, medical and surgical equipment, aircraft, space equipment, chemicals, and plastics. U.S. exports to India totaled only $7.95 billion but several American corporations established subsidiaries and other facilities in India, with General Electric been the largest presence with 19,000 employees. Its largest laboratory in the world, the John Welch Technology Centre, was set up in Bangalore. This multi-disciplinary laboratory does research in hot-air gas paths, materials design, and computer sciences. Most INFORMATION TECHNOLOGY (IT) firms including Microsoft, Intel, Texas Instruments, Sun Microsystems, Oracle, IBM, and Adobe Systems, set up major subsidiaries or collaborative ventures in India. Others, especially in bio-information, bio-technology, heavy industry, infrastructural development, entertainment and animation, too established themselves in the country. India became the premier country for U.S. information technology services with major corporations "outsourcing" its needs to Indian software engineers. The relationship became increasingly bilateral as investments by Indian companies in the United States grew rapidly in the 1990s. For example, India's United Breweries bought plants in the U.S. while other Indian companies such as Dr. Reddy's Laboratories and Ranbaxy acquired American pharmaceutical manufacturing units. In April-June 2006 Indian pharmaceutical companies filed 104 of the total of 251 Drug Master Filings (DMFs) with the FDA compared to 74 of 213 a year earlier. In the IT sector, Tata Infotech, Satyam, Infosys and Wipro set up large operations in the United States.

Another area of growth was immigration from India. The U.S. based population of Indian American grew to 2.32 million as per the Annual Survey by the Census Bureau in 2005. Almost 60 percent of all Indian Americans were college educated and earned a median family income of $60,000 compared to the national average of about $39,000. The typical income of Indians working in the SILICON VALLEY Information Technology sector in the 1990s was about $125,000 and about fifteen percent of the start-up companies were initiated by Indian-Americans. With a vested interest in promoting closer ties between their old and new homelands, Indian-Americans have been active in backing American politicians who support India.

In the new millennium, American assistance to India concentrated on the alleviation of poverty, prevention of environmental degradation, enforcement of child labor laws, and the prevention of discrimination against women. U.S. concerns also remained about nuclear safety, cooperation, and proliferation, enforcement of the rule of law, and the furtherance of human rights. In addition, both countries cooperated on challenges posed by the trafficking of people and drugs, the rise of terrorism, the presence of forced labor, and of improving access for the disadvantaged, particularly the Dalits. American NGOs were also particularly active in the management of the spread of HIV/AIDS and related awareness and destigmatization campaigns.

The most touted area of cooperation was in defense and security, as manifested by progressively sophisticated joint exercises and training. During the Cold War obsessive secrecy and mutual suspicion pervaded the two fields. In contrast, in 2003 India became eligible for EXCESS DEFENSE ARTICLES (EDA) on a grant basis under section 516 of the U.S. Foreign Assistance Act. The EDA was to support the continuing war on terrorism, to promote inter-operability of systems, and to modernize previously sold equipment. In 2007, India floated global tenders for at least 126 warplanes. Out of the six short-listed companies, two were American, and a third had substantial U.S. components in its aircraft. Another floater was the *INS Jaleshwa,* the second largest warship in the Indian Navy, and by far the largest man o' war bought by India from the U.S. The degree of operational cooperation still remains to be seen.

Indus Waters Treaty (1960)

A treaty signed on 19 September 1960 by Pakistan and India to divide and rationalize the flow of waters of the Indus River and its tributaries following the partition of 1947. By reassuring Pakistan of secure water supplies, it was hoped, more so in India, that the settlement would usher in an era of peace and trust leading to a resolution of the Kashmir dispute. Accordingly, New Delhi was also generous in settling financial differences festering since December 1948. In the same vein, NEHRU was magnanimous with the division of the Indus waters and the allocation of resources for building new canals and dams. Washington, too, strongly backed the treaty and supported it with $500 million in financial assistance. Abundant financial support was further provided by the World Bank through the establishment the Indus Basin Development Fund. Under the terms of the treaty, the three eastern rivers — Ravi, Beas, and Sutlej were given to India. Pakistan received the three western rivers — Indus, Jhelum, and Chenab. During the next fourteen years, despite two wars, nearly 400 miles of link canals were constructed for the transfer of the waters from the western to the eastern rivers at a cost of $1,070 million. The bulk of the money, $870 million, was spent in Pakistan and only the remainder was expended in India. In addition, two large storage dams were built in Pakistan at Mangla on the Jhelum River and the Tarbela on the Indus. The treaty did not fully resolve all water disputes nor settle the Kashmir conundrum. On the contrary, Kashmiris oppose the treaty for virtually all the waters flow through their land but they were not a party to the settlement. Nor did it prevent further hostilities between the two countries. The treaty may require modifications in the future.

Inter-Services Intelligence (ISI)

Pakistani intelligence agency instrumental in the creation of the TALIBAN and the latter's short-lived take-over of almost the whole of Afghanistan. One of two intelligence services run by the Pakistan Army, the ISI was formed in 1948 as a consequence of the failures of intelligence during the first Indo-Pakistan war in 1947-48. It is headed by a Lieutenant General who normally reports to the country's prime minister. About 80 percent of the personnel are drawn from the armed forces. Initially officers used to serve a single posting on deputation to the intelligence agency. This appears to have changed. Now a significant number of officers serve for much longer periods of time and others are posted repeatedly to it.

The secession of East Pakistan in 1971 was a watershed in the history of the organization. Bereft of its East Pakistani (Bangladeshi) personnel, the ISI recruited Islamists, especially non-Bengali students, for counter-insurgency operations in the eastern wing of the country. Hence the intelligence agency developed ties with Islamists and acquired experience in manipulating the domestic political situation. Later ZULFIKAR ALI BHUTTO greatly increased its budget and used its resources against his political opponents. Another watershed was the Soviet invasion of Afghanistan. The organization gained a great deal of strength, prestige and notoriety during the ten year war in Afghanistan against the Soviet Union. During the war the ISI worked closely with American, Saudi, and British intelligence agencies. It was also the sole source for providing arms, equipment, and training to all Pakistan based MUJAHIDEEN groups. The ISI, presumably directed by the pious Islamist, General ZIA, and the devout Catholic, William Casey, the director of the CIA, favored the more fundamentalist of the Mujahideen factions in a war that pitted the pious against the Godless communists. This policy led to the marginalization of royalist and secular anti-Soviet Afghan groups. The latter were smaller and less organized but equally divisive and patriotic as the Afghans supported by the ISI and the CIA. With the experience, confidence and infrastructure developed during the war against the Soviet Union, the ISI became increasingly active in India, especially in Kashmir (so called Op Topac) and in Indian Punjab (Op K-2). The operational experience and the handling of various related exigencies made the ISI into a leading agency in covert operations in the world.

J

Jammu & Kashmir Issue in U.S. Policy

At the inception of the dispute, Warren Austin, the then U.S. Representative to the U.N. asserted (4 February, 1948), "The external sovereignty of Kashmir is no longer under the control of the Maharaja. With the accession of Jammu and Kashmir to India, this foreign sovereignty went over to India and is exercised by India." However, as the politics of the Cold War reached the Indian sub-continent and Pakistan became an American ally, U.S. involvement in the dispute deepened but varied in intensity depending upon the global security environment, the strategic utility of Pakistan to the U.S., and the intensity of Indo-American relations. Hence, the U.S. variously labeled it as an issue of self-determination for an oppressed and unrepresented minority, or as a nuclear flash-point endangering international security or simply as a bilateral issue between India and Pakistan. In the early 1990s there was a complete, albeit brief, reversal of the U.S. position on the status of Kashmir when President William CLINTON's newly appointed Assistant Secretary of State, Robin Raphael (23 October,1993) opined, "We (U.S.) do not recognize the legal validity of Kashmir's accession as meaning that Kashmir is for ever an integral part of India. The people of Kashmir have got to be consulted in any kind of final settlement of the Kashmir dispute." Her remarks were followed by an intensification of the proxy war waged by Pakistan in J&K. However, six years later, the same administration acknowledged the legitimacy of the Indian presence in Kashmir when President CLINTON backed India and berated Pakistan for attempting by force to alter the Line of Control (LOC) in the Kargil region of the state.

Despite its recent rhetorical stand that Kashmir is a bilateral issue between India and Pakistan, the U.S. appears to discreetly play a mediatory role because Washington considers Kashmir as a distraction from the global war on terror. Washington also periodically cautioned

India against taking a similar approach to the American one by attacking terrorist camps and facilities in neighboring countries. Perhaps Washington has not strongly used its moderating influence on Pakistan because the longstanding strategic alliance between the two countries has been useful for U.S. agencies and forces earlier during the Cold War (1949-1989) and subsequently in the campaign against terrorism. Such structural relationships did not exist with India and are not likely to develop in the near future. Hence, Kashmir, a major point of dispute between the two largest nations of South Asia appears to be of little direct concern to the U.S. and is largely a strategic tool for use in the region.

Jinnah, Mohammed Ali (1876-1948)

Founder of Pakistan, first Governor-General of the new state (1947-8). A Hodja of the Ismaili Islamic sect, Jinnah was born in Karachi, the capital of Sindh. He received his early education at a Sindh Madrassa and at a Christian mission school. In 1892 he went to Britain and qualified for the bar to practice law. Returning to India in 1896, Jinnah rapidly ascended the intertwined and serpentine ladders of law and politics, to reach to the highest rungs of each to become a member of the Legislative Council of the Viceroy of India in 1910. Like many Muslim members of the Congress, he was also a member of the Muslim League (joined in 1913) and was elected its president in 1916 and 1920. He played a major role in negotiating the Lucknow Pact (1916) between the League and the Congress, in which the latter, a party committed to representing Indians of all religions and castes, reluctantly conceded that Muslims should have separate communal electorates to ensure their adequate representation in the legislature. However, the Congress could not accept this formulation for long and the party soon reversed its decision. In addition, by the 1920s, Jinnah's political career was being superseded by the South Africa- returned fellow lawyer and Gujarati speaker, M.K. Gandhi. The latter paid less attention to the strict constitutionalism favored by Jinnah and others. Instead, he transformed the Congress into a mass revolutionary movement characterized by civil disobedience, non-violence, and non-cooperation. Furthermore, social uplift became a major platform for the party with its disquiet about the injustices within the majority Hindu community of the country.

Jinnah a strict constitutionalist left both the Congress and the Muslim League but continued to be politically active but with little following or impact. Accordingly he left for England to resume his law practice. In 1934 he was persuaded to return to the Indian subcontinent and thereafter he headed the league until his death in 1948. His support for the London during World War II on constitutional grounds greatly increased his backing by the British in India who enhanced his role and influence in the country as the sole representative of the Muslims and as a supporter of the war effort. Jinnah's earlier, but rebuffed claim by the electorate that the League represented the Muslims of India was now substantiated in the 1946 elections for the Indian Constituent Assembly as his party won almost all the seats assigned to the Muslim electorate. Jinnah's firm stand and the widespread Hindu-Muslim riots directed by his clearly unconstitutional calls, forced the Congress to accept the establishment of the separate state of Pakistan. In August 1947, India was partitioned. Muhammad Ali Jinnah became the first governor general of Pakistan cobbled out of the seceded bits of British India. With his usual clarity of vision, he swiftly worked out an independent currency and established the State Bank of Pakistan to help bring economic stability to the new country.

When separate electorates for Hindus, Muslims, and others were instituted in the 1930s there was little reaction in the United States. However, in a series of seven articles during October to December 1939, the *New York Times* cannily observed that the rising power of the Muslin League, despite its reverses in the 1936 elections. The same year, John Günther in his widely read book, *Inside Asia*, concluded the obvious: Jinnah was among the most important leaders in the subcontinent. Three years later (1942) it was more bluntly reiterated by Herbert Matthews in the *New York Times*, who wrote, "Jinnah holds the key to peace in India." The then American aversion to the division of the subcontinent was perhaps most clearly demonstrated by *Time* magazine in the 1946. The magazine put a sinister looking Jinnah on its cover and acidly described his rise as "a story of love of country and lust for power, a story that twists and turns like a bullock track in the hills."

In November 1946, the Muslim League placed its own representatives in Washington DC. The Ispahanis, a cultured Calcutta business family was an inspired choice, perhaps reflecting Jinnah's own background. The Ispahanis concluded that," Sweet words and firm impressions count a lot for the Americans. They are inclined to quickly like or dislike an individual or organization." Jinnah took this advice to heart. Relevant Americans were thereafter targeted and by April 1947, U.S. diplomatic dispatches commented, "The present unhappy situation is as much of Congress leaders' political ineptitude and lack of vision as of Mr. Jinnah's intransigence." Hence, in Washington, the two countries were equated and both equally blamed for the troubles of the subcontinent. On 26 February 1948 while welcoming the first U.S. Ambassador to Pakistan, Jinnah emphasized the direct and intimate military relationship between the two peoples by declaring, "Though Pakistan is a new State, (the) relationship (with the United States) was strengthened and made more direct and intimate during two world wars and more particularly and more recently during the second world war when our two people stood shoulder to shoulder in defense of Democracy." The die was cast for a militarized relationship, ostensibly based on democratic ideals, between the U.S. and Pakistan.

Johnson, Lyndon Baines (1908-1973)

U.S. President (1963-1968). Born in central Texas, not far from Johnson City, which his family helped settle, Johnson, unlike his predecessor KENNEDY, knew of the pangs of rural poverty. Accordingly, his attitude towards the deprivation in the third world was directed towards problem-solving and trouble-shooting. But he was a rough-hewn, grass-roots Texas politician, virtually devoid of international experience. In South Asia, Johnson inherited the 'dual models' doctrine that KENNEDY had promulgated. However, the new president did not share his predecessor's desire to shift the focus of policy from arming Pakistan and providing much greater economic and developmental aid to India. However, his confidence was considerably soured after he dealt with the transparent wiles of the AYUB KHAN and ZUL-

ZULFIKAR ALI BHUTTO duo and concerns about a vacuum of leadership in New Delhi after the death of NEHRU in May 1964. Other major events like the outbreak of war between India and Pakistan on the summer of 1965, the drought in the eastern Gangetic plain in 1966-67, and the mounting American involvement in Vietnam made him wary, petulant and occasionally vindictive about the political obstacles he encountered in South Asia.

Soon after Johnson became president Bhutto was the rising star in Islamabad. The latter, a charismatic populist leader was attempting to create a distinct political identity for his country characterized by greater flexibility in Pakistani foreign policy including closer ties with China. A comparable evolution occurred in Johnson's relationship with INDIRA GANDHI after her ascent to power as India's prime minister in 1966. Her visit to Washington two months later went surprisingly well. Mrs. Gandhi charmed the American President. Her motive was to ameliorate Johnson's "short tether" food policy formulated by Secretary Orville Freeman and other puritanical agricultural experts who had concluded that India was profligately importing PL-480 food grains instead of stimulating its own food-growing capabilities. By doing so, Freeman and his ilk believed India and other countries, were freeing domestic capital for industrialization. In that narrow perspective Freeman was right for both Nehru and his daughter believed that it was the key to liberating India from the shackles of post-colonial paternalism. Johnson's sanctimonious support for the Freeman policy came in the midst of the Bihar famine. Ambassador BOWLES, opposed to the "short tether" tactic tried to thwart its implementation in the face of a November 1966 bipartisan joint-Congressional delegation that Johnson sent to India to provide legitimization for the new policy. He failed. With the Rupee devaluation, which many of her critics believed that a naive Mrs. Gandhi had been hoodwinked into agreeing to by American free-marketers ended the brief honeymoon between the two leaders. Mrs. Gandhi was compelled to fight for her political life and did so by abruptly turning to the Left and adopting a more populist political posture at home. In addition, she promoted closer ties with the Soviets, and was more strident in her criticism of the U.S. policy in Vietnam. By then, the positive impact of the GREEN REVOLUTION was already making India less dependent on U.S. grain shipments. By the end of the Johnson years U.S.-Indian relations had cooled considerably. The Nixon era and the August 1971 "Indo-Soviet Treaty of Peace, Friendship and Cooperation" were yet to come.

Jones, Norah (1970-)

Musician born out of wed-lock though her acknowledged father is the celebrated Indian sitarist RAVI SHANKAR. Born in New York City, Geetali Norah Jones Shankar dropped both Geetali and Shankar from her name and officially became Norah Jones at the age of 16. Her mother, Sue Jones, moved to Dallas, Texas, when Norah was four. Jones attended the prestigious Booker T. Washington High School for the Performing and Visual Arts and the University of North Texas, where she majored in jazz piano. In 1999, after finishing only two of the four year course, Norah left for New York City, where she performed with the trip hop band Wax Poetic and the guitarist Charlie Hunter. In 2002, fame and fortune came her way with the successful launch of her debut album "Come Away with Me." It sold 20 million copies worldwide and she won eight Grammy Awards in 2003. By receiving the Record of the Year, the Album of the Year, the Song of the Year, and The Best New Artist awards, Jones swept the "Big Four" in 2003. No other performer had earlier accomplished this feat. The following year, *Time* magazine listed Jones as among the Most Influential People of 2004.

Joshi, Anandibai (1865-1887)

First Indian women to obtain a medical degree from abroad. At the age of eighteen, Anandibai accompanied her husband to the United Stares and enrolled at the Medical College of Philadelphia. She returned to India as the Physician In-charge of the women's' ward at Albert Edward Hospital (now Civil Hospital) at Kohlapur in Maharashtra. Unfortunately, her impact was little for died of tuberculosis in 1887.

Judson, Adoniran (1798-1850)

American missionary in Burma. Born in Massachusetts, the 24-year-old Judson and his bride of seven days, Ann Heseltine Judson, sailed for India in February 1812. Ann was the first female missionary supported by the American Board for Foreign Missionaries. On reaching Calcutta (Kolkata), the Judsons were denied entry into India by Britain's East India Company. After many frustrations and failures, the couple finally reached Rangoon, Burma, where the xenophobic King Thiebaw promptly imprisoned the couple. However, one of Burma's larger tribes, the Karen, came to their rescue. The tribe had a legend predicting that white haired messiah bearing a powerful book would come to guide the Karen people. Since Judson was fair-haired and carried a Bible, he was considered to be the prophesied redeemer. Under Karen entreaties, King Thiebaw relented and allowed the couple to move to Upper Burma and start a school near Bhamo. By the turn of the millennium, there were about 210,000 Karen and Kachin converts, accounting for almost two percent of Burma's total population. Around 1910, the American Baptist Foreign Mission established the Judson College in Rangoon. Much earlier, Mrs. Judson was honored by the Siloam Baptist Church. The church built the Judson Female Institute at Marion, Alabama in 1839. Adoniran Judson was also a lexicographer and translated the Bible into Burmese. He died in Burma.

K

Kahn, Louis Isadore (1901-1974)

American architect who left a great imprint on the urban landscape of the subcontinent. His most celebrated works were the magical sequence of red brick buildings that appeared to float above the water-logged landscape in Dhaka, the capital of Bangladesh. He also designed the campus of the INDIAN INSTITUTE OF MANAGEMENT, in Ahmedabad, Gujarat, in neighboring India.

Born in Saaremaa, Estonia, his family emigrated to the U.S. in 1905. After graduating from the University of Pennsylvania, Kahn preferred to work with simple materials, notably brick and concrete. Therefore, he created buildings that instilled a sense of spirituality through the masterful use of space and light. In the building of Dhaka, then the capital of East Pakistan, Kahn received an opportunity to fulfill his own vision by building a city of the future. The project was disrupted by political unrest, civil war, Indian military intervention, and the eventual independence of Bangladesh. Furthermore there were logistical difficulties of building in a city prone to flooding and vulnerable to intense tropical storms. The monumental complex begun in 1962 was not completed in his lifetime. Perhaps, it was fitting that on the evening of his death, Kahn had flown back to the U.S. from India where he was supervising the ongoing construction of the campus project in Ahmedabad, India.

Kansi, Mir Aimal (1964-2002)

On 26 January 1993, Kansi in a short, swift, shooting spree killed two employees and injured three other personnel working for the American Central Intelligence Agency (CIA) while they were stopped at a traffic sign just before the road turned towards the agency's vast office complex at Langley, Virginia, near Washington DC. Kansi had earlier worked as a courier for Excel Inc., a firm with close links to the CIA. Within hours of the murders, he left for Karachi on board a

Pakistan International Airlines flight. The Federal Bureau of Investigation (FBI) and the CIA spent millions of dollars in recruiting and equipping local bounty hunters to capture him. In the meantime his name was linked with Ramzi Youssef, a participant in the bombing of the World Trade Center in 1992. Four years later, he was finally betrayed by an associate. The FBI apprehended in a seedy hotel in the dusty town of Dera Ghazi Khan in June 1997. He was quietly flown to the U.S. where a court in Virginia sentenced him to death. He was executed in 2002.

Karzai, Hamid (1957-)

President of Afghanistan. (2004-) Born in Karzai Village, Qandahar, he is an ethnic Pashtun from the powerful Populzai clan of Ahmed Shah Durrani (1722-72), the founder of modern Afghanistan. Not unexpectedly, members of the family were royalists and staunch supporters of King Zahir Shah. Karzai did his Masters in political science from Himachal Pradesh University, Shimla, India (1979-83). On returning to the Afghan-Pakistan border, he worked as the press, logistics and humanitarian relief coordinator for the royalist Mujahideen faction headed by Sibghatullah Mojadeddi. After the fall of the Soviet-backed Najibullah regime, he served as the Deputy Foreign Minister in the new Kabul government. When the Taliban emerged as a political force in the mid-1990s, Karzai briefly backed the zealots but soon broke with the new regime citing his concerns over its close links with Pakistan. In 1997, he rejoined his family in Quetta, Pakistan, and worked with other royalists to reinstate the exiled King Zahir Shah. The family paid dearly for opposing the Taliban: Karzai's father was assassinated by suspected Taliban agents in July 1999. Following the 11 September 2001 terrorist attacks in the United States, Karzai joined the American-led coalition in the overthrow of the Taliban government in Kabul. Under the 5 December, 2001 Bonn Agreement an Interim Transitional Administration was set up in Afghanistan with Karzai as the Chairman of a 29-member governing committee. The Loya Jirga of June 2002, appointed him as the interim president of the country though his authority and his popular support outside the city of Kabul was untested and he was frequently derided as simply the Mayor of Kabul and as a U.S. puppet. His credibility improved marginally after he won the nation-wide presidential elections held in October 2004. A notable guest at his inauguration as president was the country was the former king Zahir Shah. Washington was represented by Vice President Richard Cheney. Two of Karzai's brothers live in the United States.

Kennedy, John Fitzgerald (1917-63)

U.S. President (1961-63). Of Irish descent, born in Brookline, Massachusetts, educated at Harvard, he served with valor and distinction as a Patrol Torpedo (PT) Boat commander in the Navy during World War II. In 1960 he narrowly won the presidential race and became the first Roman Catholic President of the United States. His personal impact on South Asia was small because his tenure as president was out short by his assassination on 22 November 1963. Nevertheless, during his thousand day presidency, Kennedy enhanced the new policies set by President Eisenhower during his second term when a more balanced approach towards the region had emerged. It was characterized by a "dual models" policy developed in response to the changed Soviet strategy after the death of the dictator, Josef Stalin. Moscow began to cultivate the "bourgeois" ruling classes in developing countries by accepting their legitimacy, by toning down its own orthodox revolutionary Marxist-Leninist rhetoric, and by providing diplomatic, economic, military, and technological assistance. Hence, economic aid became a key weapon in the Cold War. The Kennedy administration responded by increased financial aid to India, and endorsed the development of her democratic institutions as deterrents against the spread of Communism while continuing to provide military assistance to ostensibly protect Pakistan from Soviet aggression. In addition, India was given a higher profile by the appointment of the respected Harvard professor John Kenneth Galbraith as ambassador in 1961. A well-known liberal and intellectual Galbraith had the right credentials to win the confidence of the Indian elite. The reverses suffered by New Delhi in the Sino-Indian border war in 1962 briefly created the chimera of a strategic relationship as well.

As a young congressman, Kennedy visited India and found NEHRU to be self-righteous and supercilious. As president, though Kennedy publicly professed admiration for Nehru's "soaring idealism," and called for "more cooperative relations with the uncommitted world." Nehru was in his seventies on his last to the U.S. and Kennedy found him to be "terribly passive" and in decline, yet unchanged for he remained aloof and sanctimonious. Nehru's trip was shortly followed by a visit by General AYUB KHAN. The Pakistani military dictator thought that Kennedy was unsure of his understanding of international affairs but Ayub had little success in convincing the young U.S. President on the use of economic aid to India as the means of resolving the Kashmir dispute in Pakistan's favour. In response to the two unproductive visits, Kennedy dispatched Vice President Lyndon Johnson to the subcontinent to placate the doubters and critics in both countries. The Vice President's visit was made memorable by his personal energy and his affable accessibility to the general public. Importantly, he developed a personal rapport with Ayub Khan in Pakistan. Despite his personal reservations about Nehru, Kennedy decided that not only economic aid to India should be substantially increased but that a more meaningful military relationship between the two countries must be developed as well. An agreement to this effect awaited Kennedy's signature, but was not consummated due to his assassination. Annoyed by the late President's policies, Ayub did not attend the funeral. However, both he and Pakistan were intimately connected with the burial of the slain president for the horse that walked behind the hearse was "Sardar," an animal that Ayub had presented to his wife, Mrs. Jacqueline Kennedy.

Khalilzad, Zalmay (1951-)

Afghan-born U.S. Diplomat. Born in Mazar-e Sharif, Afghanistan, Khalilzad hails from the old ruling elite of Afghanistan. His father was an aide to King ZAHIR SHAH. Khalilzad came to the United States as an exchange student after finishing college in Beirut, Lebanon. In the U.S., he obtained a doctorate from the University of Chicago. He taught at Columbia University where he worked closely with Zbigniew Brzezinski, President CARTER's National Security Advisor. In 1984 he joined the State Department under Paul Wolfowitz, the then Director of Policy Planning. Khalilzad was also a special assistant to Presidents REAGAN and GEORGE H.W. BUSH and lobbied successfully for accelerated U.S. military aid to the MUJAHIDEEN in Afghanistan.

Increased aid included the hand held STINGER anti-aircraft missile that played a key role in winning the war. During the First Gulf War (1991), he became Under Secretary of Defense in the George H.W. Bush administration. During the CLINTON years, Khalilzad was with the RAND Corporation, a leading U.S. military think tank. He was also an advisor to UNOCAL, and drew up the risk analysis of a proposed gas pipeline from Turkmenistan across Afghanistan to Pakistan and the Indian Ocean. At that stage, he considered the TALIBAN both as a stabilizing force in Afghanistan and as a counterweight to Iranian ambitions. 9/11 changed his perspective. Khalilzad headed the BUSH-Cheney transition team for the Defense Department and served as a Counselor to Secretary of Defense Rumsfeld. At the National Security Council, he reported to CONDOLEEZZA RICE the then National Security Advisor. Rice, too, had worked as an oil company consultant. She was on the Board of Directors of Chevron Corporation and was its principal expert on Kazakhstan, where the company held the largest concessions of any of the international oil companies. These fields reportedly hold more than six percent of the world's proven oil reserves and about forty percent of the global gas reserves. Khalilzad was appointed as the American ambassador to the post-Taliban KARZAI government in Afghanistan from November 2003 to June 2005. In 2005, he was shifted to Baghdad as the U.S. envoy in post-Saddam Iraq. In early January 2007, he was nominated as the U.S. representative to the United Nations. Ironically, he was replaced in Iraq by Ryan Crocker, a veteran diplomat who had once opposed the overthrow of Saddam Hussein because of the sectarian strife that would follow.

Khan, Abdul Quadeer (1935-)

Pakistani nuclear scientist and clandestine proliferators of nuclear technology. Khan trained as metallurgist in Holland in the early 1970s. On returning to Pakistan he set up a uranium enrichment laboratory at Kahuta, a small town near Islamabad. By the early 1990s, Pakistan had stocked enough enriched uranium to produce a dozen or so bombs. Around 1987, well managed news leaks informed the world that Pakistan had nuclear weapons and India should defer from military action against the country, despite the incipient insurgency in

Kashmir being fuelled by Islamabad. In the early 1990s, Khan and his associates undertook the development of missiles capable of delivering nuclear bombs. The vast complex at Kahuta was named the A. Q. Khan Laboratories in his honor. Pakistan unexpectedly launched a medium range ballistic missile named *Ghauri* in 1997. It was in fact the *Nodong* missile developed by North Korea. Later, it was revealed that A. Q. Khan traded nuclear weapons technology with North Korea in exchange for the missiles. He was also involved in secret nuclear trades with Iran and Libya. Implausibly, Pakistan blamed Khan for making these deals solely for personal gain. Nevertheless, the Pakistan military dictator, General PERVEZ MUSHARRAF pardoned Khan for any wrongdoing and refused permission to the United States to interview him.

Khan, Akhtar Rahman (1926-1988)

Pakistan Army officer. Lieutenant General Akhtar was the director-general of the Pakistani intelligence agency, the INTER-SERVICES INTELLIGENCE (ISI), during most of the Soviet intervention in Afghanistan. As director-general, he was instrumental in insuring that all aid to the MUJAHIDEEN from the United States, Saudi Arabia, and other countries was exclusively handled by the ISI. In March 1987, he was promoted to the rank of full general and appointed as Chairman of the Joint Chiefs of Staff Committee. He was killed in an air crash on 17 August 1988 in which the U.S. ambassador to Islamabad and the country's military dictator, General ZIA UL-HAQ, too perished. General Akhtar was survived by four sons, all working in the United States. After his death, all four returned to Pakistan and one of them, Humayun Akthar Khan became active in politics. The brothers have reportedly amassed large fortunes.

Khan, Habibullah (1916-1996)

Pakistani general and industrialist. General Habibullah joined the British Indian Army in 1937 and was respected for his professionalism and lack of political ambition in Pakistani military circles. His daughter married Gohar Ayub, the second son of the Pakistan military dictator, General AYUB KHAN. The latter, perhaps cognizant of Habibullah as a potential rival for power, encouraged the general to set an example and be the precedent for Pakistani military officers to go into other undertakings, industry, and businesses. Consequently, Habibullah established a large cotton textile mill at Kohat and set up Gandhara Motors, an automobile assembly plant near Karachi in collaboration with the American giant, General Motors. Later, ZULFIKAR ALI BHUTTO nationalized Gandhara Motors and merged it with other automobile plants to form the Automobile Corporation of Pakistan.

Khan, Liaquat Ali (1896-1951)

Pakistani political leader. Liaquat Ali, the brilliant scion of a family from Karnal in East Punjab (now Haryana), was called to the bar at the Inner Temple in London after completing his education at Oxford. He returned to India in 1923, and after observing both the Indian National Congress and the All India Muslim League, he opted for the latter. He then served as a member of the United Provinces Legislative Council from 1926 to 1940. He persuaded JINNAH to return to India, revive the moribund Muslim League, and take the lead in demanding the creation of a Muslim majority country, Pakistan. Liaquat was the Secretary of the Muslim League's Central Parliamentary Board in 1945 and worked closely with Jinnah during the key negotiations that led to the partition of India. He became the first Prime Minister of the newly created Pakistan and was the first Pakistani leader to visit the United States. In contrast to the India's imperious Prime Minister NEHRU, President TRUMAN found Liaquat to be agreeable and forthright. His visit set the stage for close ties between the two countries. Liaquat was assassinated in 1951. His sole assassin was killed by the police before underlying explanations or wider conspiracies could be unearthed.

Khan, Mohammed Ayub (1907-1970)

Pakistani military dictator. A Tareen Pashtun, son of a Risaldar-Major (the senior most rank then open to Indians), Ayub was commissioned in 1928 from the Royal Military Academy, Sandhurst, England. He was a Brigadier at Partition and served on the Punjab Boundary Commission. A year later, he was promoted to the rank of Major General and posted to Dhaka as the Commander of Military Garrison in East Bengal. During his tenure in Dhaka he developed an abiding contempt for the Bengali people which he transmitted to other members of the officer corps. In 1951 he became the first Pakistani to command his country's army. As the Army Chief, Ayub was unabashedly pro-American and repeatedly sought military aid and alliances with United States. In October 1958, he appointed himself President of the country. For the next seven years, despite nepotism and corruption, the country acquired a façade of a controlled democracy, stability, and growth. The dictatorship began to unravel after the failure of the Pakistan Army to wrest Kashmir from India in the September 1965 war. In addition, the unsuccessful war drained the country's financial resources. It also brought a sudden end to the highly coveted American military and economic assistance. Furthermore, the military vulnerability of East Pakistan was exposed and contributed to the secessionist movement that surfaced in the Eastern Wing. Following the war, Ayub's health and popularity declined. In the face of rising opposition that included his erstwhile protégé, ZULFIKAR ALI BHUTTO , Ayub resigned from office in 1969.

Khorana, Hargobind (1922-)

Nobel laureate (medicine, 1968) of India. Born in Raipur, West Punjab (now Pakistan), Khorana completed his Masters from Panjab University, Lahore. In 1945 he went to England on a government scholarship and obtained a PhD from the University of Liverpool (1948). After a year in Zurich as a post-doctoral fellow at the Swiss Federal Institute of Technology, Khorana returned to India in 1949. In 1960 he joined the University of Wisconsin as Professor and co-Director of the Institute of Enzyme Research and Professor of Biochemistry (1962-70). Khorana's major research was on nucleic acid synthesis and he prepared the first artificial copy of a yeast gene. His synthesis of RNA capable of replication in the laboratory, was a step towards the creation of artificial life. This pioneering work created the science of Genetic Engineering. In 1970 he became the Alfred Sloan Professor of Biology and Chemistry at the Massachusetts Institute of Technology in the United States. His numerous other awards included the *Padma Vibushan* from India (1972). He was elected as a member of the National Academy of Sciences, Washington, DC and a Fellow of the American Association for the Advancement of Science.

Khost

Strategic town in Afghanistan. The town is close to the Tora Bora Mountain caves complex, the Shah-e-kot Valley, and the Northern Waziristan region of Pakistan. During the Soviet occupation of Afghanistan, this small town (population, 15,000), located only 32 kms (about 20 miles) from the Pakistan border, was a major government base for cutting supply lines of MUJAHIDEEN forces. Khost was then commonly known as "Little Moscow" because many of the Marxist leaders were native to the area and therefore enjoyed the support of the local population. Because of its location, the town was the scene of much bitter fighting and myth-making. Successive Mujahideen attempts to capture this government stronghold failed and Kabul presented its hold on the town as an example of the rebels' weakness and of its own strength. The stalemate on the Afghan battlefield was finally broken at the end of March 1991 when the fall of Khost was hailed as evidence of new unity among the rebels because a unified Mujahideen force, headed by a twenty three member council had overseen the battle. The success was more likely due to the use of regular Pakistan Army troops than the improved cooperation among Mujahideen commanders. The surrender also resulted from secret negotiations that allowed regional militia units to change sides and quietly leave the town. Another abiding myth after the fall of the town was the conclusion by Western aid-givers that the Mujahideen showed better respect for international humanitarian law, as for the first time, captured government soldiers were promptly seen by the Red Cross. The truth was more prosaic: the relatively lenient treatment of the captured and their families reflected the fact that the battle was primarily among Pashtuns who did not want to incite blood feuds by the slaughter of prisoners belonging to other tribes. For the Kabul Government the loss was so profound that a day of official mourning was announced. The defeat marked the beginning of the slow unraveling of the communist regime in Afghanistan which collapsed thirteen months later. The region's strategic significance did not decline with the end of communist rule in Afghanistan for a sinister new force, AL QAEDA, was rising around the town. After the bombings of the American embassies in Kenya and Tanzania in August 1998, the U.S. fired Tomahawk missiles at an al Qaeda camp near Khost in a failed attempt to kill Osama BIN LADEN. In the aftermath of 9/11 U.S. Special Forces established a base near the city to fight the combined al-Qaeda and Taliban forces concentrated around Tora Bora and Shah-e-kot. However, most of the guerrillas escaped. Since then because of cross-border infiltration from Pakistan, the Khost region has been the scene of periodic intense fire fights.

Khyber Pass

A 50 Km (33 miles) passage leading through barren hills from the Afghan border to Ali Masjid, a small outpost 16 kms (10 miles) from Peshawar, Pakistan. At one point the pass, narrows to just 3 meters (15 feet) and reaches its highest elevation at 1,066 meters (3,518 feet). Britain gained control of the strategic passage by the Treaty of Gandomak (1879). Drama and intrigue have often played a prominent part in the history of the pass. Among the most unusual was one planned by Charles (Charlie) Wilson, a Democratic Congressman from Houston, Texas. Wilson was the key supporter for funding for the CIA effort against the Soviet Union in Afghanistan. The congressman, had served in the U.S. Navy, was Vietnam War veteran, and a member of the Defense Appropriations Subcommittee in the U.S. House of Representatives. He was persuaded by the Houston socialite Joanne Herring, a personal friend of General ZIA, the then Pakistani dictator, into assisting the MUJAHIDEEN in Afghanistan with congressional funds. Although the Democrats were then attacking the Reagan Administration for financing the Contras against Sandinistas in Nicaragua, Wilson managed to increase the funding for the Mujahideen from a paltry $5 million a year to over a billion dollars annually funneled through the secret budget of the CIA. During the war against the Soviets in Afghanistan, Wilson was the only U.S. Congressman to cross the Khyber Pass and see for himself the situation in the war ravaged country. He did so in 1987, despite opposition from the government of Pakistan. Islamabad was concerned about the possibility of him being killed, captured or wounded by the enemy. Later, Wilson flamboyantly planned to get married at the Khyber Pass with Afghan tribal leaders and thousands of Mujahideen in attendance. Before the scheduled wedding the congressman went to California to serve as the Grand Marshal of the Annual Mule Day Parade at Bishop, California, to honor the animals for performing to gallantly in the great anti-Communist *jihad* in Afghanistan. The planned marriage was called off when his fiancé telephoned Wilson's hotel room where a former girlfriend, answered. Doubtless, the pass will witness other dramatic events in the future. A major Hollywood movie about Wilson's exploits called *Charlie Wilson's War,* named after a best-selling book, starring Tom Hanks and Julia Roberts was released in late 2007. (See also: MULES).

King, Martin Luther, Jr (1929-1968)

African-American leader of the American Civil Rights Movement, and Nobel laureate (Peace, 1964). Born in Atlanta, Georgia, he changed his first name from Michael to Martin, perhaps reflecting his own ambitions and as a tribute to the great German pastor and reformer.

Mordecai Johnson, President of Howard University in Washington DC, first introduced King to the Mahatma GANDHI's philosophy and tactics. He was profoundly influenced by what he learnt. In 1959, King went to India to meet many of Gandhiji's surviving disciples and to further study the Gandhian strategies of non-violent non-cooperation. On landing in New Delhi he declared, "To other countries I may go as a tourist, but to India I come as a pilgrim. This is because India means to me Mahatma Gandhi, a truly great man of ages."

Through non-violent disobedience, such as boycotts, mass rallies, and sit-ins, King exposed the oppressive nature of the White establishment in the United States. The two great emancipators, Gandhi and King, shared a common fate. Both were assassinated. In a profound and poignant sketch shortly after King's assassination, the Pulitzer prize-winning cartoonist Bill Mauldin (1921-2003) had Gandhi telling the American, "The odd thing about assassins, Dr. King, is that they think they have killed you."

Kissinger, Henry Alfred, born Heinz Alfred (1923-)

Adviser, National Security Affairs (1969-75), U.S. Secretary of State (1973-77), Nobel laureate (Peace, 1973). Born in Fürth, Germany the young Kissinger immigrated to the U.S. in 1938. He was educated at Harvard — BA (1950), MA (1952), and PhD (1954). Kissinger's doctoral dissertation was a continuation of his undergraduate thesis, which at 383 pages prompted the "Kissinger rule" restricting future senior theses to less than one-half that length (150 pages). Kissinger was brought into public service by New York State's Governor Nelson Rockefeller in the 1960s. However, he was most closely associated with the Nixon presidency (1969-74). During his years in political wilderness, the latter had changed his perspectives on Communist China. By the late 1960s Nixon considered normalization of relations with Beijing as the most appropriate strategy to both contain its potential nuclear threat and to exploit the increasingly adversarial Sino-Soviet ties. Progress was slow till September 1970, when Kissinger took over the endeavor of developing the Sino-American relationship. The very next month, at a Washington meeting with Pakistani dictator Yahya Khan, Kissinger spoke of establishing secret contacts with Beijing. The Chinese Premier Zhou, reciprocated using Pakistani channels and cautiously welcomed the American overture. It culminated in Kissinger's secret trip to Beijing via Islamabad in July 1971. Earlier, in March 1971, East Pakistan was in open revolt. Despite reports of atrocities by the Pakistan military in East Pakistan, U.S.-Pakistani relations remained strong. Both personal and political factors were involved for Kissinger found the Pakistani dictator General Agha Mohammed Yahya Khan to be "a splendid product of Sandhurst" whereas the Indian Prime minister, Mrs. Indira Gandhi, was "a bitch," and Indians in general were "bastards." He may also truly have believed that an independent Bangladesh would become an unstable failed third world country. In addition, there was increasing concern in Washington over the growing Indo-Soviet hegemony in the region and hence the need to support Pakistan as an ally of both the U.S. and China. Kissinger was particularly anxious to demonstrate to Communist China the value of a tacit alliance with the United States. Hence, towards the end of the 1971 war, the U.S. Secretary of State sent a task-force from the U.S. Seventh Fleet, led by the nuclear-powered aircraft carrier, U.S.S Enterprise, into the Bay of Bengal. He claimed the move was designed to deter India from further dismemberment of Pakistan, but also to "back up the Chinese." New Delhi, shaken by such blatant "gunboat diplomacy" supposedly accelerated its nuclear program for the indigenous development of nuclear weapons culminating in its first nuclear test in 1974. By then a more sanguine Kissinger testified before the U.S. Congress that, "We objected strongly, but since there was no violation of U.S. agreements involved, we had no specific leverage on which to bring our objections to bear." Nonetheless, this non-committal response to India's nuclear test was accompanied by the resumption of military aid to Pakistan. His help to Pakistan was perhaps little appreciated in Islamabad for Pakistan's leader Zulfikar Ali Bhutto alleged that in August 1976 Kissinger threatened to make "a horrible example" of him if he did not discontinue his country's nuclear weapons program. His daughter, Benazir Bhutto, repeated this story in the country's National Assembly in June 1998 as the reason for her father's execution by another military dictator, Zia Ul-Haq in 1979. This contention notwithstanding, on the eve of President Bush's March 2006 trip to the Indian subcontinent, a more introspective Kissinger addressed the key issues in American relations with India and Pakistan, and on Washington's approach to nuclear issues by writing, "In the region between Bombay and Yemen, Indian and American interests in defeating radical Islam are nearly parallel. Relations with Pakistan are a special case. Balancing the role of Pakistan in the war against terrorism with the emerging partnership with India will require extraordinary sensitivity and an ability to keep in mind each country's national obsession(s). In 1998, I opposed the sanctions on India's nuclear tests, suggesting that India should be treated as a country whose nuclear progress had become irreversible. In such a context, nuclear cooperation with India is appropriate. The emerging cooperation between the two great democracies, India and the United States, introduces a positive and hopeful perspective."

Kurien, Varghese (1921-)

U.S. educated Father of the "White (milk) Revolution" in India. Kurien, a mechanical engineer, received his MS in metallurgy from Michigan State University in 1948. Thereafter he did his practical training at a large dairy manufacturing plant, Sheffield Farm, in Long Island, New York. The few months in Long Island were to change his life. Back in India, he did not return to the corporate world of Tata Steel. Instead, he joined as a diary engineer at the milk plant of a government-owned creamery in the sleepy hamlet of Anand in Gujarat. There he realized that milk farmers were unable to either store or effectively market their product. Kurien, therefore, started a cooperative movement mobilizing 2.2 million diary farmers into cooperatives. AMUL (acronym for Anand Milk Union Ltd) as the brand name synonymous with indigenous good quality milk products was born. Among its products was powdered milk. Earlier experts from New Zealand had concluded that it was not possible to produce powdered milk from buffalo's milk. Kurien proved them wrong. This was one of the many instances that were to reduce the credibility of foreign experts. The New Zealanders had opposed him for non-technical reasons: Their country's export of powdered milk to India would decline. Their fears were well-founded. Indian production of powdered milk was to far exceed the amount produced by New Zealand.

Kurien's pioneering project served as a model for the subsequent Operation Flood under which 180 cooperatives were established in twenty-two Indian states and five metropolitan cities. Milk production increased by 300 percent and the 100 million cooperative farmers received 60 percent of the sale price of their products. With the assistance of NGOs and Foundations (mostly American) the Indian Institute of Rural Management and the National Dairy Development Board were founded at Anand, Gujarat.

L

Lahore University of Management Science (LUMS)

In 1980 a group of industrialists led by Syed Babar Ali founded LUMS in Lahore. The mission was to train managerial staff to work in their firms and enterprises. LUMS was patterned after the Harvard Business School and partly financed by a grant from the U.S. Agency for International Development (USAID). The Lahore-based institution also established an executive training program. It followed a curriculum that approximated the one at Harvard. LUMS is widely recognized for its excellence in training.

Loya Jirga

"Grand Council" in the Pashto language. For centuries, leaders among the Pashtuns and the other factions in Afghanistan have convened loya jirgas to select kings, adopt constitutions, make important political decisions or resolve disputes. Loya jirgas were traditionally made up of tribal leaders and other elders, mostly men, representing local *shuras* (village-level councils). The quasi-democratic process was relatively representative of Afghanistan's population for its members included most of the major ethnic and religious groups including Baloch, Farsiwan, Hazara, Hindu, Nuristani, Pashtun, Shia, Sikh, Sunni, Tajik, and Uzbek. Women were largely absent except in 1964 and 1977. Under the Bonn Agreement, Chairman KARZAI and the Interim Administration was given the mandate to lead Afghanistan until a loya jirga supported by the United States selected a new Transitional Administration to succeed it. The loya jirga endorsed Karzai as the nation's ruler till elections were held to democratically elect a president of the country.

M

Madrassas

(Arabic: "school." Plural: "Madari," though Madrassas is the plural in common English language usage). Madrassas have traditionally played a leading role in imparting education in Muslim societies across the world. Washington's attention was first directed towards these seminaries by the rise of Ayatollah Khomeini in Iran and by the Soviet invasion of Afghanistan (1979). By curious coincidence, two zealots, firm in their own faiths, William Colby, the then head of the CIA and General ZIA UL-HAQ, the Pakistani dictator, were bound by the strategic and political commitment to contain communism. Both men found it opportune to support the growth of madrassas. The rise of the TALIBAN and the events of 9/11 were to come a generation later. Islam reached Afghanistan during the seventh century and gradually replaced the existing religions, Zoroastrianism, Buddhism and Hinduism. As Islam spread so did mosques and madrassas. Most mosques, even small and simple ones, have a special space or classroom for teaching and learning. The teacher, usually the *mullah* (clergyman, vicar) of the mosque, used written texts that always included the Holy *Quran* and the *hadith* (a compilation of statements or actions of the prophet Mohammed or about his tacit approval of something said or done in his presence). Most of the madrassas in Afghanistan followed the curriculum developed by the ruling Abbasids of Baghdad (750-1258). In the wake of the Mongol invasion and the destruction of Baghdad (February 1258), Herat in western Afghanistan became a major center of Islamic learning. Teachers were generally known as *mullahs, imams, or akhunds*. A few female teachers called *bibiatun*, educated girls and small boys in private homes. The situation changed dramatically under the reforming zeal of Amir Amanullah Khan (1919-1928). Western-style education was one of his priorities and by 1927 more than 300 western style schools with an enrollment of approximately 51,000 students were established in the country. In addition, several hundred students were sent for higher education to Britain, India, France, Germany, Turkey, and the newly established U.S.S.R. Consequently, the madrassas lost much of their vigor, pupils, and patronage in urban areas. The circumstances again changed dramatically when Islamic fundamentalists led the war against Soviet intervention (1979 — 1989) in Afghanistan. Madrassas were revived in the country-side and in Afghan refugee camps in Pakistan. Attendance also increased in cities as many of the secular schools were destroyed during the war. Madrassa based education peaked during the rule of the Taliban (1994-2001) as these were the only schools allowed to function during those years. In the 1980s another form of madrassas known as Arabic schools emerged in the Afghan refugee camps in Pakistan. These schools were supported by Saudi Arabia or by a few wealthy Arab individuals. Some imparted exclusively Islamic education and others followed a curriculum of both modern and Islamic subjects. After the Soviet withdrawal some Arabic schools were set up inside Afghanistan and focused on the education of male orphans. Within a few months of the U.S. intervention in Afghanistan (late 2001) education was proclaimed as a national priority. International NGOs, the biggest being the Swedish Committee for Afghanistan (SCA), acted swiftly. SCA alone enrolled an estimated 250,000 students by March 2002. By 2008, there were only 336 madrassas with an enrollment of 91,000 students. The high enrollment may be a reflection of concerns about personal safety as none of these institutions have been attacked during the on-going insurgency in the country.

The large scale building of madrassas south of Afghanistan in the northern part of the Indian subcontinent was first undertaken in the thirteenth century, perhaps by the Turks. The seminaries tried to maintain uniformity in belief and practice by enforcing such a rigid curriculum that are the great Mughal emperor Aurengzeb, though a zealot, found much to complain about. He reprimanded his own teacher for having taught him Arabic, grammar and philosophy rather than subjects more practical for a future ruler of a vast empire. With the collapse of the Muslim dominated Mughal Empire, the British systematically downgraded the prestige of the most learned man in the typical Muslim village, the *maulvi* (teacher). His decline in the village hierarchy led to a fall in grants and endowments to village madrassas and an increase in the dim-witted or the ineptitude in the ranks of the *maulvis*. The rot was stemmed by the revivalist and reformist movements in the 1860s. A group of learned theologians led by Maulana Muhammad Qasim Nanautawi established the Darul Uloom Seminary in the small town of Deoband in 1867. The location was chosen as it was close to Maulana Nanautawi's own village in northern UP (United Provinces then, Uttar Pradesh now). Others schools of thought — the Bareviles, Ahl-i-Hadith, and Shias, too, organized their respective madrassas. In most of the Sunni schools there were no formalized procedures for admission and academic schedules were often flexible. In contrast, Shias generally expected a student to complete tenth grade in a regular school before entering the seminary. Some other major madrassas, too, have institutionalized the admission, grading, and promotion of students. The madrassas in South Asia follow the curriculum known as *Dars-i-Nizami,* first introduced by Mullah Nizamuddin Sihalvi (d.1747) from Lucknow. The complete Nizami curriculum runs from seven to nine years after the completion of schooling at the elementary level. The Madrassa system has been traditionally supported by the community through trusts, endowments, charitable donations, and *zakat* contributions. About twenty subjects broadly divided into two categories known as *al-ulum an-naqliya* (the transmitted sciences) and *al-ulum al-aqliya* (the rational sciences) are taught. Only eight of the subjects were clearly religious. The remaining subjects were to equip students for the civil services and as aids to understanding religious texts. The texts for philosophy and logic were written in the thirteenth and fourteenth centuries, while medicine was taught using an eleventh-century work. About six million students in Pakistan, Bangladesh and India attend these schools.

Many Deobandis were staunch nationalists and fought for India's independence from Britain. Accordingly, many chose to remain in India rather than migrate to Pakistan at Partition in 1947. Unlike their Pakistani counterparts, Indian madrassas are not a part of mainstream politics, including the historically politicized ones like the Deobandi clerics who run several thousand of India's estimated 30,000 madrassas. Most of these schools are just a room in the back of a local mosque with fewer than 100 students. Though education for six to fourteen year olds is largely free and compulsory in India, government schools are frequently under-funded and often unavailable, especially in impoverished Muslim neighborhoods, where literacy lags behind the national average of 68 percent. Madrassas, on the other hand, are pervasive in Muslim areas, and are always free. Hence, many Muslim parents see a free madrassa education, funded largely by religious donations, as the only option for their children despite such handicaps as an education in a language of instruction that is not Hindi (India's national language) or English, the idiom of the globalizing economy. Instead, it remains Urdu, a language often identified with the Muslims of the subcontinent, and Arabic, the language of the Holy *Quran.* Students spend their first three years learning the Holy *Quran* by rote. Thereafter they study the *Hadith* (the sayings of the Prophet Mohammed), Islamic philosophy, and jurisprudence. In 1986, the Indian government initiated a project to modernize madrassas by bringing in subjects like science, mathematics, English, and Hindi. However, most seminaries were unwilling to cooperate, perhaps wary of the state's interference, particularly as their Hindu equivalents, the Sanskrit schools, were being gradually absorbed into the government school system. Thereafter efforts to assimilate the madrassas into the mainstream of Indian school education fitfully continued. One of the new initiatives undertaken by India was the government's decision to pay for the English, mathematics, and science teachers in madrassas. In 2001, 3,500 out of 6,000 madrassas in the state of Madhya Pradesh (MP) opted to receive funds for teachers of modern subjects, reaching some 175,000 students. However, this government program received a major set-back during the very next year (2002), when a secret memorandum was sent to Chief Secretaries and Education Secretaries of all State Governments and Union Territories to verify that the madrassas applying for financial assistance from the government were, "Not indulging, abetting or in any other way linked with anti-national activities. The State Governments may categorically certify that the applicant madrassas are free from security angle." The letter was promptly leaked. General outrage followed. The incensed Chief Minister of the above-mentioned state of MP with 6,000 madrassas echoed the concerns and sentiments of many Indians by declaring, "By singling out institutions of one community alone, a grave disservice has been done to sow in a suspicion about this community itself as (being) prone to anti-national activities." Independent surveys discern a higher dropout rate in madrassas than in government schools. Most attribute it to poverty and boredom, for there are few facilities for games, professional training, crafts, etc., at these institutions. Furthermore, job options for graduates are limited as most of them can only become religious leaders or rewrite and update textbooks for the madrassa system. Accordingly, few middle-class Muslims send their children to madrassas. Nevertheless, there have been numerous innovations from within the system itself including the *Darul Umoor*, a one-year institute for madrassa graduates in the southern state of Karnataka where seminarians supplement their education with courses in English literature and comparative religion before returning to their communities to teach in madrassas and preach in mosques.

Despite 9/11 and the general global hardening of theologies y appears to be low in Indian madrassas. In addition to forbidding participation in holy war abroad, Indian. Deobandi leaders specifically condemn violent jihad at home, saying Muslims have a compact to live in peace and harmony with others unless they are actively persecuted in matters of faith. Deobandis believe that in pluralistic India, to practice rigorous Islam and send their children to religious schools without being opposed to the state is a natural and acceptable state of affairs. However, since the late 1980s there is a proliferation of madrassas in the country, principally in Assam, Bihar, Meghalaya, Tripura, Uttar Pradesh, and West Bengal. All these states have weak records in the maintenance of law and order and are also impacted by violent insurgencies. According to Indian intelligence services some madrassas were being used by youths to promote a politicized curriculum oriented towards a more militant Islam. In addition, the Pakistani intelligence agency, the ISI, had reputedly infiltrated some seminaries in order to indoctrinate young, impressionable minds for future terrorist activities against a "Hindu" Indian state

In 1947, Pakistan had around 137 to 245 madrassas. Their growth picked up during the Zia dictatorship and the numbers increased rapidly to 1,953 by 1984. Twenty years later their number was generally estimated between 13,000 to 18,788 Sunni, Wahhabi, and Deobandi madrassas. The institutions ranged from those which provided elementary education to those that taught at the graduate level. In addition, there were 4,335 Barelvi madrassas, 1,625 of the Ahl-i-Hadith, and 224 run by Shias. The total enrolment was 604,421 students, including 18,000 foreigners. The majority of students were drawn from rural areas of the North West Frontier Province (NWFP), Pakistani Kashmir, and the economically depressed regions of Punjab. A survey conducted three years before the Soviet invasion of Afghanistan in 1979 revealed that 80 percent of the students in Peshawar, Multan, and Gujranwala were sons of small or landless peasants, rural artisans, or imams of the village mosques. They remaining 20 percent came from families of small shopkeepers and rural laborers.

In the mid-1960s some changes in the curriculum were instituted and included the introduction of the English language and subjects like comparative religion, history, and law. Some prominent madrassas in Punjab linked their courses with the general education curriculum in the state, thus enabling their students to acquire degrees from the government schools and colleges and thereby obtain jobs in the "secular" sector. The younger generation of prominent ulema families was especially encouraged to acquire modern (English) education to prepare them to deal with government authorities as well as their modernist and fundamentalist peers. Nevertheless, the majority of the seminaries remained privately owned and they were neither regulated nor registered by the government. An estimated ten percent of the madrassas were recruiting grounds for Muslim fundamentalist warriors mostly among Afghan refugees and other Muslims from the world over. After the Soviet withdrawal from Afghanistan, warlords plunged the country into civil war. The Pakistani intelligence service, the ISI, then fostered the rise of the TALIBAN (plural Arabic word for students; singular is *Talib*), who, too, were recruited from the madrassas. With Pakistani military and financial assistance, the Taliban conquered most of Afghanistan within a few months. The Taliban also gave refuge to OSAMA BIN LADEN after he was expelled from the Sudan in 1994. After 9/11, Islamabad moved swiftly to enact the "Pakistan Madrassa Education Board Ordinance 2001" in a belated effort to introduce secular subjects in the curriculum. The new subjects included English language, Computer Science, Economics, Law, Mathematics, Political Science, Law and Pakistan studies. It was firmly rejected by the *ulema* as being both alien and representative of Western values and systems. Another decree, the "Voluntary Registration and Regulation Ordinance", 2002 tried to catalogue the madrassas and their principals. It, too, was widely unsuccessful as only an estimated ten percent of the madrassas registered.

In the meantime, perhaps to emphasize Islam as a modern, non-fundamentalist faith, the MUSHARRAF government established 42 new seminaries in the Pakistani capital in 2006 and added another nineteen in the following year. However, an older madrassa closely identified with the Pakistani government precipitated the Lal Masjid incident in 2007. The Lal Masjid complex (Red Mosque known as such for the color of the building) included a mosque, madrassa, hostel, etc., was frequented by the Pakistani military, civilian and political leaders in the past, the most prominent being the late dictator, General MUHAMMAD ZIA UL-HAQ. After 9/11 the leadership of Lal Masjid, retained its pro-Taliban proclivities. The seemingly soft approach taken by the government in its dealings with the mosque may have emboldened its students and faculty into taking increasingly confrontational stands towards the government. Arguably, the incident may have been provoked by the government as a distraction against other pressing political and domestic issues. Events began to unfold in early 2007 with the kidnapping of ten Chinese nationals, several law enforcement officials, women and children. It escalated when a building of the Ministry of Environment was set ablaze. Clashes with government troops followed. Ultimately, it was resolved by gunfire resulting in 102 deaths and 248 injuries. It was one of the major factors in 2007 to lead to a steady decline in public confidence in the Musharraf leadership of the country.

Unlike Pakistan, Bangladesh had two kinds of madrassas: *Quomi* and *Alia* madrassas. The *Quomi* are estimated at 6,500 with about 1,462,500 students and 130,000 teachers. These madrassas were predominantly Deobandi, privately owned and receive no financial support from the government. Instead, their funding was by religious endowments or by *zakat, sadaqa*, and donations from the faithful. The overwhelming majority of the *Quomi* madrassa students (82 percent) were from poor families living in rural areas and small towns in Sylhet, Chittagong, and some northern districts. Financial autonomy made some of them into centers of religious and political power. During the three decades of independence, the *Quomi* madrassas introduced far reaching changes. Bangla replaced Urdu as the medium of instruction so as to create an indigenized Bangladeshi form of Islam, de-linked from it's the North Indian origins. New subjects such as politics, economics, and the history of Islam in the Indian subcontinent were added and the English language began to be widely taught. Elementary school education was integrated within the *Quomi madrassas* and comparative religion added to the curriculum. The second system (the *Alia madrassas*), taught modern subjects such as English, science, social studies, mathematics, geography, history, etc., along with a revised version of *Dars-i-Nizami* curriculum. The *ulema* ("Islamic scholars") showed remarkable flexibility in adapting to the changing social, economic, and political conditions, as evidenced by its acceptance of changes in education. The *Alia madrassa* system may emerge as an example of the blending of modern and traditional systems of education, notwithstanding the well-known inadequacies and shortcomings of the institutions themselves. The total number of students at all levels as 1,879,300 with 100,732 teachers. In contrast to previous governments, the ruling Bangladesh National Party (BNP) allocated public funds for the construction of 1,741 new madrassas in the private sector.

In the Maldives, the growth of Islamic fundamentalist influence can be traced in part to Saudi Arabia, which built the seven-story Islamic Studies Institute in Male. In addition, many young Maldivians have studied at madrassas in the Middle East and Pakistan, where some were recruited by militants, especially the *Lashkar-e-Tayyba*, a

Pakistani extremist group that U.S. officials have linked to al Qaeda. There are a total of 52 madrassas in the islands and most were set up under the patronage of President Gayoom. Some have been linked to militant Islam in recent years. A Maldivian identified as Ibrahim Fauzee was in the list of detainees held by the U.S. at its military base at Guantanamo Bay, Cuba. However, he was released in 2005 and returned home.

In the 1950s, Muslims were negligible in number along the Indo-Nepal border. Fifty years later, three percent of the population professed to follow the Islamic faith, especially in Nepal's Terai districts of Rupandehi, Banke, Kapilvastu and Bardiya. This rise in the Muslim population was accompanied by a proliferation of mosques and madrassas. Reportedly, within six miles (ten kilometers) of the border with India, about 820 madrassas and mosques were established in Nepal between 1999 and 2007. About 75 of them may have links with anti-India elements by facilitating the movement of terrorists, and the transport of arms, ammunition, counterfeit currency, explosives, etc., into India through the open border between the two countries.

In 2007, Muslims represented 7.36 percent of the total population of Sri Lanka and claimed to belong to a number of different ethnic groups. Three groups were recognized as such in the 1984 census: Sri Lankan Moors (1.1 million); Malays (60,000); and Indian Moors, the majority of whom were ethnic Tamils (40,000). Tamil is the established tongue of the Sri Lanka Muslims, implying that the majority are, indeed, Tamils, but, the government, in order to split the Tamil community has emphasized these divisions among the Tamil speakers. A total of 104 madrassas were functioning in the country.

The madrassas have played an important role in preserving the orthodox traditions of Islam in the Indian subcontinent despite politicization and other distortions that became prominent in some parts of the overall system since the 1980s with the flow of Iranian (mainly Shia) and Saudi (Sunni, often Wahhabi) funds and other support to these institutions.

From the U.S. perspective, education policy in South Asia, especially regarding Pakistan's madrassa system has become a security issue. It is no longer education and human development. Hence, the major goals for Washington are to support the modernization of the curriculum taught in most madrassas and in neutralizing the few that train militant students who are inimical to the United States an American interests.

(*See also:* CENTER OF AFGHANISTAN STUDIES [CAS], U.N.IVERSITY OF NEBRASKA AT OMAHA).

Maldives-U.S. Relations

Interaction between the Maldives and the United States increased as a result of the International war on terrorism (2001). The island folk were predominantly Buddhist, a faith they shared with Sri Lanka, whose Sinhala language is similar to Divehi, the native Maldivian tongue. In 1153, the king impressed by the religion and piety of an Arab traveler ordered his subjects to convert to Islam. During the past few years there was a noticeable increase in beards and headscarves among the citizens. Maumoon Gayoom, an Egyptian-trained religious scholar was the President from 1978-2008. Because the Maldives is constitutionally mandated as an Islamic nation as a matter of law, all citizens are Muslims. Gayoom was used Islam to promote the legitimacy of his regime as the parliament was not widely considered to be a democratically elected body. Hence, his official biography states that the president personally designed the calligraphy on the capital's main mosque. A single Maldivian, Ibrahim Fauzee, was detained for four years by the U.S. at the military base at Guantanamo Bay, Cuba, before being released. The Maldives provided important access for U.S. vessels and allowed aircraft during in the American-led international intervention in Afghanistan after the 9/11 terrorist attacks on U.S. soil ("Operation Enduring Freedom"). In addition, the island republic supported U.S. positions on drug trafficking, non-proliferation, international crime, and terrorism. Diplomatic exchanges with Washington are managed by the U.S. Embassy in Sri Lanka, and include a modest International Military Education and Training (IMET) program and joint exercises between the Maldivian National Security Services (NSS) and the U.S. military. The South Asian regional Economic Support Funds (ESF) to islands is channeled through the U.S. Embassy in Colombo. These funds focus on promoting the rule of law, human rights, democracy, and the empowerment of women. Though the U.S. is an important trading partner accounting for about twenty-one percent of the country's exports, there is no major American investment or grant assistance program in the Maldives. Even the tourist trade is small with only 3,000 Americans visiting the islands annually.

Masih, Iqbal (1979-1995)

Pakistani civil activist. Masih was widely honored in the U.S. for his campaign against bonded labor and as a spokesman for the Bonded Labour Liberation Front (BLLF). At the age of twelve Masih was reportedly sold for $12.00 into bondage by his mother. He was chained to a loom on which he worked for fourteen hours a day. His plight was noticed by a representative of the Bonded Labor Liberation Front on a visit to the village where Masih was working. He was taken to Lahore where he became an untiring and eloquent spokesman for BLLF. In 1994, he received the Reebok Foundation Award for his crusade against bonded labor. He was also granted a fellowship by Brandeis University in the United States. While preparing to leave for the U.S. Masih was murdered in his village near Murdike, a town well known for its carpet industries. The murder widely publicized the plight of child workers and bonded labor in the third world. About fifteen percent of the estimated 200 million such children, are in Pakistan. His slaying led to the suspension of carpet imports from Pakistan by some western countries. The Broad Meadows Middle School in Quincy, Massachusetts, took the lead in building a school in his memory at Kasur, Pakistan. The school raised an astonishing $147,000 for the project. An investigation by the Human Rights Commission of Pakistan absolved the carpet industry from any implication in the murder. It declared that the killing was just an act of random violence. This conclusion was widely doubted and disputed.

Massoud, Ahmad Shah (1953-2001)

Celebrated MUJAHIDEEN leader. The son of the police commander of Panjshir valley, north of Kabul, Massoud was a brilliant student, fluent in French, Pashto, and Urdu. While a student at Kabul Polytechnic Institute for Engineering and Architecture, he joined an insurrection against the DAUD government in 1973. It failed, but Massoud's career in politics and insurrection had begun. The Soviet intervention in Afghanistan (1979-89) made him world famous for he withstood numerous communist attacks on his territory despite little assistance from the U.S. and its allies. Called "The Lion of Panjshir" by his admirers, he organized his own supervisory council and was one of the few warlords to set up a civil administration, instill discipline in his troops and use modern military principles of tactical warfare. He was a member of the largely non-Pashtun organization, Jam'iat-i Islami-yi Afghanistan headed by the fellow Tajik, RABBANI. After the Soviet withdrawal, bloody clashes between HEKMATYAR and Massoud resulted in considerable causalities on both sides. Nevertheless, Massoud assisted by the Uzbek warlord DOSTUM, captured Kabul but other groups including Shia militants of the Hizb-I Wahdat, too, occupied parts of the city. Massoud was elected as the Minister of Defense, but relinquished the office in an attempt to accommodate Hekmatyar in the government. It failed. Instead, the divided and ineffectual government in Kabul was soon under attack from another fundamentalist movement spawned by Pakistan, the TALIBAN. In September 1996, Kabul fell to the Taliban. Massoud retreated north. On 9 September 2001, two days before 9/11, two assassins, posing as journalists, murdered him in a suicidal attack in the remote Takhar province. A wife and six children survived him. The Afghan President KARZAI posthumously awarded him with the title of "Hero of the Afghan Nation."

Matteo (1919-)

U.S. dancer and artistic director. Born as Matthew Marcellus Vittucci in Utica NY, he was one of the greatest dancers in America. Matteo was among the earliest Americans to study the Indian dance form, Bharat Natyam. He learnt the complex movements with alacrity and in a flash of insight realized the possibility of teaching Indian dances by utilizing the western ballet barre. Thereafter he established the Indo-American Dance Company in 1967. Later it became better known as the Matteo Foundation for Ethnic Dance.

Mayo, Katherine (1867-1940)

Racist American author. Her most infamous book was *Mother India.* It was rumored that Mayo went to India at the behest of British officials who had read her muckraking 1925 book, *Isles of Fear* about the chaotic conditions in the Philippines. As a well-known Anglophile she did not disappoint the British. Mother India, the product of a six month stay in the country was published in 1927. The work became an overnight sensation for the venomous portrayal of India as a degenerate, worthless society marked by sexual obsessions and the subjugation of women. *Mother India* was ranked tenth in that year's bestseller list and went through an astonishing 27 editions selling 256,697 copies. It succeeded in prejudicing two entire generations of Americans against India.

Mazari, Abdul Ali (1946-1995)

Most prominent Shia leader in Afghanistan in the late twentieth century, Chief of *Nasr* (Victory) Party, leader of *Hizb-I Wahdat*, a coalition of nine Shia factions in the country. Born at Charkant, Balkh Province, he was educated at Mazar-i-Shariff, Qum (Iran), and Najaf (Iraq). His organization was one of the three main groups to overthrow NAJIBULLAH's communist regime. However, when President RABBANI refused Mazari's nominee for the Ministry of National Security, the letter joined forces with notoriously anti-Shia HEKMATYAR AND the Uzbek DOSTUM. When the TALIBAN reached Kabul (September 1996), Mazari again shifted loyalties and surrendered frontline positions held by his forces in West Kabul to the new Sunni fundamentalists. Despite his gesture of amity, the Taliban attempted to disarm his militia. Clashes followed. Exploiting the opportunity, Rabbani struck, briefly defeating both the *Wahdat* and the Taliban. In turn, the Taliban murdered the Shia warlord. His murder caused a profound rift between Sunni Taliban and Shia Iran. Supposedly, Tehran's support for OSAMA BIN LADEN and his terrorists ceased as well.

Mehta, Ajai Singh (1952-)

India-born Editor-in-chief of U.S. publishing home Alfred A Knopf (1987-2005). Mehta, commonly known as Sonny, was born in New Delhi, the son of an Indian diplomat. As an editor, Mehta acquired the reputation for publishing some of the most outstanding and controversial books of the time. Included was Bret Easton *Ellis's American Psycho*, a novel about a serial killer in a setting of startling violence and detailed rape scenes that was rejected by other major publishers. In one of the hottest bids to acquire a book, he persuaded former President CLINTON to sign with Knopf to publish his White House memoirs (2001). The Clinton book was a triumph for Mehta at a time when he was rumored to be drinking heavily and suffering from heart disease. His personal problems were compounded by the declining fortunes of the venerable imprint, Knopf, following the acquisition of the parent company, Random House, by Germany's Bertelsmann AG. His wife, Gita, the daughter and sister of the well-known family of politicians from Orissa, the Patnaiks, is an accomplished author and poet in her own right. Her most well known book *Karma Kola* dealt with the cultural and spiritual misunderstanding between east and west.

Mehta, Zubin (1936-)

Indian-born conductor of Western classical music. Mehta made his debut at the Metropolitan Opera in December 1965 with a highly acclaimed rendering of Aida. Mehta was born in Bombay and nurtured in music by his father, Mehli Nowroji Mehta, himself an accomplished violinist. In 1958, he won the first prize at the Liverpool International Conductors Competition, thereby winning a one year contract as an Associate Conductor of Royal Liverpool Philharmonic. In 1962, he became the youngest conductor of the Los Angeles Philharmonic. He led the philharmonic on ten major tours and was invited to conduct before the United Nation's General Assembly at the twenty-fifth anniversary of the founding of the organization. In 1978, he was chosen to head the prestigious New York Philharmonic and subsequently the Israeli one as well.

Menon, V. K. Krishna (1897-1974)

Indian politician and America-baiter. The son of a successful lawyer, Menon, while still in college, became active in nationalist politics by joining Annie Besant's Home Rule Movement. As a founding member of the "Brothers of Service", Besant helped him to get to England in 1924. There he studied at the London School of Economics and at University College, London. Throughout his long years in England, Menon agitated for Indian independence while supporting himself by working as a journalist and as the secretary (1929-1947) of the India League. His activities in London attracted Nehru's attention and their association was to last a lifetime.

In 1934, he was admitted to the English bar, and joined the British Labor Party. He was elected as a Councilor in the Borough of St. Pancras, London. It was later to confer on him the Freedom of the Borough. The only other person so honored was George Bernard Shaw. At India's independence, Menon was appointed India's High Commissioner (ambassador) to Britain (1947-52). Subsequently, he led the Indian delegation to the United Nations (1952-1962), where he loudly criticized the U.S. and supported U.N. membership for Communist (Mainland) China. He also created a dubious record at the U.N.: He spoke extemporaneously on defense of the Indian position on Kashmir for nearly eight hours before melodramatically collapsing. His ready wit, brilliant repartee, and leftist perspectives made him particularly unpopular with the U.S. media and politicians. In April 1957 he became India's Minister for Defense and sought to modernize the Indian armed forces and develop a strong indigenous defense industry. However, he tried to play favorites in the officer corps and was among the many who misread the threat from China. After the Indian reverses in the Sino-Indian War of 1962, he was harshly criticized for the country's humiliation and forced to resign from office. In 1964, his mentor, NEHRU, died. Thereafter, he faded. His abiding legacy was shared by his U.S. counterpart, DULLES. Both were to strain Indo-American relations for a generation.

Missionaries

During the two centuries of British rule in South Asia, missionaries from the U.S. outnumbered those from the British Isles. The BRITISH East India Company considered proselytizing as a major cause of the decline of Portugal in India. Accordingly, after its charter was renewed in 1793, the Company actively discouraged British missionaries from entering the subcontinent. As the United States had neither political commitments nor large commercial interests in India, the

Company was more tolerant of American missionaries. The first ones arrived around 1812 and concentrated on social upliftment rather than on conversion. In 1833, despite the Company's misgivings, the subcontinent was opened to all missionaries. The backlash and the rising in 1857 led to scaling back of British missions, though the American ones were not as severely curtailed. The number of American missionaries steadily increased and peaked at 2,478 in 1922. In the 1930s the estimated U.S. investment in the Indian subcontinent was $50.5 million out of which an astonishing $22.86 million was in schools, hospitals, churches and other missionary institutions. The missionaries did much to uplift the women of the subcontinent. Among the prominent pioneers were Miss Clara Swain who started the first women's hospital in India at Bareilly in 1874 and her colleague, Isabella Thoburn, who started a school for girls in Lucknow. It later became a college named in her memory. The evangelical missionaries became more active after Indian independence, the most prominent being Mrs. Lillian Carter (1898-1983), the mother of the former U.S. President, JIMMY CARTER. For more than a year she worked as a nurse with the U.S. Peace Corps near Mumbai (Bombay) in 1967.

After independence, the situation changed. Conversions to Christianity, especially in north-eastern India were viewed as a security threat. Foreign missionaries were perceived by most of South Asia as possible spies, agents of foreign governments, and promoters of secessionist movements. Some extreme statements followed. In 1980, Indian Home Minister Zail Singh publicly blamed the U.S. Central Intelligence Agency (CIA) for channeling money through missionaries to foment unrest in Assam and neighboring tribal areas. On the other hand just before President George W. Bush's visit to three South Asian countries in March 2006, former U.S. President Jimmy Carter and U.S. Senator Barbara Boxer called on the mainly Christian Nagas of Nagaland to secede from India.

A reversal in destinations is also underway. In 2007, an estimated 5,000 Indian priests and nuns were working in western countries including the United States where a steep decline in the number of nuns has occurred. In the U.S. the number of nuns fell from 180,000 in 1965 to 70,000 in 40 years and 2,334 parishes were without resident pastors in 2004. Some cases of abuse and maltreatment of Indian missionaries was reported from time to time. Nevertheless, Tibetan Buddhist, Hindu, and Islamic missionaries, too, are increasingly active in the United States.

(*See also:* ADAM, WILLIAM; DALL, CHARLES; JUDSON, ADONIRAN: MORAN, MARSHAL; SCUDDER, JOHN: STOKES, SAMUEL EVANS JR.; UNITARIANISM; UNITARIANS OF KHASI HILLS))

Moran, Father Marshal (1906-1992)

American educator and missionary. Father Marshall Moran left Chicago in 1929 to joint a Jesuit Mission in the Indian sub-continent. In 1934, he started St. Xavier's School in a rented house at Patna, India. By the late 1940s, he was a member of the Senate of Patna University. In 1949, in that capacity, the missionary went to Kathmandu to supervise the final examinations at the Trichandra College then affiliated with Patna University. In Kathmandu, Prime Minister Mohan Shamsher Jung Bahadur Rana urged the priest to open a similar school for boys in the Nepalese capital. In 1951, Moran chartered an aircraft to transport a Land Rover and two tons of supplies. He landed at a primitive airstrip in the Kathmandu valley and promptly started the St. Xavier's School, Kathmandu. Four years later, with the king's support, he established St. Mary's School, the first institution of its kind for young women in the kingdom. Both the schools are highly regarded in the country. The Father Moran Memorial Football Tournament is the prominent soccer competition for schoolboys in the Kathmandu Valley. The Jesuit missionary was also well known among the world's fraternity of amateur radio hams. Often his transmissions directed assistance to the sick and the injured in remote parts of the country. Several years after he left Nepal it was learnt that Father Moran was also transmitting information to U.S. intelligence services. This revelation confirmed the lurking suspicion in many a native mind that the avuncular and dedicated missionary was also a spy and a secret agent.

Moynihan, Daniel Patrick (1927-2003)

American academic, U.S. Senator, and Ambassador to India. In a bid to signal an improvement of Indo-U.S. RELATIONS, President NIXON appointed Moynihan, a gregarious and distinguished academic, as the ambassador to India in 1973. Unexpectedly, Moynihan took it upon himself to maintain a low profile in New Delhi and did little to lift relations between the two countries. During his two years in New Delhi, he made only two speeches and gave just one press conference. Despite his attempts to maintain a quiet presence, he faced the question of future economic assistance to India. A central element of U.S. aid was the rupee funds accumulated under the PL-480 PROGRAM. Since 1954 under the PL-480 Program India had paid for food aid with non-convertible rupees that were deposited in a special account with Reserve Bank of India. By 1971 the funds amounted to more than $3 billion, accounting for at least 10% of the Indian currency in circulation. In 1972, despite poor rains, India used foreign exchange to commercially buy U.S. wheat rather than seek resumption of the PL-480 program because of the demeaning experience of the "ship to mouth" strategy imposed by President LYNDON JOHNSON in 1965-67. Moynihan realized that the vast sum of money could never be fully used without destabilizing the Indian currency so he engineered the write off $2.2 billion worth of rupees. On 18 February 1974, Moynihan with rare flourish presented the Government of India with a check for $ 2.2 billon in rupees. It was the largest check ever drawn. Thus, the rupee question was resolved and prospects for increased bilateral relations improved.

Mujahideen (Arabic: Freedom Fighters)

The armed resistance to the Soviet military intervention in Afghanistan (1978-89) brought the Arabic word, Mujahideen, into the English language. The guerrilla movements were largely sustained by Pakistan, the United States and Saudi Arabia. During the nine year war about $10 billion was spent on arms, ammunition, training, logistical support, safe havens, battlefield intelligence, financial support, etc. for the different guerrilla movements. The financial cost of the intervention in Afghanistan probably contributed to the collapse of the Soviet Union two years later. Hence the Mujahideen believed and claimed that they had not only defeated a super power but destroyed it as well. However, both the Afghan people and the Mujahideen, too, paid a terrible price with prolonged instability and warlordism, the rise of the TALIBAN (founded 1994) and AL QAEDA (founded 1989) and the subsequent U.S.-led intervention in the country in 2001.

Mules

Pack animals, especially mules, played a critical role in two recent wars fought by the United States. Both wars were FOUGHT in South Asia. One was against the Soviets in Afghanistan (1979-89) and the other against the Japanese in the steamy verdant hills of Burma (1942-45). Transportation is one of the key determinants of the type and nature of the war waged. In Burma and in Afghanistan tactics and equipment were often determined by the capabilities of these animals.

Mules can carry up to 250 pounds for several days in a row at the speed of about 20 miles per day. During World War I, the town of Lathrop, Missouri, shipped 350,000 mules. However, in 1941, the year that Washington entered World War II, the U.S. military had purchased 23,546 horses and only 4,279 mules. By the end of the war, in 1945, no horses were procured but 9,199 mules were acquired from the United States. Many more unaccounted for mules were bought locally or commandeered in Burma where each could carry a dismantled 75 mm howitzer.

When the Soviets intervened in Afghanistan in 1979, the country had less than 3,000 miles of hard surface roads and pack animals were already in common use. The 20 mm Oerlikan anti-aircraft gun was one of the first modern weapons to be supplied to the MUJAHIDEEN. It was too heavy (1,200 pounds) and had long and cumbersome barrel. It took twenty mules to transport it. Hence, it was not a success in Afghanistan. Instead, over the more than 300 infiltration routes into Afghanistan, mules ferried mortars, machine guns, ammunition and evacuated battle-field causalities. The mule-borne dismantled 120 mm mortar was the first successful heavy weapon to be used by the guerrillas against the fortified Soviet camps that were otherwise beyond the range of the weaponry in the Mujahideen arsenal. Large numbers of mules were killed or disabled by land mines and air attacks. As the animals died, replacements were initially sent from Tennessee at a cost of $600-1,300 per mule. However, the Mules for War Program brought American citizens directly in touch with the Mujahideen on advising the Afghan rebels as the care of the animals from the U.S. This was contrary to Pakistani and American policy of no open contact between the Mujahideen and U.S. citizens. The guerrillas also complained that the American mules were not as strong as the local ones and were not accustomed to the hot blistering arid summers or the freezing winter blizzards. The guerrillas were not the only complainers. Milt Bearden, the CIA station chief complained that, "On an annual basis we needed more mules than the world seemed prepared to breed." Hence, by 1985 mules were being imported from all over the world, especially from Egypt, Brazil, China, Argentina, and Pakistan. The Egyptians (at $1,300 per mule) and the Chinese (at $2,500 per mule) made the most money from this little-known aspect of the war.

The significance of the mule has neither declined nor been forgotten. Since 1969, the small town of Bishop, California, dubbed the "Mule Capital of the World," hosts a week-long festival called Mule days to celebrate the pack mule. The well-attended festival is held on the week of Memorial Day (late May) each year. With the changing nature of combat in the twenty-first century, the Medical Training Section of the Mountain Warfare Training Center (MWTC) in the Sierra Nevada Mountains trains medical corpsmen to work with pack mules. In addition, Boston Dynamics is developing a robot pack mule that should be ready for battle by 2014. In 2007, the Indian army, too, began to look into the possible use of robotic mules in the future.

Musharraf, Pervez (1943-)

Pakistani military dictator and U.S. ally in the war against terror. Musharraf was appointed as the Chief of Army Staff in October 1998 following the resignation of General Jahangir Karamat, who resigned from office after giving a speech criticizing the government of Prime Minister NAWAZ SHARIF at the Naval Staff College in Lahore. Musharraf, though responsible for the abortive take-over of the heights in the Kargil region of Kashmir in 1999 survived with his reputation intact. Thanks to effective favorable publicity by the army, despite Kargil, he was favorably viewed by most Pakistanis as being a straightforward and steadfast military officer who was let down by the country's timorous political leadership. Hence, Prime Minister Sharif, rather then the military, was blamed for the misadventure in Kargil.

Later that year, while returning by air from Sri Lanka General Musharraf was sacked by the Prime Minister. Within hours, the army overthrew Sharif. On landing Musharraf took over as the Chief Executive of the country but was diplomatically isolated till 9/11. Following the terrorist attacks on U.S. soil, he then publicly distanced from the Islamic fundamentalists and provided the United States with tactical, logistical and intelligence support. Despite his repeated pledges to reduce the power of Islamic fundamentalists in Pakistan there appeared to be little evidence to substantiate that he had done so. After seven years in power, President Pervez Musharraf while holding on to the dual jobs of president and army chief of staff since his 1999 coup, ruled with a relatively light touch. As in most of South Asia, he, too, lifted the government's monopoly on the broadcast media, thereby allowing the creation of new television and radio networks.

His political fortunes began to decline March 2007 when the dictator threatened and finally the suspended the Chief Justice of the Supreme Court for alleged misconduct because the General was unhappy with the former's increasing independence. Widespread protests often led by lawyers in their quaint black jackets forced the reinstatement of the chief justice in July. However, around the same time, Islamic radicals stepped up their activities to impose Taliban-style strictures in the heart of the capital, Islamabad. After initially ignoring the militants, the government besieged and then attacked their base at the Lal Masjid, the Red Mosque, in the heart of the capital on 10 July leaving 102 dead. The Islamic religious parties claim the death toll was much higher.

Meanwhile, TALIBAN and AL QAEDA militants, based in Pakistan's loosely controlled Federally Administered Tribal Areas (FATA) along the Afghan border increased cross-border attacks on NATO and U.S. troops in Afghanistan. In response to Western complaints, Pakistani army and Para-military forces tried to half-heartedly curb the militants only to sustain casualties that invited scorn from friend and foe alike.

This situation energized the splintered and dormant opposition leaders, both in exile. One of them, Nawaz Sharif, exiled in Saudi

Arabia, eventually returned with overt backing from Riyadh in November 2007. The other, BENAZIR BHUTTO, opened negotiations with him to share power in return for dropping all legal charges filed against her and her husband, mostly for alleged corruption. She returned to Karachi on 18 October 2007. An estimated crowd of 1.5 million was on hand to receive her. It included at least two suicide bombers. As her convoy inched its way from the airport to Jinnah's mausoleum, in the darkness of the midnight hour, the two assassins struck. She narrowly escaped. About 140 other did not. Another 450 were seriously injured. A month later another suicide bomber succeeded in assassinating her in Rawalpindi.

Earlier on 6 October 2007 General Musharraf was re-elected as president by the lame-duck national and provincial assemblies. The main opposition parties had boycotted the electoral proceedings. As expected this sham election was challenged in the nation's Supreme Court. Musharraf, anticipating an unfavorable judgment from the apex court, imposed a state of emergency on 3 November 2007. Thousands of people were detained, judges were dismissed, and independent television stations were forced off the air. The move was widely condemned.

However bowing to domestic and international pressure, General Musharraf reluctantly fulfilled his pledge to shed the army uniform and became a civilian president. He also pledged free and fair parliamentary elections in late November 2007-08, though it was assumed that he expected the two major parties to split the vote so neither would emerge with a clear-cut majority. As there was well-known bitter rivalry and suspicion between the two ex-prime ministers the dictator hoped to divide the opposition and create enough support for himself to get a pliant prime minister and a facade of democratic governance. However, the assassination of Bhutto in December 2007 and his possible complicity in it, led to a further decline in his approval ratings. His party was routed in elections held in Pakistan in February 2008. His two main opponents, Nawaz Sharif and Benazir's widower, ASIF ALI ZARDARI, both won a substantial number of seats in the National Assembly. The military retained a neutral stance in the subsequent machinations. By August 2008, it was clear that Musharraf, without support at home or abroad or within the army had to go. He resigned. Next month (September 2008), his long-held prisoner, Asif Ali Zardari was duly elected as President of the country.

Mutual Defense Agreement (MDA)

An agreement signed by Pakistan and the United States in 1954. General MOHAMMED AYUB KHAN, the then army chief of Pakistan, was mainly responsible for Pakistan entering into an alliance with the United States. Washington's strategic interest was to control the spread of communism whereas Pakistan's predominant reason for signing the agreement was to balance India's military power. As the two countries had such divergent imperatives for signing the MDA, it did not survive the Indo-Pakistan war of September 1965 when Islamabad had expected American support. Instead, Washington imposed an embargo on the sale and transfer of military equipment and developmental aid to Pakistan on the premise that MDA was solely aimed at the containment of global communism.

N

Najibullah, Mohammed (1947-1996)

Fourth and last President of the (communist) Democratic Republic of Afghanistan (May 1986-April 1992). A Pashtun born in Kabul, he graduated from the College of Medicine in 1975. After the communists seized power in Afghanistan, Najibullah, a member of the *Parcham* faction of the party, was sent as the ambassador to Tehran (July 1978) as a part of the planned removal of leading *Parchamis* out of the country. He returned to Kabul with KARMAL after the ouster of AMIN in the final days of December 1979. Under Amin's successor, Karmal, he became the General-President of the dreaded secret police, KHAD (1980-86). In 1986 Najibullah replaced Karmal as Secretary-General of communist party and shortly afterwards as the president of the country. The Soviets had obviously selected him for the presidency because of his success in running KHAD. As president, he purged the central committee, brought in new members, and set up a National Compromise Commission as the means of bringing in various rebel factions into the government. Thus he managed to create enough political stability to provide the Soviets with the rationalization to leave Afghanistan. Consequently, on 20 July 1987 Moscow announced the phased withdrawal of Soviet troops from the country.

Meanwhile, in an attempt at both reconciliation and at splitting the opposition, Najibullah declared Afghanistan to be an Islamic non-aligned state. Accordingly the name of the country reverted to the Republic of Afghanistan, the State Council was replaced by a National Assembly and Mir Hussein Sharq, a non-communist, was appointed as the new Prime Minister. The MUJAHIDEEN, anticipating the swift fall of government, scorned the overtures to join the government. In response, Najibullah declared a state of emergency, removed Sharq and the other non-communist ministers and sought and received a great deal of Soviet military equipment ($ 3 billion a year from 1990 onwards). Most of it was shipped from Eastern Europe.

The Afghan army, well armed and lavishly supplied by the Soviet Union, survived for another four years. Eventually, divisions within its own ranks, especially the defection of DOSTUM, fatally weakened the government. Therefore, on 16 April 1992, Najibullah resigned as president and took refuge in the U.N. compound in Kabul. The Mujahideen militias refused to let him leave the country, but made no attempt to arrest him. Najibullah spent the next four years in virtual detention in the U.N. building. In September 1996 the TALIBAN captured Kabul. A special unit of five men ignored the laws of international immunity and seized Najibullah from the U.N. complex. He was driven to the presidential palace, tortured and killed along with his brother. The two mutilated bodies were then hanged outside the presidential palace for two days.

Narain, Jaiprakash (1902-1979)

Indian patriot and revolutionary. Narain, commonly known as JP, opted for college in the United States because he refused to be educated by the British either in India or in the United Kingdom. Accordingly, in October 1922 he joined the University of California, Berkeley. However, he could not afford the high fees. Therefore, he shifted to Iowa State University in Iowa City, Iowa. Later he studied at the University of Wisconsin, Madison, Wisconsin, where he met a young Polish Jew, Abraham Landy, a member of the American Communist Party. JP's Marxist leanings were thus kindled. He later taught at Ohio State University before returning to India in 1929 to join the freedom struggle. After independence he was a social activist rather than a political leader till the mid-1970s when his grassroots campaign against Prime Minister INDIRA GANDHI and her Congress Party paved the way for the first non-Congress Party government in New Delhi.

Nehru, Jawaharlal (1889-1964)

Independent India's first Prime Minister (1947-64). Nehru also took charge of the Foreign Ministry and the nascent Department of Nuclear Energy (the only nuclear physics laboratory in the subcontinent was left in Pakistan at the Punjab University, Lahore). Jawaharlal was the only son of Motilal Nehru, a wealthy Allahabad based barrister and political leader. Educated at the elite British public school, Harrow and at Trinity College, Cambridge, Nehru was called to the bar at Inner Temple, London. He returned to India in 1912, briefly practiced law and then followed his father into politics. He soon attracted the attention of Mahatma GANDHI. Nehru soon abandoned western clothes and pastimes and adopted Hindustani as the language of common use. The young political leader switched to a white *khadi kurta-pyjama* and Gandhi cap, the new uniform of the Indian nationalist. In 1929, Nehru became first major Indian political figure to seek for full independence and not just Home Rule within the British Empire. Eighteen years of further agitation, seven jail sentences, a world war and Partition of the subcontinent brought Nehru to power as India's Prime Minister from 15 August 1947 to 27 May 1964 — the day he died. His years in power laid the foundations of India's social, political and economic development, as well as its defense, education and foreign policies for more than four decades. Nehru, though a liberal was fascinated by the Russian Revolution (1917) and the economic success of the Soviet Union's *Piatiletka* or 5-year plans. His socialist instincts favored the control of the commanding heights of the economy by the state (public sector) instead of private ownership. The Soviet Union was to emerge as the only major power during Nehru's tenure to assist India in developing independent capabilities in heavy industry, engineering, and technology. This fact, combined with Nehru's preference for state-led development, promoted suspicion about the sincerity of India's non-aligned foreign policy. American policy-makers drew the bleak and simplistic conclusion that Nehru was more likely to bend backwards to appease communism; to hoist the white flag of neutralism, and get other wavering nations to join him in order to create a global nuisance value for the themselves; to intimidate and threaten an American ally, Pakistan, and to abuse the West, especially the U.S., whenever it suited him. Furthermore, Nehru's pursuit of a non-alignment foreign policy was widely considered in Washington to be "immoral." His support for decolonization resonated well with the communists, and exasperated the major colonial powers who were allied to the United States. His opposition to apartheid in the staunchly anti-communist South Africa was yet another irritant. Despite his perceived anti-Americanism, there were only two table ornaments on Nehru's office desk: a bronze statue of Mahatma Gandhi and a model of the hands of the U.S. President Abraham Lincoln.

As a founding leader of the Non-Aligned Movement (NAM), Nehru's was a voice of moderation. Nehru also took further satisfaction in the rate of India's economic growth of more than four per cent whereas the strongly capitalist United States grew more slowly, as did most of the newly independent countries. Hubris followed in 1962 when Communist China delivered stinging reverses to India in a brief border war. Perhaps in his last year he derived some consolation from the signing of the Partial Nuclear Test Ban Treaty (1963), for as early as 27 November 1946, Nehru, then a private citizen, had appealed to both the United States and the Soviet Union to end nuclear testing and to start nuclear disarmament, stating that such an action would "save humanity from the ultimate disaster." Nehru also sired the most powerful political dynasty in India's modern history. His daughter, INDIRA GANDHI, and his grandson, RAJIV GANDHI both became prime ministers of India. Into the new millennium, Rajiv's widow, Sonia Gandhi, became President of the Congress Party. Speculation is rife that her children would lead India sooner than later.

Nepal Civil War (1996-2006)

Conflict between Maoist rebels and the government of Nepal. About 13,500 people were killed in the war and an estimated 100,000 to 150,000 persons were internally displaced before the conflict was formally terminated by the conclusion of the Comprehensive Peace Agreement (CPA) between the Maoists and the ruling Seven Party Alliance (SPA). The king's role in the settlement was negligible and the abolition of the monarchy followed after the election of a Constituent Assembly in April 2008.

The civil war increased in intensity in 2001, after King Gyanendra, then the Commander-in-Chief of the armed forces, deployed the Royal Nepalese Army (RNA) against the Maoists. The new king assumed the throne in June that year after Crown Prince Dipendra had supposedly shot and killed his father, King Birendra, and nine other members of the royal family before committing suicide. Under the new monarch, the strength of the army increased from 46,000 to

90,000 and was organized into six divisions. The U.S. supported the fight against the Maoists by providing Kathmandu with more than $8.3 million in weapons and services during 1994-2003. After February 2005 aid declined dramatically as the king ousted the parliamentary government and assumed direct control over the country. Nevertheless, the U.S. Pacific Command (USPACOM) coordinated military training and assistance through the Office of Defense Cooperation. Nepal received a total of $21.95 million in grants under Foreign Military Financing (FMF) and about $2 million as a part of the Enhanced International Peacekeeping Capabilities (EIPC) from the United States. After more than ten years of conflict, punctuated by four ceasefires, the Maoists controlled about half the countryside. The military failure was paralleled by a series of political crises in the country as prime ministers changed every few months. In April 2006, a people's movement for the restoration of democracy toppled the king's government. Parliament was reinstated and Gyanendra was stripped of most of his authority. An octogenarian former Prime Minister Girija Prasad Koirala of the Nepali Congress Party was elected by the opposition Seven Party Alliance (SPA) to again form a government. The Maoists declared a ceasefire in April 2006, and the newly formed Koirala government followed suit and peace talks with the insurgents were instituted. Both India and the U.S. maintained firm but discrete pressure on the Maoists and kept the army intact as an apolitical and well armed lever to exercise their influence. Earlier, in November 2005 the insurgency acquired an international character when PRANCHANDA and Ganapathy, the general secretary of the Communist Party of India (Maoist), signed a joint statement about fighting together to establish socialism and communism in the two countries. Indian Maoists, active in five states, Andhra Pradesh, Jharkhand, Chattisgarh, Orissa and Bihar, declared their aim was to construct a "compact revolutionary zone" by connecting these states with the lands controlled by their co-revolutionaries in Nepal. The first major coordinated attack was in June 2006 when 21 policemen were killed in Bihar. Maoist violence also spread to other states in India. The revolutionaries do not expect an Indian military response against their safe havens in Nepal and consider the U.S. as too overextended to meaningfully intervene in the region. However, the return of the Nepalese Maoists to mainstream political activity that year put the future of such combined actions into doubt.

Despite the traditional anti-American Maoist talk, considerable U.S. presence was established in the country by the Atlanta-based Carter Center. The Center became active in 2003 and inducted a thirteen member international election observation mission in Nepal in March 2007. Shortly afterwards, in June 2007, the former U.S. President Jimmy Carter, the founder of the eponymous Atlanta-based Center, visited Nepal and helped ease the return of the guerillas to the mainstream of the Nepalese political process following his fruitful talks with the Maoist leaders, Prachanda and Bhattarai. Not unexpectedly, he was invited by the government of Nepal, several political parties, and the election commission of the country to be an observer during the elections for the constituent assembly. Instead, Carter's representatives met with members of all political parties, election officials, civil society, domestic observer groups, and the international community. Observers from the Center visited all 75 districts and took steps to ensure free and fair elections with the peaceful participation of all political factions, parties and groups. Despite widespread misgivings the polls were a great success and the political and constitutional landscape of the country changed dramatically. The monarchy was abolished, and Prachanda, now the Prime Minister of the country again met the former U.S. President in Nepal in April 2008.

(*See also*: NEPAL-U.S. RELATIONS)

Nepal-U.S. Relations

On 25 April 1947 formal diplomatic relations were established between the United States and Nepal. Initially, the U.S. embassy in New Delhi was concurrently accredited to Nepal. In March 1959 a full scale revolt against the Chinese broke out in Lhasa, Tibet. It FAILED. Consequently, the Dalai Lama, Tibet's theocratic ruler, fled to India. Possibly in response to these developments, a full-time U.S. ambassador was posted to Kathmandu and an embassy was established there. However, the American presence was greatest in two districts in Nepal that bordered Tibet, Walanchung-gola in the east and Mustang in the west. In these two districts CIA trained and financed Tibetan guerrillas operated with impunity against the Communist Chinese from the early 1960s until 1973. These clandestine operations were discontinued following U.S. President NIXON's visit to Beijing in 1972.

Notwithstanding the CIA's sinister presence in the country, Kathmandu was one of the first to welcome PEACE CORPS volunteers and the program became the largest in Asia. In addition, with American assistance malaria was largely eradicated and life expectancy doubled from 28 to 56 years. Clearly American economic assistance beginning in 1951 and amounting to a total of $791 million in the next 55 years had substantially benefited the Nepalese people. Most of the bilateral U.S. developmental assistance is channeled through the U.S. Agency for International Development (UASID). The American agency focused on agriculture, health, family planning, protection of the environment, democratization of the political process, good governance, and the development of hydropower in the country. Washington also contributed to international institutions and private voluntary organizations working in Nepal.

Military ties between the two countries grew as Nepalese forces interacted with American troops in U.N. peacekeeping operations. Military aid for counter-insurgency operations and for U.N. Peacekeeping Operations totaled around $ 35 million during 1997-2007. The largest amount of military aid was provided in 2003. The $ 6.6 million military assistance that year included equipment for raising an elite new ranger battalion for counter insurgency operations against the Maoist guerrillas.

The Peace Corps suspended its operations in Nepal in 2004 due to increasing security concerns, and officially terminated then in 2006. However, the U.S. along with Britain and India were the key factors in moderating abuses during counter-insurgency operations and in maintaining the professionalism and integrity of the Nepalese Army. At the same time the three countries were instrumental in bringing the Maoists into the political process in the country.

NGOs in Bangladesh

The nineteen storey BRAC Centre (Bangladesh Rural Advancement Committee) is the headquarters of the largest NGO in the world. BRAC has over 100,000 Bangladeshis on its payroll. In addition to running 30,000 schools and employing thousands of teachers, this huge Non-Governmental Organization (NGO) has on its pay-roll health-care workers, computer analysts, bankers, etc. BRAC is emblematic of the NGO presence in Bangladesh. The country has the largest presence of NGOs with a density of 3.5 foreign NGOs per square mile of the country. More than one thousand of these institutions receive foreign funding. Advocates of NGOs point to some truly impressive achievements: Life expectancy has risen by 12 years; female literacy rates have doubled; Bangladesh can feed itself; family sizes have been cut in half. Others argue that public services have suffered as NGOs have grown larger. Furthermore, there is the danger of delegitimization of the government itself as it becomes more marginalized and increasingly cut off from the citizenry. Some Bangladeshis charge that most Christian NGOs give employment to those who covert to Christianity. In addition, it is alleged that certain NGOs make Bible reading compulsory for their staff that included Hindus and the Muslims. Reportedly, one of the big missionary NGOs employed only Christian teachers in its schools and only Christian students were given boarding and lodging in its hostels. According to one estimate, during the twenty years between 1971 and 1991, the number of Christian converts in Bangladesh doubled from 200,000 to 400,000. Apart from missionary activities, NGOs increasingly assume the role of an invisible government with little regard for the history, culture, and customs of the people. Others fear that the NGOs may become more powerful than the Government of Bangladesh. They cite the inability of the NGO Bureau of the government to take action against two powerful NGOs — ADAB (Association of Development Agencies of Bangladesh) and SEBA (Society for Economic and Basic Administration) by canceling their registration on the grounds of defalcation of funds and receiving money from foreign embassies without prior permission from the government. The foreign embassies supposedly compelled the government to withdraw the cancellation order within three hours of its issuance. A backlash may be developing for there have been recent attacks against NGO premises resulting in a number of injuries. Some Islamic groups have been implicated in these attacks.

Nixon, Richard Milhous (1913-1994)

U.S. President (1969-74). Born in California, Nixon had a brilliant academic record at Whittier College and Duke University Law School. He was elected to Congress from California in 1946 and to the U.S. Senate four years later. In 1952, General EISENHOWER selected him as his running mate for the presidential election. As Vice President, Nixon took on major responsibilities in both domestic and foreign policy. Nevertheless, Senator JOHN F. KENNEDY defeated him in the race for the White House in 1960. Nixon returned to California, ran for governor of the state and lost again. Completely out of office, he then methodically set out to rebuild his political career. While doing so he undertook a global tour to re-establish his bona fides as an authority on international relations. His itinerary included stops in South Asia. He first visited India and then Pakistan. In New Delhi, Prime Minister INDIRA GANDHI hosted him with undisguised disdain whereas the military dictator AYUB KHAN rolled out the red carpet in Pakistan. This difference in receptions made a lasting impression on him and he was not one to forget slights.

On entering the White House in 1969, Nixon's animus against India drove him to fully revitalize the militarized grand strategy of the DULLES era. Accordingly, his presidency marked the nadir of U.S.-India relations. The worst period started in 1971. That year, on 26 March, Pakistan's military dictator, General Yahya Khan, turned his country's army against his own people in a brutal but unsuccessful attempt to suppress secession in East Pakistan. India under Indira Gandhi countered U.S. hostility through an explicit strategic alliance with the Soviet Union. The ensuing Bangladesh War was marked by a clear "tilt" in U.S. policy towards Pakistan. The most prominent aspect of the tilt was gunboat diplomacy characterized by the dispatch of a carrier task force to the Bay of Bengal, ostensibly to signal to India against the further destruction of West Pakistan and to impress upon the Chinese that they could count on American steadfastness in times of trouble.

As in the past, some measures were then taken to reduce Indo-U.S. frictions. A key gesture was the appointment of DANIEL PATRICK MOYNIHAN to replace Senator Kenneth Keating as Ambassador in New Delhi. Moynihan, like JOHN KENNETH GALBRAITH, an ambassador to India during the Kennedy administration, was an eminent scholar whom both the Indian intellectual and political establishments respected even when there were serious political or policy differences. Unexpectedly, Moynihan was low-keyed, remote and paternalistic and defined his posting in India as waiting "until the Indians were prepared to settle for a more traditional relationship of diplomacy rather than tutelage."

Two years later the Nixon Administration was deeply mired in the "Watergate" scandal, stemming from a break-in at the offices of the Democratic National Committee during the 1972 presidential campaign. Faced with almost certain impeachment, Nixon announced his resignation from the presidency on 8 August 1974. Three months earlier India exploded a nuclear device signaling its determination to preserve its independence.

(*See also*: KISSINGER, HENRY ALFRED)

Nonalignment and Non-Aligned Movement (NAM)

The ideological basis of newly independent India's foreign policy was non-alignment. Prime Minister Jawaharlal Nehru first enunciated it principles in April 1954 in a trade agreement with China it and adopted as a keystone of relations among nations at the Asian-African Conference (the Bandung Conference) held in the eponymous city of Bandung , Indonesia, in 1955.The five guiding principles, collectively known as Panch Shila were: mutual respect for territorial integrity and sovereignty, mutual nonaggression, mutual non-interference in internal affairs, equality and mutual benefit, and peaceful coexistence.

The Non-Aligned Movement (NAM) was formally established in September 1961 with the mission of promoting political and military nonalignment among its member countries to differentiate them from the traditional East and West blocs. India was among the original members. The Movement peaked in 1995 with 107 members plus the

Palestine Liberation Organization, 21 observer nations and organizations, and an equal number of "guest" nations. The end of the cold war and the attendant dismantling of the East Bloc reduced the relevance of the Movement. Washington generally considered NAM to be a pro-Soviet irritant.

Nuclear Non-Proliferation Treaty (NPT)

The treaty was opened for signature in 1968 with an original life of 25 years. It was renewed indefinitely in 1995. The vast majority of countries signed it, some with reluctance, many others with reservations. Only India, Israel, and Pakistan refused to join it. The treaty effectively divided the world into two parts, one consisting of countries that possessed nuclear weapons — Britain, China, France, the Soviet Union and the United States. All five were also the only permanent members of the U.N. Security Council with veto powers. In addition, under NPT no other country across the globe could acquire nuclear weapons, regardless of the security threats and strategic imperatives faced by them. In return, the five recognized nuclear powers undertook to work towards nuclear disarmament and the Non-Nuclear States were to receive assistance for their civilian nuclear industries. India opposed the NPT on grounds that treaty discriminated among countries by perpetuating the five nuclear "haves" and remainder as nuclear "have-nots." Opposition to Israeli refusal to sign the treaty was muted and Pakistan said it was willing to do so if India were to sign it. The Vienna based International Atomic Energy Commission (IAEC) enforces the provisions of the treaty and keeps an inventory of the fissionable material stockpiled by Non-Nuclear States. Additional powers were given to the IAEC following a new protocol in the NPT in 1997. The flaws in the treaty are obvious, as India, North Korea, and Pakistan have subsequently tested nuclear weapons. Israel is widely assumed to possess a stock-pile of nuclear weapons and Iran appears to be developing the capability for producing such weapon. South Africa, though a signatory to the treaty developed six nuclear bombs that were subsequently dismantled after the sweeping political changes in that country.

O

Obama Barack Hussein (1961-)

U.S. President-elect, 2008. The charismatic African-American U.S. Senator won the historic race for the White House in November 2008. His candidacy made a deep impression on both the countries and the peoples of South Asia. The new Maldivian President Mohamed Nasheed, was being acclaimed as the Maldivian Obama, even before the latter was elected U.S. president. At the other edge of South Asia region, in Nepal, Hindu astrologers had already predicted his victory. South Asia itself received more prominence during the 2008 elections than in previous polls in the United States. The reasons were multiple. Concerns about terrorism, the off-shoring of American jobs, nuclear proliferation, and narcotics trafficiking were important election issues involving South Asian countries. The changing times were reflected by Obama's long familiarity with the region; in 1981, after his second year in college, he undertook a round the world trip that included a stop in Hyderabad, India, and a three-week holiday in Karachi, Pakistan, where he had stayed with his roommate's family.

The Obama Administration is expected to focus more clearly on the war in Afghanistan. The Indo-U.S. relationship may be complex though as a candidate he had described ties with india as a "natural partnership" and he has a picture of Gandhiji in his office. However, some of Obama's early campaign rhetoric was directed against his rival Senator Hillary Clinton's "Indian connections." In addition, India was concerned about Obama's lukewarm support for the U.S.-India Civil-Nuclear Agreement and for his well-known commitment towards nuclear non-proliferation. Similarly, his protectionist stance may lead to job losses in India. Obama may also be pro-active on the Kashmir issue and appoint a high-profile figure as a mediator, a step not likely to find favor in New Delhi because of traditional Indian wariness towards third party mediation in the region. According to some experts, 90 percent of Muslim voters were expected to have cast their ballot in favor of the Senator. Hence, Pakistani-Americans were likely to have voted for him despite the President-elect's stated willingness to attack Islamic terrorists inside Pakistan with or without approval from Islamabad. He had also accused Pakistan of misusing American funds to increase Islamabad's capacity to wage war against India.

Obama had encouraged India, among others, to press for reforms in Burma (Myanmar). He had also voiced concerns about the internal repression in Sri Lanka, especially as the conservative Tamil community in the U.S. had strongly supported him. Little change is expected in the American policies towards Bangladesh, Bhutan, the Maldives, and Nepal under the Obama Administration.

Oil and Gas Pipelines

In the 1990s, ambitious plans were made to lay pipelines to South Asia from the oil and gas fields located to the north of Afghanistan in Turkmenistan, Uzbekistan, Kazakhstan and Russia. The most studied was the Turkmenistan-Afghanistan-Pakistan (TAP) pipeline. UNOCAL, then described as the largest independent energy company in the world, took the lead in the formation of a multinational consortium called Cent Gas (Central Asia Gas). The consortium planned to develop one of the world's largest known reserves, the Dauletabad Field, in south-eastern Turkmenistan. In May 1995 the Cent Gas consortium met with the TALIBAN leaders of Afghanistan. Important figures like HENRY KISSINGER, the former U.S. Secretary of State, attended the 1995 meeting at which the first plans to lay a trans-Afghan pipeline were announced. A paid adviser to the company was ZALMAY KHALILZAD, an Afghan émigré and later U.S. ambassador to Afghanistan, Iraq, and the U.N.. He drew up the risk analysis of the proposed gas pipeline from Turkmenistan across Afghanistan to Pakistan (TAP). The proposed route for the 42-inch oil pipeline was southwards through the Afghan cities of Herat and Qandahar, before crossing into Pakistan near Quetta and linking with existing pipelines at Multan. The 1,040-mile long pipeline would cost about $2.5 billion and could be further extended to the Pakistani port of Gwadar where natural gas would be liquefied for export to other countries. For an additional $600 million, an extension to India could also be undertaken. Under the proposed plan, Taliban could earn up to $150 million annually in royalties and transit fees. As a part of the deal, Unocal was to provide $900,000 for a contract with the UNIVERSITY OF NEBRASKA AT OMAHA to train 400 Afghans in the management of the pipeline. After the dismissal of the BENAZIR BHUTTO government in Pakistan in 1996, the newly elected Prime Minister, NAWAZ SHARIF too, encouraged Unocal to expeditiously start construction. The political motive for supporting Unocal was the belief that the pipeline would legitimize Taliban rule in Afghanistan. Other more ambitious pipelines, for both gas and oil, including some from Iran were also mooted. The cost of such pipelines was estimated to be two to three times greater than the $2.5 billion project. Security of the pipelines is another major concern not only in Afghanistan and Balochistan (Pakistan) but in other countries as well. Optimistic statements about pipelines are routinely made, for example in December 2007 the Indian Secretary for Petroleum and Natural Gas publicly hoped that work would start on Iran-Pakistan-India (IPI) Gas pipeline project by March 2008. At the same time he cautioned that talks with Pakistan on transit fee and other related issues were stopped due to the political uncertainty in that country. Nevertheless, other reports suggested that India has already negotiated the price of gas and its transportation with Islamabad and only the issue of transit fees remained. At the other end of the subcontinent, Burma has 2,056 kilometers of gas and 558 kilometers of oil pipelines. New pipelines from both Bangladesh and Burma to neighboring countries were also under discussion or in the planning stage.

(*See also*: ENERGY OVERVIEW OF SOUTH ASIA)

Ojhri Camp Explosion (1988)

The camp was the ISI command post for the war against the Soviets in Afghanistan (1979-1989). The camp occupied an area of about 75 acres in the northern outskirts of Rawalpindi, about eight miles from Islamabad. The complex included a training area, a psychological warfare unit, a stinger missile training school, and mess halls for about 500 men. Importantly, it warehoused 70-80 percent of all U.S. supplied weaponry for equipping the Afghan MUJAHIDEEN. In early 1988, the depot was stocked to capacity with four months' supply for the forthcoming spring offensive in Afghanistan. On 10 April 1988 the entire stock was lost in a giant explosion. A fire supposedly started in a box of Egyptian rockets, which had not been de-fused before shipping. One of the boxes was dropped and burst into flames. Several workers were injured and the fire continued to burn while the wounded were taken away for medical treatment. Ten minutes later, the whole depot blew up and secondary explosions continued to rock the camp for another two days. By one account about "30,000 rockets, thousands of mortar bombs, millions of rounds of small-arms ammunition, countless anti-tank mines, recoilless rifle ammunition and stinger missiles were sucked into the most devastating and spectacular firework display that Pakistan is ever likely to see." About 100 died and over 1,000 were injured, some as far away as eight miles (thirteen kilometers) from the site by falling debris. An estimated $120-130 million of stock was lost. The Government of Pakistan ordered an inquiry into the blast and the then Prime Minister Junejo informed the National Assembly that the findings would be placed before the House. On 29 May, a day before the conclusions were to be made public, General ZIA dismissed the prime minister on charges of corruption, inefficiency and procrastination in the pace of Islamization of the country. It was widely believed that Junejo was sacked because the report would reveal corruption and disclose the names of military personnel responsible for the mishap. The findings of the inquiry were not made public.

Opium Production in South Asia

An addictive narcotic generally derived from illegally grown poppies. Most of the world's opium is cultivated in the 2,900 miles that span the South Asia. The two countries that form the rim of the region, Afghanistan and Burma, are the largest producers of the illicit product on the planet. Sandwiched between the golden crescent (Afghanistan) and the golden triangle (Burma), India provides about half of the opium legally utilized by the world's pharmaceutical industries to produce codeine, morphine, thebaine, papaverine, and other medical products.

In 1991, Afghanistan overtook Burma as the world's biggest cultivator of the narcotic. An estimated 2.3 million Afghans (356,000 households) were directly involved in the opium economy. Hence, approximately ten percent of the total population of the country was engaged in this trade. Despite the overthrow of the TALIBAN in late 2001, the narcotic was grown in an unprecedented 131,000 hectares of land by 2004. Washington, greatly concerned by this unexpected growth, increased developmental aid and more counter-narcotics assistance and equipment to Kabul. Consequently, cultivation fell slightly during the next year. However, the small decline in 2005 was dramatically reversed in 2006 with the rise in the area under cultivation to 165,000 hectares and the estimated production of 6,100 tons of drug, far surpassing the previous 4,200-ton record during the bumper year of 2004. The acreage still accounted for only two to three percent of the total agricultural land in the country. The earlier phenomenal declines in the two provinces, Nangarhar (96 percent) and Badakshan (53 percent), too, were reversed. These two provinces were among the three to receive the largest amount of aid for alternative development. Nangarhar got $70.1 million and Badakshan collected $47.3 million. The additional cause for the short-term decline in Nangarhar may have been the capture of Baz Mohammed, a warlord with ties to the Taliban who had controlled the opium trade in the province since 1990. President Bush designated Baz Mohammed as a foreign narcotics kingpin under the so-called “Kingpin Act” which targeted prominent foreign drug traffickers, their organizations, and their operatives. However, in the next four years no other Afghan Kingpins were arrested despite on-going counter-narcotics operations. By 2007, opium cultivation was present in almost all thirty-four provinces of the country making it the main engine of economic growth. Unexpectedly, in August 2008 the United Nations Office on Drugs and Crime (UNODC) reported in its Afghanistan Opium Survey 2008 that the drought, improved governance, and the anti-drug campaigns cut the country’s opium cultivation by nineteen percent when compared to the previous year. However, there was little decline in the poppy crop in the south where the Taliban insurgency is the strongest. Perhaps an important factor was overproduction in the past few years led to the reduced cultivation in 2008 as the price of fresh opium at harvest dropped by twenty percent from $86 to $70 per kilogram. Hence, the value of harvest fell from $1 billion in 2007 to $732 million in 2008. Another factor may be the increased cultivation of cannabis, the precursor of marijuana. Both crops are important sources of income for terrorist groups including *Hezb-e-Islami* GULBUDDIN (HIG), Islamic Movement of Uzbekistan (IMU), and the resurgent Taliban and AL QAEDA. As in previous years, about 87 percent of the estimated fifteen million heroin users worldwide were supplied from the Afghan poppy fields. The overall value of the crop rises two to four times once it reaches Europe.

In the early 1950s, the Wa and Kokang regions of northern Shan State emerged as the main opium producing areas in Burma. Allegedly Washington had then assisted the trapped Chinese Nationalist (KMT) forces in Shan State to grow the crop as a source of income. Fifty years later about 350,000 households (2 million people) in the State relied on opium as their primary source of income. The 380 tons of opium produced in 2006 comprised 70 percent of their cash flow. Under pressure from China, Thailand and the United States, the armed semi-autonomous regional force with the fanciful name of the United Wa State Army (UWSA) implausibly declared that as of 26 June 2005 the areas under their control were free from opium production. This declaration was in response to a January 2005 indictment by the U.S. Department of Justice of eight leaders of the UWSA on charges of trafficking in heroin and methamphetamine. The indictment included the chairman of UWSA, Bao You Xiang, and Wei Xue Kang, the former commander of the 171 Brigade of the UWSA's Southern Command located near the Thai border. The UWSA was described 'as one of the largest heroin-producing and trafficking groups in the world.' The indictments were the result of a long investigation led by the U.S. Drug Enforcement Agency (DEA) in cooperation with the Thai Police. However, little tangible change occurred and the situation in Burma remains unchanged.

In India cultivation of poppies has been regulated and taxed since the days of the great Mughal Emperor Akbar (1543-1605). In 1773, the British-owned East India Company wrested the monopoly from the Mughals for the cultivation of the narcotic in Bengal, Bihar, Benares, and Orissa. Following independence in 1947 production was confined to three states: Uttar Pradesh (UP), Madhya Pradesh (MP) and Rajasthan. The average yield per hectare is almost twice as great in India as compared to Afghanistan because the selected land is quite dry, flat, well-fertilized, weeded, and tended under the supervision of the Indian Government's Central Bureau of Narcotics (CBN). The Narcotics Control Bureau (NCB) is the nodal agency for coordination of intelligence and enforcement operations with various Central (Federal) and State organizations within the country and with relevant foreign agencies like the DEA. The latter first established an office in India in 1972 and cooperation with its Indian counterparts increased substantially after 9/11. Indian farmers are usually licensed to grow 0.1 hectare of opium poppies (0.24 acre), and sell 4.5 kilograms of unadulterated raw opium paste at a fixed government price of 320 Rupees ($8) per kilogram. The raw opium is processed at the two government factories located at Ghazipur, UP (since the 1860s) and at Neemuch, MP (founded in the 1930s). The headquarters of the Industry is in the central Indian city of Gwalior. The Indian production is about 425 tons per annum. About 72,000 Indians are employed in this industry and the Government of India's gross profit is approximately $40 million per year.

The crop is also grown in Nepal and Pakistan. Cultivation in both countries is unregulated and generally believed to be quite small.

In June 2007, the Europe based international policy think tank, the Senlis Council, launched a "Poppy for Medicines" project that proposed that village-cultivated poppy be transformed into morphine tablets in Afghanistan's rural communities. By this project the Europeans hoped to reduce the flow of the illegally produced opium that is converted into heroin to Europe and elsewhere. Another part of the proposal was to alter "80-20 rule" that requires the U.S. and others to purchase 80 percent of its legal opium from India and the remaining twenty percent from Turkey. The Senlis Council expected to include Afghanistan in the system by establishing a second-tier of supply that complements the current regulations established by the U.N.'s International Narcotics Control Board (INCB) for providing poppy-based medicines to countries that cannot meet their requirements under the present rules.

Notwithstanding projects like "Poppy for Medicine," the sustainability of the drive against illicit opium production in Afghanistan and Burma is seriously questioned. For example, the total amount pledged for developmental purposes in the two regions of Burma was less than $15 million by UNODC in partnership with other U.N. agencies and NGOs. This paltry sum included emergency food assistance. In Afghanistan, an earlier crackdown led to the virtual collapse of the informal credit system based on opium and caused great hardship to many indebted former poppy farmers. Heroin of Burmese origin, pushed off the international market by another South Asian country (Afghanistan), was consumed principally in China, South-East Asia and Australia. Afghanistan served Iran, Pakistan, Central Asia, Russia and Eastern Europe. The U.S. heroin market was supplied increasingly from Latin America. Mexico was the only source of opium in the Americas until the early 1990s when Colombia emerged as a significant producer.

P

Pakistan-U.S. Relations

Pakistan's relations with the United States developed against the backdrop of the Cold War. Hence, the military aspects of the alliance were particularly prominent. For Washington, South Asia was a peripheral theater in the global struggle against communism, but for Islamabad the main focus was balance of power vis-à-vis its larger neighbor, India. Accordingly, the U.S.-Pakistani relationship was warm when interests coincided, but otherwise there remained much doubt and frustration especially in Washington since 9/11. The Pakistani basic objective was to ensure sufficient defense capability with U.S. assistance to prevent its neighbors, especially Afghanistan and India, from using coercive means to settle outstanding disputes. A distant second objective was economic development, and a third was general protection against a possible long-range communist threat. General AYUB KHAN, the primary architect of the relationship, shared with most Pakistanis, before and since, the belief that the U.S. did not sufficiently use American economic assistance to India as the instrument to settle the Kashmir dispute in its favor. Therefore, Pakistan expected to eventually resolve the impasse by imposing its own military solution. With this prospect in mind, in 1954 the country signed the MUTUAL DEFENSE AGREEMENT with the U.S. Next year Pakistan became a member of two American led defense pacts, SEATO and CENTO. Over the next ten years Pakistan received $1.5 billion in military aid far more than the economic support to the country. The military assistance included 120 F-86 fighters, 26 B-57 bombers, and 460 Main Battle Tanks. Assistance continued till 1965 but was stopped, much to Islamabad's shock, at the onset of the Indo-Pakistan War that year. The arms embargo was not lifted until 1975, long after the secession of Bangladesh and the attendant Indo-Pakistan War of 1971. In the wake of that disaster, the new ruler of the country ZULFIKAR ALI BHUTTO followed a foreign policy of befriending other Islamic nations and "Bilateralism," implying neutrality in the Cold War with equal treatment accorded to both superpowers. The resumption of aid in 1975 was abruptly stopped in April 1979 by President JIMMY CARTER who cut off economic assistance, except for food aid, as required under the Symington Amendment (adopted in 1976 as a modification of the Foreign Assistance Act of 1961) because Pakistan was suspected of developing nuclear weapons. Barely six months later another U-turn followed. In the wake of the December 1979 Soviet military intervention in Afghanistan, Islamabad received $8 billion in aid between 1979 and 1990. As in the past, the assistance was disproportionately military (40 percent). The restraints of the Symington Amendment were circumvented by the passage of the PRESSLER AMENDMENT in 1985 that allowed for a Pakistani conventional arms build-up if the U.S. President could certify to Congress on an annual basis that Islamabad did not possess nuclear weapons. After the Soviet withdrawal from Afghanistan in 1989, President GEORGE H.W. BUSH refused to make the required certification. Assistance to Pakistan was again terminated and further sanctions were imposed following the nuclear tests in 1998 and the coup by General MUSHARRAF in 1999. Ties between the two countries were revived by another conflict for Pakistan, a frontline state during the cold war, again acquired the same role in the Global War on Terror (GWOT). Pakistan's logistical and operational support for Operation Enduring Freedom (the designation used for the U.S.-led military intervention in Afghanistan since 2001) and in the maintenance of some stability in Afghanistan were considered important enough contributions to the U.S. war an international terrorism. Islamabad handed over about 500 suspected terrorists but the number included only four major figures from the AL QAEDA leadership. In 2003, as a part of the overt and tangible commitment to GWOT, 25,000 Pakistani troops were deployed to support limited U.S. military operations in the Federally Administered Tribal Areas (FATA) of Pakistan. Most of the American attacks were carried out by drones or manned aircraft. The intensity of the attacks increased in June 2008. However, Islamabad refused to allow foreign combat forces to operate in these regions. Not only national pride was involved but committing either U.S. or Pakistani forces would be as an attack on its own people on the behest of the United States. In addition, the TALIBAN were Pashtuns, the majority ethnic group in Afghanistan where the de facto rulers were smaller minorities like Tajiks and Uzbeks. Therefore, support and sympathy from fellow Pashtuns in FATA for the Taliban was widespread. Consequently, the Pakistan Army was withdrawn from military operations in 2006 but again in 2008.

The war on terror also brought economic benefits to Pakistan for despite American and other bilateral and multilateral aid, the country's foreign debt had climbed from $3 billion in 1970 to over $25 billion by 1999. In the immediate aftermath of 9/11 the United States provided Pakistan with $600 million in cash, $350 million in military aid, and cancelled $1.5 billion in debt. Other nations, too, wrote off or restructured some of the debt. The Camp David package (June 2003) followed with another $3.2 billion in economic and military aid over five years. By 2007 Pakistan had received an estimated $11billion in aid including $5.6 billion from the little-known Pentagon's Coalition Support Fund. In return, accountability and results were not emphasized. In 2008 the Biden-Lugar Legislation aimed to transform the U.S.-Pakistan relationship from what Senator Biden termed as "transactional" toward deeper and broader effort by providing Islamabad $15 billion in development aid over a ten year period.

Relations continued to progress though underlying hostility and suspicion between the two was also present. For instance, in June 2004 the country was designated as a major non-NATO ally of the U.S. and in March 2006 Presidents Bush and Musharraf issued a joint statement about the partnership between the two countries that called for strategic dialogue and significant expansion of bilateral economic ties. The latter are comparatively insignificant as Pakistan's export base to the U.S. has remained dependent on two agricultural products: cotton and rice. In addition, trade with the United States has stagnated at about thirteen percent of Pakistan's exports and approximately eleven percent of its imports.

Pashtunistan (or Pakhtunistan) Issue

Amir Abdur Rahman, the ruler of Afghanistan (1880-1900) bitterly resented the boundary line drawn as the frontier between his country and the British Indian Empire by Sir Mortimer Durand, the then Foreign Secretary of the Government of British India. Known as the eponymous Durand Line it divided the Pashtun people into two halves and Kabul effectively lost its historical claims to vast territory includes Kashmir much of Pakistani Punjab (up to the river Jhelum in the east and the city of Multan in east-central Punjab), the and the Pashtun areas of Balochistan including the capital Quetta. This territorial claim while not formally declared is still mentioned by Afghans. None of Abdur Rahman's successors relinquished either the concept of Pashtun unity under the leadership of the *Amirs* of Kabul or their territorial claims to lands lost to the Sikhs and the British. However, the *Amirs* in Kabul reluctantly cooperated with the British Indian Government and bided their time. The Afghans perceived an opportunity to reclaim territory and tribes in the immediate aftermath of World War I. In a short-lived campaign (The Third Anglo-Afghan War 1919), the British succeeded in preserving the status quo but had to concede full independence to the Kingdom of Afghanistan. Earlier it was formally recognized as a British protectorate. At the creation of Pakistan in 1947 the issue of Pahtunistan and of the validity of the Durand Line were again raised were again raised by the Kabul government.

By 1947 the situation had changed greatly. Kashmir was a part of the Princely State of Jammu and Kashmir and was being actively contested for by for by both India and Pakistan. The Pashtun tribes in British India had been reorganized in 1901 by the creation of a new administrative area, the North-West Frontier Province (NWFP). The new province was further divided into Settled Districts and Tribal Agencies, with the latter being supervised by British political agents who reported directly to the imperial government in Delhi. In 1935 Britain extended limited self-government to the Provinces, including NWFP. By then, the Indian National Congress (Congress Party), which many Muslims saw as a predominately Hindu organization, had expanded its political activities in the province. The links between the political leaders of the NWFP and the leaders of the Congress Party were such that the elected majority in the North-West Frontier Province assembly originally voted to join India at partition in 1947. However, in July 1947, the British held a referendum in the

Settled Districts of the province offering the population the choice of either joining an independent India or the now-inevitable Pakistan. An estimated 56 percent of the eligible voters participated and over 90 percent elected to join Pakistan. A LOYA JIRGA held in the Tribal Agencies opted for Pakistan as well.

During a tribal uprising in 1949, a Pakistani air force plane bombed an Afghan village just across the frontier. This incident was the *casus belli* for the Kabul government to summon a loya jirga, which dutifully proclaimed that it recognized "Neither the imaginary Durand nor any similar line" and that all treaties starting with the 1893 Durand agreement pertaining to the issue were null and void. Irregular forces led by a local Pashtun leader crossed the border and attacked Pakistani forces in 1950 and 1951. The Pakistanis successfully beat back these incursions. The issue periodically flared up, but not with the same intensity except during the DAUD regime in Kabul (1973-78). The United States has consistently recognized the Durand Line as the frontier between the two countries.

Pandit, Vijayalaxmi (1900-1990)

JAWAHARLAL NEHRU's sister, Indian political activist and diplomat. Mahatma GANDHI decided to send a young beautiful articulate woman as a member of the delegation led by Sir Tej Bahadur Sapru to represent India in the United States in the mid-1940s. His choice was Mrs. Pandit. It was an inspired decision for she was received in New York by the Nobel Laureate, Pearl S. Buck, and in Washington DC by Mrs. Eleanor Roosevelt, the first lady. The conference to draft the Constitution of the freshly mooted United Nations was then being organized in San Francisco, California. Sapru's delegation opposed the official British-chosen mission to represent India. It did not succeed in San Francisco, but the articulate Mrs. Pandit was invited by the new American President, HARRY S. TRUMAN, to Washington, DC. Later she was the Indian Ambassador to the U.S. (1949-1952). With Washington's strong support, Mrs. Pandit became the first woman President of the United Nations General Assembly (1955).

Peace Corps

An American program which called on university students to serve their country in furthering peace and prosperity by sharing their knowledge and experience with the peoples of the third world. First proposed in 1960 by Senator JOHN F. KENNEDY, then a U.S. Presidential candidate, it was officially founded a year later. Within two years about 7,300 Peace Corps volunteers were serving in 44 countries. Their total more than doubled by June 1966 to 15,000 and marked the all-time high in the number of volunteers to serve abroad in the history of the organization.

In 1981, the U.S. Congress established the Corps as an independent agency of the federal government. Perhaps in response to its newly established independent status, the corps was reenergized and branched away from its traditional emphasis on education and agriculture into business-related programs. The altered focus brought more conservatives and more Republicans into the agency, reflecting the changing political and social spectrum within the U.S. After 9/11 President GEORGE W. BUSH sought to double the number of volunteers sent abroad, especially to Islamic and middle-eastern countries by 2007. Therefore, the Corps' budget, too, doubled to approximately $350 million per annum.

The Peace Corps was initially, viewed in some countries, especially in Africa, as an American scheme for sending spies or neo-colonialists to undermine their newly won independence. In contrast, both the major countries in South Asia, India and Pakistan, were among the first to whole-heartedly welcome its volunteers. In the following year, perhaps taking a cue from the larger countries in South Asia, Afghanistan, Nepal and Sri Lanka, too, accepted workers from the Corps. Political tensions between host countries and the U.S. often led to curtailment of its activities. Incrcased education and experience in the countryside led to cessation of the program in India in 1976. Altogether 4,325 young Americans had served and included President JIMMY CARTER's mother, Mrs. Bessie Lillian Carter ("Miz Lillian"). In 1966, at the age of 68 she worked in a clinic near Mumbai for 21 months. A biannual Lillian Carter Peace Corps Award for senior volunteers (50 years and older) was instituted in 1986.

The Peace Corps program was discontinued in Pakistan in 1967 and briefly revived in 1988-91. Only 517 worked in the country during the nine years of intermittent operations in that country. In Afghanistan, the communist revolution (1979) terminated the Corps' presence. A total of 1,652 had been to the country. Nepal had the longest continuous presence of workers: 3,629 from 1962 to 2004. It was abruptly shut down after bombings and violence by Maoists against the Corps that year. A total of 372 workers went to Sri Lanka in 1962-64, 1967-70, and 1983-98. In 1998, Bangladesh, heavily dependent on NGOs, allowed the Peace Corps into the country. For the first time in thirty years the corps had returned to the region and concentrated on education and youth development. However, after a series of bomb attacks, the Peace Corps pulled out in 2006. During its eight year presence in Bangladesh a total of 280 workers served in the country.

Very few went to the reclusive Maldives and Bhutan. A notable exception was Edward C. Dolby, President, Bank of America-Carolinas (Bhutan 1966-68).

As the Peace Corps reinvented itself by changing its focus and getting more diverse volunteers of different ages to work in the demanding international environment, its mission, too, was enlarged. Initially there were two main objectives. The first was to provide educated altruistic young Americans the opportunity to assist the less fortunate, especially in third world. The second was to promote better understanding about Americans among the peoples of the host country. Later a third objective was added. It was for Americans to get a better awareness of other peoples and their cultures. In 1996, a sub-group designated as the Crisis Corps was formed by utilizing the services of exceptionally qualified volunteers to return to the field during an acute crisis for short-term assignments that typically ranged from three to six months. Their knowledge of the local language, technical and professional experience, and cross-cultural skills gained through earlier service with the Corps were expected to be positive assets in critical situations, natural disasters and other calamities. In ten years (1996-2006) the Natural Disaster Relief and Reconstruction Program grew into the largest of the Crisis Corps undertakings with 380 international assignments. In South Asia its only role was the dispatch of about 25 volunteers to Sri Lanka to work with local and other international assistance groups in the aftermath of the 26 December 2004 Tsunami.

People's Democratic Party of Afghanistan (PDPA)

It was founded on 1 January, 1965 by Nur Mohammed Taraki, a business man who also translated materials for foreign organizations. The twenty-eight founding members elected him as the party Secretary-General and BABRAK KARMAL another avoided communist as Deputy Secretary-General with five others as members of the Central Committee (the Politburo). However, the two main leaders differed strongly in their ideology. Karmal was more nationalistic and felt that the country was too under-developed for a Marxist revolution. Accordingly, he advocated a gradual progression towards socialism and cooperation with other political parties. In contrast, Taraki believed that a Marxist revolution in Afghanistan could be achieved by building a tightly disciplined membership from the proletariat led by a highly educated leadership committed to violent and revolutionary change. The PDPA's influence was limited because it was widely known as a political party that survived on financial aid received from the Soviet Union. Accordingly, its membership was small and limited to cities. The majority of Afghans were rural and suspicious of politicians especially those with ties to the "Godless" Soviet Union. Taraki's faction was called *Khalq* ("People"), after his defunct newspaper, and Karmal's was *Parcham* ("Banner") named for the weekly magazine he had briefly published. In 1967, the party formally split into its two groups, the *Khalq* and the *Parcham*. After ten years of bickering, the two factions reluctantly reunited under of Soviet pressure. Within a year the unstable PDPA surprised both the U.S. and the Soviet Union by overthrowing the DAUD regime. Initially the façade of party unity was maintained with the cabinet being carefully constituted with alternate ranking positions allotted to *Khalqis* and *Parchamis*. Hence, on 1 May 1978 Taraki became the president and prime minister; Karmal was senior deputy prime minister, and AMIN, a *Khalqi,* the foreign minister. However, party unity was remarkably short-lived. In July that year, *Khalqis* purged their rivals and Karmal was banished as ambassador to Czechoslovakia. As a result of the purge, Amin emerged as the main beneficiary for he became the prime minister in March 1979. Meanwhile, a rebellion broke out against the narrow-based ideologically extreme regime in Nuristan Province in eastern Afghanistan. In Kabul, the intense rivalry between Taraki and Amin, both *Khalqis*, culminated in the former's assassination in September 1979. Amin assumed power but his Soviet backers soon realized that he was too rigid a Marxist-Leninist to succeed in a conservative and religious country like Afghanistan. Within three months (December 1979), Amin was shot and killed by Soviet forces and replaced by the *Parchami* exile, Karmal, as president. Though more moderate than his predecessors, he too was unable to consolidate power beyond a few urban areas in the country. Hence, in 1986 Karmal was replaced by Najibullah. The latter tried to widen the base of the party changed its name from the discredited PDPA to the *Watan* ("Homeland") Party in 1988. Most members of *Watan* were from his faction, *Parcham*. In 2002 long after its fall from power, the name was further changed to Democratic *Watan* Party of Afghanistan. Some *Parchamis* with connections in the bureaucracy and security services formed the *Hezb-e-Mutahed Mili*. The remaining Khalqis established *Hezb-e-Mili Afghanistan* and *Hezb-e-Wahdat-e-Mili Afghanistan*. The latter enjoys some support among non-communist Pashtun intellectuals.

PL 480 Food Aid

The Agricultural Trade Development and Assistance Act, 1954, became U.S. Public Law 480. It is widely known as PL 480. Over the next 54 years, the program distributed about 360 million metric tons of food aid to millions of the poor and the hungry around the world. The program is comprised of three titles. Title I is administered by U.S. Department of Agriculture (USDA), and Titles II and III are run by the Agency for International Development (AID). Title I is government-to-government sales of agricultural commodities to developing countries under long-term credit arrangements. Title II covers donation of agricultural commodities as humanitarian aid and Title III provides for government-to-government grants for long-term economic growth to the least developed countries. Financing of sales on long term credit at concessional rates is handled by Commodity Credit Corporation (CCC), an agency within USDA. In addition to the low rates of interest charged by the U.S., another attractive feature of PL 480 was that repayment could be in either dollars or in the currency of the recipient country. An unappealing aspect of the program was its requirement that at least 75 percent of the foodstuffs be shipped on privately owned U.S. flagged commercial vessels. This provision added considerably to the cost of the aid, except under Title III where the expense of shipping, too, was borne by the U.S. Government. All of South Asia benefited greatly from the program till the mid-1960s when the JOHNSON administration tried to use humanitarian aid as a lever for applying political pressure. India, facing famine, with MRS. INDIRA GANDHI as prime minister, reacted by making the goal of self-sufficiency in food as a national priority. As such, Johnson's attitude contributed to the spread of the GREEN REVOLUTION. An unintended consequence of the program was accumulation of approximately $3 billion in Indian Rupees by the United States by 1974. The funds were held in a special account by the Reserve Bank of India. The $3 billion amounted to approximately 10 percent of all currency in circulation in the country. Both Washington and New Delhi considered this situation could lead to financial destabilization in India. This problem was adroitly handled by Ambassador MOYNIHAN in 1974. He convinced the U.S. Congress to write off $2.2 billion in Rupee funds. The remaining money was utilized for a variety of educational undertakings, especially for the development of specialized libraries. In the new millennium, all South Asian countries continue to intermittently avail of Title II donations.

Prachanda, *Nom De Guerre* used by Pushpa Kamal Dahal (1954-)

Dahal is the leader, Communist Party of Nepal (Maoist) [CPN (M)]. As Prachanda he launched the Nepalese People's War, known as the Prachanda Path on 13 February 1996. The war was based on combining the strategy followed by the Shining Path insurrectionists in Peru and the Maoist tactics used by the communists in their successful revolution in China. After ten years of intermittent conflict, the Maoists controlled large portions of Nepal.

Dahal, born in an inconspicuous Brahmin family in Chitwan, western Nepal, was initially motivated by the Cultural Revolution in

China. He obtained a Bachelor's Degree from the Institute of Agriculture and Animal Sciences, Chitwan and was studying for a Masters in Public Administration when he quit academics to join politics. He became a communist radical in the early 1970s and remained underground even after the restoration of democracy in Nepal in 1990. He then took control of the party's covert wing while the parliamentary representation was headed by BABURAM BHATTARAI as a part of the United People's Front. The duo issued a list of forty demands to the Nepalese Government and threatened civil war if their conditions were not met. The government rejected their stipulations. Prachanda then established a "base area" in the remote regions of western Nepal. After almost ten years of intermittent, low intensity conflict punctuated by ceasefires, Prachanda declared a unilateral three-month ceasefire on 3 September 2005. In November before the expiration of the ceasefire he released a "twelve-point agreement" that reiterated CPN (M) political positions and defined the areas of agreement between the Maoists and seven other Nepalese parties whose members constituted 190 out of the 205 representatives in the dissolved National Assembly. Parliament was reconvened and the 84-year old Girija Prasad Koirala was sworn in as Prime Minister as the head of the Seven-Party Alliance (SPA). Further meetings followed and culminated in a Comprehensive Peace Agreement (CPA) signed on 21 November 2006 signaling the end of the civil war and paving the way for an elected Constituent Assembly. Both he and Bhattarai met former U.S. President CARTER. The meeting gave the communists greater international legitimacy and further impetus to participate in the political process in the country. After repeated postponements elections for the Constituent Assembly were held in April 2008. To the surprise of most experts, Prachanda's party, CPN (M)), placed first in the election with 220 out of 575 elected seats, and it became the largest party in the Constituent Assembly. A distant second was the veteran Nepali Congress with exactly half as many seats (110 seats). The monarchy was swiftly abolished. After months of discussions Prachanda was elected as the Prime Minister of a coalition government in August 2008. However, numerous new groups with differing political agendas mushroomed in the small country. The Nepali experience of a newly formed republican country and a democratic election that led to an elected coalition led by former insurgent communists is unique and is likely to evolve with time.

Pressler Amendment

A Pakistan-specific U.S. legislation to control nuclear proliferation while allowing Islamabad to receive American conventional weapons. In 1996, U.S. Senator Larry Pressler, a Republican from South Dakota, attached an amendment to the foreign aid bill in which all assistance from the United States to Pakistan would be stopped if the Administration believed that Islamabad was developing nuclear weapons. The Amendment also gave the President the authority to waive any penalty against Pakistan on the grounds of American strategic interests. Accordingly the transfer of conventional arms to Pakistan was maintained as long as the U.S. president issued a waiver that Islamabad was not developing nuclear weapons. Such waivers were granted as long as Pakistan was engaged in the effort to dislodge the Soviet Union from Afghanistan. However, in 1992, President GEORGE H.W.BUSH refused to give such a waiver and U.S. aid to Pakistan was stopped. Neither country was prepared to sustain such a complete break. Hence, nine years later the Brown Amendment was passed. This amendment, sponsored by a Republican Senator and promoted by a Democratic Administration, reflected a bipartisan consensus in Washington to repair the bilateral relationship. It removed restrictions on all non-military assistance and resumed the IMET (International Military Education Training) program. In addition, as a one-time waiver of the Pressler Amendment, embargoed military equipment worth $368 million was released. Only the 28 F-16s for not sold to Pakistan but President CLINTON made a good-faith pledge to reimburse Islamabad for the money it had already paid for the warplanes. From Pakistan's perspective the Brown Amendment was a political message marking the first concrete step taken by the United States in five years to improve the military aspect of the longstanding but tenuous the U.S.-Pakistani military relations. In 1998, Pakistan detonated five nuclear devices and conclusively demonstrated that Islamabad was already in possession of a significant nuclear arsenal. The Pakistan-specific Pressler Amendment had failed to prevent Pakistan from developing nuclear weapons. Accordingly it became obsolete and irrelevant.

Provincial Reconstruction Teams (Afghanistan)

During Operation Enduring Freedom in Afghanistan, the U.S. Central Command (U.S. CENTCOM, headquartered in Tampa, Florida) developed Joint Reconstruction Teams (JRTs) to facilitate humanitarian relief and reconstruction operations. The teams consisted of both military personnel and civilian staff from the diplomatic corps and developmental agencies. From the outset, in December 2002, HAMID KARZAI the then interim President of the Afghan Transitional Authority was an enthusiastic supporter of the concept. At his request, the name was changed from JRTs to "Provincial Reconstruction Teams" (PRTs). Their mission was further enlarged to extend the authority of the Afghan central government by enhancing security in the countryside. Twenty-five PRTs were operationalized by 2007. Twelve were led by the United States. The PRTs varied in size, scope, and mission. An average American PRT consisted of about 100 personnel and focused on force protection and quick impact assistance projects. In contrast, the German team was three times as large and contained a more robust civilian component. American PRTs were funded by the U.S. Department of Defense's Overseas Humanitarian Disaster and Civic Aid (OHDACA) and the Commander's Emergency Response Program (CERP). As most of the PRTs operating in 2003 and 2004 had virtually no civilian or NGO presence, the average Afghan regarded the teams as a part of the military campaign. Hence, even after the civilian component was increased most Afghans viewed them as threats rather than as providers of aid. Civilian agencies also pointed out that if the PRTs were intended to enhance security, they should be deployed in the least secure areas. Instead, PRTs were often located in regions where long-standing civilian humanitarian assistance providers were already functioning. Though the Terms of Reference for PRTs were published in February 2005 concerns about the role and effectiveness persisted. Nevertheless, despite their drawbacks, PRTs probably added to the creation of an environment that allowed three million refugees to resettle and for successful elections to be conducted. However, by 2007 most authorities felt that a complete overhaul of the PRT mechanism was overdue.

Q

Qureshi, Moeenuddin Ahmed (1931-)

Economist, IMF bureaucrat, and Prime Minister of Pakistan (1993). Qureshi a member of a distinguished family from Kasur, a small town near Lahore, received a Fulbright Fellowship for Post Graduate work in Economics at the University of Illinois. On completing his PhD he returned to Pakistan in 1955 and joined the country's Planning Commission. A year later he joined the International Monitory Fund (IMF). From the IMF, he was appointed as the Head of the International Finance Corporation (IFC). In 1987, he was became the Senior Vice President of Operations of the World Bank. He retired in November 1991 and founded his own investment company. In July 1993 he was invited by Pakistan's President Ghulam Ishaq Khan to serve as the caretaker Prime Minister in a government of technocrats. During his three months in Islamabad, he introduced a number of economic reforms, improved the governance of the country, and tried to retrieve money from defaulters on loans from public sector banks. After the October 1993 elections, Qureshi returned home to Washington, DC.

R

Rabbani, Burhanuddin (1940-)

Leader, *Jam'iat-i Islami-yi Afghanistan* (Islamic Society of Afghanistan, a largely non-Pashtun group), President of the Islamic Republic of Afghanistan (1993-96, 2001). A Tajik, born in Faizabad, Badakhshan Province, educated in Islamic studies at Kabul University and at Al-Azhar University, Cairo, Egypt (M.A., 1968), Rabbani then joined the Faculty of Theology at Kabul University. In the then highly politicized environment of the university, he organized his students to counter secular trends in Afghanistan and to attack leftists on campus. In 1970 his credentials as a leader and theologian were further strengthened when he became the editor of *Majallat-i Shari'at* (Journal of Islamic Law) and was elected as head of *Jam'iat-i Islami* in 1971. After DAUD's crackdown in 1974, he fled to Pakistan, where he was supported by the government and the Pakistani fraternal organization, *Jam'iat-i Islami.* In 1975, the *Jamiat* carried out raids into Afghanistan to destabilize Daud but had little impact. The failure of the armed attacks led to disagreements in policy and tactics between Rabbani and HEKMATYAR. The two split and Hekmatyar created the *Hisb-i Islami* in 1976. Rabbani continued to lead the *Jamiat.* At the fall of the NAJIBULLAH regime, Rabbani's forces under MASSOUD entered Kabul and swiftly ousted Hekmatyar's troops from such key locations as the presidential palace and the interior ministry. Meanwhile, Uzbeks under DOSTUM and other groups, most notably the Shiite organization, *Hisb-i Wahdat* occupied different parts of the Afghan capital. In March 1993, Rabbani succeeded Sibghatullah Mojadeddi as president of the Islamic Republic of Afghanistan, but he did not control either Kabul or the rest of the country. Nevertheless, he refused to step down after a two year term as president. Consequently, the civil war intensified and Kabul was heavily shelled especially by Hekmatyar and Dostum. In this chaotic situation the TALIBAN forces captured the capital in September 1996. The Rabbani regime was forced to move northwards in the country and he remained the titular head of the de jure government of Afghanistan for his *Jam'iat-i-Islami* was the largest component of the anti-Taliban grouping known as the Northern Alliance. His government was still recognized by most countries and the U.N. as the legitimate authority in Afghanistan. After the 9/11 terrorist attacks, he joined U.S. and NATO forces to oust the Taliban from Afghanistan. Rabbani returned as president but soon, under U.S. pressure, he reluctantly relinquished the presidency to HAMID KARZAI.

Rai, Lala Lajpat (1865-1928)

Indian patriot. At the turn of the twentieth century, Rai was among the three predominant members of the Indian freedom movement. The trio was popularly known as Lal-Pal-Bal. Lal being Rai's abbreviated name. As a freedom fighter he sought American support and first landed in New York in November 1904. He was surprised by the color prejudice in the country and the widespread ignorance about India. The indifference in some schools was so profound that students simply skipped over the few pages devoted to India in their schoolbooks. He responded by giving a series of lectures across the country and wrote two books, one about the United States and the other on India. He left for Japan from San Francisco, California, in July 1905. He returned to the U.S. in 1914, spurned German and Afghan offers of assistance, and tried to remedy the anti-Indian propaganda by the British Government in America by giving speeches throughout the United States. In October 1915, he founded the Indian Home Rule League (Home Rule was a term used to describe self-rule or independence). In January 1917, the League launched a small monthly called *Young India.* Rai's League was only effective enough to make a formal presentation in support of Indian home rule before the Foreign Relations Committee of U.S. Senate. It achieved little. Rai returned to India after five years in United States.

Rao, P.V. Narasimha

Indian Prime Minister (1991-96). Rao decisively moved the country towards free market reforms and advocated relations closer with the

U.S.A. poet, lawyer, and linguist, Rao joined the Indian National Congress during the struggle for independence. After a long stint in state politics, he was first elected to the Lok Sabha in 1972. After five years of dutiful service in parliament, he was rewarded with a succession of key cabinet posts under the GANDHIS, INDIRA and RAJIV. As the foreign minister (1980-84), Rao had the difficult task of reconciling New Delhi's reservations about the Soviet intervention in Afghanistan and the need to sustain a close working relationship with Moscow as India was heavily dependent on the U.S.S.R. for defense supplies and equipment. Nevertheless, he pointed out to the Soviets that the Afghan intervention would negatively affect the U.S.S.R.'s. international credibility and drain its military and economic resources.

In semi-retirement, he was summoned as an unelected prime minister in 1991. Rao was subsequently elected to the Lok Sabha and faced a myriad of economic and security challenges that had built up in the country during the previous decade. With an imminent balance of payments crisis on hand, the new prime minister moved decisively towards free-market reforms and in reducing the government's role in the economic life of the country. He also instituted austerity measures, and encouraged foreign investment. In addition, he concentrated on improving ties with Washington and publicly urged the U.S. to erase "old perceptions" about India. With uncharacteristic enthusiasm, in an interview, he declared that "the sky was the limit" in terms of potential American investment in his country. In that context he visited the U.S. twice during his tenure as prime minister. Perhaps, to further reassure Washington of the altered circumstances, in 1992 he made public the Indian ties with Israel, which had been kept secret since they were first established under Indira Gandhi's government in 1969. Accordingly, Israel finally opened an embassy in New Delhi. However, he was not averse to confronting Washington on other issues like nuclear non-proliferation and U.S. military aid to Pakistan, while the latter was clearly developing nuclear weapons.

Rao lost the general elections in May 1996 but did not fade into quiet retirement. Instead, he was embroiled in legal tangles culminating in his conviction in 2000 for conspiring to buy votes in parliament prior to a 1993 no-confidence vote. However, the judgment was overturned in 2002.

Rapti Valley Multi Purpose Project

Rapti Valley is 90 miles (145 kilometres) southwest of Kathmandu, Nepal, and is 600 square miles (1,535 square kilometres) in area. Around 1950 its population was estimated at 25,000 with only 42,000 acres of land under cultivation. An American study concluded that another 80,000 acres of land could be tilled, as the soil was suitable for growing cereals, maize, sugar cane, oil seeds and fruit and vegetables. In addition, grasslands could support cattle breeding and the surrounding forests might provide timber for woodworking and derivative industries like the manufacture of furniture, matches, paper, etc. After the floods of 1951-53, the few rudimentary roads were washed away. Therefore, an airstrip was built, equipment flown in, and a road was bulldozed to the Valley. The region was full of peacocks that had never seen humans and were therefore unafraid of them. Hence, American officers had the rare treat of having peacock eggs for breakfast. This project was the main focus of American aid to Nepal in the 1950s. An integrated system of administration was set up as the Rapti Valley Development Board. Nepali refugees from Burma and Assam and ex-servicemen from the British and Indian armies were resettled in the valley. The newcomers more politicized and more worldly wise than other Nepalese, sought to change the feudal system of the country. Thirty years later, the Rapti Valley became one of the major strongholds of Maoist insurgents in Nepal.

Reagan, Ronald Wilson (1911-2004)

U.S. President (1981-89). In 1952 Reagan married Nancy Davis, an actress, embroiled in disputes over the issue of communists in the film industry. Her activism was a factor in shifting Reagan's own political views from liberalism to conservativism In South Asia, the Reagan administration was marked intensified American involvement in Afghanistan and the aggressive utilization of Pakistan as a base for promoting the Afghan insurgency against the Soviet occupation. President Reagan in a new spirit of measured bilateralism succeeded in forging a "limited strategic relationship" with Pakistan which did not at the same time, commit the U.S. against India. Both INDIRA GANDHI and her son, RAJIV GANDHI, reciprocated by being less stridently opposed to Washington. Rajiv's amiable relationship with the much older Reagan initiated crucial economic and diplomatic changes that created greater long-term compatibility in the Indo-American ties.

Rice, Condoleezza (Condi) (1954-)

U.S. National Security Advisor (2001-2005), U.S. Secretary of State (2005-). After a brilliant academic career Rice worked on German reunification and collapse of the Soviet Union in the GEORGE H.W. BUSH administration. Rice was Senior Fellow at the Hoover Institution and Professor of Political Science at Stanford University when she became a key advisor on foreign policy to the then Republican presidential candidate, George W. Bush. In a seminal article titled "Campaign 2000: Promoting the National Interest" published in the influential journal *Foreign Affairs* (January-February 2000 issue), she outlined the contours of the Bush foreign policy. Regarding the Indian subcontinent, she asserted, "The United States must deepen its cooperation with Japan and South Korea and maintain its commitment to a robust military presence in the region. It should pay closer attention to India's role in the regional balance. There is a strong tendency conceptually to connect India with Pakistan and to think only of Kashmir or the nuclear competition between the two states. But India is an element in China's calculation, and it should be in America's, too. India is not a great power yet, but it has the potential to emerge as one." Accordingly, the newly elected President George W. Bush and his National Security Advisor, Condi Rice, considered India as a natural strategic partner. She viewed the series of detailed discussions between Deputy Secretary of State Strobe Talbott and the prominent BJP leader Jaswant Singh during 1999-2000 as the basis for furthering relations between the two countries. Accordingly, she advised President Bush to meet with Jaswant Singh, on his visit to Washington in 2001 as India's Foreign Minister. This gesture set into motion a major change in U.S. policy towards the region. After Bush's re-election in 2004, Rice took over as Secretary of State and became instrumental in giving India access to high technology and nuclear expertise and equipment under a framework labeled as the Next Steps in the Strategic Partnership (NSSP).

Rockefeller Foundation

Established in May 1913, it is knowledge based global foundation with wide-ranging commitments especially in the areas of public health, medical education, arts and culture, housing, globalization and social, scientific and agricultural research. One of the earliest grants made by the Foundation was in South Asia: Research funds were given to the All India School of Hygiene and Public Health, Calcutta in 1913. During 1930s and 1940s the Foundation supported various medical programs, especially in rural areas to control epidemics and endemic diseases, establishment of nursing colleges, rat trapping to prevent plague and mosquito control especially in Sindh after a barrage across the River Indus caused an upsurge of malaria. The Foundation reduced its activities in India during the years of Cold War because of New Delhi's foreign policy of NON-ALIGNMENT. Nonetheless, it continued to support the teaching of the Hindi language, Indian history, art and social sciences at 41 American universities. Its assets totaled $3.1 billion at the turn of the new millennium. Like FORD FOUNDATION, Rockefeller, too, has had its share of controversy especially in the 1920s when it supported eugenics and other pseudo-scientific programs in Germany.

Roosevelt, Franklin Delano (1882-1945)

U.S. President (1933-45). Roosevelt, like his predecessors in the White House and those who succeeded him to the presidency had little experience of South Asian affairs before entering office. However, unique among the U.S. Presidents, Roosevelt's family had long ties with South Asia through a well-known trading family, the Sassoons. Warren Delano, a Huguenot from New York, was a senior partner in the firm, Russell & Company, whose merchant fleet carried the Sassoon opium from India to China and returned with tea. Warren Delano moved to Newburgh in New York state. In 1851 his daughter Sara married their well-born neighbor, James Roosevelt, the father of Franklin Delano Roosevelt.

Because of Roosevelt's and other New Dealers' anti-colonialist predilections, the U.S. was favorably disposed towards Indian independence. His administration viewed political autonomy coupled with democracy for India at the end of World War II as a model for post-colonial nations elsewhere as well.

Long after the president's untimely death, his widow, Eleanor Roosevelt, was to leave her mark on South Asia. In 1952, at the invitation of Prime Minister NEHRU the 67 year old Eleanor journeyed to India for the first time. The impulse to visit the region may have been related to her experiences as the Chairperson of the United Nations Commission on Human Rights (1946-51). In Pakistan though there was an absence of cordiality, she was shown every consideration, whereas in India she was received with great warmth. In turn, she made a deep impression, especially on students and on the Indian press. Thereafter she wrote a 237 page book, *India and the Awakening East.* In the book, the former first lady wrote about the thrilling challenges of nation-building that lay ahead for the country and complimented the leaders of independent India for their dedication and zeal. In 1963, on the fifteenth anniversary of the Declaration of Human Rights, India honored her by issuing postage stamp bearing her likeness. At the turn of the new millennium, her five story townhouse in the upper east side of Manhattan was bought by an Indian-American family.

Rushdie, Salman (1947-)

Author. Rushdie, born in Bombay, migrated to Pakistan and then to England and the United States. His first book, *Midnight's Children* won the coveted Booker Prize and brought him international fame. The book was a semi-autobiographical account of the partition of India in 1947. His maternal uncle General Shahid Hamid, himself an author and India-baiter was a major character in the novel. His other books were not as successful till he published the *Satanic Verses*, a novel peopled with several characters that closely resembled the Prophet Mohammed and his wives. In February 1989, the book was banned in India. A few days later, Ayatollah Khomeini of Iran issued an edict (*Fatwa*) against the novelist and offered $1.6 million as reward for the author's assassination. The *fatwa* forced Rushdie into hiding for more than six years. Relations between Iran and the western countries were greatly soured by the *fatwa*. The *fatwa* expired with the death of the Ayatollah and Rushdie resumed a normal lifestyle, shuttling between London, New York, and the Indian subcontinent. His subsequent books have not attracted the same financial or critical appeal. He was knighted by the British government in 2007.

S

Sabu (1924-1963)

Actor. He was the twelve -year old son of an Indian *Mahout* (elephant handler) working for the Maharaja of Mysore, when he was cast to play the title role in Alexander Korda's film, "The Elephant Boy." Shortly afterwards he starred as the little robber in the film, "The Thief of Baghdad," a great box-office hit. He acted in a number of other films with Indian characters, but all his roles were stereotypical of the American view of India as a land of holy men, jungles, Maharajas, snakes and poverty. His son Paul was a music composer in Hollywood and his daughter, Jasmine, owned a horse farm in California.

Salam, Abdus (1926-1996)

Pakistani Nobel laureate (Physics, 1979). The Punjab and Cambridge University educated physicist was passionately committed to the creation of an international center dedicated to theoretical physics that could meet the needs of scientists from the developing world. He first outlined the proposal for such a center at the Tenth Annual International Conference on High Energy Physics in Rochester, New York (1960). Ultimately, such an institution, the International Center for Theoretical Physics (ICTP), was set up in Trieste, Italy in 1964 with Salam as its director. Among the key early donors was FORD FOUNDATION WITH a four-year $200,000 grant. American academics and physicists also supported him by donating their time, expertise, and services. As a member of Pakistan Atomic Energy Commission (1958-74), Founder-Chairman of SUPARCO, Pakistan's Space and Upper Atmosphere Research Committee (1961-64), and as Chief Scientific Adviser to the President of Pakistan (1961-1974), Salam dealt extensively with his U.S. counterparts and won their respect and confidence. After long years of service to his country, he resigned from the key positions he held because ZULFIKAR ALI BHUTTO pressed for a nuclear weapons program, and Salam was opposed to the non-peaceful uses of atomic energy. It was a further tribute to his altruism and integrity that both Marshal N. Rosenbluth, of the University of California, San Diego, California, and Roald Z. Sagdeev, head of the Plasma Physics Laboratory, Institute of Nuclear Physics, Novosibirsk, U.S.S.R., joined him in Trieste to launch the plasma physics group at ICTP. Rosenbluth's and Sagdeev's partnership made ICTP into one of the few institutions in the world where scientists from the communist East and the capitalist West could work side-by-side during the Cold War.

Salinity Control and Reclamation Programme (SCARP)

In the latter half of the nineteenth century, the British developed a vast system of canals to irrigate the arid districts of western Punjab (now Pakistan). Most of the water was taken from the Indus River. Though the water brought fertility to the fields, no provision was made for its subsequent drainage. Consequently, by the 1950s, vast areas of Central Punjab developed signs of salinity and waterlogging. President AYUB KHAN sought assistance from President JOHN F. KENNEDY during his visit to Washington in 1961.Kennedy sent a team of experts under John Revelle, a well-known Harvard University geologist. The SCARP program was successfully completed by the end of 1990.

Sanctions as a Stratagem in U.S. Foreign Policy

Economic sanctions have a hallowed history in U.S. foreign policy. Before American independence, the colonialists frequently used economic sanctions to challenge London by boycotting British goods. As early as 1807, the U.S. Congress formalized the use of sanctions as an instrument of foreign policy by imposing trade embargoes against Britain. During the American Civil War, economic sanctions in the form of a blockade of the Confederate States provided the resource-rich North with a significant strategic advantage. The statutory basis for U.S. economic sanctions in the twentieth century was the enactment of the Trading with the Enemy Act (TWEA) in 1917; six months after the U.S. entered World War I. The Act was amended in 1933 to give the President authority to exercise TWEA powers in peacetime during national emergencies. Accordingly, it was under TWEA that sanctions were enforced against Japan prior to the formal onset of hostilities in 1941. Additional legislation called the Export Control Act was passed in 1949. In the following year, the Act was incorporated into the foreign policy export control authority in the Export Administration Act. The latter expired on 20 August 1994 and was replaced by the International Emergency Economic Powers Act (IEEPA) in 1977. IEEPA is administered by the U.S. Department of Commerce. Congress occasionally imposes sanctions aimed at specific situations like the Helms-BURTON Act which authorizes suits for damages against the Cuban government for confiscation of private property.

However, supporters of sanctions can only cite a few instances when sanctions were successful as an instrument of foreign policy. For example, sanctions were widely acknowledged in forcing the apartheid government of South Africa to make way for majority rule in the country; economic sanctions pushed Serbia to the negotiating table over the war in Bosnia, and embargoes limited Iraq's ability to rebuild its military after the 1991 Gulf War. However, in all these instances the sanctions were either multi-lateral or imposed by international institutions such as the U.N. or NATO.

The effectiveness and relevance of unilateral sanctions, on the other hand, is more debatable. Among the failures were the grain embargo against the U.S.SR in retaliation for its 1979 military intervention in Afghanistan and sanctions in 1982 against firms that were building the Soviet natural gas pipeline to Western Europe. In both cases American exporters and investors lost business to foreign companies whereas Soviet policies remained unchanged. Similarly, 45 years of U.S. sanctions against Cuba did not topple the Castro government. In 1997, a number of studies examined various aspects of U.S. sanctions. The Congressional Research Service (CRS) found 191 different sanctions were imposed by the U.S. that year. The Institute for International Economics found that since 1970, unilateral U.S. sanctions had achieved foreign policy goals in only thirteen percent of cases at a cost to the U.S. of around $15-19 billion per annum in lost potential exports. During the same year, the National Association of Manufacturers (NAM) calculated that forty-two percent of the world's population lived under some sort of sanctions imposed by the USNAM also stated that "the economic implications of the unilateral actions have been seriously underestimated" since the above figures did not take into account other countries affected by "secondary boycott" measures, which applied restrictions and penalties under U.S. law to foreign companies doing business in a targeted country. Furthermore, the study did not calculate the effects of sanctions that were imposed at the state and local level. According to the U.S. Council on Competitiveness, more than $6 billion in export sales and 120,000 jobs in the United States were put at risk by American unilateral sanctions. Not unexpectedly, Washington's allies, especially European governments, are increasingly reluctant to support unilateral U.S. punitive measures. Consequently, American sanctions are often unilateral.

In 1963, South Asia faced U.S. sanctions for the first time. Ironically, the country impacted was a much touted ally, Pakistan. On 30 August, 1963, the United States indefinitely postponed the $4.3 million in aid for modernization of the airport at Dhaka (then in East Pakistan) for it was slated as the terminus for flights to Communist China from Pakistan at a time when a U.S. — led embargo banned all air-links with the Chinese mainland. More substantive sanctions were to follow in 1965 after the outbreak of war between India and Pakistan. Washington suspended all military and economic aid to both sides. Even food aid under PL-480, a program that was based on commercial exports at concessional rates was restricted to both the countries. More sanctions were imposed on India after its solitary nuclear test in 1974. The sanctions were not just on goods and services but also restricted Indian scientists and technicians from interacting or training with their counterparts in the U.S. and elsewhere. In April 1979, in response to the Pakistan government's on-going nuclear weapons program, the CARTER administration suddenly suspended aid to the country only to resume it after the Soviets intervened in Afghanistan eight months later. Both Indian and Russian firms were sanctioned in 1992 when New Delhi tried to purchase cryogenic engines and technology for its space program from Moscow. In 1998, and with the support of Japan and a number of other nations, Washington slapped further sanctions on both countries in response to their nuclear tests. The U. S. embargo on the sale of GE F-404 jet engines which was to be fitted into the Indian Light Combat Aircraft (LCA) was a serious blow to the country's aeronautical industry. Similarly, helicopters whether on the drawing board or on board ships were grounded for lack of key components. Pakistan was pushed to the brink of a financial crisis, so the CLINTON administration removed a number of the sanctions, allowing the International Monetary Fund to resume assistance to the country. In the wake of 9/11, President GEORGE W. BUSH lifted almost all U.S. sanctions on Pakistan and India. Nevertheless, newer ones appear. In late 2006, sanctions were imposed on nine companies, six in China, two in India, and one in Austria for selling materials to Iran that could allegedly be used in the production of missiles and weapons of mass destruction. Another South Asian country, Burma, was under severe sanctions since the 1990s. Even state governments in the United States have tried to impose embargoes on Rangoon. However, state governments have generally had little success in doing so and a federal district court late 2005 struck down a Massachusetts law restricting state transactions with companies doing business in Burma.

Sanger, Margaret (1879-1966)

Nurse. Margaret Sanger was the founder of the American Birth Control League in 1921. She first went to India in 1935 at the invitation of the All India Women's' Conference and met Mahatma Gandhi as well. Both agreed on the need for family limitation in India. However, the Mahatma considered abstinence as the only moral way for family control. Instead, Sanger, with a greater understanding of human desires, launched the first birth control program in India. The program was based on contraception and abortion. Both theses forms of birth control found limited appeal in India. Accordingly, her return visit to India in 1952 was not a great success. Undaunted, she continued to visit India and published extensively on the need for family planning.

Saund, Dalip Singh (1899-73)

India-born U.S. Congressman (1956-64). Born in Chhajalwadi village, Amritsar district, Punjab, Saund was educated in a boarding school in Amritsar and at the Prince of Wales College in Jammu. He graduated with a BA in Mathematics from Panjab University in 1919. He then enrolled at the University of California, Berkeley in 1920 to study food preservation in the Department of Agriculture. Later, he switched to mathematics and received his MA in 1922 and Ph.D. in 1924. While a student in India, Saund had become an ardent follower of Mahatma GANDHI at a time when the latter's political star was just rising. His early perspicacity was reflected in his 1924 monograph, *Gandhi: The Man and his Message*. Saund was later to state, "My guideposts were two of the most beloved men in history, Abraham Lincoln and Mahatma Gandhi." In 1930 he wrote a full-length book, *My Mother India* as a stinging rebuttal to *Mother India* a muck-racking book on India by KATHERINE MAYO. Despite a doctorate, under U.S. immigration laws Saund had little choice but to work as a foreman on a cotton farm in Imperial Valley, California. Later, like other Indians in the region, he bought a farm but unlike most of his compatriots, he married a white woman, Marian Kosa, who under the laws of the day became stateless. Nevertheless, both actively participated in numerous civic activities. Saund also lobbied for Indian independence and citizenship rights along with others like J J SINGH, a New York based businessman who arrived in the U.S. in 1926 and formed India League of America in 1938 and Mubarak Ali Khan, a prosperous Arizona farmer who had established the India Welfare League a year earlier. Saund himself organized the Indian Association of America in the 1940s to fight racial discrimination. At long last in 1946, U.S. Congress passed the Luce-Celler Bill granting naturalization and immigration quotas for Indians. Saund took up American citizenship in 1949. Four years later, he was elected as a judge in the Riverside and Imperial counties solely due to his grassroots campaign in 1953. He was elected to the U.S. Congress in 1956 and was re-elected till he was incapacitated by a stroke in 1964. In Congress he opposed giving foreign aid solely to central governments because he thought it led to graft and corruption. Despite being the first elected

Congressman from Asia, Saund is little remembered perhaps because his last book, *Congressman From India*, was a disappointment. Unlike his forceful earlier writings, this later book was not insightful. Instead, it glossed over the racism, prejudice, personal and professional challenges that Saund encountered during his long years in America. Nevertheless, his contributions to American society were formally acknowledged in 2007 for his portrait was hung in the U.S. Capitol building in that year. It was also the golden jubilee of Indian independence.

Saur Revolution

Marxist coup in Kabul, Afghanistan on 27 April 1978 named after the Afghan month (Saur 1357). It was an unusual revolution for it enjoyed neither domestic nor international support. Nur Mohammad Taraki, the leader of the revolt, was told that a coup would not be welcome in Moscow. Later he was to boast, "(Though) we are a backward country not ready for revolution (but) I am now sitting in the presidential palace." However, the Soviets knew that the communist's radical domestic program of putting a limit on large landholdings and rural indebtedness, controls on bride wealth, commitment to modern education, etc., enjoyed little public support in the deeply conservative country. Furthermore, Taraki, despite persistent calls from Moscow, did little to enhance his personal credibility among the people. Though opposed to using Soviet forces to save an unpopular government, the Kremlin felt impelled to do so, especially as the Americans were supporting rebellion in the country since July 1979. Moscow's intervention in support of the Saur revolution contributed to the eventual unraveling of the Soviet Union itself and to the rise of widespread, confident, and militant Islamic fundamentalism.

(*See also*: ANTI-SOVIET RESISTANCE GROUPS IN AFGHANISTAN, GENEVA ACCORDS, and PEOPLE'S DEMOCRATIC PARTY OF AFGHANISTAN)

Sayyaf, Abdul Rasool (1946-)

Afghan warlord. Sayyaf studied theology in Egypt and Saudi Arabia and was a leading member of the Egyptian inspired Muslim Brotherhood (*Ikwan-i-Musalamin*). He returned to Afghanistan and was promptly jailed. However, he was soon released by his cousin,

HAFIZULLAH AMIN. Hence, he was the last of the significant anti-Soviet party leaders to be recognized by Pakistan during the Soviet intervention in Afghanistan. Despite his late arrival on the scene, he was elected to head the front of all anti-Soviet parties, the *Ittehad-i-Islami B'rai Azadi-i-Afghanistan* (Islamic Union for the Liberation of Afghanistan). The front soon imploded and Sayyaf was left with rump organization, *Ittehad-e Islami Sayyaf.* Consequently, among the Pakistan based anti-Soviet Afghan factions Sayyaf's was smaller but different. It included more militant Arabs than other Afghan faction and it had closer financial links to Saudi Arabia. Accordingly, Sayyaf maintained recruiting and liaison offices in the desert kingdom and shared strong ideological ties with Riyadh because unlike most Afghans, Sayyaf followed the Wahhabi sect of Islam, the dominant one in Saudi Arabia. Hence, he was opposed to the presence of U.S. troops in Saudi Arabia and was a fierce opponent of women's rights, refusing to meet or talk to females outside his family circle. Among his wealthy benefactors was OSAMA BIN LADEN. The two established common military camps and related infrastructure that was used for training and indoctrination of new recruits to fight in conflicts in other regions of the world like Chechnya, Bosnia-Herzegovina, and Southern Philippines. In the latter his name inspired the eponymous Abu Sayyaf terrorist group. His followers included the infamous, Kuwait-born, AL QAEDA senior commander, Khalid Sheikh Mohammed. He had joined the organization in 1987. In 1996 Sayyaf invited bin Laden back to Afghanistan from his Sudanese exile though the former had misgivings about the like-minded Taliban movement.

After 9/11, Sayyaf joined the Northern Alliance, notwithstanding his different religious and ideological affinities with other members of the alliance. He then joined the LOYA JIRGA to draft a new national constitution for the country. In the council he proved to be a trenchant and decisive leader. He put the word "Islamic" into "The Transitional Islamic State of Afghanistan," the country's name after the ouster of the TALIBAN from Kabul. Clerics loyal to him occupied the highest legal positions in the country's judicial system, and included the country's chief justice, Fazl Ahmad Shinwari. His future role is Afghanistan is likely to remain strong.

Scudder, John (1793-1855)

Missionary, physician. Scudder came to Ceylon (present day Sri Lanka) in 1819 on behalf of the Dutch Reformed Church. Twenty years later he moved to Madras (now Chennai). Thereafter three generations of Scudders devoted their lives to the Indian subcontinent. In 1918 his granddaughter, Ida, started a small hospital that became the Women's Christian Medical College and Hospital, Vellore. Male students were admitted 30 years later. The Scudders also set up numerous inter-faith programs including the Institute of Sikh Studies at the Baring Union Christian College in the small town of Batala in Punjab, the Henry Martyn Institute for Islamic Studies, Hyderabad, and the Christian Institute for Study of Society and Religion in Bangalore.

Sen, Amartya Kumar (1933-)

Indian economist. Winner of the Bank of Sweden Prize in Economic Sciences, 1998 (informally known as the "Nobel Prize for Economics"). The award recognized for his work on welfare economics, the underlying mechanisms of poverty, and political liberalism. Sen was born in Shantiniketan, West Bengal, the university town established by the poet and Nobel Laureate RABINDRANATH TAGORE. The poet supposedly gave the child the name Amartya (Bengali: "Out of the world"). He earned his PhD from Trinity College, Cambridge in 1959 and taught economics at a number of institutions including the University of Calcutta, Jadavpur University, Delhi University, Oxford University, London School of Economics, and Harvard University. Sen's seminal papers in the late 1960s and early 1970s developed the theory of social choice, which was conceptualized in the 1950s by the American economist, Kenneth Arrow, at RAND Corporation. Arrow proved that all voting rules, must inevitably contradict some basic democratic norms. Sen enriched the theory by using his interpretation of the history of economic thought and philosophy. It culminated in his 1981 book, *Poverty and Famines: An Essay on Entitlement and Deprivation*. He demonstrated that famines occur not simply from lack of food, but from the inequalities built into mechanisms for its distribution. Sen's revolutionary contribution to developmental economics and social indicators was the concept of "capability". He contended that governments should be measured against the concrete capabilities on their citizens. For instance, in the United States, citizens have a hypothetical "right" to vote. To Sen, such a right to vote was an empty concept as long as all the requisite conditions were not met so that the citizen had the capability to vote. These conditions could range from the very broad, such as the availability of education, to the very specific, such as transportation to the polls. Not unexpectedly, his work in developmental economics considerably influenced the formulation of the *Human Development Report* by the United Nations. Sen was exceptional among late twentieth-century economists in his insistence on asking questions related to "value," a subject long removed from "serious" economic consideration. He mounted one of the few major challenges to the economic model positing "self-interest" as the prime motivating factor of human activity. He was awarded India's highest civilian award, *Bharat Ratna*, in 1999, soon after having received the Nobel Prize. Sen is the Thomas W. Lamont University Professor at Harvard since 2003.

Shankar, Ravi (1920-)

Legendary Indian sitarist and musical composer. A disciple of Ustad Allaudin Khan, the founder of the *Mahar Gharana* of Indian classical music, Shankar is the best-known Indian musician in the West.

His career began in 1944 and he remains active to this day. He has composed musical scores for numerous films and ballets in India and the West. His musical score in films include such notable ones as the award-winning "Gandhi" and Satyajit Ray's acclaimed the "Apu Trilogy." By the 1960s Shankar became an intrinsic part of popular Western music following his collaboration with George Harrison in "Shankar Family & Friends" and his participation in the year long "Festival of India." In the U.S. he was featured on such legendary occasions as the Monterey Pop Festival, Concert for Bangladesh and the Woodstock Festival. His numerous accolades include honorary membership of the American Academy of Arts and Letters, fourteen doctorates, the two Grammy Awards. His recording "Tana Manna," brought Indian classical music into the "New age" with its unique blend of traditional Indian instruments and electronics. In other syncretic works, he wrote with Allaudin Khan, his tutor, the very first two concertos for the sitar and orchestra. Similarly, he recorded the original violin-sitar compositions with Yehudi Menuhin, music for the flute with virtuoso Jean Pierre Rampal, and with Japanese musicians like Hosan Yamamoto, the master of the *Shakuhachi* (an end blown flute made from the root of the bamboo), and Musumi Miyashita, the *Koto* (a 13 string zither) virtuoso. His elder brother, Uday, was a notable Indian classical dancer. His two daughters, the American NORAH JONES and Anoushka, are both talented musicians. He established the Ravi Shankar Foundation in Delhi to create the atmosphere, along with modern facilities, of the ancient traditions of the Gurukul System of learning for the few extremely talented and hardworking students.

Sharif, Mian Nawaz (1950-)

Pakistan's former prime minister. In 1986, the Pakistani military dictator, General ZIA UL-HAQ hand-picked Nawaz, an industrialist turned politician as the Chief Minister of Punjab. In the elections held in November 1998, after the death of Zia, Nawaz emerged as the most powerful political figure outside the Pakistan People's Party (PPP). With the help of Islamic Jamhurie Ittehad (IJI) he continued as the Chief Minister in Lahore, while BENAZIR BHUTTO, the leader of the PPP, took over as the Prime Minister in Islamabad. Each tried to unseat the other and failed. Finally the President, Gulam Ishaq Khan, dismissed both of them and ordered fresh elections. Nawaz, with covert support from the army, won and became the new prime minister in 1990. He then began feuding with the president. The army chief sacked both of them and a general election followed in 1993. Bhutto replaced Nawaz as the prime minister and kept him out of power in Punjab as well. Instability continued till the 1997 election, when Nawaz won with a huge majority in the National Assembly. As prime minister he moved the Thirteenth Constitutional Amendment to divest the president of the power, under Article 52(b) of the Eighth Amendment, to dismiss the Prime Minister and dissolve the National Assembly. He added another milestone to the Constitution when his Parliament adopted the anti-defection Bill as the Fourteenth Amendment. Nawaz also moved to control the judiciary and the armed forces. Pre-occupied with political maneuvering, the prime minister had little time for administration or for fiscal reforms. The U.S.-led economic sanctions following the nuclear tests in May 1998 brought the country close to bankruptcy. Undeterred, Pakistan tried to occupy the heights of Kargil to Kashmir in May 1999. The unexpectedly forceful but restrained Indian response apparently unnerved Pakistan, including Sharif, who rushed to Washington to seek a way out. The Pakistani military deflected blame for defeat in the Kargil war to weakness on the part of the prime minister and ousted him in bloodless coup when he tried to sack by Army Chief, General PERVEZ MUSHARRAF. Sharif though he was land-bound was charged with attempted hijacking, since the General was on board a commercial flight, when the prime minister had tried to sack him. Under American and Saudi pressure, the military government in Pakistan allowed him and his family to go into exile in Saudi Arabia. In 2007, the Pakistan Supreme Court reversed the agreement and allowed Sharif to return to Pakistan. On his return to Pakistan in September 2007, he was hastily dispatched back to Saudi Arabia only to return to Lahore under Saudi aegis in late November 2007. A lesser crowd than the one that welcomed Benazir Bhutto on her return to Karachi a month earlier was present a Lahore. In November 2007, unlike in September that year, Nawaz was accompanied by his brother Shahbaz, who too was a former chief minister of the key state of Punjab. In addition, in striking contrast, to Benazir Bhutto's homecoming no savage bomb attacks marked his return. Following her assassination on 27 December 2007, the effective control of her party, the PPP, passed to her husband the controversial ASIF ALI ZARDARI. He soon formed an unlikely electoral alliance with Nawaz Sharif. Both parties won substantial seats in the elections for the National Assembly in February 2008. A coalition government was formed by the two rivals with the PPP holding the key appointments including that of the prime minister. Subsequently, a legal judgment prevented Sharif from contesting a by-election seat for the National Assembly. Nevertheless the two parties stayed in the coalition government till the former General Pervez Musharraf resigned as the President of Pakistan. After much prevarication, Zardari refused to restore to office the sacked Chief

Justice Iftikhar Muhammad Choudhary. Sharif then formally withdrew from the coalition government in August 2008. He remains a powerful, perhaps more mature and introspective political leader in Pakistan, and even more so in key province of Punjab.

(*See also:* CLINTON, WILLIAM JEFFERSON)

Silicon Valley

The term was first used by the journalist Don Hoefler in 1971 in a couple of articles he wrote about the semiconductor industry around Palo Alto, California. Silicon first came to the valley in 1955, when a Stanford graduate student, William Shockley, who, along with some talented young scholars from the East Coast developed the transistor, based on the amplification of electrical current using silicon as the solid semi-conducting material. Semiconductors are usually solid elements or compounds that can selectively conduct electricity under some conditions but not under others, making them as useful mediums for the control of electrical current. Semiconductors are essential for the functioning of most electrical and electronic devices ranging from computer to digital audio players. Silicon is utilized to create most of the semiconductors commercially though dozens of other materials are in use as well. Since then the valley had acquired its name (silicon) and its image (association with high technology).

The initial impetus for the growth of high-technology industry in the region was Stanford University, founded 1891, by the eponymous Governor Leland Stanford. In the 1920s the university sought to improve its academic standing and strengthen its financial base by hiring highly respected faculty members from prestigious East Coast universities. An important newcomer was Professor Frederick Terman from Massachusetts Institute of Technology (MIT). Concerned by the loss of his most of his graduates to the East Coast because of a lack of jobs in the Valley, Terman encouraged his students to launch companies near the university on land leased from the institution itself. Among them were William Hewlett and David Packard. In 1937 their company, Hewlett-Packard, was started in the now-iconic garage in Palo Alto. In the same year, William Hansen, a professor of physics, teamed with Sigurd and Russell Varian to develop the klystron tube, a device for bunching of electrons to produce electric fields which could be used for the generation and amplification of ultra-high frequencies. Radar and microwaves were to follow. During World War II and the Cold War, further funding and development of the high-technology industry in the region continued.

Twenty years after the transistor, in March 1975, some students formed the Homebrew Computer Club to experiment with the building of compact computers that could be used at home. The PC (Personal Computer) revolution had begun. It coincided with increased immigration of technocrats from the Indian subcontinent. The software engineers gravitated to the Silicon Valley to write software for applications from mainframe computers for use in the burgeoning PC market. Twenty years later, the same engineers, familiar with the software they had written earlier were busy making sure that systems were capable of handling the changes from 1900 to 2000 (the Y2K PROBLEM). The Immigration and Nationality Act of 1990 further favored the immigration of engineers by almost tripling the number of visas granted occupational skills from 54,000 to 140,000 annually. Hence, between 1975 and 1990, Silicon Valley's technology companies created more than 150,000 jobs and the foreign-born population of the region more than doubled to almost 350,000. One third of all scientists and engineers were foreign-born. The majority were of Chinese or Indian descent. Of the 11,443 firms launched during this period, 2,001 (seventeen percent) were run by Chinese and 774 (seven percent) by Indians. Among the latter was a sizable subset of engineers who, though of Indian origin, had grown up in Africa and few had actually lived or studied in India. Another three percent were from other countries of the Indian subcontinent. The vast majority worked well together and launched a number of cooperative ventures. It is highly probable that the number of companies owned by these immigrant groups was much higher because many firms though owned and started by Asians had non-Asian CEOs as venture capital financing at the time often mandated that non-Asian senior executives be present in the company.

A young Intel engineer and his three Indian roommates started the Silicon Valley Indian Professionals Association (SIPA) in 1987 to provide an organization to tackle professionals challenges, the most common being the presence of a glass ceiling in the region's established companies. Most Indians responded to the glass ceiling by starting their own businesses and by joining SIPA instead of other pre-existing professional associations. SIPA's mission, too, changed from individual professional advancement to furthering Indo-U.S. business ties and to "fill the information gap" between the U.S. and India. Accordingly, the association sponsored regular seminars and workshops where the U.S.-based Indian professionals attempted to provide their employers and peers with a better understanding of the recently opened Indian market and to concomitantly explore professional opportunities for themselves in India. SIPA lost some of its momentum when its founder returned to India in 1992. By coincidence, during the same year, an older generation of sub-continental immigrants started The Indus Entrepreneur (TiE) with the goal of nurturing fledgling companies founded by younger South Asians. Its founding members included three of the region's most successful Indian entrepreneurs: Suhas Patil, a professor from MIT and founder of Cirrus Logic, Prabhu Goel, founder of Gateway Design Automation, and Kanwal Rekhi, who started and ran Excelan until it merged with Novell. Forty charter members formed the core of the organization. Charter membership was by invitation only and included successful entrepreneurs, corporate executives, and senior professionals with roots in or an interest in South Asia. The founders called themselves Indus (rather than Indian) entrepreneurs so as to encourage other South Asians such as Pakistanis, Bangladeshis, and Nepalese to join them. However, the vast majority of members continued to be of Indian origin. TiE instituted monthly meetings with the objective of creating a forum for networking among themselves as well as for assisting younger South Asians to start their own businesses. It also launched chapters in other parts of the country and in various Indian cities like Bangalore, but the center of gravity remained in Silicon Valley. TiE's most distinguishing role was in cross-generational investing and mentoring of younger members by providing business and financial advice, and professional contacts. Vinod Khosla, a co-founder of Sun Microsystems and then a partner at venture capital firm Kleiner, Perkins summarized the situation in the new millennium and its challenges by stating, "the ethnic networks clearly play a role here: people talk to each other, they test their ideas, they suggest other people they know, who are likely to be of the same ethnicity. There is more trust because the language and cultural approach are so similar." This emerging *esprit de corps* may be of great help to the next generation of Indian-American technocrats.

(*See also:* BUSSINESS PROCESS OUTSORCING AND INFORMATION TECHNOLOGY IN INDIA)

Singh, Jagjit (J.J.) (1897-1984)

Political activist. Singh the son of a prominent civil servant, born in Rawalpindi (now Pakistan), came to the U.S. in 1926. During World War II, he was president of Indian League and Indian Chamber of Commerce and arranged for the Connecticut Republican Congresswoman Claire Booth Luce to visit India. He convinced the former journalist and editor of *Vanity Fair* magazine to support Indian independence. She was the wife of the media mogul and *Time* magazine founder Henry Luce, and used her considerable influence in the media to endorse an end of British colonialism, especially in India. Meanwhile, Mrs. Luce and New York Democrat Congressman Emanuel Cellar, Chairman of the House Judiciary Committee, jointly introduced a bill in Congress to the grant of U.S. citizenship to Indian immigrants. For four years, the bill languished in Congressional Committees. Finally, on 3 July 1946, President TRUMAN signed the Luce-Celler Bill granting Indians the right of naturalization and established a small quota for immigrants from the subcontinent. It was an enormous achievement as the Indian community in the U.S. numbered less than 4,000 and the country was still under British rule. Singh's pre-eminent role in the passage of the new legislation was acknowledged by Mahatma GANDHI himself. After independence, Singh returned to India and lived out his remaining years in prosperous anonymity in Delhi's suburban sprawl.

Singh, Manmohan (1932-)

India's first Sikh Prime Minister. Dr. Singh was sworn in on 22 May 2004 after the Congress party alliance won an unexpectedly large number of seats in the Parliamentary elections. Mrs. Sonia Gandhi, the Italian born widow of the slain former Prime Minister RAJIV GANDHI and the elected leader of the Congress Parliamentary Party sprang another surprise when she declined the prime ministership and nominated Singh instead. His appointment was especially notable as it came twenty years after India witnessed significant tensions between the Indian central (federal) government and the Sikh community. Singh, an economist, received his doctorate in 1962 from Oxford University (Nuffield College) and served in the International Monetary Fund. Before becoming prime minister, he was an advisor to the party president Sonia Gandhi and had earlier served as finance minister under Prime Minister PV NARASIMHA RAO (1991-96). The economic liberalization in 1991 was prompted by an acute balance of payments crisis whereby the Indian government was left without sufficient reserves to meet its obligations. The Rao-Singh duo to persist with reforms after the balance of payments crisis had passed and did not yield to opposition from entrenched interests in the country. As a political leader he was relatively insignificant and was considered as a stop-gap figure before Sonia's son and heir-apparent, Rahul Gandhi took over the Congress Party. Even the Leftist parties, who supported the government from the outside, rarely addressed Singh directly on major political issues. Furthermore, Singh's lack of knowledge about party affairs and key decisions made by Congress leaders has left him embarrassed on numerous occasions. Despite these handicaps Singh developed a powerful working relationship with U.S. President GEORGE W. BUSH. The two leaders signed a landmark nuclear deal that ended India's exclusion from the global trade in civilian nuclear fuels and technologies. One of his three daughters is a Yale Law School graduate and works in New York City with the American Civil Liberties Union (ACLU).

Sino-Pakistan-American Connection

In 1955, Pakistan was the recipient of American military aid to resist communist expansionism, and Sino-Indian relations were close and effusive. Nonetheless, Pakistani Prime Minister, Mohammed Ali Bogra, at the Afro-Asian Summit at Bandung, Indonesia pointedly distinguished the differences between the two Communist giants, the Soviet Union and China. Bogra portrayed the Soviets as imperialistic, hegemonic, and expansionist, but urged the conferees not to apply the same label to China. This remarkable speech was made despite negligible Sino-Pakistani ties and marked the first step in the development of a triangular nexus between China, Pakistan and the United States. Following the U-2 incident in 1960, when an American spy-plane took off from Peshawar and was shot down deep over Soviet territory, Pakistani dictator AYUB KHAN, despite his cloying pro-Americanism, cautiously tried to reduce his country's total dependence on the United States. A younger minister, ZULFIKAR ALI BHUTTO, had already contended that better ties with Beijing would strengthen Pakistan's international position. Hence, in 1961, Ayub agreed with him that Pakistan should vote at the United Nations to admit the mainland Chinese Communists into the U.N. and expel the Taiwan based Chinese Nationalists. The sudden and dramatic move caught the KENNEDY administration by surprise. The gap between the United States and Pakistan further widened when civil aviation links between Pakistan and China were established in 1963. Such a linkage was a breach in the then Western ban on commercial ties with Communist China. Washington responded by refusing to provide the $4.3 million loan needed for the construction of a new airport at Dhaka, East Pakistan (now Bangladesh). This airport was slated for the Pakistan International Airlines (PIA) flights to China. The Chinese then stepped in and built the airfield. After the U.S. arms embargo in the 1965 Indo-Pakistan War, Islamabad looked northeast towards Beijing to weapons and political support. China promptly obliged and became Pakistan's "all-weather" ally. The bilateral relationship became trilateral on 9 July 1971, when the U.S. Secretary of State, HENRY A. KISSINGER., flew from Islamabad to Beijing on a PIA aircraft for secret talks with the Chinese Premier Zhou En Lai. RICHARD M. NIXON, a well-known friend of Pakistan, then became the first U.S. President to visit China. Over the years, Beijing has steadfastly supported Pakistan, notwithstanding the vicissitudes in Sino-American relations and Pakistani-U.S. ties. Chinese assistance to Pakistan in the development of nuclear weapons and ballistic missile technologies has repeatedly exacerbated tensions between Islamabad and Washington but the American response, in general, has been under-stated. The Sino-

Pakistan ties apparently remain so strong that General MUSHARRAF flew to Beijing for consultations before hosting President Bush in Islamabad in March 2006.

South East Asia Treaty Organization (SEATO), 1954-1977

American led anti-communist pact. An alliance initially formed in 1954 as the Southeast Asia Collective Defense Treaty with the mission of preventing further Communist gains in Southeast Asia after the French collapse in Indochina. Members of the grouping were Australia, Britain, France, New Zealand, Pakistan, the Philippines, Thailand and the United States, with the treaty was supplemented by a Pacific Charter, affirming the rights of Asian and Pacific peoples to equality and self-determination and set goals of economic, social and cultural cooperation between member countries. However, when the U.S. tried to get SEATO to buttress the American effort in Vietnam, both France and Pakistan withheld their support. Due to its rule of unanimous action, the alliance was thus unable to intervene in Indo-China. After the U.S. withdrawal from Indo-China, SEATO lost its relevance and was dissolved in 1977.

Spelling Bee Contests

Spelling bee contests are dominated by the Indian-American community. The term first appeared in print in 1875, but the word was used orally for several years before that. The United States National Spelling Bee was started in 1925 by the *Louisville Courier-Journal*, a major newspaper in the eponymous city in Kentucky. The objective of the contests was to promote excellence in the proper usage of English language among children. In 1941, the EW Scripps Company, headquartered in nearby Cincinnati, Ohio, acquired sponsorship of the program and made it into the nation's largest educational promotion that was administered on a not-for-profit basis. Known as the Scripps National Spelling Bee, the contest attracts about 260 sponsors in the United States, Europe, Canada, New Zealand, Guam, Jamaica, Puerto Rico, the U.S. Virgin Islands, The Bahamas, and American Samoa. After a series of qualifying rounds, the finals are held in Washington, DC in May-June each year. In recent years, descendants of Indian immigrants have dominated the contest, winning the first place six times during 1995-2005. Enthusiasm for the contest spread throughout the community with chat rooms and blogs where Indian-Americans would discuss the spellings of words. At times, the contests acquired obsessive levels of parental participation and the pressure on children to win at the exclusion of other activities. Some winners became celebrities for a while like the thirteen year-old eighth grader who won the title in 2005. He appeared on all major television networks and was prominently featured in various mass-circulation publications. On returning to his school in California, he even received a marriage proposal. Perhaps, the hype was too much for a two year drought followed. Then 2008 turned out to be a bumper year with three out of the final four being of Indian origin. By then television ratings for the show had slipped perhaps because it was slotted on Fridays against popular entertainment shows. Previously the finals were held in mid-week and the ratings were higher. In 2008 the winner, an Indian-American, had correctly spelled guerdon which means "something that one has earned or gained." Some in the community wondered whether Spelling Bee contests were indeed guerdon. Others had little doubt for contest winners are often invited on Broadway shows for Guest-Spots. A musical, too, was launched on Broadway in 2005. That year it won two Tony awards for being the "Best Book of a Musical" and having the "Best Featured Actor in a Musical." Other countries and other organizations within the U.S. have promoted similar contests. The first South Asian Spelling Bee Contest in the United States was announced in New York City in June 2008. Two years earlier, Annapurna, an enterprise of the giant multinational company, Hindustan Lever, had instituted the first such competition in India.

Sri Lanka-U.S. Relations

American whalers and merchant ships first harbored on the island of Sri Lanka, then called Ceylon in 1789, while the U.S. Constitution was being drafted. Within 20 years, American missionaries were active, especially around Jaffna. Among them was Harriet Winslow, the great-great-grandmother of JOHN F. DULLES, the U.S. Secretary of State (1953-59). She founded the Uduvil Girls' School in 1824. It was the first boarding school for young women in Asia. In turn, by the 1830s, the island greatly contributed to American education for it was the major exporter of graphite to the United States. Graphite is the form of carbon commonly known as lead used in lead pencils. The first U.S. Consulate opened in Colombo in 1870. Ten years later, Colonel Henry Olcott, the president of the THEOSOPHICAL SOCIETY moved to Sri Lanka, became a Buddhist and was instrumental in the revival of Theravada Buddhism on the island.

Substantial U.S. involvement in Sri Lanka began in World War II. The country was then a British colony and served as the headquarters of the South East Asia Command. U.S. warships used the fine facilities at Trincomalee harbor and American servicemen were entertained by radio broadcasts from two transmitters on the island. This tradition endures: The International Broadcast Bureau, formerly the Voice of America (VOA), uses transmission facilities in Sri Lanka. Since independence in 1948, ties between the two countries have been cordial based partly on shared democratic traditions. For five years from 1960 onwards there were tensions related to the amount of compensation paid to U.S. companies nationalized by the left-leaning government led by Sirimavo Bandaranaike the world's first woman Prime Minister. In 1977, the island became the first country in South Asia to liberalize its economy. Washington strongly supported the new economic policies and focused its aid on the reduction of unemployment and on improving the general quality of life by developing new roads, housing, sanitation, etc. In addition, the U.S. encouraged various NGOs and foundations to actively participate in the country's growth. As a result, the country had received $1.63 billion in foreign aid by 2005, and the U. S. imported 63 percent of the island's most important export, garments. The result was the highest rise in social indicators in the region. Despite progress, the island is not self-sufficient in food, has high rates of inflation and is wracked by political and sectarian violence. Since 1983, the latter has bordered on civil war between the Tamil minority and Sinhala majority. However, Washington steadfastly supports the country's territorial integrity and democratic institutions. Accordingly, the U.S. branded the most powerful Tamil secessionist group, the Liberation Tigers of Tamil Eelam

(LTTE, often called Tamil Tigers) as a terrorist organization in October 1997. In the wake of the 2004 tsunami, America provided an additional $67 million in relief aid.

Stars and Stripes

A possible Indian connection with the U.S. flag. The origins of the American flag, commonly known as the Stars and Stripes, are unclear but not for want of contenders. Among them is the seventeenth century flag of the East India Company. It consisted of thirteen alternating red and white stripes with the odd numbers being red. The upper stripes were broken by a canton at the corner and contained the red cross of St. George on a white field. The ensign was in use at the time of the American Revolution. It may have been one of the models for the American flag.

Star Spangled Banner and India

Indian connections with the U.S. National Anthem. On 13 September 1814 an American lawyer, Francis Scott Key (1779-1843), was detained overnight on board the British warship, HMS *Minden*, constructed at Duncan Docks, Bombay by Wadia Master Ship Builders from Surat. That night Key witnessed the British attack on Fort McHenry, eight miles away in Baltimore Harbor. By next dawn's early light, amidst the rockets' red glare, Key was delighted to find the American flag still flying over the fort. The bedazzling rockets were designed by Robert Congreve. Fifteen years earlier, as an artillery officer, he had taken the rocket technology from the defeated forces of Tipu Sultan in India and then inducted missiles into the British army and navy. Key composed a poem called "The Defense of Fort McHenry." It was written to match the meter of the English song, "To Anacreon in Heaven." It was later put to music and sung as the Star Spangled Banner and became the national anthem of the United States in 1931.

Stinger

Portable shoulder-fired American infrared heat seeking anti-aircraft missile with a high explosive warhead. The missile weighed 34.5 pounds and has a range from three to five miles depending on the model. The missile first entered service with the U.S. forces in 1981. Three hundred were first supplied to the Afghan MUJAHIDEEN in 1986. Altogether, an estimated total of 250 grip stocks and 2,000 missiles were shipped to the guerrillas during the Soviet-Afghan War. The number that actually reached the guerrillas is unclear. Perhaps 80 percent did. The Afghans achieved the remarkable strike rate of 65-75 percent, three times better than their Pakistani or American counterparts. The effect on the battlefield was stunning. In the next three years, Soviet backed forces lost 200-275 aircraft and the much-feared Hind D helicopter gunship never regained its tactical dominance. In a controversial move, the U.S. Central Intelligence Agency rewarded Mujahideen commanders with two additional stingers for each one used in the successful downing a Soviet aircraft. Apparently, the guerrillas stockpiled 300-500 stingers and sold some of them. A second rung commander, Mullah Malang, reportedly sold four launchers and sixteen missiles for one million dollars each to Iran. So did a first-rung commander, HEKMATYAR. China, too, obtained several stingers and was supposedly trying to reverse engineer the missile. The U.S. responded by instituting a buy-back program paying between $80,000-200,000 per missile. Reportedly, it netted only seventy. The number still operational in Afghanistan is unclear but does not appear to be much as NATO forces have not encountered them since the U.S. led intervention in 2001. AHMAD SHAH MASSOUD paid the missile the ultimate compliment stating, "There are only two things that the Afghan's love to have: the Koran and stingers."

Stokes, Samuel Evans Jr. (1888-1946)

American missionary and horticulturist. Stokes, a Quaker from Philadelphia, Pennsylvania, arrived in India in 1904 to work in a leper colony. While he was recuperating from the summer heat in the Simla Hills a severe earthquake, struck the region. He went to Kotgarh (north of Simla) to help out. At Kotgarh Stokes was moved by the extreme poverty of the people and decided to stay there and work with the hill-folk. In 1911, his mother visited him and realized that he planned to settle down in the area. Therefore, she bought a 200-acre tea plantation to provide him with financial support. The following year he married Agnes, a Christian Rajput girl from the neighboring hills. On a visit to the States in 1915 he came across the newly patented strain of apples called "Red Delicious." After careful study, he concluded that the climate in the Simla Hills was suitable for growing this strain of the fruit. In 1920 his mother sent him some saplings as a Christmas gift. The saplings bore their first fruit in 1926. Seventy years later the annual crop of apples from Kotgarh was 1.2 million cases, each case containing 100 apples. By then 75 percent of the population was engaged in the prosperous business of apple farming. Stokes joined the Indian National Congress and was the only American to serve on the All-India Congress Committee. He was also one of the few Americans to be charged with sedition by the British and was sentenced to jail for six months. He also joined the *Arya Samaj* (a reformist Hindu movement) in 1932 and changed his name to Satyanand. Hence, a missionary sent to convert the natives became one of them and then he led a movement for the reconversion of local Christian converts back to Hindus. He was partially successful. His eldest son Prem Chand, though trained as a mechanical and electrical engineer, stayed in Kotgarh to further develop the orchards. His youngest daughter-in-law, Vidya Stokes, joined politics and was the President of the Congress Party in Himachal Pradesh and Speaker of the State Legislature. In 2005, she became the President of the Indian Women's Hockey Federation.

Stone, Edward Durrell (1902-1978)

American modernist architect. Educated at the University of Arkansas, Harvard, and at the Massachusetts Institute of Technology (MIT), Durrell was influenced by the use of marble, grills and functional use of space and running water in Indian architecture. Major examples include are the American Embassy building in New Delhi (1958) the National Assembly and Presidential Palace in Islamabad, Pakistan (1960s), and the Kennedy Center for the Performing Arts, Washington, DC (1971). His other strikingly similar works were the Pakistan Institute of Nuclear Science and Technology (PINSTECH), Nilore (near Islamabad) and the State University of New York at Albany, New York.

SubbaRow, Yella Pragada (1895-1948)

Renowned Indian Pharmaceutical scientist. In medical college SubbaRow insisted on wearing homespun (*khadi*) surgical gowns as a symbol of his nationalism. The British professor of surgery blocked him from receiving the MBBS degree. Accordingly, SubbaRow was given the lesser qualification, LM&S. Thereafter, he became a researcher at the Madras Ayurvedic College where the British had little influence. However, as facilities for research were scarce in India, he sought opportunities in the United States. Accordingly, in 1923 with borrowed funds he enrolled at the School of Tropical Medicine, Harvard University. At Harvard he collaborated with Dr. Cyrus H. Fiske in the calorimetric determination of phosphorous thereby elucidating biochemical processes in the physiology of the contraction of muscles. He also worked on the identification and isolation of nicotinic acid, whose deficiency causes the disease known as pellagra. But, his anti-British past caught up with him. At Harvard, he could not be promoted since he did not have the MBBS degree. However, academe's loss was industry's gain. In 1940 he joined Lederle Laboratories at Pearl River, New York. For the next eight years he was instrumental in synthesizing an important array of medicines such as folic acid, teroptrin, sulfamethazine, aureomycin and hetrazan. The SubbaRow Memorial Library was established in his honor at Pearl River, New York.

Subrahmanyan, Chandrasekhar (1910-1995)

American astrophysicist of Indian origin, Nobel laureate (Physics, 1983). The Nobel Prize was awarded "for his theoretical studies of the physical processes of importance to the structure and evolution of the stars." Subrahmanyan received his doctorate in 1933 from Trinity College, Cambridge, England. At Cambridge, the astrophysicist first calculated the eponymous Chandrasekhar Limit while working with a Brazilian colleague, Mario Schenberg. His calculations were challenged by the British physicist Arthur Eddington. Racial prejudice was also involved. Embittered, Chandrasekhar moved to the United States becoming one of the first Indian scientists to do so. He was also among the first to become a naturalized citizen of the United States (1953). He served on the faculty of the University of Chicago from 1937 until his death in 1995. In 1999, NASA named the third of its four 'Great Observatories' Chandra in his honor. The name for the observatory was selected by a contest which attracted 6,000 entries from all 50 states and 61 other countries. The asteroid, 1958 Chandra, also bears his name.

Suu Kyi, Aung San (1945-)

Burmese political leader, Nobel laureate (Peace, 1991). She is the daughter of the late Burmese nationalist leader, General Aung San, who had negotiated the end of British colonial rule in Burma in 1948. After early education in Burma and India (her mother, Khin Kyi, was the Burmese ambassador in New Delhi in the 1960s), she moved to Oxford University. In 1972 she married Michael Aris, a well-respected Oxford University academic specializing in Tibetan culture. The couple and their two sons lived quietly in England until she returned to Burma in April 1988 to be with her ailing mother. Suu Kyi had not planned for a lengthy stay in Burma as per her husband and their two sons who had stayed behind in Britain. However, her return to her native land coincided with student disturbances in response to the worsening economic situation in the country. On 15 August 1988, India's Independence Day, Suu Kyi, a follower of Mahatma GANDHI's philosophy of non-violence, committed her first political act. She sent an open letter to the government asking for the formation of an independent consultative committee to prepare for multi-party elections in the country. Then in keeping with the south Asian tradition of daughters following their parents into politics (INDIRA GANDHI, BENAZIR BHUTTO, Chandrika Kumaratunga, Megawati. Sukarnoputri, and others), she became a founding member of the National League for Democracy (NLD) on 27 September 1988. A week earlier, the military had deposed one of their own, General Ne Win and his Burmese Socialist Program Party (BSPP). A new ruling junta called the State Law and Order Restoration Council (SLORC) was established. In response to SLORC's brutal suppression of the students, NLD swiftly transformed itself into a political party and surprised the military by getting 82 percent of the vote in national elections in 1990, though Suu Kyi herself was under house arrest since July 1989. The military regime, however, refused to relinquish power and further intensified political repression. She was offered her personal freedom on the condition that she would leave the country. Suu Kyi refused. Cut off from the world at large, she met her husband for the last time during Christmas 1995. In March 1999, Michael Aris died of prostate cancer in London, England, having been denied permission by the Burmese dictatorship to visit her. She remains in Burma, in and out of house arrest. Since 2004, the U.S. has periodically pressured the Burmese government to unconditionally release her. In 2006 she was voted as the number one "Hero of our Time" in a poll conducted by the respected British news magazine, *New Statesman.* Occasionally the military rulers allowed her access to other leaders. That year she was allowed to meet Ibrahim Gambari, U.N. Undersecretary General (USG) of Department of Political Affairs. It was the first meeting with a foreign official since 2004. On the other hand, her house arrest, set to expire on 27 May 2006, was extended for yet another year despite a personal appeal by Kofi Annan, the then Secretary-General of the United Nations. Further pressure was mounted on her in early 2007, for she was accused of tax evasion by spending her Nobel Prize money outside of the country. The accusation followed the defeat of a U.S.-sponsored United Nations Security Council resolution condemning Myanmar as a threat to international security.

Anti-government protests again erupted on 15 August 2007, the 60th anniversary of Indian independence. The immediate cause was the unannounced decision of the ruling junta, the State Peace and Development Council (SPDC, the successor to the equally secretive and brutal SLORC), to remove fuel subsidies which caused the price of diesel and petrol to suddenly double and the cost of Compressed Natural Gas (CNG) used for buses, etc., to increase by 500 percent. Led by students and opposition political activists, the demonstrations were at first dealt with quickly and harshly by the dictatorship. About a month later, the protests acquired a different character. The widely respected Buddhist clergy, too, joined the protest marches, but to little avail. After a week of unrest, another government crackdown succeeded in containing the opposition. However, at the same time the government launched a diplomatic offensive. On Mahatma Gandhi's birthday, 2 October 2007, Gambari again met her after seeing General

Than Shwe and other members of the ruling junta. For the first time in four years the state television broadcasts showed Suu Kyi with Gambari. It was considered a small step in the revival of the political process in the country. It was followed by talk in November between Suu Kyi and specially appointed liaison minister Aung Kyi, a senior member of the ruling junta. Another first in three years was meeting with her political allies in National League for Democracy. Despite these gestures and the promulgation of a pathway to democracy, there has been little substantive action by the ruling junta. Her older brother, a U.S. citizen, lives in San Diego, California.

Swami Vivekananda, (1863-1902)

Hindu missionary, Pre-Monastic Name Narendranath Dutta. In 1893 at the Parliament of Religions held in conjunction with the World's Fair in Chicago, Illinois, in 1893, a then unknown monk from Calcutta, Swami Vivekananda, spoke of Hinduism as the mother of all religions and as the faith that that bestowed on humanity both tolerance and universal acceptance. The Swami's short address brought hundreds of parliamentarians to their feet as they applauded him for two full minutes. Vivekananda had become the first Hindu celebrity-monk. Before his trip to the United States few Hindu high caste ecclesiastical scholars ventured beyond India's shores for fear of losing their caste by crossing the seas. Accordingly, Swami Vivekananda he was the first well-known Hindu Swami to introduce Hinduism, Yoga (a philosophy that focuses on meditation as the conduit to self-knowledge and liberation, though it is now primarily associated with physical postures and exercises), and Vedanta to the West. Vedanta is a combination of two words, *Veda* (knowledge) and *anta* (the goal of). The philosophy forms the foundations of Hinduism based on the sacred scriptures, the four Vedas. During his stay in United States the Swami's outspoken, witty, and courageous remarks were widely disseminated. In March 1896 Swami Vivekananda was invited to lecture before the Graduate Philosophical Society at Harvard University. After his lecture, he was the first Indian to be offered the Chair in Eastern Philosophy. Being a monk, he declined. Nevertheless, he founded the first American Vedanta Society in New York City before returning to India in 1896. Swami Vivckananda was the most celebrated disciple of the nineteenth century sage, Swami Ramakrishna Paramhansa. The latter normally taught duality (good and evil) and Bhakti (devotion) to his devotees but he singled out the young Vivekananda for the study of Advaita Vedanta for five years. It is the philosophy of non-dualism and examines the relationship between Brahman, the source of everything, and Atman, the self. The *Upanishads* are the primary source for exploring these issues from different perspectives. Following Swami Ramakrishna's demise in August 1886, Vivekananda became a monk and later established the Ramakrishna Mission in honor of his mentor. After his triumphs in the West, Swami Vivekananda had a tremendous impact on society in India itself. Hindus developed greater self-confidence in their faith and the rate of conversion to Christianity slowed down significantly. Swami Vivekananda did not limit himself to the spiritual. For example, he advised the industrialist, JAMSETJI NUSSERWANJI TATA, to set up the Indian Institute of Science in Bangalore.

T

Tagore, Rabindranath (1861-1941)

Indian poet and Nobel laureate (Literature, 1913). Tagore was fascinated by the United States and admired the country for its scientific and technological achievements. Accordingly, he sent his son, Rathindra Nath, to study agriculture at the University of Illinois, rather than to the traditional centers of higher learning in England, Oxford or Cambridge. The great poet himself first visited the country in 1912 accompanied by his son and daughter-in-law. The son persuaded the father to spend a few quiet months at Urbana, Illinois. While at the university of Illinois at Urbana, Tagore wrote his first original prose in English, which he later delivered as a lecture at Harvard University. He was still at Urbana when the India Society published his greatest work, *Geetanjali*, in London. Altogether, Tagore visited the United States on five occasions, commanding huge fees for his speeches and appearances. The *Minneapolis Tribune* noted that he managed to admonish America at the rate of $700 per scold and plead for Indian independence at the same time. His last trip was in 1930 and was a greater success than his penultimate one when he was harassed by immigration officials at the Canadian border and spent his time in widely criticizing KATHERINE MAYO's shallow, muckraking book, *Mother India*.

Tahir-Kheli, Shirin Raziuddin (1944-)

Special Assistant to the U.S. President and National Security Council, Senior Director for Democracy, Human Rights and International Operations (2003-). Born in Hyderabad, India. Tahir-Kheli's father migrated to Pakistan after Partition. Tahir-Kheli did an M.A. and PhD in International Relations from the University of Pennsylvania and was an Associate Professor for Political Science at Temple University when she was tapped by the REAGAN administration to join the Policy Planning Staff in the Office of the U.S. Secretary of State in 1982.

Subsequently, she was the Director for Political-Military Affairs at the National Security Council (NSC) in 1984-1986 and Director for Near East and South Asia (1986-1988). She was given the rank of an ambassador on being appointed as the Alternate U.S. representative for Special Political Affairs at the United Nations (1990-1993) and on the Presidential Commission on Public Service (1992-1993).

With the return to office of the Republican administration in 2001, Tahir-Kheli was back in public service as the head of the U.S. Delegation to the U.N. Commission on Human Rights in 2001 and on the U.S. Commission on International Religious Freedom. On South Asia she considers that "India's role as a regional power suffers from its distraction in the dispute with Pakistan. An openly hostile and nuclear-armed Pakistan is not in India's interest, nor does it help foreign investment throughout the region."

Taliban

Religious students. Seminaries were first established in Afghanistan soon after the arrival of Islam in the country in the seventh century. Students (Taliban in Arabic) were an important part of the social fabric in most Islamic countries, including Afghanistan. Young men assisted in running schools, mosques, and shrines, performed various religious and social services, and served as *Mujahideen* when necessary. Hence, groups of Taliban were loosely organized on a regional basis during the war against the Soviet intervention in Afghanistan (1979-89). The politicized, sinister, militarized, mostly ill-educated zealots that emerged in the Afghanistan-Pakistan region in late 1994 were a new phenomenon. Their beginnings were mundane: Afghan youth were recruited from select madrassas by Pakistani trucking interests to provide security to convoys of commercial trucks as they traversed through lawless Afghanistan on the trade routes from Pakistan to Central Asia. Most recruits were from madrassas established by the *Jamiat Ulema-e-Islam* (JUI) for Afghan refugees in Pakistan. Two madrassas, the *Dar-ul-Uloom Sarhad* at Peshawar, the largest religious school of its kind in the Northwest Frontier Province (NWFP) and *Darul uloom Haqqania* at Akora Khattak provided most of the leadership in the Taliban. Both the JUI and the Taliban were dominated by Pashtuns, an ethnic group that straddles the Pakistan-

Afghan border. The leader of JUI, Maulana Fazl ur-Rehman, was a political ally of Prime Minister BENAZIR BHUTTO. Hence, Rehman in collaboration with the army and the INTER-SERVICES INTELLIGENCE (ISI) trained and equipped the Taliban. The new militia first took control of the city of Qandahar in 1994 and then steadily advanced with little bloodshed to Kabul by September 1996.

While members of the Taliban were Sunni Muslim Pashtuns (also referred to as Pathans), their rivals for power, the Northern Alliance was dominated by Tajiks, Hazaras, Uzbeks, Turkmen and Ismailis. The latter, along with the mongoloid Hazaras were Shiites and suffered the most in Taliban-occupied areas. With the seizure of Mazar-i Sharif on August 1998, the Taliban consolidated its hold over 90 percent of Afghanistan. Though the Taliban regime, proclaimed the Islamic Emirate of Afghanistan the new rulers in Kabul received diplomatic recognition from just its three patron states: Pakistan, Saudi Arabia and the United Arab Emirates. The Northern Alliance continued to retain the country's seat at the United Nations, though it held only a thin sliver of land in the northeast. Initially the Taliban's widespread support among the country's population surprised the other warring factions. Most Afghans, weary of conflict and anarchy, were relieved by the ouster of the corrupt and often brutal warlords. In contrast, the devout Taliban, under the direction of the little-educated, secretive one-eyed veteran of the Anti-Soviet war, Mullah Muhammad Omar, eliminated much of the corruption, restored law and order, and facilitated the resumption of trade and commerce. However, the young zealots also instituted a very strict interpretation of *Sharia*, or Islamic law. Public executions and punishments (such as floggings) became regular events at Afghan soccer stadiums. Joyful activities like kite-flying were outlawed. In order to root out other "non-Islamic" influences, television, music, and the internet were banned. The ire of the Taliban also fell on the two 1,400 year old giant statutes of the Buddha carved in the Indo-Greek style at Bamiyan, 230 kilometers (143 miles) north-west of Kabul. The two statues measuring 55 and 37 meters (180 and 121 feet) high were the largest examples of the standing Buddha carvings in the world and UNESCO had listed the entire complex as a world heritage site. Despite world-wide pleas to spare the monuments, the Taliban deemed the structures as idols and therefore un-Islamic. Accordingly, both monuments were systematically dynamited and destroyed in 2001.

Other aspects of the Islamization of the country required men to wear beards, girls were forbidden from going to school, and women were barred from working outside the home. These severe restrictions precipitated a crisis in the healthcare system and education in the country. The cities in particular suffered greatly as access to food, clean water, and employment declined. The countryside was not spared as a continuing drought and a very harsh winter (2000–2001) brought famine and an increase in the flow of refugees to Pakistan.

In contrast to their strict beliefs, the Taliban reportedly profited from smuggling operations (primarily electronics) and the cultivation of opium. Despite its lack of widespread international recognition, the Kabul regime was courted by Western energy interests who were gearing up to tap the estimated fifteen billion barrels of oil and nine trillion cubic meters of natural gas in the former Soviet republics of Central Asia. Transit through Afghanistan instead of the U.S. sanctioned Iran was favored by most of the companies. The leading contender was a consortium led by the U.S. Oil company UNOCAL. In this context, in late 1997, a Taliban delegation arrived at Unocal's offices in Sugarland, Texas to negotiate transit rights though a month earlier, the then Secretary of State Madeleine Albright had chastised the regime for its gross violations of human-rights in Afghanistan. Further visits and negotiations about pipelines continued and little was discussed about the Taliban's support for terrorist organizations, especially the AL QAEDA run by OSAMA BIN LADEN. The situation changed dramatically after 9/11. Washington then unsuccessfully pressed Kabul to turn over bin Laden and his men to the United States. Accordingly, on 7 October 2001 the U.S. began bombing Taliban military sites and stepped up aid to the Northern Alliance. The 25,000 strong Taliban military being more like a traditional tribal militia than a regular modern army quickly melted away. Kabul fell to the Northern Alliance on 21 November 2001. While some of the Taliban's leaders and supporters were killed or captured, most simply returned to their homes or moved into neighboring Pakistan. By 2003, the United

States had shifted its military effort to Iraq, and attacks on American-led forces intensified under the regrouped Taliban and al-Qaeda. By 2008 the fighting in the country become the deadliest since the U.S. led intervention in 2001.

Earlier, in September 2007, seven militant groups in Pakistan formed an umbrella group, called the *Tehrik-i-Taliban* and became commonly known as the "Pakistani Taliban." Prominent leaders included Maulana Sufi Mohammad, head of the *Tehrik Nifaz-e-Shariah Mohammedi* (TNSM), his deputy Faqir Mohammed who assumed control in the Bajaur tribal agency, Mullah Fazlullah in the districts of Swat and Shangla, and Baitullah Mehsud in South Waziristan. The latter was accused of masterminding the December 2007 assassination of former Prime Minister BENAZIR BHUTTO, though it was widely assumed that the MUSHARRAF government, too, was involved. Intermittent clashes, truces withdrawals, ceasefires, etc., between the Pakistan government and the Taliban followed. In August 2008, after two suicide bombers blew themselves up at the gates of Pakistan's main weapons complex at Wah, twenty miles (thirty-two kilometers) west of Islamabad, killing 79 and injuring 103, the organization was officially banned by the Pakistan Government. The fundamentalists, unmindful of bans, continued to be active in Pakistan. In addition, there is a growing number of leaders and opinion makers who support the development of working relationships with select sections within the Taliban. This approach may be an important part of a deal to restore peace in both Pakistan and Afghanistan. Afghans ranging from the former president BURHANUDDIN RABBANI to the renegade GULBUDDIN HEKMATYAR have suggested as much.

Tata, Jamsetji Nusserwanji (1839-1904)

Industrialist, philanthropist. Tata, a contractor for the army in Central India, learnt of iron deposits at Chanda in Central India and planned to build an iron works there. The British rulers of the country discouraged him from doing so. Undaunted, he went to United States in September 1902. In the steel town of Pittsburgh, Pennsylvania, he met Julian Kennedy, the head of Julian Kennedy, Sahlin & Company, one of the foremost metallurgical engineering firms in the world. Kennedy suggested the name of an eminent consulting engineer in

New York City. The man was not available, but his associate C.M. Weld was. Weld accompanied Tata to India and helped establish the Tata Iron and Steel Company (TISCO). Known as Tata Steel the company produced 26.6 million tons of the steel in 2008 and is the sixth largest producer of the metal in the world.

Terrorism, the United States, and South Asia

In the wake of the September 2001 terrorist attacks on the United States, Washington faced the major challenge of balancing the American national interest with the individual security concerns, rivalries, and suspicions among the countries of South Asia. In addition, some were aiding and abetting both fundamentalism and terrorism though none of their nationals were directly involved in the September attacks. However, Washington singled out al Qaeda AL QAEDA with its Arab leadership headquartered in Afghanistan as the main culprit. Accordingly, the first major U.S. anti-terrorism effort, Operation Enduring Freedom, launched in October 2001, was targeted against Afghanistan. The mission's major goals were the destruction of terrorist training camps and infrastructure, the capture of the AL QAEDA and the TALIBAN leadership, to procure data and information about the organization, and to deny the country of Afghanistan as a safe haven for terrorists and for their training and other activities. Substantive assistance from neighboring Pakistan was vital for the success of the U.S.-led invasion. Such assistance was given and ever more widely acknowledged though key members of both al Qaeda and its Taliban supporters escaped alive and regrouped in Pakistan itself. Subsequently, al Qaeda reportedly strengthened ties with indigenous Pakistani terrorist groups that had been implicated in anti-Western attacks in Pakistan and in acts of terrorism in Indian Kashmir and elsewhere. Within three years of Operation Enduring freedom, some fundamentalists launched terrorist attacks against the government of President PERVEZ MUSHARRAF. Another notable development was the continued presence of foreign nationals especially from China, Central Asia, Indonesia and Malaysia in the militant-run MADRASSAS in the country.

New Delhi, too, provided some logistical and intelligence support for the invasion, but also consistently blamed Pakistan-based militant groups for continued lethal attacks on Indian civilians and security forces, in both Kashmir and in other parts of India. American designated Foreign Terrorist Organizations (FTOs) like *Lashkar-e-Taiba*, *Jaish-e-Mohammed*, *Harakat ul-Mujahideen*, and *Hizbul Mujahideen* were the most active in India. In broad strategic terms some in Washington believed that the eventual suppression of terrorism, depended on better education, increased economic growth and the liberation of women, especially in a major Islamic country like Pakistan. Among the steps to achieve these goals, the U.S. expected the two major countries in South Asia, India and Pakistan, to exercise nuclear restraint and through dialogue resolve conflicts, especially Kashmir, among themselves with Washington providing economic and military inducements to Islamabad and New Delhi. Reality was different: By 2004, echoing the long-standing Indian complaints, both U.S. and Afghan officials stated that insurgents were crossing into Afghanistan to attack American-led forces before returning to safe havens in Pakistan. In response, in 2005, the then Pakistani Prime Minister Shaukat Aziz visited Kabul and pledged "seamless cooperation." Nevertheless, U.S. officials continued to urge Islamabad and Kabul to "do more" to quell the fundamentalist led insurgency in the region. Undeterred by public pledges and actions taken by the Pakistan government, the Taliban clearly continued to recruit and train cadres in Pakistani territory without significant government interference. On the other hand, Indo-U.S. cooperation expanded especially after the June 2005 ten-year Defense Framework Agreement was signed. It listed the defeat of "terrorism and violent religious extremism" as one of four key shared security interests. Such frameworks and assurances notwithstanding, Islamic fundamentalists chose their own targets (the assassination of BENAZIR BHUTTO in December 2007) and took their own stands (at the Lal Masjid in Islamabad in July 2007, in FATA and the valley of Swat in 2007-8).

On 17 August 2005, about 350 small bombs exploded almost simultaneously across Bangladesh, killing two and injuring more than 125. No one claimed responsibility for the widespread attacks, but leaflets issued by the banned militant organization, *Jamatul Mujahideen*, calling for the institution of Islamic laws in Bangladesh were found at most sites. Numerous suspects were subsequently arrested, and another group called the *Jagrata Muslim Janata Bangladesh* was banned. From the U.S. perspective, Bangladesh was "an unavoidable partner" in bridging religious divides across the world. This stated perspective may be at odds with the changes brought about by returning migrant laborers from Saudi Arabia and elsewhere in the Middle East. Apparently a lot of the labor has been inculcated with a more radical version of Islam that makes them more open to collaboration and recruitment by terrorists. Economics, too, plays a vital role in this development. Bangladeshis with their established ties and means of transportation can move money (Hindustani: "Hawala"), explosives, information, etc., without being directly involved in terrorist activities.

Theosophical Society and Theosophists

A nineteenth century society of religious mysticists founded in the United States that had great impact on South Asia both an individual and as an organization. Theosophy or Divine Wisdom considers all religions are attempts by man to understand 'the Divine.' Hence, every religion contains a portion of the true knowledge about God. However, according to theosophy, coherent and comprehensive understanding can only be achieved through spiritual ecstasy, especially by the blending of Hindu, Buddhist, and Zoroastrian philosophical traditions. Theosophists also believe in special individualized relationships with the esoteric and the mystical can reveal the great secrets of ancient wisdom.

The Society was founded in 1875 in New York City with Colonel Henry Steel Olcott (1832-1907) as the president and the Russian-born Helena Blavatsky (1831-1891) as the corresponding secretary. The two moved to India and set up temporary headquarters in Bombay (Mumbai) before moving to Adyar (Chennai). Colonel Olcott went to Sri Lanka in 1880, became a Buddhist and was prominent in the revival of Theravada Buddhism these. A major thoroughfare in Colombo is named after him and a couple of statues on the island were erected in his honor. Blavatsky converted a young Irishwoman, Annie Besant (1847-1933), to theosophy. The latter, too, moved to India, discovered and nurtured the teenaged Jiddu Krishnamurti (1895-

1986), the unconventional philosopher. Besant became an ardent advocate for Indian independence and was the first woman to be elected as President of the Indian National Congress (1917). She was credited with coining the term Commonwealth for Britain's relationship with its erstwhile dependencies. Meanwhile, Krishnamurti, renounced Besant's attempts to project him as the world teacher (*Maitreya Buddha*, "Jesus of the East") and disbanded the Order of the Star, the organization established to support him. He moved to England and then to Ojai, California. Working through charitable trusts, he founded several independent schools around the world. He spoke and wrote extensively on peace and awareness and received the United Nations Peace Medal in 1985.

Thoreau, Henry David (1817-1862)

American philosopher, transcendentalist, conservationist. Around 1840 a fellow New Englander RALPH WALDO EMERSON probably aroused Thoreau's interest in Indian philosophy and religion, because after 1841 the latter was fulsome in his admiration for Hindu scriptures. In addition, he often referred to himself as a Yogi. On a July evening in 1846, Thoreau was placed under house arrest and jailed overnight for refusing to pay a poll tax that he considered was exclusively for use by a government that did not meet his approval. Consequently, in early 1848 he gave two lectures at the Concord Lyceum on "The Rights and Duties of the Individual in Relation to Government." In the following year the lecture was published in Elizabeth Peabody's magazine, *Aesthetic Papers*. It was largely ignored until 1866 when it was republished under the heading "Civil Disobedience." At the turn of the twentieth century MAHATMA GANDHI read the work. It profoundly influenced him for in 1908 in South Africa, Gandhi, too, refused to pay what he considered as an unjust tax and was jailed On his release, Gandhi published extensively from "Civil Disobedience" in the newspaper, *Indian Opinion*. However, Gandhi was uncomfortable with the term and finally coined a new one: *Satyagraha* (Sanskrit: "Truth-force"). Gandhi was to make *Satyagraha* into action for the masses by giving it various forms ranging from non-cooperation and passive resistance to fasting and prayer meetings. Thoreau's own reputation was more mixed. In general, he was regarded as a powerful literary radical who was too aloof to be a man of the masses.

Truman, Harry S. (1884-1972)

U.S. President (1945-52). The S in his name has no known attached to it. It is a standing middle initial. Born in the tiny hamlet of Lamar, Missouri, Truman grew up in Independence, a small settlement close to the much more metropolitan town of Kansas City, Missouri. Elected to the U.S. Senate in 1934, Truman finally gained national prominence as Chairman of the Senate Special Committee to Investigate the National Defense Program during World War II. Consequently, he was picked as the running mate for Roosevelt's 1944 presidential race and was sworn in on 12 April, 1945 as the nation's thirty-third president after the latter's death only eighty-two days into his fourth term. Truman, with his cumulative experiences in France during World War I, his long association with the Jewish haberdasher Eddie Jacobson, and his years in the U.S. Senate, was better equipped to handle international relations than many of his predecessors, peers, and erstwhile critics.

Two years later profound changes shook South Asia. The demise of the British Raj had given way to Indian independence, but the price paid was the division of the unitary sub-continental entity into two antagonistic countries, India and Pakistan. India, under the Congress Party, led by JAWAHARLAL NEHRU and imbued with the spirit of MAHATMA GANDHI adopted liberal democracy, secularism, a socialist idiom for economic development, and a non-aligned approach to international relations. Pakistan, led by the Muslim League and MUHAMMAD ALI JINNAH would establish itself as a notionally Islamic homeland for the Muslims of the Indian subcontinent and governed by a viceregal political system, with a quasi-capitalist economy, a polity controlled by feudal landlords, colonial-era bureaucratic elite, and a Punjabi-dominated military establishment. Both countries emerged with a bitter legacy of religious conflict and mutual hostility over the princely state of Jammu and Kashmir. Meanwhile, the U.S. pre-occupied with the spread of world communism created a foreign policy defined by the doctrine of containment of the Soviet dominated part of the world. Policy-makers in Washington, with little knowledge and experience of the Indian subcontinent, were swayed by Sir Olaf Caroe and other traditional British imperialists, to incorporate newly created Pakistan into the contemplated *cordon sanitaire* around the potentially expansive and obviously bellicose Soviet Union. After some public debate and little private deliberation, a regional strategy for South Asia evolved with the five explicit aims of preventing the Communist Bloc's penetration into the region; deter the rise of domestic communism; prevent intra-regional wars, especially between India and Pakistan over Kashmir and Pakistan and Afghanistan over the Pashtun issue; promote economic development throughout the subcontinent based on free-market economics, and encourage the evolution and preservation of democratic political institutions. Without Indian participation, militarization of the region was not one of the goals of the administration. However, Pakistan, backed by some British "old India Hands" aggressively sought and established military ties with the U.S. Accordingly, even at its inception the grand design for the region was warped by contradictory decisions. Among the most important being the appointment of CHESTER BOWLES as the ambassador to India in 1951. Bowles was opposed to the militarization of South Asia by the inclusion of Pakistan into the West's alliance against the Soviet Union, because he expected this would have a destabilizing effect on the region. He also believed that American diplomatic support and economic assistance would prevent India from slipping into the communist camp. Bowles also hoped that New Delhi, with American support would become a bulwark against the rising tide of totalitarianism that was engulfing most of the newly freed nations of the world. This could be accomplished, Bowles believed, by simply assuring Nehru's political survival when many experts were calling him as the Kerensky of India (Alexander Kerensky, the stop-gap ill-fated leader of Russia after the fall of the Tsars and before the rise of the communists to power in that country was being compared with Nehru in 1947-8). But Nehru, a fellow lawyer, was much more clear eyed and intellectually coherent than Kerensky. He charted out a fresh course for India by keeping the country NON-ALIGNED from both Moscow and Washington and yet maintain New Delhi as an active mediatory third force between the two rival power blocs. However, neither the Truman administration nor the U.S. Congress paid enough attention to South Asia. Instead, the doctrine of non-alignment was interpreted as being the equivalent of "fellow traveler," a pejorative connotation for a crypto-communist in the McCarthyist atmosphere that prevailed in the domestic American political environment.

Tsunami 2004

Officially, the Sumatra-Andaman Earthquake, 2004. The undersea earthquake with its epicenter just north of Simeulue Island off the west coast of Sumatra, Indonesia, occurred at 07:58:53, local time, on 26 December 2004. The tsunami (Japanese: "Harbor wave") generated by the tremor killed approximately 275,000 people, making it one of the deadliest disasters in modern times. Included were about 9,000 foreign tourists (mostly Europeans) with Swedes being the hardest hit with the death toll of about 500. It was the second largest earthquake ever recorded. Its magnitude was 9.15 on the Richter scale. The quake itself lasted for almost ten minutes whereas the duration of most major tremors is no more than a few seconds. It caused the entire planet to vibrate. The resulting wave devastated the shores of Indonesia, Sri Lanka, South India, Thailand and other countries with waves up to 30 meters (100 ft) high. The farthest death recorded due to the tsunami was at Port Elizabeth in South Africa, 8,000 km (5,000 mi) from the epicenter. Tsunamis behave differently in the deep than in shallow water. In deep ocean water, tsunami waves form only a small hump, barely noticeable and harmless, which generally travel at a very high speed of 500 to 1,000 kilometres per hour (310 to 620 mph) whereas in shallow waters near coastlines, the wave slows down to speeds of only tens of kilometres (miles) an hour but in doing so it forms large destructive waves. The warning signs are the ocean receding from the shore accompanied by frothing bubbles. The 2004 tsunami was not a single devastating wave, but a succession of several ones, occurring in retreat and rise cycles with a period of more than thirty minutes between each peak. Four times as many women were killed as men as they were waiting on the beaches for the fishermen to return and were in beach-front homes looking after their children. The dynamiting of many reefs around the Indian

Ocean, the destruction of coastal mangroves, and the removal of coastal dunes to make way for residential development were cited as major causal factors for such massive devastation. Some saw the wrath of God in the disaster and asserted that the tsunami was divine punishment for sex tourism and drug abuse in southeast Asia. Others contend to the contrary by pointing out that the hardest hit area, Aceh, was a conservative Islamic region with no tourist industry nor any other substantial Western presence due to a long-standing insurgency against the Indonesian state by Acehnese separatists. The U.S. government initially offered just $35 million in aid. However, after the extent of the damage became known and after the widespread scorn at American parsimony, Washington increased its commitment to a total of $950 million. Other countries, foundations, and Non Governmental Organizations (NGOs) were quick to offer generous assistance. However, two years after the tsunami, only twenty-three percent of the $10.4 billion in promised aid was given. Corruption and mismanagement had further reduced effectiveness of the aid, e.g., thousands of mangrove seedlings perished for want of proper handling. In addition, the role of foreign NGOs raised a number of sensitive issues. It appeared that NGOs were more concerned about preserving their independence by resisting government oversight and were indiscriminate in doling out cash grants. Washington remained deeply involved as former President WILLIAM J. CLINTON was the U.N. Special Envoy for Tsunami recovery.

Twain, Mark

(pseudonym), born Samuel L Clemens (1835-1910). Widely loved and celebrated American writer since his first books were released in the late 1860s. His fascinating travelogue *Following the Equator* (1897), detailed his many experiences in India. Some of his observations were, "So far as I am able to judge, nothing has been left undone, either by man or nature, to make India the most extraordinary country that the sun visits on his rounds. Nothing seems to have been forgotten, nothing overlooked. Land of religions, cradle of human race, birthplace of human speech, grandmother of legend, great grandmother of tradition. The land that all men desire to see and having seen once even by a glimpse, would not give up that glimpse for the shows of the rest of the globe combined. She had the first civilization; she had the first accumulation of material wealth; she was populous with thinkers and subtle intellects; she had mines, and woods, and a fruitful soul. Varanasi or Banaras has been continuously populated for more than 3,000 years, and often been called the oldest city in the world. It was the contemporary of Thebes and Babylon. Early visitors were struck by the "spectacle" and the "panorama" of the Banaras riverfront. The Ganges front is the supreme showplace of Benares. (It's) soaring stairways, sculptured temples, majestic palaces, softening away into the distances; and there is movement, motion, human life everywhere, and brilliantly costumed and massed in metaphorical gardens on the great platforms at the river's edge. India has two million gods, and worships them all. In religion all other countries are paupers India is the only millionaire."

Despite Twain's extensive and ecstatic write-ups on India, the American people were not enthused by the British colony on the other side of the globe.

U

U.S. Covert Operations in South Asia

As a super power, the United States has engaged in covert operations around the globe. Various U.S. intelligence agencies were active in Pakistan during the early years of the country's participation in the SEATO and CENTO alliances. These activities, mostly directed against the Soviet Union, were quietly scaled down after the U-2 incident in 1960 when a Pakistan based American U-2 spy plane was shot down deep inside the Soviet Union. The revival of ties began with the increasing Soviet influence in Afghanistan after the assassination of President DAUD 1978. In Washington it is generally considered that clandestine involvement in Afghanistan (1978-89) during the Soviet intervention in that country was the largest and most successful CIA operation in history and the one morally unambiguous crusade of the Cold War. The attacks on U.S. soil on 9/11 changed that perception. Before the Soviet intervention in Afghanistan in 1979, most Pakistanis believed that the 1971 secession of the eastern wing of their country was a sinister American plot engineered by CIA to separate East Pakistan and convert it into a pliant vassal state of the United States. After Pakistan's 1998 nuclear tests, Washington's demonization of A.Q. KHAN, the proclaimed father of the Pakistani atom bomb, was regarded as particularly hypocritical. Covert U.S. involvement in Khan's activities was also alleged by the former Dutch Prime Minister Ruud Lubbers in a radio interview in August 2005. Lubbers stated that the CIA had prevented the Dutch from prosecuting Khan in the mid 1970s after he was caught copying drawings of the URENCO centrifuge plant in Holland. The CIA disingenuously had argued that if Khan was left free, then the agency would be better able to keep track of the Pakistani nuclear program. According to Lubbers the CIA should have also known about Khan's numerous trips to North Korea after the BENAZIR BHUTTO visit to Pyongyang in 1994 when she apparently hand-carried sensitive blueprints for use by the North Koreans.

The trips were related to a deal for the supply of North Korean ballistic missiles in exchange of Pakistani uranium enrichment technology and materials. However, in the shadowy world of covert activities the credibility of sources that become public is often in doubt. For instance, Lubbers may have acted to protect Henk Slebos, the Dutch academic, who was Khan's personal friend and business partner. Regardless, the Khan saga acquired another twist when U.S. Senator Kerry's Senate Committee Report in 1992 referred to connections between the infamous, now defunct, Bank of Credit and Commerce International (BCCI), Khan, the Iranian nuclear program, and the unwillingness of the CIA to reveal the details about its ties with the bank. Reportedly, the U.S. agency had good reasons not to cooperate because BCCI was financing the Pakistani nuclear program while the CIA was using it in the Iran-Contra deal to covertly sell U.S. arms to Iran in return for the release of hostages in Lebanon and the use of the money from the sales to support Nicaraguan resistance groups known as contras.

The post-Cold War era, more so after 9/11, revealed the need for the U.S. military to respond to fast-moving, rapidly evolving contingencies around the globe. Ready access to overseas installations, foreign territories and airspace assumed particular importance for the United States Air Force (USAF), whose aircraft were mostly configured to operate from bases relatively close to their intended targets. Accordingly, a global access strategy for USAF was developed. In the Indian subcontinent it included plans to significantly increase "electronic and other intelligence assets" in the territories of potential partners in the region. Sri Lanka was a prime candidate, as the country's military and intelligence services already had long-standing institutional ties with the British MI-6, MI-5, and the U.S. Central Intelligence Agency (CIA). The MI-6 provided most of the training for Sri Lanka's Special Branch, which became the National Intelligence Bureau (NIB) in 1984 and was later reorganized as the Directorate of Internal Intelligence (DII). The world's largest intelligence gathering organization, America's National Security Agency (NSA), reportedly functions through the U.S. army/Defense Intelligence Agency office at the U.S. mission in Colombo. The Defense Special Missile and

Astronautics Centre (DSMAC), another arm of the NSA, whose mission was to perform "initial analysis and reporting on all foreign space and missile events," reportedly stepped up its monitoring on India after the 1998 nuclear tests. The NSA's operations in Sri Lanka may benefit from the substantial infrastructure developed by the Voice of America (VOA) station on the island's west coast. VOA facilities may also accommodate NSA's electronic surveillance assets though the VOA hotly disputes all such assertions. In addition, the escalation of the war between the Sri Lankan government and the Liberation Tigers of Tamil Eelam (LTTE, AKA Tamil Tigers) was important enough for the U.S. to further expand its military and intelligence relations with Sri Lanka.

In India, during the NEHRU years (1947-64), financial aid to various political parties and front organizations was the major covert activity carried out by the U.S. Perhaps the clearest instance of such support was in the wake of the unexpected win by the communists in the South India state of Kerala in the 1957 elections. The state government was dismissed in 1959. Since then the involvement of CIA in removing the Communist Government has remained a murky subject. Apparently the American role was limited to providing financial help necessary to organize agitations against the state government. In 1975, the former U.S. Ambassador to India, Daniel Patrick Moynihan stated as much, "We had twice, but only twice, interfered in Indian politics to the extent of providing money to a political party. Both times this was done in the face of a prospective communist victory in state elections, once in Kerala and once in West Bengal, where Calcutta is located. Both times the money was given to the Congress Party which had asked for it."

In the aftermath of the Indian reverses in the October-November 1962 Sino-Indian border war, New Delhi hastily created the Special Frontier Force (SFF) on 14 November 1962. The SFF soon acquired the nom de guerre, 'Establishment 22,' as its first Inspector General, a Brigadier in the artillery, had earlier commanded the 22 Mountain Regiment of the Indian Army. The SFF was based at Chakrata, a small remote mountain town with a large Tibetan refugee population, located about 100 kilometres north-west of the famous cantonment city of Dehra Dun. An initial force of 5,000 men was raised. The U.S. provided the small arms, mortars, and machine guns to equip the men who were primarily to be used for gathering intelligence and or for conducting commando operations in the Sino-Indian Theater. Both countries agreed that heavy weapons would not be appropriate for such a force.

The U.S.-Indian collaboration also included teams of Indian and American mountaineers and intelligence officers making seven trips between 1965 and 1968 to two mountain peaks in northwest India, just south of the Chinese border. The two peaks were Nanda Devi (25, 645 ft.) and Nanda Kot (22, 538 ft.). The missions were to place nuclear-powered monitoring devices as high on the mountains as possible. The second mission to Nanda Devi managed to place an instrument, only to lose it shortly afterwards for it plunged down the mountain slope. The device placed on Nanda Kot stopped functioning after three months. Therefore, a team was sent to repair it, but it again failed a few months later. The devices each contained 1,734 grams (3.8 lbs.) of plutonium; mainly the Pu-238 isotope. The equipment consisted of two transceivers and a generator powered by seven plutonium capsules designed to last for 1,000 years. None lasted long. An additional set of sensors installed in the Nanda Kot was dismantled in 1968 and sent back to the U.S. By November 1968 the CIA had developed a more reliable gas powered sensor. Therefore, joint expeditions were sent to position these safer instruments on a mountain in Ladakh in 1968 and 1969. In mid-1969 climbers also put an apparatus on a 16,000 ft. mountain in Arunachal Pradesh as well. By then newer technologies had overtaken these heroic and unsuccessful attempts to monitor the Chinese nuclear program.

Active U.S. covert operations in Nepal probably date to March 1951, when the U.S. Ambassador to India (and concurrently to Nepal) advised the young Dalai Lama to leave his country and seek asylum abroad. Thereafter, Nepal was used in a modest effort to gather intelligence in Tibet and for the exfiltration and infiltration of Tibetan rebels. After the Dalai Lama finally fled Tibet in 1959, CIA-trained agents in the Dalai Lama's convoy reportedly laid out markers in the snow to guide airdrops from a U.S. military C-130 aircraft that was specially modified to fly in the thin Tibetan air. Halfway to India, a radio operator joined the group so that the whole operation could be directly monitored from the CIA station in Dacca (now Dhaka), East Pakistan (now Bangladesh). For the next fifteen years the CIA provided the Tibetan movement in exile with $1.7 million annually for operations against China. Most Tibetan forces operated out of hapless, impoverished Nepal as a combined U.S.-Indian-Tibetan mission with the remote little principality of Mustang being the major base. After the U.S.-China rapprochement in 1971 these secret operations were wound up. Without U.S. assistance, Tibetan armed resistance was over by 1974. However, American support did persist and a number of successful Tibetan businesses including carpet manufacturing, hostel and hotel operations in Nepal resulted from CIA contributions to the Tibetan fighters in Mustang who were relocated and retrained for leading civilian lives. CIA operations in India and Nepal surface under odd circumstances as well. In 2004, a defector to the U.S. from India's external intelligence service, Research and Analysis Wing (RAW), used his own Indian passport to travel to Nepal, where he supposedly received false travel documents issued by the Americans to enter the United States. Washington again focused on Nepal in the 1990s with the onset of the Maoist movement in the country. The U.S. State Department designated the Maoists as a terrorist group while other entities like the Revolutionary Internationalist Movement (RIM) with its headquarters in Chicago, Illinois, openly lent its support to the movement.

Washington has no direct ties with the reclusive Himalayan Kingdom of Bhutan. The U.S. Embassy in New Delhi handles diplomatic relations and aid is largely through multilateral organizations. In an unusual move, in October 2006, the U.S. announced its willingness to resettle up to 60,000 of the 106,000 Nepali-speaking refugees expelled by Bhutan. Though the little Himalayan kingdom is itself largely free from terrorist violence, the existence on Bhutanese soil of camps of terrorist organizations like the United Liberation Front of Asom (ULFA), the National Democratic Front of Bodoland (NDFB) and the Kamtapur Liberation Organisation (KLO) that operate in India's Northeast continue to arouse apprehensions in the U.S. and India.

Covert operations in the Maldives and Burma, if any, are on a small scale in the new millennium.

U.S. Immigration Laws

Though a land peopled by immigrants, the United States passed various laws to regulate immigration shortly after the nation was founded. Since then changes in the pattern of immigration into the country has been a feature of American society. To start with, the 1790 Naturalization Act restricted American citizenship to white races only.

Successive variants of the Asian Exclusion Acts (1882, 1892, 1902, 1904, 1917, 1924, and 1934) prevented legal immigration from Asian countries. The Asian Exclusion laws included Japanese nationals as well. However after Japan's stunning victory in the Russo-Japanese War of 1905, Washington became more tolerant towards immigration from Japan. Tokyo responded by issuing only a limited number of travel documents to its citizens. The changed American attitude towards a victorious Asian power was not lost upon Indian and Chinese immigrants. The fervor for Indian independence picked up and the Chinese determination to get rid of foreign concessions gained momentum.

The unexpected migration from the Indian subcontinent to the West coast of the United States around 1900 led to the formation of the Asiatic Exclusion League in 1908. Canada swiftly followed suit, curtailing immigration in 1909. By 1910, the League successfully lobbied for restrictions on the immigration of Asians, including those from the Indian subcontinent. Thereafter, Alien Land Law Acts (1913, 1920, and 1923), precluded immigrants from owning or leasing land, making it particularly difficult for South Asians as most of them were farmers. The "Asia Barred Zone" (1917) further denied entry to natives of India, Siam, Indo-China, Afghanistan, Arabia and parts of Siberia. The Cable Act (1922) was the most draconian of legislations for it revoked citizenship of those Americans who married Asians. It was repealed in 1931. Immigration for the Indian subcontinent had effectively ceased a few years earlier after the 1923 judgment passed by the U.S. Supreme Court (U.S. vs. Thind 261,

U.S. 204). The Court's verdict was that though Bhagat Singh Thind was Caucasian by scientific methods but he was not a "white" man as understood by the common American. Hence, by 1923, Asian immigration, except from Japan, was negligible and the "Thind" case of 1923 specifically declared Indians as ineligible for citizenship on the basis that they were not white. The situation slowly Magnuson Act (1943) and the Asian Exclusion Repeal Act (1946, the Luce-Celler Bill) allowed for small quotas of immigrants from China, India, and the Philippines. However, the McCarran-Walter Act (1952), reflecting the sentiments of the Cold War, established strict quotas for immigrants based on "strategically territorial mapping".

In 1965, immigration laws were radically modified under the Hart-Cellar Act. Quotas based national origins that were in place since 1882 were abolished. The Act allowed 170,000 immigrants form the Eastern hemisphere with a limit of 20,000 per country. From the Western hemisphere immigration was pegged at 120,000 with no consideration for national boundaries. This was an enormous change from a European allocation of 149,667 and an Asian quota of only 2,990. Under the Act, "Employment based immigration" admitted those with specific skills and professions that were needed in the country. "Family based immigration" was for the unification of families. Both had a system of "preferences" that were changed periodically. After 1965 other immigration laws were also enacted. For instance, a law in 1986 legalized the status of 3 million illegal immigrants. The Immigration and Nationality Act of 1990 further increased the total quota of immigrants to 700,000 per annum and favored the immigration of technocrats by almost tripling the number of visas granted to those with occupational skills from 54,000 to 140,000 annually. Immigration remains a dynamic process with subsequent Acts that have sought to legalize or rationalize the massive illegal immigration of Hispanics into the country.

U.S. Military Aid in South Asia After 9/11

The United States has periodically applied sanctions to the two most powerful countries in South Asia. The most recent ones were imposed after the 1998 nuclear tests by both Pakistan and India. The sanctions prohibited the export of goods listed on the U.S. Munitions

List, the transfer of certain military technologies, and aid through the Foreign Military Financing (FMF) program. After 9/11 countries receiving FMF increased from 48 to 71. Two of the three biggest gainers were countries from the Indian subcontinent — Pakistan ($300 million) and Afghanistan ($396 million). Within two months of 9/11, the U.S. agreed to provide Pakistan with $73 million in "border security" military hardware, including Huey helicopters and spare parts for F-16 fighter planes. In July 2004, Bell Helicopters instituted the delivery of twenty-six 412EP medium twin-engine helicopters and associated equipment. The transactions were estimated at $230 million. Further military aid included six used C-130E cargo aircraft with spare engines, six Aerostat L-88 radar systems, 400 grenade launchers and other riot control gear, spare parts for the PAF's C-130s, UH-1H helicopters, and M-113 armored personnel carriers. Less than a year later, in March 2005, President GEORGE W. BUSH reversed 15 years of policy begun under his father by offering F-16 fighter planes to Islamabad with no formal limits being set on the number of aircraft that could be purchased. Estimates of the cost of the deal range up to $3 billion. Other military aid included a grant of $75 million in FMF in 2002, supplemented by an anti-terrorism grants and aid. Altogether, by 2007, the total U.S. aid to Pakistan was conservatively estimated at $ 11 billion. Before the institution of the ten year, two stage $15 billion Biden-Lugar Bill for developmental aid to Pakistan, 96% of the funds were spent on the military, three percent on the Border Security Program and one percent on civil assistance. According to the U.S. General Accountability Office (GAO) report released in 2008, about twenty percent of the more than $10 billion in funds dispersed has not been accounted for. Egregious examples include $45 million earmarked for bunkers that were never built.

India, too, received some military equipment. Military hardware included were twelve Firefinder artillery-locating readers; spare parts for Sea King helicopters and Hawk trainer aircraft, and air defense radars. Economic Support Funds (ESF) as unrestricted grants modestly increased from $10.5 million in 2003 to $14 million in 2006. Altogether the total security assistance to India in five years since 9/11 was $78 million. The country was also made eligible for free or deeply discounted weapons and military equipment through the Excess Defense Articles program. In 2004, President Bush unveiled a new agreement to increase technical cooperation between the two countries, permitting the export of sensitive nuclear and space technology to India.

In Nepal after the restoration of democracy and the participation of the Maoists in the political activity in the country in 2006, the modest military aid was further was scaled down. Hence, about $1 million in FMF was given in 2006. During the active insurgency, despite the autocratic rule of the king, Washington provided $2.9 million in 2004 and $3.9 million in 2005. Nevertheless, ESF remained steady at an average of $4.5 million over the three years. Earlier, Washington delivered M-16 rifles, grenade launchers, and M-4 carbines to outfit a new ranger battalion. In 2005 Nepal was also made eligible to receive Excess Defense Articles (EDA). Select Nepali and U.S. soldiers underwent in joint military training along with soldiers from Uganda, Bhutan, Sri Lanka and India for six weeks at the Counter Insurgency Jungle Warfare School in north-eastern India.

In Kabul, President HAMID KARZAI was dependent on Washington for his personal protection, which is provided by the multifaceted American security firm, DynCorp. The rebuilding of Afghan security forces was complicated by low morale, tribalism, and the involvement of both officers and men in the drug trade. U.S. aid to Afghanistan in 2005 totaled around $930 million, with 80 percent of it being earmarked for the military and the police. Future U.S. aid was similarly skewed with only ten percent of it being spent on developmental assistance, human resource development, etc. Overall, the effort to eliminate AL QAEDA, the TALIBAN, and other militants met with limited success at great cost, both in terms of lives and the possibility for a stable and democratic future for the country.

In Sri Lanka, the Tamil-Sinhala armed conflict since 1984 evoked little military response from Washington. On the political and financial level, the U.S. supported Colombo by designating the most powerful militant Tamil outfit, the LTTE, as a Foreign Terrorist Organization (FTO) well before 9/11. In addition, the U.S. granted $500,000 annually under IMET and about $1 million in FMF in 2006, down from a high of $2.5 million two years earlier.

U.S.-India Agricultural Knowledge Initiative on Agriculture (AKI)

In July 2005, the U.S. — India Knowledge Initiative on agricultural education, teaching, research, service, and commercial linkages (AKI) was announced. AKI was one of the initiatives undertaken by Presidential George W. Bush to strengthen the agricultural relationship between the United States and India by facilitating technology transfer, trade, and investment, and by strengthening partnerships in agricultural research, education, and outreach. The Initiative was in keeping with the long history of cooperation in agriculture and the success of India's GREEN REVOLUTION launched with U.S. assistance forty years earlier. In addition, as a nod to free markets, the initiative was to promote public-private partnerships and create outreach programs into the community whereby the results of the work in the academic institutions could reach directly to the farmer. Four institutions, University of Florida (UF) at Gainesville, the International Crops Research Institute for the Semiarid Tropics (ICRISAT), Acharya N. G. Ranga Agricultural University (ANGRAU) and Punjab Agricultural University (PAU), were to take the lead. The two countries also created a board of academics, government officials, and private sector representatives to draw up a three year work plan that envisioned an "Evergreen Revolution" based upon environmentally sustainable and market-oriented agriculture. The plan also focused on establishing a U.S. — India Joint Working Group for training and faculty exchanges, and to organize workshops, increase outreach activities, enlarge library resources, and promote leadership development. The holistic and comprehensive aspects of AKI also targeted joint research, quality assurance, food safety, and reduction in post-harvest losses. In addition, increased investment in agribusinesses, induction of advanced processing technologies, and better utilization of by-products and bio-fuels was envisaged. Furthermore, development of transgenic crops that were more resistant to viruses, to drought, heat and salinity was planned. Research in the sustainable use of water resources, micronutrients, molecular technology, genomics, and vaccines against animal diseases was also announced. Other areas of shared interests included food safety, biosafety, and protection of intellectual property rights. However, for such an ambitious and far-reaching venture, the U.S. pledged a mere twenty-four million dollars in funding over a three year period. Perhaps a better funded and more focused project may be more effective in an era of rising food and energy costs, a decline in grain buffers stocks, and increased wariness towards the use of bio-engineered agricultural products.

United States Military Aid, Categories

American military aid is provided through complex systems and controls. Hence, the market value of aid is difficult to quantify. The important categories are enumerated below:

Foreign Military Financing (FMF): The U.S. Congress appropriates grants to finance foreign nations' purchases of American-made weapons, services and training. It is the Pentagon's most widely used program for providing weapons to other countries.

Economic Support Fund (ESF): While U.S. law makes clear that ESF is not intended for military expenditure, the grants are frequently used as a de facto military aid, with foreign governments using the funds to free up their own resources for military programs.

International Military Education and Training (IMET): These grants are given to foreign governments to pay for military training provided by American military officials.

Foreign Military Sales (FMS): These sales are government-to-government agreements negotiated by the Pentagon and the purchasing country.

Direct Commercial Sales (DCS): These sales are agreements negotiated between the manufacturing company and the purchasing country and then licensed by the State Department.

Excess Defence Articles (EDA): The U.S. government transfers weapons from its stocks for free or at greatly reduced prices through the EDA program.

Emergency Drawdown Program: This program enables allied governments to receive fast track grants of weapons during crisis situations.

Defence Security Cooperation Agency (DSCA): This Pentagon agency handles government-to-government weapons sales. The DSCA established the "Enduring Freedom Response Cell" to "fast track weapons requests from our allies".

Arms Export Control Act (1976): The Act stipulates that arms transfers can only be used by the recipient nation for self-defense, internal security and in United Nations sanctioned operations.

The Foreign Assistance Act (1961): The Act bars military aid and arms sales to countries that demonstrate "gross and consistent" patterns of human rights abuses.

Export Administration Act (1979): The Act regulates the sale of "dual-use" items that could have civilian or military applications.

U. Thant, Maha Thray Sithu (1907-1974)

Secretary-General of the United Nations (1962-72). Born in the delta of the Irrawaddy River in British-ruled Burma, U. Thant was educated at Rangoon University. As the permanent representative of Burma, he chaired the U.N. Congo Conciliation Commission in 1962. Therefore, he was appointed as the acting secretary-general of the United Nations when the incumbent Dag Hammarskjöld's was killed in an air-crash in the Congo that year. Just over a year later, the General Assembly voted unanimously to make him the secretary-general of the organization.

U. Thant believed, "that the world will not live in harmony so long as two thirds of its inhabitants find difficulty in living at all." Hence, he established many of development and environmental agencies, funds, and programs, including the U.N. Development Program (UNDP), the U.N. University, United Nations Conference on Trade and Development (UNCTAD), United Nations Institute for Training and Research (UNITAR) and the U.N. Environmental Program (UNEP).

In addition, he led a number of successful largely forgotten mediation efforts like the transfer of Netherlands New Guinea (now Papua and West Irian Jaya) to Indonesia (1962); the removal of Soviet missiles from Cuba (1962); controlling the conflict in Yemen in 1962; the resolution of the civil war in the Congo in 1963; the establishment of a peacekeeping force on Cyprus (1964) and the establishment of a cease-fire in the 1965 India-Pakistan War.

Elected to a second term in 1966, U. Thant was less successful in dealing with the major crises of the period, which included the Vietnam War, the six day war between the Arabs and Israel, the Prague Spring and subsequent Soviet invasion of Czechoslovakia, and the Indo-Pakistani War of 1971 leading to the birth of Bangladesh. He was widely criticized in the U.S. and Israel for succumbing to Egyptian President Nasser's demand to pull out U.N. troops from the Sinai in 1967. His cordial relations with the U.S. further declined after he publicly criticized the American conduct of the war in Vietnam.

U. Thant died of lung cancer in New York City in November 1974. By then Burma was under military rule and he was buried in Yangon (Rangoon) without appropriate pomp and ceremony. Student demonstrators, who had briefly seized the coffin, were brutally crushed. A pattern was thus set for student demonstrators, repression, and unceremonial burials of leaders of Burma.

Unitarianism

Religion. A liberal form of Protestantism that emphasized the unity of God despite the differences in various forms of religion. The Christian concepts of the Holy Trinity and of the divinity of Jesus Christ were discarded and tolerance for all other religions and beliefs encouraged. It became popular in eastern India after its close association with Raja Ram Mohan Roy (1772-1833), the great Indian social reformer. This Indo-U.S. relationship also stirred considerable controversy as Roy's, *The Three Steps of Jesus,* was widely circulated in the United States and was sharply critical of the Baptist Missionaries in India. Nevertheless, the author's perspective on Christianity was widely interpreted as one of the early fusions of the Eastern and Western religious thought.

Within a radius of 50 miles in the highlands of northeast India live 98 percent (about 10,000) of India's Unitarians. The Khasis were one of numerous tribes in the region that practiced neither Hinduism nor Islam. Instead, most tribes possessed their own indigenous religions until the British intervened. The British conquest of eastern India brought waves of Christian missionaries into the hills and forests of the region despite resistance by the East India Company. Welsh Calvinists constituted the most numerous and aggressive of the early missionaries. By the 1840s, the Calvinists gave the Roman alphabet to the Khasi language and translated the Bible into the local tongue. Thereafter missionary schools were established and monopolized education among the hill tribes. However, Hajom Kissor Singh (1865-1923), a Khasi lay preacher, reasoned that the Calvinist preoccupation with sin, hellfire and damnation was incompatible with the teachings of Jesus Christ. Accordingly, Singh preached that Jesus was not the actual son of God but a gifted tutor and his two main teachings were the love of God and affection for fellow humans. Singh further reasoned that the Bible was written by other well-meaning folk who, too, were in search of God and the book had both truths and errors in it. Therefore, holy books from other religions could help one gain better understanding of God. Similarly, heaven and hell were not geographic locations but states of the mind and the soul on earth itself. In collaboration with the American, Rev. GEORGE APPLETON DALL, a well-known Unitarian, Singh named his faith as *Ka Niam Unitarian* (The Unitarian Religion). The flaming chalice, a symbol of Unitarianism, is used lavishly in the Khasi Hills. It is atop buildings, in windows, on gates, and on clothes as a pattern knitted into sweaters.

Most of the hill tribes in north-eastern India converted to various Christian denominations in the nineteenth century but few have as charming a historical progression to Christianity as the Unitarians of the Khasi Hills.

(*See also:* ADAM, WILLIAM; MISSIONARIES; UNITARIANISM)

Unocal

American Energy Company (1890-2005). During the last few years of its existence as an independent company, it was active at both edges of South Asia, Afghanistan and Burma. The corporation, headquartered in El Segundo, California, was founded in 1890 as Union Oil. It was the ninth largest oil company in the United States when it merged Chevron Corporation in August 2005. Earlier, in 1996 lawsuits were filed in U.S. Federal Court against the company for alleged human rights violations and for breaking international treaties that prohibit slavery. These cases were instituted in connection with building of the Yadana pipeline for pumping gas from Burma to a power plant in Thailand. Unocal was an investor in the pipeline though Totalfina, a French firm, was the project manager. Following lawsuits, Unocal issued a statement reconfirming the Report by a French Parliamentary Committee that concluded that forced labor was, indeed, used during the early phases of the construction of the pipeline. Though the company also declared its determination to conduct business in "an absolutely ethical, honest, and moral manner," it was forced into an out of court settlement of the suits in 2004. Since August 2005, there has been a series of attacks against the pipeline, some resulting in injuries and deaths. At the other edge of South Asia, women's rights groups, across the globe, incensed by TALIBAN's suppression of women, had decried Unocal for holding discussions with the group on building pipelines through Afghanistan.

(*See also*: ENERGY OVERVIEW OF SOUTH ASIA; OIL AND GAS PIPELINES; KHALILZAD, ZALMY; TALIBAN)

V

Vajpayee, Atal Bihari (1924-)

Journalist and social worker, Prime Minister of India (16-31 May 1996 and 1998-2004). During his tenure as prime minister, India energetically courted the U.S. and moved towards a closer strategic, economic, and diplomatic relationship with Washington. This drive was based on ideological considerations and the imperatives of keeping up with the major changes in the global environment in the wake of the Soviet Union's collapse. Furthermore, new paradigms were needed to cope with the increased globalization of trade and commerce. At the same time, some long standing predicaments persisted. These included Pakistani supported insurgency Indian Kashmir. For about ten years India had already sought for American acknowledgment that such terrorism with its undertones of Islamic fundamentalism was as a major global menace and platforms such as an alliance of democracies were needed to counter it. In this context, Vajpayee hoped that improved Indo-U.S. ties would lead to enough American pressure on Pakistan to persuade Islamabad to discontinue its proxy war in Kashmir

However, in May 1998, the BJP stunned the world by testing three nuclear devices on a single day followed by two more tests a couple of days later. Shortly thereafter, neighboring Pakistan, too, detonated some of its own nuclear devices. The U.S. incensed by the altered international situation and embarrassed by the failure of American intelligence to detect the impending tests, imposed a variety of sanctions against both countries. Till then, the U.S. had considered India as peripheral to its other major strategic interests.

The nuclear tests, India's economic growth, and 9/11 changed that. India's unprecedented offer of its bases for the American intervention in Afghanistan in 2001 further emphasized the altered circumstance. Before 9/11, U.S. Navy ships visited India at intervals of approximately one every three years. After 9/11 such visits became routine. In addition, India's strategic location in the center of Asia, astride the frequently traveled Sea Lanes of Communication (SLOC) linking the Middle East to East Asia, made the country particularly attractive to the U.S. military. The shift had begun earlier with the then President WILLIAM J. CLINTON's visit to India in March 2000, and the lifting of most U.S. sanctions imposed after the nuclear tests. The process was further boosted by the new U.S. President, GEORGE W. BUSH and New Delhi capitalized on the Republicans' opposition to the Comprehensive Test Ban Treaty (CTBT). In addition, Vajpayee sought to further enhance the strategic aspect of the relationship by becoming the first government to support Bush's plans for Ballistic Missile Defense (BMD) systems.

In economic terms, too, India achieved remarkable growth under the BJP though reforms were started at least ten years earlier under the Congress government. In the first year under Vajpayee (1998-90), and despite global recession, India achieved a 5.8 per cent growth in the GDP, which was to rise steadily in succeeding years and was accompanied by massive increases in the foreign exchange reserves of the country. Despite Vajpayee's pro-Americanism, his adroit handling of the nuclear issues, and of the Kargil war (1999), the BJP was perceived as a political party that was too polarizing, too complacent in power, and not enough pro-rural or pro-poor to be rewarded with another win in the general election. After the 2004 loss, Vajpayee took an unusual step in Indian politics by declining to serve as the leader of the opposition in parliament.

W

Walden Pond

A small (64 acres) 102- foot deep glacial kettle-hole pond in Concord, Massachusetts. A kettle hole pond is a shallow, sediment-filled body of water formed by retreating glaciers or draining floodwaters. HENRY DAVID THOREAU lived near this pond from July 1845 to September 1847. His experiences inspired the book, *Walden*, or, *Life in the Woods*, and made the spot famous. The book was a celebration of living the simple life in natural environment. Because of its association with Thoreau, Walden Pond was designated as a National Historic Landmark and is considered as the birthplace of the conservation movement. Boston's "Ice King," Fredric Tudor, harvested ice from Walden Pond each winter and shipped it to India and other countries. One winter at the sight of Tudor's ice harvesters, Thoreau rhapsodized, "The sweltering inhabitants of Charleston and New Orleans, of Madras and Bombay and Calcutta, drink at my well . . . The pure Walden water is mingled with the sacred water of the Ganges."

Watumull Foundation

A Foundation set up in the U.S. by India America to promote better understanding between India and the United States by supporting educational, cultural and philanthropic institutions in Hawaii. Gobindram J. Watumull left India in early 1917 to help his brother run a shop in Honolulu, Hawaii. The business prospered and in the 1940s he became active in the "Committee for India's Freedom." In 1942, the Watumull Foundation was set up. It encourages the writing of books by sponsoring annual book awards.

Whitman, Walt(er) (1819-1892)

American poet, essayist, and a remarkable visionary on Indo-U.S. ties. Born in Long Island, he grew up in the rapidly enlarging city of New York. Whitman was moved by the expansive energy of the age.

In 1855 he paid for the publication of *Leaves of Grass*, a book of twelve poems. His poetry was inspirational, simple in style without orthodox meter or rhyme and full of erotic candor. The book was greatly enlarged and revised five times. In his long poem, "Passage to India," Whitman revels at the laying of the transatlantic cable (1866) and of the opening of the Suez Canal in1869, thus shortening the passage to India. To him it was not the physical journey. Instead, it was a prelude to the spiritual pathway to India and ultimately to God. Whitman regarded India as, "reason's early paradise." With his correct use of Sanskrit words, the work was described as blend between the *Bhagwad Geeta* and the newspaper, *The New York Herald*. His exhortation to the peoples of the two countries may be prophetic for he called upon them to, "Sail forth – steer for deep waters only, Reckless O soul exploring, I with thee, and thou with me, For we are bound where mariner has not yet dared to go." E.M. Foster later used the title for his famous novel on India.

Y

Yale, Elihu (1649-1721)

American businessman and philanthropist. Though born in Boston, Massachusetts, Yale spent little time in America. As a three year old he moved with the family to England. He started as a writer (clerk) at the generous salary of £500 per annum for the East India Company in December 1671. During his twenty-one years in India, Yale rose steadily through the ranks of the Company to become the Governor of Madras and amass great wealth through private trade. He was one of the first to return to England after having made his fortune in the East. When the trustees of Collegiate School of Connecticut in New Haven, Connecticut sought funding for an engineering college Yale sent a donation that included two trunks of textiles that sold for £562 and 12 Shillings. In gratitude, the trustees named the University after him.

Youssef, Ramzi (1968-)

Terrorist. Youssef allegedly entered the United States on a false Iraqi passport in 1992. His uncle, Khalid Shaikh Mohammed, was a leading figure in AL QAEDA. On 26 February 1993, the second anniversary of the end of the first Gulf War, Ramzi drove a van filled with a mixture of paper, urea, nitric acid, three cylinders of compressed hydrogen, and four containers of nitro-glycerin into the parking lot of the World Trade Center in New York City. The expectation was that the explosion would destroy structural parts of the foundation and make one tower collapse into the other. Six other immigrant Muslims were involved in the plot. The explosion did not bring down the twin towers but killed six and injured a thousand. Undeterred, he then plotted to blow-up a dozen American airliners over the Pacific in 1994 by planting explosives inside toy cars that were to be packed in checked-in luggage. His co-plotter, Istaique Parker, a South African Muslim of Pakistani origin backed out. Ramzi returned in disgust to Pakistan.

Parker, familiar with the $2 million bounty for the capture of Ramzi, betrayed him. Hence, Ramzi was apprehended and brought back to New York City. In 1998 he was sentenced to 240 years in solitary confinement.

Yunus, Muhammad (1940-)

Nobel Prize laureate (Peace, 2006), economist, banker. The $1.4 million prize was split between the Grameen Bank and Yunus, its founder and managing director. Born in Chittagong, Bangladesh, educated in economics at Dhaka University (BA 1960, MA 1961), Yunus, earned a Ph.D. in economics from Vanderbilt University in 1971, on a FULBRIGHT SCHOLARSHIP. The Nobel laureate was named as the university's first Distinguished Alumnus in 1996 and refers to Vanderbilt as his second home. Between 1969 and 1972, Yunus was an assistant professor of economics at Middle Tennessee State University (1969-72) where he put up posters and cartoons in support of Bangladeshi independence. He returned to an independent Bangladesh in 1972 to become the head of the economics department at Chittagong University. During the terrible famine of 1974 he met a woman who made bamboo stools but she had no capital of her own, as she had to pay 93% of her earnings to middlemen. Yunus then gave $27 to 42 self-employed crafts workers in a similar quandary. He reasoned that if financial resources were made available to the poor on reasonable terms, then economic activity would be generated and poverty alleviated. Accordingly, Yunus founded the Grameen (Hindi/Bengali: "Rural") Bank in 1976 to provide credit to the poorest in rural Bangladesh. Though credit without collateral was advanced by the bank it was only to those who owned their own homes. This requirement meant that it was not the poorest of the poor or the homeless whc received loans. In addition, borrowers were required to maintain and improve their houses, grow vegetables, plant seedlings, build and repair pit-latrines, do regular physical exercise, and neither accept nor offer dowries. The guidelines also stressed that the whole community (of 8–10 groups) must not allow anyone to fall behind in their repayments or in the activities outlined above. In this manner social capital became the collateral used by the bank. The bank's profitability and liquidity was further enhanced by its ability to borrow at low rates of interest from governments around the world, and lend the same money at higher rates of interest to the poor. In addition, unlike other banks in Bangladesh, the Grameen does not pay corporate taxes. With this unique approach and support systems, the bank claims that the loan repayment rate is at an astonishing 99 percent. However, in 2001 the *Wall Street Journal's* correspondents concluded that the repayment rate of loans was much lower than the professed 99 percent. The Journal also discovered that at least twenty-five percent the loans were used for consumption and not for commercial activity and defaulters were given repeated extensions for making repayments. Nevertheless, it is widely perceived that micro-credit banking as promoted by Yunus is cost-effective in reducing some poverty and spurring overall development. An unexpected and underestimated impact of lending to females was the empowerment of women in the household and community resulting in better educational standards and higher levels of confidence in their off-spring. On the other hand, it has led to a backlash as men-folk in several communities joined local politicians who disapproved of the bank's role in turning women into entrepreneurs as un-Islamic. Despite such tensions and questions about the bank's practices and performance, it has more than six million borrowers, 97 percent of them being women. It services 71,000 villages through approximately 2,300 branches in the country. Micro-credit banking has been emulated in about 100 other countries with varying degrees of success. Yunus' international recognition began in the U.S. in 1994 he received the World Food Prize in Des Moines, Iowa. Numerous other honors followed including the Magsaysay Award, Gandhi Peace Prize, and Sydney Peace Prize.

Y2K Problem

Y2K was the short-hand for Year 2000. From the 1960s to the late 1980s it was common in computer software programs to save disk and memory space by using two digits instead of four to represent a particular year. The major Programming languages of the time were COBOL (an acronym for COmmon Business-Oriented Language) and RPG (Report Program Generator). COBOL processed text using ASCII (American Standard Code for Information Interchange). RPG used the EBCDIC (Extended Binary Coded Decimal Interchange

Code) for its representations. Most of this programming for the big mainframe computers was done by Indian software engineers.

As the 1990's approached experts realized that in the year 2000 computer systems could interpret 00 as 1900 thereby distorting many programs. For instance, if the difference between 1 January 2000 and 31 December 1999 was computed as -100 years rather than 1 day, then there would be major complications in finance, banking, utilities, manufacturing, telecommunications, airlines operations and schedules.

While the new computers were manufactured with the four digit year 2000 as an operating system, the entire application source code of most of the older mainframe systems had to be fixed. Since most of it was initially written by Indian software engineers, they were the most proficient in fixing it. And so they did. At the turn of the millennium, many utilities and other companies switched off their main computers and put backup computers to work. When the clock ticked 1 January 2000, no major problems were reported. Almost all financial and banking systems worked seamlessly, time-bound security locks operated without glitches, there were no major power outages, and aircraft took off and landed without incident. Billions of dollars were generated for the Indian Information Technology (IT) industry to fix the Y2K problem. It was a major stimulant for the growth and development of the IT industry in India.

(*See also*: BUSINESS PROCESS OUTSOURCING (BPO) and INFORMATION TECHNOLOGY (IT) IN INDIA, SILICON VALLEY).

Z

Zahir Shah, Mohammed (1914-2007)

Last King of Afghanistan (1933-1973). Zahir succeeded to the blood-stained throne of Afghanistan after his father, Mohammed Nadir Shah, was assassinated in 1933. The first thirty years of his reign were dominated by members of the royal family, initiall*y by his uncles, and later his cousin, SARDAR MOHAMMED DAUD. In 1951, an uncle, the then prime minister dissolved the Kabul University Students' Union, shut down newspapers critical of the government, and jailed many opposition leaders. In the wake of the crisis, younger members of the royal family replaced him in 1953 with Daud as the new Prime Minister. Ten years later, in March 1963, with the backing of the royal family, Zahir sought Daud's resignation because Pakistan had closed the border with land-locked Afghanistan in August 1961 in retaliation to the Prime minister's obsessive support for PASHTUNISTAN. The closure had increased Afghan dependence on the Soviet Union for trade and in-transit facilities. Both were greatly limited and led to a significant decline in the economic well-being of the country. Two months after Daud's resignation Pakistan reopened the border, much to the relief of the Afghan people. Hence, by 1964, the king, now respected and popular in the country, was finally his own master. He then promulgated a new constitution that included a democratically elected legislature and greatly improved opportunities for the education of women. In addition, it provided for a constitutional monarchy, and instituted political and economic modernization of the country. The implementation of the reforms was timid and tentative creating a "vague atmosphere of a political crisis" by 1972. Earlier, in January 1970, as a gesture of support for his policies Vice President Spiro Agnew became the highest ranking U.S. leader to meet the king since President EISENHOWER visited the country in 1959. At the same time the American ambassador, the French speaking Robert Neumann (1967-1973), developed close ties with the Zahir, who, too, hir, who, too, was fluent in the language. The envoy stressed the dire consequences of the long drought in the country and the likelihood of its negative impact on the monarchy. Meanwhile, the cagey Daud, reportedly backed by both India and the Soviet Union, sought tacit American backing to overthrow the monarchy. Through Wahid Abdullah, an official in the Afghan Foreign Ministry, Daud provided the exact details of the planned coup. Neumann, well-remembered for his probity, informed the intermediary that the U.S. government "cannot properly comment" on the "internal nature of the Afghan government," and Washington's position towards any country was "based on that government's policies and actions, in particular toward U.S. interests and towards peace and stability." Thus reassured, Daud deposed Zahir in July 1973 and proclaimed a republic. Neumann quietly left as ambassador to Morocco, another kingdom with French-speaking Muslim monarch (incidentally, Neumann's son was later to serve as the U.S. Ambassador to Afghanistan). Within months, Zahir formally abdicated. He was ignored by major powers and stayed in quiet exile in Italy. He was back in the political calculus in 1982. In May that year the U.S. tried to establish a coalition of anti-Soviet resistance under the leadership of the exiled king. Six of the seven leaders rejected him and U.S. contacts with Zahir again declined. Around the same time, the Soviets, too, wooed him. However, he refused to return as a puppet ruler of a Soviet-backed regime in Afghanistan. Hence, he had little choice but to remain aloof from the blood feuds that followed the Soviet withdrawal from his country in 1989. After another ten years of fratricidal blood-letting in Afghanistan, he offered to help restore peace and stability. In July 2000 the U.S. faintly acknowledged the offer of "His prestige as elder statesman in an attempt to restore peace to his shattered homeland" but did little. In 2001 when U.S. launched air-strikes against AL QAEDA and the TALIBAN, a Congressional and CIA delegation met with deposed king with the forlorn hope that he could persuade *Pashtun* tribesmen to defect from the Taliban. Another factor in the revival of the "Zahir Shah option" was the king's popularity among refugees, especially among political moderates and the exiled elite. An estimated 70 percent of the Afghan refugees living in Pakistan favored his return. So he did in 2002 but only to support the U.S.-backed former royalist, HAMID KARZAI for the presidency of Afghanistan. He formally did so at the LOYA JIRGA, the traditional legislative council that had ruled the country's tribal society. Zahir was allowed to move back into his old palace in central Kabul but had to again renounce all claims to the throne. As a symbol of unity for Afghanistan he was proclaimed as the "Father of the Nation." Zahir, like Zafar (Bahadur Shah II, 1775-1862), the last Mughal Emperor of India, was a well-meaning, ineffectual ruler buffeted throughout his life by family and foreigners.

(*See also:* AFGHANISTAN-U.S. TIES)

Zardari, Asif Ali Khan (1956-)

President of Pakistan (September 2008-), Director, M/S Zardari Group (Pvt.) Ltd. A Shia and scion of one of the lesser Sindhi tribes, he briefly attended St. Patrick's School, the alma mater of a number of Pakistani leaders including the former Prime Minister Mir Zafarullah Khan Jamali and ex-President PERVEZ MUSHARRAF. His father owned the Bambina Cinema in Karachi which featured a risqué neon sign and the young Zardari's main claim to fame was that he had a private disco in his home. However, As early as 1969, Zardari was already in the public eye for he played the role as the child of the character portrayed as the adult by the famous movie star Waheed Murad in the blockbuster Urdu film *Salgirah* ("Anniversary").

His sudden appearance on the international scene was the announcement of his engagement to BENAZIR BHUTTO in 1987. Zardari, three years her junior was considered as an unusual match for the thirty-five year old brainy Oxford and Harvard graduate who was carefully groomed for the leadership of the Pakistan Peoples' Party (PPP) founded by her father, ZULFIKAR ALI BHUTTO. However, despite her initial misgivings, the polo-loving, hard-living charmer wooed and won her. Nevertheless, it was apparently understood that he would stay out of politics. That was not to be. During Benazir's first tenure as Prime Minister, Zardari's associates were appointed to her secretariat whereas he himself reportedly peddled his influence and took kick-backs on government contracts. In 1990, following the dismissal of the Benazir government on allegations of corruption, nepotism, and abuse of power, he was arrested for kidnapping, extortion, and loan fraud. Zardari was imprisoned for three years though none of the charges resulted in a conviction. When Benazir returned to power in 1993, Zardari was unmistakably a political figure with a substantial role in the governance of the country. It was formalized by his election to the National Assembly and his appointment as the Federal Minister for the Environment (1993-95). Then, much to the establishment's consternation, Benazir sprang a surprise in 1995 by installing him as the Federal Minister of Investment, a post specially created for him. Some considered Benazir's judgment had faltered because her intense love for him, others, less romantic, merely regarded him and his minister-ship as a liability to the party and to her political career. The post was reportedly used by the two to acquire a personal fortune of $1.5 billion. A year later Benazir's government was ousted for alleged nepotism and corruption by the President of Pakistan who was supposedly a Bhutto loyalist. Thereafter, Zardari was a senator from 1997 to 1999 with the nickname "Mr. Ten Percent" for his alleged reputation as a vigorous collector of kickbacks. In the wake of the 1999 coup by General Musharraf, the senate was dissolved and Zardari spent the next eight years in prison from 1996 to November 2004, shuttling between Lahore, Rawalpindi, and Karachi. Numerous charges, including the 1996 murder of his brother-in-law, Mir Murtaza Bhutto were filed against him. None led to a conviction. Meanwhile his wife went into exile. Zardari's release by President Musharraf in 2004 was seen as an early sign in a possible alliance between Musharraf and Benazir Bhutto.

With the decline of the Musharraf presidency in 2007, both Britain and the U.S. stepped up their efforts to shore-up his government by establishing a Bhutto-Musharraf alliance. By passing the National Reconciliation Order (NRO) in October that year, the faltering Pakistani dictator absolved the Bhutto-Zardaris from charges of corruption and related offenses from 1988 to October 1999. The passage of the NRO was followed by the swift return of Benazir to Pakistan. Two assassination attempts followed. The second succeeded on 30 December 2007. Zardari inherited the co-leadership of the PPP and was clearly was the chief beneficiary from the tragedy.

In the aftermath of the assassination, Zardari revealed a combination of finesse and decisiveness. He was a moderating influence on the public backlash the followed his wife's murder. He formed a coalition with archrival NAWAZ SHARIF. The two successfully then successfully forced Musharraf's resignation from the presidency. Thereafter Zardari outmaneuvered Nawaz Sharif, the two-time prime minister, by denying him the chance of running for elections to the National Assembly through an adverse judgment by the Lahore High Court. He then forced Sharif to quit the coalition by reneging on the commitment to reinstate the chief justice of the Supreme Court, Iftikhar Muhammad Chaudhry, whom President Musharraf had removed earlier. Zardari's opponents alleged that the latter was concerned that independent-minded Chaudhry might reverse the amnesty under the NRO. The new co-leader of the PPP also sidelined Bhutto loyalists like Makhdoum Amin Fahim who was the leader of the legislative party and the main negotiator of the deal that facilitated the Bhutto-Zardaris return to Pakistan. He publicly favored subsidizing the cost of wheat to the consumer, an inflationary step that would further dip into the depleted exchequer. In addition, he scrapped a proposed capital gains tax thereby reducing government revenues. Zardari also stated that a fresh perspective was needed on Kashmir and the battle against Islamic militants in the country would continue. As in the past, he soon dropped his protestations about not seeking a role in the government. Instead, he ran for the presidency of the country and was elected in September 2008. His election may have further hardened the perception of him being a street-smart schemer, and an unbridled opportunist. Accordingly, instead of uniting the country he may have further splintered the political spectrum thereby ultimately paving the way for the return of the military to power in an increasingly unstable Pakistan.

In Washington, his election he also raised concerns about the oversight of the two stage, ten-year, bipartisan $15 billion package of non-military aid to Pakistan proposed by Senators Biden and Lugar and backed by the Bush administration. Despite their reservations, American officials apparently prefer him to Sharif because the PPP has better secular credentials and Washington may also find it easier "to do business" with Zardari as he is viewed as a "pragmatic businessman" in the U.S. capital.

Another unknown factor is his health. He apparently suffers from diabetes and perhaps a spinal ailment. However, a host of western newspapers quoted court documents listing a range of psychiatric illnesses, including dementia, depression, and post-traumatic stress disorder. These diagnoses may be exaggerated for their use in courts instead of the purposes of treatment.

The marble presidential palace in Islamabad designed by EDWARD DURRELL STONE whose own inspiration lay in the sublime structure of the Taj Mahal, may sway Zardari, perhaps mellowed and tempered by age and experience, his years of incarceration, and the loss of Benazir, to be the right man at the right place for his country.

Zia ul-Haq, Mohammed (1924-1988)

Pakistani general and military dictator. Zia was born in Julundhar, India, and educated at the Government High School, Simla and at the elite St. Stephens College, Delhi. Nevertheless, he championed MADRASSAS as a good source of schooling with such vigor and knowledge that many assumed that he himself had attended one. Zia joined in the British-Indian Army in 1943. He received further training in the United States and served as an Advisor to the government of Jordan in 1967-70. He was appointed as Chief of the Army Staff by ZULFIKAR ALI BHUTTO in March 1976. It was a carefully made choice by the Pakistani leader for he wanted a pliable quiet officer who was personally beholden to him. Zia seemed to fit the bill for he was a comparatively junior Lieutenant General (sixth in seniority) with a reputation for piety, professionalism and little interest in political matters. He was also from the Arain community, which had little representation in the army. After a prolonged and bitter confrontation between Bhutto and a coalition of parties known as the Peoples' National Alliance (PNA), following the blatantly rigged elections in 1977, the army under Zia seized control on 5 July 1977. Zia and his fellow commanders set a limit of 90 days for the completion of a fair general election, but were probably dissuaded by the legal consequences of their actions as the Constitution of 1973 explicitly defined a coup against the government as a capital offence punishable by death. Instead, Zia had Bhutto sentenced to death by the Lahore High Court for the attempted murder of political opponent. Consequently, Zia and the country were treated as political pariahs till late 1979 when both became key allies of the United States in the war against communism following the Soviet military intervention in Afghanistan in December that year. Zia's legacy includes the global rise of pugnacious, xenophobic triumphalistic, Islamic fundamentalists some of whom had fought as the MUJAHIDEEN against the Soviet supported Afghan Government (1979-89) and for the growth of MADRASSAS in Pakistan. His policies led to the general Islamization of society in his country. He was killed in an ill-explained air-crash in August 1988.

Bibliography

Note

The internet has greatly eased access to information. It has also replaced the physical transportation and storage of knowledge from traditional forms like books on paper to the medium of cyberspace. In addition to search engines such as Google and Yahoo, web-sites like Amazon.com and Barnes & Noble.com offer many more books, periodicals, papers, reviews, etc., than any traditional library can. In addition, a great deal of data is available in the public domain especially from the U.S. Central Intelligence Agency's *World Factbook*, the Country Pages in the Background Notes prepared by the U.S. Department of State, and the Congressional Research Service. Among the other remarkable resources on the internet are various blogs, specific sites and many of the entries on *Wikipedia.* However, the accuracy of internet based sources remains a problem.

During the last century, the first comprehensive work on the Indian Subcontinent was the *Cambridge History of India*, published between 1922 and 1937. It was particularly good in formulating a chronology of Indian history and in describing the administrative structures of government in India. In 1970 its scope has been greatly widened and publication of *The New Cambridge History of India* as a series of forty short, self-contained volumes, each dealing with a separate theme within an overall four-part structure under the editorship of C.A. Bayly, Gordon Johnson, and John F. Richards was launched. As it remains an on-going work, the bibliography does not list any of these excellent volumes. Similarly, various Historical Dictionaries and A to Zs related to the region and written, edited, and published by leaders in the field are not mentioned below for these works, too, are a part of an on-going series. The multivolume Reports by Louis Dupree on Afghanistan as a part of the Asia series for the Hanover, New Hampshire, based American Universities Field Staff

(AUFS) are acknowledged here. Therefore, the works are not individually listed in the bibliography. Numerous other sources ranging from various government archives to newspaper articles and radio or television transcripts are not included in this bibliography. What remains, for the most part, are singular works or an eclectic selection of works by authors who have written extensively on South Asia. Hence, the works listed are often representative samples of their much wider and deeper scholarship. All material cited or recommended is in a predominant language used in both the United States and South Asia: English.

General

Ahmad, Aziz. *An Intellectual History of Islam in India.* Chicago: Aldine, 1969.

Ali, Chaudhri Muhammad. *The Emergence of Pakistan.* New York: Columbia University Press, 1967.

Ambedkar, B. R. *Pakistan, or the Partition of India,* Bombay: Thacker, 1945.

Al-Mujahid, Sharif. *Quaid-i-Azam Jinnah: Studies in Interpretation.* Karachi: Quaid-i-Azam Academy, 1981.

Arasaratnam, Sinnappah. *Ceylon.* Englewood Cliffs, New Jersey: Prentice-Hall, 1984.

Aris, Michael. *Bhutan: The Early History of a Himalayan Kingdom.* Warminster, Wiltshire, United Kingdom: Aris and Phillips, 1979.

Bahadur, Lal. *The Muslim League: Its History, Activities and Achievements.* Lahore: Book Traders, 1979.

Barrier, N. Gerald. *India and America: American Publishing on India, 1930-1985.* New Delhi: American Institute of Indian Studies, 1986.

Basham, A. L. *The Origin and Development of Classical Hinduism.* Edited and completed by Kenneth G. Zysk. New York: Oxford University Press, 1989.

Basham, A. L. *The Wonder That Was India, 1: A Survey of the History and Culture of the Indian Sub-Continent before the Coming of the Muslims.* London: Sidgwick and Jackson, 1967.

Basham, A. L. *The Wonder That Was India.* New York: Grove Press, 1954.

Basham, A. L., ed. *A Cultural History of India.* Oxford: Clarendon Press, 1975.

Baxter, Craig. *Bangladesh: A New Nation in an Old Setting.* Boulder: Westview Press, 1984.

Bayly, C. A. *Rulers, Townsmen, and Bazaars: North Indian Society in the Age of British Expansion, 1770-1870.* Cambridge: Cambridge University Press, 1983.

Bennett-Jones, Owen. *Pakistan: Eye of the Storm.* New Haven: Yale University Press, 2002.

Bhattacharjee, Arun. *Rajiv Gandhi: Life and Message.* New Delhi: Ashish, 1992.

Binder, Leonard. *Religion and Politics in Pakistan.* Berkeley and Los Angeles: University of California Press, 1963.

Bolitho, Hector. *Jinnah: Creator of Pakistan.* New York: Macmillan, 1954.

Bondurant, Joan V. *The Conquest of Violence: The Gandhian Philosophy of Conflict.* Princeton: Princeton University Press, 1958.

Brecher, Michael. *Nehru: A Political Biography.* London: Oxford University Press, 1959.

Brown, Judith M. *Gandhi and Civil Disobedience.* London: Cambridge University Press, 1977.

Brown, Judith M. *Modern India: The Origins of an Asian Democracy.* New Delhi: Oxford University Press, 1985.

Burki, Shahid Javed. *Pakistan: A Nation in the Making.* Boulder: Westview Press, 1986.

Cafaro, Philip. *Thoreau's Living Ethics: Walden and the Pursuit of Virtue.* Athens: University of Georgia Press. 2004.

Chawla, Subash. *The New Maldives.* Colombo, Sri Lanka: Diana, 1986.

Collins, Larry, and Dominique Lapierre. *Freedom at Midnight.* New York: Simon and Schuster, 1975.

Cohen, Stephen P. *Emerging Power: India.* Washington DC: Brookings, 2001.

Cohen Stephen P. *The Idea of Pakistan.* Washington DC: Brookings, 2004

Das, Nirmala. *The Dragon Country: The General History of Bhutan.* Bombay: Orient Longman, 1974.

Das, Veena. *Mirrors of Violence: Communities, Riots, and Survivors in South Asia.* New Delhi: Oxford University Press, 1992.

Davies, C. Collin. *An Historical Atlas of the Indian Peninsula.* London: Oxford University Press, 1959.

de Silva, Chandra Richard. *Sri Lanka: A History.* New Delhi: Vikas, 1987.

de Bary, Wm. Theodore, et al. (comp.). *Sources of Indian Tradition.* New York: Columbia University Press, 1958.

Dunn, Rose E. *The Adventures of Ibn Battuta.* London: Croom Helm, 1986.

Dupree, Louis. *Afghanistan.* Princeton: Princeton University Press, 1973.

Eaton, Richard M. *The Rise of Islam and the Bengal Frontier, 1204-1760.* Comparative Studies on Muslim Societies, No. 17. Berkeley: University of California Press, 1993.

Edwardes, Michael. *A History of India.* Bombay: Asia, 1961.

Embree, Ainslie T. *1857 in India: Mutiny or War of Independence.* Lexington, Massachusetts: Heath, 1963.

Embree, Ainslie T., ed. *Alberuni's India.* New York: Norton, 1971.

Erickson, Erik H. *Gandhi's Truth: On the Origins of Militant Nonviolence.* New York: Norton, 1970.

Fischer, Louis. *The Life of Mahatma Gandhi.* New York: Harper, 1950.

Fisher, Michael. *Indirect Rule in India: Residents and the Residency System, 1764-1857.* New Delhi: Oxford University Press, 1991.

Gandhi, Mahatma. *An Autobiography: The Story of My Experiments with Truth.* Trans., Mahadev Desai. Boston: Beacon Press, 1957. Reprint. Boston: Beacon Press, 1993.

Gandhi, Mahatma. *Essential Writings of Mahatma Gandhi.* Ed., Achaean Iyer. New Delhi: Oxford University Press, 1991.

Gascoigne, Bamber. *The Great Moghuls.* London: Jonathan Cape, 1971.

Gilmartin, David. *Empire and Islam: Punjab and the Making of Pakistan.* Berkeley: University of California Press, 1988.

Glazer, Sulochana Raghavan, and Nathan Glazer, eds. *Conflicting Images: India and the United States.* Glenn Dale, Maryland: Riverdale, 1990.

Gopal, Sarvepalli. *Jawaharlal Nehru: A Biography.* 3 vols. London: Cape, 1975-84.

Gould, Harold A. *Sikhs, Swamis, Students, and Spies: The India Lobby in the United States, 1900-1946.* New Delhi: Sage Publications, 2006.

Gupte, Pranay. *Mother India: A Political Biography of Indira Gandhi.* New York: Scribner's, 1992.

Gupte, Pranay. *Vengeance: India after the Assassination of Indira Gandhi.* New York: Norton, 1985

Habib, Irfan. *An Atlas of the Mughal Empire.* Delhi: Oxford University Press, 1982.

Hadi Hussain, Muhammed. *Syed Ahmed Khan: Pioneer of Muslim Resurgence.* Lahore: Institute of Islamic Culture, 1970.

Hamid, Abdul. *Muslim Separatism in India.* Karachi: Oxford University Press, 1971.

Hasan, K. Sarwar. *The Transfer of Power.* Karachi: Pakistan Institute of International Affairs, 1966.

Hasan, Mushirul. *India Partitioned: The Other Face of Freedom.* Delhi: Roli Books, 1995.

Heinsath, Charles. *Indian Nationalism and Hindu Social Reform.* Princeton: Princeton University Press, 1964.

Heyerdahl, Thor. *The Maldives Mystery.* London: Allen and Unwin, 1986.

Hill, John L., ed. *The Congress and Indian Nationalism: Historical Perspectives.* Westwood, Massachusetts: Riverdale, 1991.

Hodson, H. V. *The Great Divide: Britain, India, Pakistan.* London: Hutchinson, 1969.

Hosseini, Khaled. *The Kite Runner.* New York: Riverhead Books, 2003.

Humbers, Philippe. *The Rajiv Gandhi Years: Sunshine and Shadows.* New Delhi: Vimot, 1992.

Ikram, S. M., and Percival Spear, eds. *The Cultural Heritage of Pakistan.* Karachi: Oxford University Press, 1955.

Irschich, Eugene F. *Politics and Social Conflict in South India: The Non-Brahman Movement and Tamil Separatism.* Berkeley: University of California Press, 1969.

Jalal, Ayesha. *The Sole Spokesman: Jinnah, the Muslim League, and the Demand for Pakistan.* Cambridge: Cambridge University Press, 1985.

Javed, Hassan, *India: A Study in Profile,* Rawalpindi: Army Book Service, 1990.

Jayakar, Pupul. *Indira Gandhi: A Biography.* New Delhi: Penguin, 1992.

Kamath, M. V. *The United States and India 1776-1996.* New Delhi: Indian Council for Cultural Relations. 1998.

Kapur, Rajiv. *Sikh Separatism: The Politics of Faith.* New Delhi: Vikas, 1987.

Kashyap, Subhash. *The Politics of Defection.* Delhi: National, 1969.

Khan, Fazal Muqeem. *Pakistan's Crisis in Leadership.* Islamabad: National Book Foundation, 1973.

Khilnani, Sunil. *The Idea of India.* New York: Farrar, Straus and Giroux, 1998.

Korbel, Josef. *Danger in Kashmir.* Princeton: Princeton University Press, 1966.

Kumar, Satish. *Rana Polity in Nepal: Origin and Growth.* New York: Asia, 1967.

Lamb, Alistair. *Kashmir: A Disputed Legacy, 1846-1990.* Karachi: Oxford University Press, 1992.

Lelyveld, David. *Aligarh's First Generation: Muslim Solidarity in British India.* Princeton: Princeton University Press, 1978.

Low, David A, ed. *Congress and the Raj.* London: Arnold-Heinemann, 1977.

Ludden, David. *Peasant History in South India.* Princeton: Princeton University Press, 1985.

Manor, James, ed. *Sri Lanka: In Change and Crisis.* New York: St. Martin's Press, 1984.

Lumby, E. W. R. *The Transfer of Power in India.* London: George Allen and Unwin, 1954.

Macintyre, Ben. *The Man Who Would Be King: The First American in Afghanistan.* New York: Farrar, Straus and Giroux, 2004.

Majumdar, R. C. *History of the Freedom Movement in India, (3 vols.)* Calcutta: Firma Mukhopadhyay, 1962-3.

Maldives Islands: Monograph on the History, Archaeology, and Epigraphy. Colombo: Government Printers, 1940.

Maldives Department of Information and Broadcasting. *Maldives: A Historical Overview.* Male: 1985.

Maldives Department of Information and Broadcasting. *Maldives: Social Development.* Male: 1985.

Malik, Hafeez, ed. *Iqbal: Poet-Philosopher of Pakistan.* New York: Columbia University Press, 1971.

Maniku, Hassan Ahmed. *Changes in the Topography of the Maldives.* Maldives: Forum of Writers on the Environment, 1990.

Mansergh, N., and E. W. R. Lumby, eds. *The Transfer of Power, 1942-47.* (5 vols.) London: Her Majesty's Stationery Office, 1970-83.

Masani, Zaheer. *Indira Gandhi: A Biography.* Farmington, New York: Brown, 1976.

Mehta, Ved. *Portrait of India.* New Haven: Yale University Press, 1993.

Menon, Vapal Pangunni. *The Story of the Integration of the Indian States.* Madras: Orient Longman, 1956. Reprint. Madras: Orient Longman, 1985.

Menon, Vapal Pangunni. *The Transfer of Power in India.* Princeton: Princeton University Press, 1957.

Metcalf, Barbara Daly. *Islamic Revival in British India: Deoband, 1860-1900.* Princeton: Princeton University Press, 1982.

Michel, Aloys A. *The Indus River: A Study of the Effects of Partition.* New Haven: Yale University Press, 1967.

Minault, Gail. *The Khilafat Movement: Religious Symbolism and Political Mobilization in India.* Studies in Oriental Culture, No. 16. New York: Columbia University Press, 1982.

Misra, H. N. *Bhutan: Problems and Policies.* New Delhi: Heritage, 1988.

Mojumdar, Kanchanmoy. *Anglo-Nepalese Relations in the Nineteenth Century.* Calcutta: K.L. Mukhopadhyay, 1973.

Moon, Penderel. *Divide and Quit.* London: Chatto and Windus, 1962.

Moon, Penderel. *The British Conquest and Dominion of India.* London: Duckworth, 1989.

Mascarenhas, Anthony. *Bangladesh: A Legacy of Blood.* London: Hodder and Stoughton, 1986.

Myint-U, Thant. *The River of Lost Footsteps: Histories of Burma.* London: Faber and Faber, 2006.

Naipaul, V. S. *India: A Million Mutinies Now.* London: William Heinemann, 1990.

Narain, Harsh. *The Ayodhya Temple Mosque Dispute.* New Delhi: Penman, 1993.

Narashimhan, C. R. *Rajagopalachari: A Biography.* New Delhi: Radiant, 1993.

Nehru, Jawaharlal. *Towards Freedom: An Autobiography.* New York: Day, 1941.

Nugent, Nicholas. *Rajiv Gandhi: Son of a Dynasty.* New Delhi: UBS, 1991.

O'Donnell, Charles Peter. *Bangladesh: Biography of a Muslim Nation.* Boulder: Westview Press, 1984.

Ostheimer, John M., ed. *The Politics of the Western Indian Ocean Islands.* New York: Praeger, 1975.

Panikkar, K. M. *Asia and Western Dominance.* New York: Collier, 1969.

Panikkar, Kerlam Madhava. *A Survey of Indian History.* NewYork: Asia, 1971.

Papanek, Gustav V. *Pakistan's Development.* Cambridge: Harvard University Press, 1967.

Philips, C. H., and Mary Doreen Wainwright, eds. *The Partition of India: Policies and Perspectives, 1935-1947.* London: Allen and Unwin, 1970.

Qureshi, Ishtiaq Hussain, ed. *A Short History of Pakistan.* (4 vols.) Karachi: University of Karachi Press, 1967.

Rahula, Walpola. *History of Buddhism in Ceylon: The Anuradhapura Period, 3rd Century B. C. — 10th Century A. D.* Colombo: M. D. Gunasena, 1966.

Rangarajan, L. N., trans. and ed. *Kautilya: The Arthasastra.* New York: Penguin, 1992.

Ray, N. R., ed. *Himalaya Frontier in Historical Perspective.* Calcutta: Institute of Historical Studies, 1986.

Rizvi, S. A. A. *The Wonder That Was India, 2: A Survey of the History and Culture of the Indian Sub-Continent from the Coming of the Muslims to the British Conquest, 1200-1700.* London: Sidgwick and Jackson, 1987.

Rose, Leo E. *The Politics of Bhutan.* Ithaca: Cornell University Press, 1977.

Rose, Leo E., and John T Scholz. *Nepal: Profile of a Himalayan Kingdom.* Boulder, Colorado: Westview Press, 1980.

Schwartzberg, Joseph E, ed. *A Historical Atlas of South Asia.* New York: 1992.

Sisson, Richard, and Leo E. Rose. *War and Secession: Pakistan, India, and the Creation of Bangladesh.* Berkeley: University of California Press, 1990.

Smith, Vincent Arthur. *The Oxford History of India.* Oxford: Clarendon Press, 1968.

Smith, Wilfred Cantwell. *Modern Islam in India.* Lahore: Ashraf, 1963.

Spear, Percival. *A History of India, 1.* Harmondsworth, United Kingdom: Penguin, 1965.

Spear, Thomas George Percival. *A History of India, 2.* Harmondsworth, United Kingdom: Penguin, 1965.

Syed, Anwar H. *The Discourse and Politics of Zulfikar Ali Bhutto.* New York: St. Martin's Press, 1992.

Tahir-Kheli, Shirin. *The United States and Pakistan: The Evolution of an Influence Relationship.* New York: Praeger, 1982.

Thapar, Romila. *A History of India, 1.* Harmondsworth, United Kingdom: Penguin Books, 1966.

Thapar, Romila. *A History of India, 2.* Harmondsworth, United Kingdom: Penguin Books, 1966.

Tharoor, Shashi. *India: From Midnight to the Millennium.* New York: Arcade, 1997.

Vertzberger, Yaacov. *The Enduring Entente: Sino-Pakistan Relations, 1960-80.* New York: Praeger, 1983.

Wheeler, Richard S. *The Politics of Pakistan: A Constitutional Quest.* Ithaca, New York: Cornell University Press, 1970.

Wink, André. *Al-Hind, the Making of the Indo-Islamic World, 1: Early Medieval India and the Expansion of Islam, 7th-11th Centuries.* 2d. ed., rev. Leiden: Brill, 1991.

Winnius, George Davison. *The Fatal History of Portuguese Ceylon: Transition to Dutch Rule.* Cambridge: Harvard University Press, 1971.

Wintle, Justin. *Life of Aung San Suu Kyi.* London: Hutchinson, 2007.

Wolpert, Stanley A. ed., *Encyclopedia of India* (4 Volumes). Chicago: Charles Scribner's Sons, 2005.

Wolpert, Stanley. *Jinnah of Pakistan.* New York: Oxford University Press, 1984.

Wolpert, Stanley. *Tilak and Gokhale: Revolution and Reform in the Making of Modern India.* Cambridge: Cambridge University, 1962. Reprint. Delhi: Oxford University Press, 1989.

Wolpert, Stanley. *Zulfi Bhutto of Pakistan: His Life and Times.* New York: Oxford University Press, 1993.

Woodruff, Philip (pseudo.) *The Men Who Ruled India (Vol. I): The Founders.* London: Jonathan Cape, 1953

Woodruff, Philip (pseudo.). *The Men Who Ruled India,(Vol. II): The Guardians.* London: Jonathan Cape, 1954.

Zimmer, Heinrich. *The Art of Indian Asia.* New York: Pantheon, 1955.

Ziring, Lawrence. *The Ayub Khan Era: Politics in Pakistan, 1958-1969.* Syracuse, New York: Syracuse University Press, 1971.

Ziring Lawrence. *Pakistan at the Crossroads of History.* Oxford: Oneworld, 2003.

Society and Culture

Abbedin, Namjul. *Local Administration and Politics in Modernizing Societies: Bangladesh and Pakistan.* Dhaka: National Institute of Public Administration, 1973.

Abel, Evelyn. *The Anglo-Indian Community: Survival in India.* Delhi: Chanakya, 1988.

Aggarwal, J. C., and Sarita Aggarwal. *Education in India: A Comparative Study of States and Union Territories.* New Delhi: Concept, 1990.

Aggarwal, Santosh. *Three Language Formula: An Educational Problem.* New Delhi: Sian, 1991.

Agnihotri, R. K., and A. L. Khanna. *Second Language Acquisition: Socio-Cultural and Linguistic Aspects of English in India, 1: Research in Applied Linguistics.* New Delhi: Sage, 1994.

Agwani, Mohammed S. *Islamic Fundamentalism in India.* Chandigarh: Twenty-First Century India Society, 1986.

Ahir, D. C. *Buddhism in Modern India.* Delhi: Sri Satguru, 1991.

Ahmad, Aijuzuddin. *Muslims in India: Their Educational, Demographic, and Socio-Economic Status with Inter-Community Comparisons Based on Field Survey Conducted in 1991.* New Delhi: Inter-India, 1993.

Ahmad, Imtiaz, ed. *Caste and Social Stratification among Muslims in India.* New Delhi: Manohar, 1978.

Ahmad, Kamruddin. *The Social History of East Pakistan.* Dhaka: Pioneer Press, 1967.

Ahman, Anis. *Women and Social Justice: Some Legal and Social Issues in Contemporary Muslim Society.* Islamabad: Institute of Policy Studies, 1991.

Ahmed Rafiuddin. *Islam in Bangladesh: Society, Culture, and Politics.* Dhaka: Bangladesh Itihas Samity, 1983.

Ahmed, Akbar S. *Discovering Islam: Making Sense of Muslim History and Society.* London: Routledge and Kegan Paul, 1988.

Ahmed, Akbar S. *Pakistan Society: Islam, Ethnicity, and Leadership in South Asia.* New York: Oxford University Press, 1986.

Akbar, M. J. *The Siege Within: Challenges to a Nation's Unity.* London: Penguin, 1985.

Ali, A. K. M. Ayyub. *History of Traditional Islamic Education in Bangladesh down to A.D. 1980.* Dhaka: Islamic Foundation of Bangladesh, 1983.

Ali, Banuazizi, and Myron Weiner, eds. *The State, Religion, and Ethnic Politics: Afghanistan, Iran, and Pakistan.* Syracuse, New York: Syracuse University Press, 1986.

Andersen, Walter K., and Shridhar D. Damle. *The Brotherhood in Saffron: The Rashtriya Swayamsevak Sangh and Hindu Revivalism.* Boulder, Colorado: Westview Press, 1987.

Arnold, Fred, and Nasra Shah. eds., *Asian Labor Migration: Pipeline to the Middle East.* Boulder, Colorado: Westview Press, 1986.

Arumugam, Shanmugam. *Some Ancient Hindu Temples of Sri Lanka.* Colombo: Ranco Printers and Publishers, 1980.

Ashraf, Ali, ed. *Ethnic Identity and National Integration.* New Delhi: Concept, 1994.

Attanayake, Abhaya, et al. *Mahaweli Saga: Challenge and Response.* Colombo: Mahaweli Authority of Sri Lanka, 1985.

Aziz, K. K. *The Making of Pakistan.* London: Chatto and Windus, 1967.

Babb, Lawrence A. *Redemptive Encounters: Three Modern Styles in Hindu Tradition.* Berkeley: University of California Press, 1986.

Bagwe, Anjali. *Of Woman Caste: The Experience of Gender in Rural India.* New York: Zed, 1995.

Baxi, Upendra, and Bhikhu Parekh, eds. *Crisis and Change in Contemporary India.* New Delhi: Sage, in association with The Book Review Literary Trust, New Delhi, 1995.

Bharati, Agehananda. *The Ochre Robe.* London: Allen and Unwin, 1961.

Bhutan. Department of Education. *Dzongkha Reader.* (4 vols.) Thimphu: Royal Government of Bhutan Press, 1979.

Brass, Paul R. *Language, Religion, and Politics in North India.* London: Cambridge University Press, 1974.

Bumiller, Elisabeth. *May You Be the Mother of a Hundred Sons: A Journey among the Women of India.* New York: Fawcett Columbine, 1990.

Burki, Shahid Javed. *Pakistan: The Continuing Search for Nationhood.* Boulder, Colorado: Westview Press, 1991.

Calman, Leslie J. *Towards Empowerment: Women and Politics in India.* Boulder, Colorado: Westview Press, 1992.

Caplan, Lionel. *Class and Culture in Urban India: Fundamentalism in a Christian Community.* New York: Oxford University Press, 1987.

Carrithers, Michael, and Caroline Humphrey. eds. *The Assembly of Listeners: Jains in Society.* Cambridge: Cambridge University Press, 1991.

Cartman, James. *Hinduism in Ceylon.* Colombo: M. D. Gunasena, 1957.

Chaklader, Snehamoy. *Sociolinguistics: A Guide to Language Problems in India.* New Delhi: Mittal, 1990.

Chanchreek, K. L., and Saroj Prasad, eds. *Mandal Commission Report. Myth and Reality: A National Viewpoint.* Delhi: H.K. Publishers, 1991.

Chauhan, R. R. S. *Africans in India: From Slavery to Royalty.* New Delhi: Asian Publication Services, 1995.

Chowdhury, Rafiqul Islam. *Tribal Leadership and Political Integration: A Case Study of Chakma and Mong Tribes of Chittagong Hill Tracts.* Chittagong: University of Chittagong, 1979.

Clark, Alice W., ed. *Gender and Political Economy: Explorations of South Asian Systems.* Delhi: Oxford University Press, 1993.

Coomaraswamy, Ananda K. *The Dance of Shiva.* New York: Noonday Press, 1958.

Datta, Prabhat Kumar. *Regionalism of Indian Politics.* New Delhi: Sterling, 1993.

de Silva, Lynn. *Buddhism: Beliefs and Practices in Sri Lanka.* Colombo: Wesley Press, 1980.

Dhamothara, Ayyadurai, ed. *Word-Borrowing and Word-Making in Modern South Asian Languages.* Heidelberg: South Asia Institute, University of Heidelberg, 1978.

Donnan, Hastings, and Pnina Werbner, eds. *Economy and Culture in Pakistan: Migrants and Cities in a Muslim Society.* Basingstoke, United Kingdom: Macmillan, 1991.

Downs, Frederick S. *Christianity in North East India.* Delhi: Indian Society for Promoting Christian Knowledge, 1983.

Drury, David. *The Iron Schoolmaster: Education, Employment, and the Family in India.* Delhi: Hindustani, 1993.

Dutta, Pratap C. *The Great Andamanese: Past and Present.* Calcutta: Anthropological Survey of India, 1978.

Elst, Koenraad. *Decolonizing the Hindu Mind.* New Delhi, India: Rupa, 2001.

Engineer, Ashgar Ali, ed. *Mandal Commission Controversy.* Delhi: Ajanta, 1991.

Fuller, Christopher J. *Servants of the Goddess: The Priests of a South Indian Temple.* Cambridge: Cambridge University Press, 1984.

Furer-Haimendorf, Christoph von. *Himalayan Traders: Life in Highland Nepal.* London: Murray, 1975.

Fürer-Haimendorf, Christoph von. *Tribes of India: The Struggle for Survival.* Berkeley: University of California Press, 1982.

Galanter, Marc. *Competing Equalities: Law and the Backward Classes in India.* Berkeley: University of California Press, 1984.

Gopalakrishnan, Ramamoorthy. *The Geography and Politics of Afghanistan.* New Delhi: Concept, 1982.

Gregory, Robert G. *South Asians in East Africa: An Economic and Social History, 1890-1980.* Boulder, Colorado: Westview Press, 1993.

Gross, Susan Hill. *Wasted Resources, Diminished Lives: The Impact of Boy Preference on the Lives of Girls and Women.* St. Louis Park, Minnesota: Upper Midwest Women's History Center, 1992.

Haaland, Gunnar. *Evolution of Socio-economic Dualism in the Maldives.* Bergen, Norway: Michelsen Institute, DERAP (Development Research and Action Program), 1987.

Hamid, Mohsin. *The Reluctant Fundamentalist.* New York: Harcourt Brace, 2007.

Hasnain, Nadeem, and Sheikh Abrar Husain. *Shias and Shia Islam in India: A Study in Society and Culture.* New Delhi: Harnam, 1988.

Hiltebeitel, Alf. *Criminal Gods and Demon Devotees: Essays on the Guardians of Popular Hinduism.* Albany: State University of New York, 1989.

Hiro, Dilip. *The Untouchables of India.* Rev. ed. MRG Report, No. 26. London: Minority Rights Working Group on Untouchables, 1982.

Hluna, John V. *Church and Political Upheaval in Mizoram: A Study of the Impact of Christianity on the Political Development in Mizoram.* Aisawl: Mizo History Association, 1985.

Huntington, Susan L. *The Arts of Ancient India: Buddhist, Hindu, and Jain.* New York: Weatherhill, 1985.

Iqbal, Javed. *Islam and Pakistan's Identity.* Lahore: Vanguard Books, 2003.

Islam, Nazrul. *Internal Migration in Bangladesh: A Review of Literature.* Dhaka: Centre for Urban Studies, 1983.

Israel, Benjamin J. *The Jews of India.* New Delhi: Centre for Jewish and Inter-Faith Studies, Jewish Welfare Association, 1982.

Ives, Jack D., and Bruno Masserli. *The Himalayan Dilemma: Reconciling Development and Conservation.* The United Nations University and Routledge: New York, 1989.

Jacobson, Doranne, and Susan S. Wadley. *Women in India: Two Perspectives.* Columbia, Missouri: South Asia Books; and New Delhi: Manohar, 1994.

Jeffery, Roger. *The Politics of Health in India. Comparative Studies of Health Systems and Medical Care,* No. 21. Los Angeles: University of California Press, 1988.

Kachru, Braj B. *The Indianization of English: The English Language in India.* Delhi: Oxford University Press, 1983.

Kakar, Sudhir. *The Colors of Violence: Cultural Identities, Religion, and Conflict.* Chicago: University of Chicago Press, 1996.

Karan, Pradyumna P., and William M Jenkins, Jr. *The Himalayan Kingdoms: Bhutan, Sikkim and Nepal.* Princeton, New Jersey: Van Nostrand, 1963.

Karat, Prakash. *Language and Nationality Politics in India.* Bombay: Orient Longman, 1973.

Katz, Nathan, and Ellen S. Goldberg. *The Last Jews of Cochin: Jewish Identity in Hindu India.* Columbia: University of South Carolina Press, 1993.

Keith, Arthur Berriedale. *The Religion and Philosophy of the Veda and Upanishads.* 2 vols. Reprint. Westport, Connecticut: Greenwood, 1971.

Kinsley, David R. *Hinduism: A Cultural Perspective.* Englewood Cliffs, New Jersey: Prentice-Hall, 1982.

Knipe, David M. *Hinduism: Experiments in the Sacred.* San Francisco: Harper, 1991.

Kohli, Shanta. *Family Planning in India: A Descriptive Analysis.* New Delhi: Indian Institute of Public Administration, 1977.

Kopf, David. *The Brahmo Samaj and the Shaping of the Modern Indian Mind.* Princeton: Princeton University Press, 1979.

Korson, Henry J. ed. *Contemporary Problems of Pakistan.* Boulder, Colorado: Westview Press, 1993.

Kulke, Eckehard. *The Parsees in India: A Minority as Agent of Social Change.* Munich: Weltforum Verlag, 1974.

Lamb, Christina. *Waiting for Allah: Pakistan's Struggle for Democracy.* New York: Viking, 1991.

Lebra, Joyce, J. Paulson, and J. Everett, eds. *Women and Work in India: Continuity and Change.* New Delhi: Promilla, 1984.

Mahmood, Tahir, ed. *Minorities and State at the Indian Law: An Anthology.* New Delhi: Institute of Objective Studies, 1991.

Malik, M. Saeed. *The Musical Heritage of Pakistan.* Islamabad: Idara Saqafat-e-Pakistan, 1982.

Maloney, Clarence, ed. *Language and Civilization Change in South Asia.* Contributions to Asian Studies, No. 11. Leiden: Brill, 1978.

Mann, Rann Singh. *Culture and Integration of Indian Tribes.* New Delhi: M. D. Publications, 1993.

Massey, James. *A Concise History of Dalits.* Delhi: Indian Society for Promoting Christian Knowledge, 1994.

Mathema, Padma. *Primary Health Care in Nepal.* Kathmandu: Vijaya Ram Mathema, 1987.

McLeod, W. H. *The Sikhs: History, Religion, and Society.* New York: Columbia University Press, 1989.

Mencher, Joan P. *Female Cultivators and Agricultural Laborers: Who They Are and What They Do.* Michigan State University Working Papers on Women in International Development, No. 192. East Lansing: November 1989.

Michell, George. *The Hindu Temple: An Introduction to Its Meaning and Forms.* New Delhi: B.I. Publications, 1977.

Miller, Barbara D. *The Endangered Sex: Neglect of Female Children in Rural North India.* Ithaca: Cornell University Press, 1981.

Misra, Bhaskar D., Ali Ashraf, Ruth S. Simmons, and George B. Simmons. *Organization for Change: A Systems Analysis of Family Planning in Rural India.* New Delhi: Family Planning Association, 1982.

Misra, Kamal Kant. *Tribal Elites and Social Transformation.* New Delhi: Inter-India, 1994.

Mitter, Sara. *Dharma's Daughters: Contemporary Indian Women and Hindu Culture.* New York: Penguin, 1991.

Moorhouse, Geoffrey. *To the Frontier.* New York: Holt, Rhinehart, and Winston, 1985.

Mujib, Muhammad. *The Indian Muslims.* Montreal: McGill University Press, 1967.

Mumtaz, Khawar, and Farida Shaheed. *Women of Pakistan: Two Steps Forward, One Step Back?* London: Zed Press and Karachi: Vanguard, 1987.

Mukhopadhyay, Carol Chapnick, and Susan Seymour, eds. *Women, Education, and Family Structure in India.* Boulder, Colorado: Westview Press, 1994.

Naidu, K. Munirathna, ed. *Peasant Movements in India.* New Delhi: Reliance, 1994.

Naim, C. M., ed. *Iqbal, Jinnah, and Pakistan: the Vision and the Reality.* Syracuse, New York: Maxwell School at Syracuse University, 1979.

Nigosian, S. A. *The Zoroastrian Faith: Tradition and Modern Research.* Montreal: McGill-Queen's University Press, 1993.

Norman, Ayesha. *Status of Women and Fertility in Bangladesh.* Dhaka: University Press, 1983.

O'Flaherty, Wendy Doniger, ed. and trans. *The Rig Veda: An Anthology.* New York: Penguin, 1981.

Ostor, Akos, Lina Fruzetti, and Steve Barnett, eds. *Concepts of Person: Kinship, Caste, and Marriage in India.* Cambridge: Harvard University Press, 1982.

Papanek, Hanna, and Gail Minault, eds., *Separate Worlds: Studies of Purdah in South Asia.* Columbia, Missouri: South Asia Books; and New Delhi: Chanakya, 1982.

Quddus, Naseem Jaffer. *Problems of Education in Pakistan.* Karachi: Royal Book Company, 1990.

Ramadan, Tariq. *In the Footsteps of the Prophet: Lessons from the Life of Mohammad.* Oxford: Oxford University Press, 2007.

Rashiduzzaman, M. *Rural Leadership and Population Control in Bangladesh.* Washington: University Press of America, 1982.

Rekhi, Upjit Singh. *Jharkhand Movement in Bihar.* New Delhi: Nunes, 1988.

Reynolds, C. H. B. *Linguistic Strands in the Maldives.* London: School of Oriental and African Studies, 1978.

Riyaz, Fahmidah. *Pakistan Literature and Society.* New Delhi: Patriot Publishers, 1986.

Robb, Peter G. *Dalit Movements and the Meanings of Labor in India.* SOAS Studies on South Asia. Delhi: Oxford University Press, 1993.

Robert, Michael. *Caste Conflict and Elite Formation: The Rise of a Karava Elite in Sri Lanka, 1500-1931.* Cambridge: Cambridge University Press, 1982.

Routledge, Paul. *Terrains of Resistance: Nonviolent Social Movements and the Contestation of Place in India.* Westport, Connecticut: Praeger, 1993.

Ruberu, Tantrige Ranjit. *Education in Colonial Ceylon.* Kandy, Sri Lanka: Kandy Printers, 1962.

Sahasrabuddhe, P. G., and Manik Chandra Vajpayee. *The People Versus Emergency: A Saga of Struggle.* Trans., Sudhakar Raje. New Delhi: Suruchi Prakashan, 1991.

Sankaia, H. D. *Aspects of Indian History and Archeology.* Delhi: B. R. Publishing, 1977.

SarDesai, D. R., and Anand Mohan, eds. *The Legacy of Nehru: A Centennial Assessment.* New Delhi: Promilla, 1992.

Sarkar, Jadhunath. *Fall of the Mughal Empire* (4 vols.) Bombay: Orient Longman, 1964-72.

Sarma, Sunil Sen, ed. *Farakka, A Gordian Knot: Problems on Sharing Ganga Water.* Calcutta: Ishika, 1986.

Seal, Anil. *The Emergence of Indian Nationalism: Competition and Collaboration in the Late Nineteenth Century.* London: Cambridge University Press, 1968.

Seddon, David. *Nepal: A State of Poverty.* New Delhi: Vikas, 1987.

Segal, J. B. *A History of the Jews of Cochin.* London: Vallentine Mitchell, 1993.

Seligmann, C. G., and Brenda Z. Seligmann. *The Veddas.* Cambridge: The University Press, 1911.

Sen, Makhan Lal, trans. *The Ramayana of Valmiki.* New Delhi: Munshiram Manoharlal, 1978.

Sethi, V. K. *Kabir: The Weaver of God's Name.* Amritsar: Radha Soami Satsang Beas, 1984.

Sharma, Kususm. *Ambedkar and Indian Constitution.* New Delhi: Ashish, 1992.

Sharma, Miriam. *The Politics of Inequality: Competition and Control in an Indian Village.* Honolulu: University of Hawaii Press, 1984.

Sharma, Pitamber. *Urbanization in Nepal.* (Papers of the East-West Population Institute, No. 110.) Honolulu: East-West Center, 1989.

Shearer, Alistair, and Peter Russell, trans. *The Upanishads.* New York: Harper and Row, 1978. Reprint. Boston: Unwin Paperbacks, 1989.

Shourie, Arun. *Indian Controversies: Essays on Religion in Politics.* New Delhi: Manohar, 1993.

Shourie, Arun. *Symptoms of Fascism.* New Delhi: Vikas, 1978.

Shukri, M. A. M, ed. *Muslims of Sri Lanka: Avenues to Antiquity.* Beruwala, Sri Lanka: Jamiah Naleemia Institute, 1986.

Siddiqi, A. H. *Baluchistan: Its Society, Resources, and Development.* Lanham, Maryland: University Press of America, 1991.

Singh, Gopal. *A History of the Sikh People, 1469-1978.* New Delhi: World Sikh University Press, 1979.

Sisson, Richard, and Stanley Wolpert, eds. *Congress and Indian Nationalism: The Pre-Independence Phase.* Berkeley: University of California Press, 1988.

Smith, Vincent, ed. *The Oxford History of India.* New Delhi: Oxford University Press, 1981.

Spear, Thomas George Percival, ed. *The Oxford History of Modern India, 1740-1975.* New Delhi: Oxford University Press, 1978.

Srivastava, Sushil. *The Disputed Mosque: A Historical Inquiry.* New Delhi: Vistaar, 1991.

Stein, Burton, ed. *Peasant, State, and Society in Medieval South India.* New Delhi: Oxford University Press, 1980.

Subramaniam, Chitra. *Bofors: The Story Behind the News.* New Delhi: Viking, 1993.

Suleri, Sara. *Meatless Days.* Chicago: University of Chicago Press, 1989.

Tahseen, Rana. *Education and Modernisation of Muslims in India.* New Delhi: Deep and Deep, 1993.

Talwar, S. N. *Under the Banyan Tree: The Communist Movement in India, 1920-1964*. New Delhi: Allied, 1985.

Tandon, Prakash. *Punjabi Century, 1857-1947*. Berkeley: University of California Press, 1968.

Tapper, Richard, ed. *The Conflict of Tribe and State in Iran and Afghanistan.* London: CroomHelm, 1983.

Thapar, Romila. *From Lineage to State: Social Formations in the Mid-First Millennium B.C. in the Ganga Valley.* New Delhi: Oxford University Press, 1984.

Thurston, Edgar. *Caste and Tribes of Southern India.* 7 vols. Madras: Government Press, 1909.

Tisserant, Eugene. *Eastern Christianity in India: A History of the Syro-Malabar Church from the Earliest Time to the Present Day.* Trans., E. R. Hambye. London: Longmans, Green, 1957.

Torwesten, Hans. *Vedanta: Heart of Hinduism.* New York: Grove Weidenfeld, 1985.

Trautmann, Thomas R. *Dravidian Kinship.* Cambridge Studies in Social Anthropology. New York: Cambridge University Press, 1981.

Troll, Christian W., ed. *Muslim Shrines in India: Their Character, History, and Significance.* Delhi: Oxford University Press, 1989.

Vatuk, Sylvia, ed. *American Studies in the Anthropology of India.* New Delhi: Manohar, 1978.

Vincent, Rose, ed. *The French in India: From Diamond Traders to Sanskrit Scholars.* Trans., Latika Padgaonkar. Bombay: Popular Prakashan, 1990.

Webb, Paul A. *Maldives: People and Environment.* Male: Department of Information and Broadcasting, 1989.

Weiner, Myron, and Banuazizi Ali, eds. *The State and the Restructuring of Society in Afghanistan, Iran, and Pakistan.* Syracuse, New York: Syracuse University Press, 1993.

Weiner, Myron. *The Child and the State in India: Child Labor and Education Policy in Comparative Perspective.* Princeton: Princeton University Press, 1991.

Weiss, Anita M. *Walls Within Walls: Life Histories of Working Women in the Old City of Lahore.* Boulder, Colorado: Westview Press, 1992.

Weiss, Anita M., ed. *Islamic Reassertion in Pakistan: The Application of Islamic Laws in a Modern State.* Syracuse, New York: Syracuse University Press, 1986.

Worthington, Vivian. *A History of Yoga.* London: Routledge and Kegan Paul, 1982.

Writer, Rashna. *Contemporary Zoroastrians: An Unstructured Nation.* Lanham: University Press of America, 1994.

Zaehner, Robert Charles. *Hinduism.* 2d ed. New York: Oxford University Press, 1966.

Economics, Trade, and Development

Acharya, K. C. S. *Food Security System of India: Evolution of the Buffer Stocking Policy and Its Evaluation.* New Delhi: Concept, 1983.

Ahluwalia, Isher Judge. *Industrial Growth in India: Stagnation since the Mid-Sixties.* Delhi: Oxford University Press, 1985.

Ahmad, Masood, and Gary P. Kutcher. *Irrigation Planning with Environmental Considerations: A Case Study of Pakistan's Indus Basin.* (World Bank Technical Paper, No. 166.) Washington: World Bank, 1992.

Alderman, Harold, George Mergos, and Roger Slade. *Cooperatives and the Commercialization of Milk Production in India: A Literature Review.* Washington: International Food Policy Research Institute, 1987.

Attwood, D. W., and B. S. Baviskar, eds. *Who Shares? Co-operatives and Rural Development.* New Delhi: Oxford University Press, 1988.

Awasthi, Dipesh. *Regional Patterns of Industrial Growth in India.* New Delhi: Concept, 1991.

Bag, A. K. *Science and Civilization in India.* New Delhi: Navrang, 1985.

Bagchi, Kathkali S. *Drought-Prone India: Problems and Perspectives.* (2 vols.) New Delhi: Agricole, 1991.

Bansil, P. C. *Ceylon Agriculture: A Perspective.* Delhi: Dhanpat Rai & Sons, 1971.

Bhagwati, Jagdish, ed. *India in Transition: Freeing the Economy.* Oxford: Clarendon Press, 1993.

Bhalla, A. S., and A. K. N. Reddy, eds. *The Technological Transformation of Rural India.* New York: St. Martin's Press, 1994.

Bhutan and United Nations Development Programme. *Report of the Workshop on the Evaluation and Planning of Human Resources Development, Thimphu, May 27-June 2, 1985.* Thimphu: 1985.

Brown, Douglas, and Scott Wilson. *The Black Book of Outsourcing: How to Manage the Changes, Challenges, and Opportunities.* Hoboken, N. J.: Wiley, 2005.

Byres, Terence J., ed. *The State and Development Planning in India.* Delhi: Oxford University Press, 1994.

Cameron, John, and Mohammad Irfan. *Enabling People to Help Themselves: An Employment and Human Resources Strategy for Pakistan in the 1990s.* Geneva: World Employment Programme, International Labour Organisation, 1991.

Chakravarty, Shubhra. *Atomic Energy in India.* New Delhi: Batra, 1992.

Chanda, Nayan. *How Traders, Preachers, Adventurers, and Warriors Shaped Globalization.* New Haven: Yale University Press, 2007.

Das, Gurcharan. *India Unbound: The Social and Economic Revolution from Independence to the Global Information Age.* New Delhi: Viking, 2000.

Dasgupta, Ajit K. *A History of Indian Economic Thought.* Routledge History of Economic Thought Series. London: Routledge, 1993.

de Janury, Alain, and K. Subbarao. *Agricultural Price Policy and Income Distribution in India.* New Delhi: Oxford University Press, 1986.

Davies, Paul. *What's This India Business?: Offshoring, Outsorcing, and the Global Services Revolution.* London: Nicholas Brealey International, 2004.

Farrington, John, and David J. Lewis, eds., *Non-Governmental Organizations and the State in Asia: Rethinking Roles in Sustainable Agricultural Development.* Non-Governmental Organizations Series. London: Routledge, 1993.

Fisher, William C., ed. *Working Toward Sustainable Development: The Narmada Dam Project.* Armonk, NY: Sharpe, 1994.

Friedman, Thomas. *The World is Flat.* New York: Farrar, Straus and Giroux, 2005.

Fry, Maxwell J. *The Afghan Economy: Money, Finance, and the Critical Constraints to Economic Development.* Leiden: Brill, 1974.

Gadgil, Madhav, and Ramachandra Guha. *This Fissured Land: An Ecological History of India.* Berkeley: University of California Press, 1993.

Gandhi, P. Jegadish, ed. *Economic Development and Policies in India.* New Delhi: Har-Anand, 1994.

Ghosh, Arun, K. K. Subrahmanian, Mridul Eapen, and Haseeb A. Drabu, eds. *Indian Industrialization: Structure and Policy Issues.* Delhi: Oxford University Press, 1992.

Ghosh, Udipto. *Bhutan's Economic Development: Objects, Strategies and Problems.* (Centre for Himalayan Studies, Special Lectures, No. 3.) Raja Rammohunpur, India: University of North Bengal, 1984.

Gillespie, Stuart, and Geraldine McNeill. *Food, Health, and Survival in India and Developing Countries.* New Delhi: Oxford University Press, 1992.

Guhan, S. *The World Bank's Lending in South Asia.* Brookings Occasional Papers. Washington: Brookings Institution, 1995.

Gunasekera, H. M. *Land to the Tiller: The Political Economy of Agrarian Reform in South Asia.* New Haven: Yale University Press, 1983.

Gupta, Suraj B. *Black Income in India.* New Delhi: Sage, 1992.

Gupta, Suraj B. *Monetary Planning in India.* London: Oxford University Press, 1979.

Hazell, Peter B. R., and C. Ramasamy. *The Green Revolution Reconsidered: The Impact of High-Yielding Rice Varieties in South India.* Baltimore: Johns Hopkins University Press, 1991.

Iqbal, Badar Alam. *Indo-U. S. Economic Relations — Then and Now.* Hyderabad, AP: Icfai University Press, 2005.

Iqbal, Munawar, ed. *Pakistan: State of the Economy in a Long-run Perspective.* Islamabad: Institute of Policy Studies, 1989.

Ishiguro, Masayasu, and Takamasa Akiyama. *Energy Demand in Five Major Asian Developing Countries: Structure and Prospects.* World Bank Discussion Papers, No. 277. Washington: World Bank, 1995.

Jalal, Ayesha. *The State of Martial Rule: The Origins of Pakistan's Political Economy of Defence.* Lahore: Vanguard, 1991.

Jalan, Bimal. *India's Economic Crisis: The Way Ahead.* Delhi: Oxford University Press, 1991.

James, William, and Subroto Roy, eds. *Foundations of Pakistan's Political Economy: Towards an Agenda for the 1990s.* Newbury Park, California: Sage, 1992.

Jha, Prem Shankar. *India: A Political Economy of Stagnation.* Bombay, Oxford University Press, 1980.

Joshi, S. C. *Forestry Handbook of Bhutan.* Dehra Dun, India: International Book Distributors, 1986.

Kamdar, Mira. *Planet India: How the Fastest Growing Democracy is Transforming America and the World.* New York: Scribner, 2007.

Kanuk, Alan R. *Capital Markets of India: An Investor's Guide (Wiley Finance).* Hoboken, NJ: Wiley, 2007.

Keay, John. *The Honourable Company: A History of the English East India Company.* London: Harper Collins, 1991.

Khan, Mahmood Hasan. *Underdevelopment and Agrarian Structure in Pakistan.* Boulder, Colorado: Westview Press, 1981.

Khan, Shahrukh Rufi. *Profit and Loss Sharing: An Islamic Experiment in Finance and Banking.* Karachi: Oxford University Press, 1987.

Kobayashi-Hillary, Mark. *Outsourcing to India: The Offshore Advantage.* Berlin: Springer, 2005.

Kohli, Atul. *The State and Poverty in India.* Cambridge: Cambridge University Press, 1987.

Kohli, Rajan. *Structural Change in Indian Industries.* New Delhi: Capital Foundation Society, 1994.

Kuppuram, G., and K. Kumudamani, eds. *History of Science and Technology in India.* 12 vols. Delhi: Sundeep Prakashan, 1990.

Lal, Deepak. *The Hindu Equilibrium: India C1500-2000.* New York: Oxford University Press, 2005.

Lipton, Michael, and John Toye. *Does Aid Work in India? A Country Study of the Impact of Official Development Assistance.* London: Routledge, 1990.

Luthfi, M., and Zubair, H. *Innovation in Primary School Construction: Maldives Community Schools.* Bangkok: UNESCO Regional Office for Education in Asia and the Pacific, 1987.

Mandal, Gobinda. *Technology, Growth, and Welfare in Indian Agriculture.* New Delhi: Agricole, 1989.

Michel, Aloys A. *The Indus Rivers.* New Haven: Yale University Press, 1987.

Mitra, Subrata K. *Power, Protest, and Participation: Local Elites and Development in India.* New York: Routledge, 1992.

Moore, Mick. *The State and Peasant Politics in Sri Lanka.* Cambridge: Cambridge University Press, 1985.

Mydral, Gunnar. *Asian Drama: An Inquiry into the Poverty of Nations.* 3 vols. New York: Pantheon, 1968.

Nehru, Jawaharlal. *The Discovery of India.* New York: Day, 1946.

Noman, Omar. *Pakistan: A Political and Economic History since 1947.* London: Kegan Paul, 1990.

Qasir, Nadeem. *Pakistan Studies: An Investigation into the Political Economy, 1948-1988.* Karachi: Oxford University Press: 1991.

Rajakarunanayake, Lucien, ed., *Mahaweli Saga: Challenge and Response.* Colombo: Mahaweli Authority of Sri Lanka, 1985.

Regmi, Mahesh Chandra. *Land Tenure and Taxation in Nepal.* Kathmandu: Ratna Pustak Bhandar, 1978.

Reich, Michael R., and Toshiteru Okuba, eds. *Protecting Workers' Health in the Third World: National and International Strategies.* New York: Auburn House, 1992.

Rodriguez, Deborah, and Kristin Ohlson. *Kabul Beauty School: An American Woman Goes Behind the Veil.* New York: Random House, 2007.

Rosen, George. *Contrasting Styles of Industrial Reform: China and India in the 1980s.* Chicago: University of Chicago Press, 1992.

Shah, Nasra M., ed. *Pakistani Women: A Socioeconomic and Demographic Profile.* Islamabad: Pakistan Institute of Development Economics; and Hawaii: East-West Population Institute, 1986.

Sharma, Pitamber. *Urbanization in Nepal.* (Papers of the East-West Population Institute, No. 110.) Honolulu: East-West Center, 1989.

Shrestha, Babu Ram. *Managing External Assistance in Nepal.* Kathmandu: Jamuna Shrestha, 1990.

Siddiqa, Ayesha. *Military Inc.: Inside Pakistan's Military Economy.* London: Pluto, 2007.

Sinha, Ajit Kumar, ed. *New Economic Policy of India: Restructuring and Liberalizing the Economy for the 21st Century.* New Delhi: Deep and Deep, 1994.

Sinha, R. K., ed. *The Great Ascent: The Rural Poor in South Asia.* Baltimore: Johns Hopkins University Press, 1990.

Sondhi, Sunil. *Science, Technology, and India's Foreign Policy.* Delhi: Anamika Prakashan, 1994.

Subbarayappa, B. V. *In Pursuit of Excellence: A History of the Indian Institute of Science.* New Delhi: Tata McGraw-Hill, 1992.

Varma, Roli. *Harbingers of Global Change: India's Techno-Immigrants in the United States.* Lanham, MD: Lexington, 2006.

Verghese, B. G. *Integrated Water Resources Development and Regional Cooperation within the Himalayan-Ganga-Brahmaputra-Barak Basin.* New Delhi: Oxford University Press and IBH, 1990.

Verghese, B. G., and Ramaswamy R. Iyer, eds. *Harnessing the Eastern Himalayan Rivers: Regional Cooperation in South Asia.* New Delhi: Centre for Policy Research, 1993.

Wallich, Christine, Raja J Chelliah, and Narain Sinha, eds. *State Finances in India.* 3 vols. World Bank Staff Working Paper, No. 523. Washington: World Bank, 1982.

Weiss, Anita M. *Culture, Class, and Development in Pakistan: The Emergence of an Industrial Bourgeoisie in Punjab.* Boulder, Colorado: Westview Press, 1991.

Governance and Politics

Abbas, Borhanuddin Mohammad. *The Ganges Water Dispute* Dhaka: University Press, 1982.

Abbas, Hassan, Jessica Stern (Foreword). Pakistan's Drift Into *Extremism: Allah, The Army, And America's War On Terror.* Westport, Connecticut: Praeger, 2000.

Ahamed, Emajuddin, ed. *Foreign Policy of Bangladesh: A Small State's Imperative.* Dhaka: University Press, 1984.

Ahmad, Munir. *The Civil Servant in Pakistan.* Karachi: Oxford University Press, 1964.

Ahmed, Moudud. *Bangladesh: Era of Sheikh Mujibur Rahman.*Dhaka: University Press, 1983.

Ahuja, Gurdas M. *BJP and the Indian Politics: Politics and Programmes of the Bharatiya Janata Party.* New Delhi: Ram, 1994.

Aijazuddin, F. S., ed. *The White House & Pakistan: Secret Declassified Documents, 1969-1974.* New Delhi, Oxford University Press, 2002.

Akbar, M. J. *Kashmir: Behind the Vale.* New Delhi: Viking, 1991.

Ali, A. M. M. Shawkat. *Politics and Land System in Bangladesh.* Dhaka: National Institute of Local Government, 1986.

Ali, Tariq. *An Indian Dynasty: The Story of the Nehru-Gandhi Family.* New York: Putnam, 1985.

Ali, Tariq. *The Leopard and the Fox.* Oxford, England: Seagull, 2007.

Arnold, Anthony. *Afghanistan's Two-Party Communism: Parcham and Khalq.* Stanford: Hoover Institution Press, 1983.

Austin, Dennis. *Democracy and Violence in India and Sri Lanka.* Chatham House Papers. London: Royal Institute of International Affairs, 1995.

Austin, Granville. *Working a Democratic Constitution: The Indian Experience.* New Delhi: Oxford University Press, 2000.

Balasingham, A. S. *Liberation Tigers and Tamil Eelam Freedom Struggle.* Madras: Makkal Acchakan, 1983.

Braibanti, Ralph, ed. *Asian Bureaucratic Systems Emergent from the British Imperial Tradition.* Durham: Duke University Press, 1966.

Baraith, Roop Singh. *Transit Politics in South Asia: A Case Study of Nepal.* Jaipur, India: Aalekh, 1989.

Barnett, Marguerite Ross. *The Politics of Cultural Nationalism in South India.* Princeton: Princeton University Press, 1976.

Basu, Amrita. *Two Faces of Protest: Contrasting Modes of Women's Activism in India.* Berkeley: University of California Press, 1992.

Baxi, Upendra. *Courage, Craft, and Contentions: The Indian Supreme Court in the Eighties.* Bombay: Tripathi, 1985.

Baxter, Craig, Yogendra K. Malik, Charles H. Kennedy, and Robert C. Oberst. *Government and Politics in South Asia.* Boulder, Colorado: Westview, 1993.

Bertocci, Peter J. *Emergence of Bangladesh and Role of the Awami League.* New Delhi: Vikas, 1982.

Bhattarai, Baburam. *Monarchy Vs. Democracy: The Epic Fight in Nepal.* Delhi: Samkaleen Teesari Duniya, 2005.

Bhutto, Benazir. *Daughter of Destiny.* New York: Simon and Schuster, 1989.

Bhutto, Zulfikar Ali. *The Great Tragedy.* Karachi: Pakistan People's Party, 1971.

Bhutto, Zulfikar Ali. *The Myth of Independence.* Karachi: Oxford University Press, 1969.

Boyce, James K. *Agrarian Impasse in Bengal: Institutional Constraints to Technological Change.* Oxford: Oxford University Press, 1987.

Bradsher, Henry S. *Afghanistan and the Soviet Union.* Durham: Duke Press Policy Studies, 1983.

Brass, Paul R. *Ethnicity and Nationalism: Theory and Comparison.* New Delhi: Sage, 1991.

Burke, S. M., and Lawrence Ziring. *Pakistan's Foreign Policy: An Historical Analysis.* Karachi: Oxford University Press, 1990.

Butler, David, Ashok Lahiri, and Prannoy Roy. *India Decides: Elections 1952-1991.* New Delhi: Living Media India, 1991.

Canfield, Robert L, ed. *Revolutions and Rebellions in Afghanistan: Anthropological Perspectives. Berkeley:* Institute of International Studies, University of California, 1984.

Centre for Women and Development. *Women and Politics in Bangladesh.* Dhaka: 1985.

Chopra, J. K. *Women in the Indian Parliament: A Critical Study of Their Role*. New Delhi: Mittal, 1993.

Crossette, Barbara. *India: Facing the Twenty-First Century*. The Essential Asia Series. Bloomington: Indiana University Press, 1993.

Day, Richard H., and Inderjit Singh. *Economic Development as an Adaptive Process: The Green Revolution in the Indian Punjab*. New York: Cambridge University Press, 1977.

Dhar, Pannanlal N. *Preventive Detention under Indian Constitution*. New Delhi: Deep and Deep, 1986.

Echeverri-Gent, John. *The State and The Poor: Public Policy and Political Development in India and the United States*. Berkeley: University of California Press, 1993.

Feroz, Ahmad, *Ethnicity and Politics in Pakistan. Oxford* University Press, 1998.

Frankel, Francine R. *India's Political Economy*. Delhi: Oxford University Press, 2006.

Franda, Marcus F. *The Death of Ziaur Rahman*. (American Universities Field Staff, Fieldstaff Reports, South Asia Series, 1982/2.) Hanover, New Hampshire: AUFS, 1982.

Ghosh, Sucheta. *The Role of India in the Emergence of Bangladesh*. Calcutta: Minerva Associates, 1983.

Ghosh, S. K. *Women and Crime*. New Delhi: Ashish, 1993.

Graham, B. D. *Hindu Nationalism and Indian Politics: The Origins and Development of the Bharatiya Jana Sangh*. Cambridge: Cambridge University Press, 1990.

Hachten, William A. *The Growth of Media in the Third World*. Ames: Iowa State University Press, 1993.

Hafiz, M. Abdul, and Abdur Rab Khan, eds. *Nation Building in Bangladesh: Retrospect and Prospect*. Dhaka: Bangladesh Institute of International and Strategic Studies, 1986.

Hammond, Thomas T. *Red Flag over Afghanistan: The Communist Coup, the Soviet Invasion, and the Consequences*. Boulder: Westview Press, 1984.

Hardgrave, Robert L. Jr., and Stanley A.Kochanek. *India: Government and Politics in a Developing Nation*. Fort Worth: Harcourt Brace Jovanovich, 1993.

Harrison, Selig S. *In Afghanistan's Shadow: Baluch Nationalism and Soviet Temptations*. Washington: Carnegie Endowment for International Peace, 1980.

Hasan, Mubashir. *The Mirage of Power: An Inquiry into the Bhutto years,* 1971-77. Oxford University Press, 2002.

Haqqani, Husain. *Pakistan: Between Mosque And Military*. Washington DC: Carnegie Endowment for International Peace, 2005.

Heginbotham, Stanley J. "Sri Lanka's Gamble for Ethnic Peace." (Library of Congress, Congressional Research Service, Major Issues System, IB87183.) January 22, 1988.

Hossain, Mahabub. *Credit for Alleviation of Rural Poverty: The Grameen Bank in Bangladesh.* (Research Report, No. 65.) Washington: International Food Policy Research Institute in collaboration with Bangladesh Institute of Development Studies, February 1988.

Hyman, Anthony. *Afghanistan Under Soviet Domination, 1964-81*. New York: St. Martin's Press, 1982.

Hyman, Anthony. *Pakistan: Toward a Modern Muslim State*. (Conflict Studies Series, No 227.) London: Research Institute for the Study of Conflict and Terrorism, 1990.

Iqbal, Muhammed. *The Reconstruction of Religious Thought in Islam.* London: Oxford University Press, 1934.

Jagmohan. *My Frozen Turbulence in Kashmir*. New Delhi: Allied, 1991.

Jain, C. K., ed. *Rajiv Gandhi and Parliament*. New Delhi: CBS, 1992.

James, Morrice. *Pakistan Chronicle. Oxford* University Press, 1993.

Jansen, Eirik G. *Rural Bangladesh: Competition for Scarce Resources.* Oslo: Norwegian University Press, 1986.

Jiggins, Janice. *Caste and Family in the Politics of the Sinhalese, 1947-1976*. Cambridge: Cambridge University Press, 1979.

Khan, M. R. *Some Population Characteristics and Fertility Differentials in Four Microregions of Bangladesh.* (Research Report, No. 43.) Dhaka: Population Division, Bangladesh Institute of Development Studies, 1985.

Khan, Mohammad Asghar. *Generals in Politics: Pakistan, 1958-1982.* New Delhi: Vikas, 1983.

Khan, Mohammad Asghar, ed. *Islam, Politics, and the State*. London: Zed Books, 1985.

Khan, Mohammad Ayub. *Friends Not Masters: A Political Autobiography*. New York: Oxford University Press, 1967.

Khan, Zillur Rahman. *Leadership Crisis in Bangladesh: Martial Law to Martial Law*. Dhaka: University Press, 1984.

Kochanek, Stanley A. *The Congress Party of India*. Princeton: Princeton University Press, 1968.

Kohli Atul, ed. *India's Democracy: An Analysis of Changing State-Society Relations.* Princeton: Princeton University Press, 1988.

Kothari, Rajni. *State Against Democracy: In Search of Humane Governance.* Delhi: Ajanta, 1988.

Lamitare, Devi Bhakat. *Murder of Democracy in Himalayan Kingdom.* New Delhi: Amarko, 1978.

LaPorte, Jr., Robert. *Power and Privilege: Influence and Decision-Making in Pakistan.* Berkeley: University of California Press, 1975.

Limaye, Madhu. *Janata Party Experiment.* Delhi: B.R. Publishing, 1994.

Maheshwari, Shriram. *The Mandal Commission and Mandalisation: A Critique.* New Delhi: Concept, 1991.

Mallick, Ross. *Indian Communism: Opposition, Collaboration, and Institutionalization.* Delhi: Oxford University Press, 1994.

Mehrotra. N. C. *The Socialist Movement in India.* New Delhi: Radiant, 1995.

Mitra Subrata K., and James Chiriyankandath, eds. *Electoral Politics in India: A Changing Landscape.* New Delhi: Segment, 1992.

Mizanur, Rahman Shelly. *Chinese Attitudes Towards Bangladesh.* Dhaka: Study Group, 1981.

Mukherjee, Bimal Chandra. *Administration in Changing India.* New Delhi: Blaze, 1994.

Nadkarni, M. V. *Farmers' Movement in India.* Ahmedabad: Allied, 1987.

Nayak, Pandav. *Pakistan, Political Economy of a Developing State.* New Delhi: Patriot Publishers, 1988.

Nayar, Kuldip, and Kushwant Singh. *Tragedy of Punjab: Operation Bluestar and After.* New Delhi: Vision Books, 1984

Nossiter, T. J. *Marxist State Governments in India.* London: Pinter, 1988.

Oberst, Robert. *Legislators and Representation in Sri Lanka: The Decentralization of Development Planning.* (Westview Special Studies on South and Southeast Asia.) Boulder, Colorado: Westview Press, 1985.

Parmanand. *The Nepali Congress since Its Inception: A Critical Assessment.* Delhi: B.R. Publishing, 1982.

Rahman, Atiur. *Rural Power Structure: A Study of the Local Level Leaders in Bangladesh.* Dhaka: Bangladesh Books International, 1981.

Rahman, Syed Tayyebur. *Global Geo-Strategy of Bangladesh, OIC, and Islamic Ummah.* Dhaka: Islamic Foundation of Bangladesh, 1985.

Rudolph, Lloyd I., and Susanne Hoeber Rudolph. *In Pursuit of Lakshmi: The Political Economy of the Indian State.* Chicago: University of Chicago Press, 1987.

Rudolph, Lloyd I., and Susanne Hoeber Rudolph. *The Modernity of Tradition: Political Development in India.* Chicago: University of Chicago Press, 1967.

Schaffer, Teresita C. *Profile of Women in Bangladesh.* Dhaka: United States Agency for International Development, 1986.

Sen Gupta, Bhabani. *Communism in Indian Politics.* New York: Columbia University Press, 1972.

Singh, Prakash. *The Naxalite Movement in India.* New Delhi: Rupa, 1995.

Singhal, Arvind, and Everett M. Rogers. *India's Information Revolution.* Newbury Park, California: Sage, 1989.

Sisson, Richard, and Ramashray Roy, eds. *Diversity and Dominance in Indian Politics.* New Delhi: Sage, 1990.

Smith, Chris. *The Diffusion of Small Arms and Light Weapons in Pakistan and Northern India.* London: Center for Defence Studies, 1994.

Sobhan, Rehman. *The Crisis of External Dependence: The Political Economy of Foreign Aid to Bangladesh.* London: Zed Books, 1984.

Symonds, Richard. *The Making of Pakistan.* London: Faber, 1950.

Srinivasan T. N., and P.K Bardhan, eds. *Rural Poverty in South Asia.* New York: Columbia University Press, 1988.

Tambiah, Stanley Jeyaraja. *Sri Lanka: Ethnic Fratricide and the Dismantling of Democracy.* Chicago: University of Chicago Press, 1986.

Tewary, I. N. *People, Panchayat, and Parliament.* New Delhi: Print Media, 1994.

Thakur, Ramesh Chandra. *Government and Politics of India.* New York: St. Martin's Press, 1995.

Tully, Mark, and Satish Jacob. *Amritsar: Mrs. Gandhi's Last Battle.* London: Cape, 1985.

Varshney, Ashutosh. *Ethnic Conflict and Civic Life: Hindus and Muslims in India. New Haven:* Yale University Press, 2001.

Varshney, Ashutosh. *Democracy, Development, and the Countryside: Urban-Rural Struggles in India.* Cambridge: Cambridge University Press, 1995.

Weiss, Anita M., and Gilani, S. Zulfiqar. *Power and Civil Society in Pakistan.* Oxford University Press, 2001.

Who Are the Guilty? Report of a Joint Inquiry into the Causes and Impact of the Riots in Delhi from 31 October to 10 November. New Delhi: People's Union for Democratic Rights and People's Union for Civil Liberties, 1984.

Wilson, A. Jeyaratnam. *The Gaullist System in Asia: The Constitution of Sri Lanka, 1978.* London: Macmillan, 1980.

Ziring, Lawrence. *Pakistan: The Enigma of Political Development.* Folkestone, United Kingdom: Dawson, 1980.

Defense, Security, International Relations

Ahmar, Moonis. *Superpower Rivalry in the Indian Ocean since the Withdrawal of Great Britain.* Karachi: Area Study Centre for Europe, University of Karachi, 1986.

Akbar, Ahmed S. *Islam under Siege: Living Dangerously in a Post-Honor World,* Oxford, UK: Polity Press, 2003.

Ali, S. Mahmud. *The Fearful State: Power, People, and Internal War in South Asia.* London: Zed, 1993.

Augustus, Rayol J. *In Defense of My Country: Indo-U.S. Defense Technology Cooperation.* Boca Raton, FL: Universal, 1998.

Ayoob, Mohammed. *India and Southeast Asia: Indian Perceptions and Policies.* New York: Institute of Southeast Asian Studies; and Singapore: Routledge, 1990.

Banerjee, B. N. *Indian Ocean: A Whirlpool of Unrest.* New Delhi: Paribus, 1988.

Beazley, Kim C., and Clark, Ian. *The Politics of Intrusion: The Super Powers and the Indian Ocean.* Sydney: Alternative Publishing, 1979.

Bergen, Peter L. *Holy War Inc.: Inside the Secret World of Osama Bin Laden.* New York: The Free Press, 2001.

Bhasin, Vijay Kumar. *Super Power Rivalry in the Indian Ocean.* New Delhi: Chand, 1981.

Bokhari, Imtiaz H., and Thomas Perry Thornton. *The 1972 Simla Agreement: An Asymmetrical Negotiation.* Washington: Foreign Policy Institute, Johns Hopkins University, 1988.

Bose, Sumantra. *Kashmir: Roots of Conflict, Paths to Peace.* Cambridge, Massachusetts: Harvard University Press, 2003.

Brar, Bhupinder, ed. *Collapse of the Soviet Union: Lessons for India.* Delhi: Ajanta, 1993.

Brar, K. S. *Operation Blue Star: The True Story.* New Delhi: UBS, 1993.

Brines, Russell. *The Indo-Pakistani Conflict.* New York: Pall Mall, 1968.

Burke, S. M., and Lawrence Ziring. *Pakistan's Foreign Policy.* Karachi: Oxford University Press, 1990.

Buzan, Barry, and Gowher Rizvi. *South Asian Insecurity and the Great Powers.* New York: St. Martin's Press, 1986.

Cohen, Stephen P. *The Indian Army: It's Contribution to the Development of a Nation*, Los Angeles and Berkeley University of California Press, 1971.

Cohen, Stephen P. *The Pakistan Army.* Los Angeles and Berkeley: University of California Press, 1989.

Coll, Steve. *Ghost Wars: The Secret History of the CIA, Afghanistan, and Bin Laden, From the Soviet Invasion to September 10, 2001.* New York: Penguin, 2004.

Cordovez, Diego, and Selig Harrison. *Out of Afghanistan.* New York: Oxford University Press, 1995.

Damodaran, A. K., and U. S. Bajpai, eds. *Indian Foreign Policy: The Indira Gandhi Years.* New Delhi: Radiant, 1990.

Das, Rabindra K. *Nepal and Its Neighbors.* Banaras, India: Konark, 1986.

DeSilva, Kingsley. *India in Sri Lanka, 1983-1991.* Occasional Paper, No. 25. Washington: Asia Program, Woodrow Wilson Center, 1992.

Dutt, V. P. *India and the World.* New Delhi: Sanchar Publishing House, 1990.

Fay, Peter Ward. *The Forgotten Army: India's Armed Struggle for Independence, 1942-45.* Ann Arbor: University of Michigan Press, 1993.

Franda, Marcus F. *Bangladesh Nationalism and Ziaur Rahman's Presidency*, Part 1 & 2 (American University Field Staff, Fieldstaff Reports, South Asia Series, No. 7.) Hanover, New Hampshire, AUFS, 1981.

Ganguly, Sumit. *The Origins of War in South Asia: The Indo-Pakistani Conflicts since 1947.* 2d ed. Boulder, Colorado: Westview Press, 1994.

Ganguly, Sumit, and Andrew Scobell, eds. US-Indian Strategic Cooperation: An Elusive Partnership? (Asian Security Studies). Abington, Oxon: Routledge 2006.

Ghosh S. K., and Rustamji, K. F,eds. *Encyclopedia of Police in India.* (2 vols.) New Delhi: Ashish, 1993-94.

Gordon, Sandy. *India's Rise to Power in the Twentieth Century and Beyond.* New York: St. Martin's Press, 1995.

Grover, Verinder, ed. *International Relations and Foreign Policy of India*. 10 vols. New Delhi: Deep and Deep, 1992.

Gupta, Sisir. *Kashmir: A Study in India-Pakistan Relations*. Bombay: Asia Publishing House, 1966.

Harrison, Selig S., and K. Subrahmanyam, eds. *Superpower Rivalry in the Indian Ocean: Indian and American Perspectives*. London: Oxford University Press, 1989.

Hoffmann, Steven. *India and the China Crisis*. Berkeley: University of California Press, 1990.

Jha, Shankar Kumar. *Indo-Nepal Relations*. New Delhi: Archives Books, 1989.

Joshi, Manoj. *Combating Terrorism in Punjab*. Conflict Studies, No. 261. London: Research Institute for the Study of Conflict and Terrorism, May 1993.

Kadian, Rajesh. *India and Its Army*. New Delhi: Vision Books, 1990.

Kadian, Rajesh. *The Kashmir Tangle*. Boulder, Colorado: Westview Press, 1993.

Kapur, Harish. *India's Foreign Policy, 1947-92: Shadows and Substance*. New Delhi: Sage, 1994.

Karnad, Bharat, ed. *Future Imperilled: India's Security in the 1990s and Beyond*. New Delhi: Viking, 1994.

Khan, Fazal Muqeem. *The Story of the Pakistan Army*. Karachi: Oxford University Press, 1963.

Khan, Riaz Mohammed. *Untying the Afghan Knot: Negotiating the Soviet Withdrawal*. Durham: Duke University Press, 1991.

Knaus, John Kenneth. *Orphans of the Cold War: America and the Tibetan Struggle for Survival*. New York: Public Affairs, 1999.

Kolff, Dirk H. *Naukar, Rajput and Sepoy: The Ethnohistory of the Military Labour Market in Hindustan, 1450-1859*. Cambridge: Cambridge University Press, 1990.

Kukreja, Veena. *Civil-Military Relations in South Asia: Pakistan, Bangladesh, and India*. New Delhi: Sage, 1991.

Kux, Dennis. *India and the United States: Estranged Democracies*. Washington DC: National Defense University Press, 1993.

Kux, Dennis, *India-Pakistan Negotiations: Is Past Still Prologue?* Washington DC: USIP Press, 2006.

Kux, Dennis. *The United States and Pakistan, 1947-2000*. Washington DC: Woodrow Wilson Center Press, 2001.

Levy, Adrian, and Catherine Scott-Clark. *Deception: Pakistan, the United States and the Secret Trade in Nuclear Weapons: Pakistan's Nuclear Programmme*. New York: Walker, 2007.

Liu, Xuecheng. *The Sino-India Border Dispute and Sino-India Relations*. Lanham, Maryland: University Press of America, 1994.

Magnus, Ralph and Eden Naby. *Afghanistan Mullah, Marx and Mujahid*. Boulder: Westview Press, 1998.

Mansingh, Surjit. *India's Search for Power: Indira Gandhi's Foreign Policy, 1966-82*. New Delhi: Sage, 1984.

Maxwell, Neville. *India's China War*. New York: Doubleday, 1972.

Menon, Raja. *A Nuclear Strategy for India*. New Delhi: Sage Publications, 2000.

Moraes, Frank. *The Revolt in Tibet*. New York: Macmillan, 1960.

Mudiam, Prithvi Ram. *India and the Middle East*. London: British Academic Press, 1994.

Muni, S. D. *Foreign Policy of Nepal*. New Delhi: National, 1973.

Musharraf Pervez. *In the Line of Fire: A Memoir*. New York: Free Press, 2006.

Nadeem, Azhar Hasan. *The Punjab Police in a Comparative Perspective*. Lahore: Progressive Publishers, 1989. .

Nirmal, Anjali. *Role and Functioning of Central Police Organisations*. New Delhi: Uppal, 1992.

Onesto, Li. *Dispatches from the People's War in Nepal*. London: Pluto, 2004.

Palit, D. K. *War in the High Himalaya*. London: Hurst, 1991.

Perkovich, George. *India's Nuclear Bomb*. New York: Oxford University Press, 2000.

Pettigrew, Joyce J. M. *The Sikhs of the Punjab: Unheard Voices of State and Guerrilla Violence*. Atlantic Highlands, New Jersey: Zed, 1995.

Phadnis, Urmila, and Ela Dutt Luithui. *Maldives: Winds of Change in an Atoll State*. New Delhi: South Asian, 1985.

Phadnis, Urmila, S. D. Muni, and Kalim Bahadur, eds. *Domestic Conflicts in South Asia*. New Delhi: South Asian Publishers, 1986.

Pipes, Daniel, and Adam Garfinkle, eds., *Friendly Tyrants: An American Dilemma*. New York: St. Martin's Press, 1991.

Raja Mohan, C. *Crossing the Rubicon: The Shaping of India's Foreign Policy*. New Delhi: Viking, 2002.

Richardson, John. *Paradise Poisoned: Learning About Conflict, Terrorism and Development from Sri Lanka's Civil Wars*. Colombo, Sri Lanka: International Centre for Ethnic Studies, 2005.

Riza, Shaukat. *The Pakistan Army, 1: War 1965*. Lahore: Army Education Press, 1984.

Riza, Shaukat. *The Pakistan Army, 2: 1966-71*. Lahore: Services Book Club, 1990.

Rizvi, Hasan-Askari. *Internal Strife and External Intervention: India's Role in the Civil War in East Pakistan (Bangladesh)*. Lahore: Progressive, 1981.

Rizvi, Hasan-Askari. *Military, State and Society in Pakistan,* New York: St. Martin's Press, 2000.

Rose, Leo E., and Eric Gonsalves, eds. *Towards a New World Order: Adjusting India-U.S.. Relations*. Research Papers and Policy Studies, No. 38. Berkeley: Institute of East Asian Studies, University of California, 1992.

Ross Babbage, and Sandy Gordon, eds., *India's Strategic Future: Regional State or Global Power?* New York: St. Martin's Press, 1992.

Roy, Olivier. *Islam and Resistance in Afghanistan.* Cambridge: Cambridge University Press, 1986.

Rudolph, Lloyd I., and Susanne Hoeber Rudolph, eds. *The Regional Imperative: U.S. Foreign Policy Towards South Asian States*. New Delhi: Concept, 1980.

Rustomji, Nari. *Bhutan: The Dragon Kingdom in Crisis*. Delhi: Oxford University Press, 1978.

Rustomji, Nari. *Imperilled Frontiers: India's North-Eastern Borderlands*. New Delhi: Oxford University Press, 1983.

Sharma, Gautam, and K. S. Nagar, eds. *India's Northern Security: Including China, Nepal and Bhutan*. New Delhi: Reliance, 1986.

Sen, Lionel Protip. *Slender Was the Thread: Kashmir Confrontation, 1947-48.* Bombay: Orient Longman, 1969.

Singh, Jaswant. *Defending India*. New York: St. Martin's Press, 1999.

Sinha, P. B. *Armed Forces of Bangladesh.* (Occasional Papers, No. 1.) New Delhi: Institute for Defence Studies and Analyses, 1979.

Sisson, Richard, and Leo Rose. *War and Secession: Pakistan, India and the Creation of Bangladesh.* Berkeley: University of California Press, 1990.

Smith, Chris. *India's Ad Hoc Arsenal: Arms Procurement in Historical Perspective.* Oxford: Oxford University Press, 1994.

Spector, Leonard. *Nuclear Weapons and South Asian Security.* Washington: Carnegie Endowment for International Peace, 1988.

Talbott, Strobe. *Engaging India: Diplomacy, Democracy and the Bomb.* Washington DC: Brookings, 2004.

Tanham, George K. *Indian Strategic Thought: An Interpretive Essay.* Santa Monica, California: RAND, 1992.

Taylor, Jay. *The Dragon and the Wild Goose: China and India. With New Epilogue.* New York: Praeger, 1991.

Tetley, Brian. *Defenders of Pakistan.* Lahore: Ferozsons, 1988.

Tharoor, Shashi. *Reasons of State: Political Development and India's Foreign Policy under Indira Gandhi, 1966-1977.* New Delhi: Vikas, 1982.

Thomas, Raju G. C. *Democracy, Security, and Development in India.* New York: St. Martin's Press, 1996.

Thomas, Raju G. C. *Indian Security Policy.* Princeton: Princeton University Press, 1986.

Thomas, Raju G. C., ed. *Perspectives on Kashmir: The Roots of Conflict in South Asia.* Boulder, Colorado: Westview Press, 1992.

Thornton, Thomas P. *Pakistan: Internal Developments and theU.S. Interest.* Washington: Foreign Policy Institute, 1987.

Tirmazi, Syed A. I. *Profiles of Intelligence.* Lahore: Combined Printers, 1995.

Tiwari, Chitra K. *Security in South Asia: Internal and External Dimensions.* Lanham, Maryland: University Press of America, 1989.

Verma, Ravi. *India's Role in the Emergence of Contemporary Bhutan.* Delhi: Capital, 1988.

Yousaf, Mohammed, and Mark Adkin.. *The Bear Trap: Afghanistan's Untold Story.* London: Leo Cooper, 1992.

Appendix I

Major Political Parties and Regional Institutions in South Asia

Association of Southeast Asian Nations (Asean)

Founded in 1967 for the purpose of promoting regional stability, economic development, and cultural exchange between the countries of the region. ASEAN's membership includes Brunei, Indonesia, Malaysia, the Philippines, Singapore, Thailand, and Vietnam. India is a "dialogue partner" along with Austria, Canada, China, Japan, New Zealand, the Republic of Korea (South Korea), Russia, and the United States.

Awami League

Political party led by Sheikh Mujibur Rahman. Founded in 1949, it won absolute majority in putative Pakistan Constituent Assembly in 1970, an event leading to the 1971 civil war and Bangladesh independence.

Bangladesh National Party

Political party founded by General Ziaur Rahman (Zia) in 1978. It was the majority party during Zia's presidency.

Bharatiya Janata Party (BJP)

Major political party in India. The party was founded as the Jan Sangh in 1952. It was revived as the BJP in 1980. The BJP briefly came to power in May 1996 as the single largest party in the Lok Sabha. The party emphasized nationalism, revivalist Hinduism, less state control over the economy, a hard line against Pakistan, and closer ties with the United States. In March 1998, a BJP-led coalition was re-elected. On May 11, 1998 India tested three nuclear devises followed by two more a couple of days later. The BJP also made a conscious effort to develop cordial ties with the United States. The nuclear tests were a temporary set back to those efforts. The party was defeated in the general elections of 2004.

Jatiyo Party

Political party established by General Hussain Muhammed Ershad in 1985. The party won parliamentary majorities in the 1986 and 1988 elections.

Liberation Tigers of Tamil Eelam (LTTE or Tamil Tigers).

The organization has a military and a political wing . It was founded in 1975 by Velupillai Prabhakaran. The Tigers are the largest, the best known, the most ruthless, and best equipped of any of the numerous Sri Lankan secessionist organizations and parties. The LTTE fought the Indian Peace Keeping Force (IPKF) to a stalemate (1987-90). It also carried out numerous high profile assassinations using suicide bombers. Among the victims were the former Indian Prime Minister RAJIV GANDHI (1991) and the Sri Lankan President Ranasinghe Premadasa (1993). The United States declared it as a Foreign Terrorist Organization (FTO) in 1997. Numerous ceasefires and agreements with various governments have not led to lasting peace or to a mutually satisfactory political solution of the Tamil secessionist movement on the island. Despite splits, internecine bloody conflicts, and the fascist character of the organization, it remains a potent and cohesive force. Though the LTTE also has a political wing, it has not formally created a political party. Instead, in the 2004 parliamentary elections, it openly supported the TAMIL NATIONAL ALLIANCE, which won over 90% of votes in Jaffna, in the Northern Province, once again underscoring the public support and acclaim that the Tigers enjoy among the Tamils of Jaffna

Muslim League

The All India Muslim League was founded in 1906 in Dacca (Dhaka), in what then was the province of Eastern Bengal and Assam. The inaugural session was attended by Muslim representatives from throughout India and Burma as a counterpoise to the Indian National Congress. After the creation of Pakistan, its relevance and party base withered. As early as September 1947, Mohammed Ali Jinnah resigned from the presidentship of the party. Since 1962 it was revived under various names as the Pakistan Muslim League (PML). During the February 2008 elections five different Pakistan Muslim Leagues were in the fray. The one led by former prime minister Nawaz Sharif, the PML (N) was the second largest party in the National Assembly following the February 2008 elections. The Musharraf backed PML (Q) finished a distant third.

The All India Muslim League is active in Kerala and has formed coalition governments with other parties. In 1976 the Muslim League was revived in Bangladesh.

Pakistan Peoples Party (PPP)

Founded in 1967 by Zulfikar Ali Bhutto in Lahore. The party is ideologically socialistic and secular. It was headed by his daughter, Benazir till her assassination in December 2007. Subsequently, it is cochaired by her son, Bilawal Bhutto Zardari and her husband, Asif Ali Zardari. The party was in power in Pakistan in 1972-77, 1988-90, and 1993-96. It emerged as the largest single party in the February 2008 general elections and formed a coalition government in Islamabad.

South Asian Association for Regional Cooperation (SAARC)

The association comprises of the seven nations of South Asia: Bangladesh, Bhutan, India, Maldives, Nepal, Pakistan, and Sri Lanka. SAARC was founded at a meeting of foreign ministers in New Delhi on 1-2 August 1983. the inaugural meeting of the heads of state and governments was held in Dhaka on 7-8 December 1986. The stated mission of the Association is to promote economic, technical, and cultural cooperation and to provide the setting for the discussion of South Asian political issues in a multi-lateral regional forum.

Sri Lanka Freedom Party (SLFP)

Political party in the eponymous island. The party ruled from 1956-65, with a short hiatus in 1960, first under S.W.R.D. Bandaranaike and after his assassination in 1959, under his widow, Sirimavo, the world's first female chief executive in modern times. In 1970, Mrs. Bandaranaike again assumed the premiership. A year later, an insurrection by the Maoist "Janatha Vimukthi Peramuna" (JVP, or "People's Liberation Front") broke out. The SLFP government suppressed the revolt and declared a state of emergency that lasted 6 years. In 1972, SLFP introduced a new constitution, that changed the country's name from Ceylon to Sri Lanka, and declared it as a republic, with a weak president appointed by the prime minister. In a momentous policy decision, the new charter made the protection of Buddhism as a constitutional principle. The party's economic policies during this period were highly socialistic and included the nationalization of large tea and rubber plantations and other private industries. The economic paradigm shifted shortly but the Sinhala-Buddhist policy did not.

United National Party (UNP)

Sri Lankan political party. First ruled from 1948-56 under three Prime Ministers, D.S. Senanayake, his son Dudley, and Sir John Kotelawala. Dudley Senanayake and the UNP returned to power in 1965. The UNP, under J.R. Jayewardene, was back in office in 1977 and introduced sweeping changes in the country. The new government opened the economy and, in 1978, introduced a new constitution based on the French model with a strong executive president. Jayewardene was then elected as an executive president by Parliament in 1978 and by nationwide elections in 1982.

Appendix II

Systems of Governance in South Asia

In AFGHANISTAN, after decades of turmoil and changing political systems, the current constitution was adopted on 4 January 2004. It was largely based on the 1964 constitution. The monarchy was replaced by an executive presidency but most of the arrangements for the division of power between the executive and legislature remained unchanged. The parliament consisted of a 249 member Wolesi Jirga, or lower house, and an upper house, the Meshrano Jirga, with 102 seats. With the exception of the Taliban and Hizb-e-Islami (Khalis faction), all political parties and entities were allowed to participate in the process. However, the Single Non-Transferable Voting (SNTV) system meant that candidates were contested as individuals and not as members of a particular party. The SNTV also limited the level of electioneering or of the formation of coalitions by parties. Nevertheless, the legislature was quite representative of the established leadership in the country and the sectarian, ethnic, and gender based segments of society. This was reflected in the number of warlords, Mujahideen commanders, religious and factional leaders, and some drug barons as members of the legislature. Most of them have floated a political organization or a party or two. Hence, there is a proliferation of parties in the country. The system of governance is still evolving in the country and has not come to grips with those who are excluded from the system, i.e., the Taliban and some major Pashtun factions.

In BANGLADESH the Parliament (Jatiya Sangsad) has 330 seats. Three hundred members are directly elected while thirty seats are reserved for women who are elected by the MPs. The tenure of the Parliament is five years. A caretaker government is supposed to run the country for three months prior to parliamentary elections. This unique arrangement is to ensure fair and fair elections. This arrangement may also be considered as an indictment of the parliamentary process for it reflects a lack of faith in the orderly transfer of power from a democratically defeated party to a freely elected winner with popular mandate garnered through the ballot box. These underlying insecurities, the suspicion that political parties committed to democracy are not willing or capable of conducting reasonably free and fair elections, and on the reliance on other institutions of state (the civil services, the armed forces, judiciary, etc.) all highlight the inherent weaknesses of the political system of parliamentary democracy in the country. Furthermore, the role of the Non- Governmental Organizations (NGOs) remains undefined in a country where political institutions possess limited legitimacy.

In 1972 when asked about the backwardness of his nation, the ruler, King Jigme Singye Wangchuck, the absolute monarch of the reclusive Himalayan Kingdom of Bhutan presented the concept of Gross National Happiness, as the guiding philosophy for the modernization of his country. About thirty years later, in 2003, the king initiated a draft constitution which was published in 2005 for the stepwise conversion of the government from an absolute monarchy to parliamentary democracy. In 2006 King Jigme abdicated in favor of his India and Oxford-educated son, the twenty-five year-old Jigme Khesar Namgyel Wangchuck. The latter presided over the notional transformation of the country's system of governance. After a practice election, voting was held for the twenty-five member National Council of Bhutan, the upper house of the new bicameral parliament in late 2007. Three months later, in March 2008, elections were held for the lower house. Only two parties, People's Democratic Party (PDP), headed by Sangay Nidup, the maternal uncle of the King, and the Druk Phuensum Tshogpa (DPT) led by Jigme Thinley, another relative of the royal family were allowed to compete. A third party, Bhutan People's United Party (BPUP) was disqualified by the Election Commission because it was out of tune with the "noble aspirations of the Constitution of Bhutan." Other parties were in exile and were therefore totally excluded from the elections. These included the ethnic Nepalese-dominated Bhutan State Congress (BSC), the militant Bhutan People's Party (BPP), the Bhutan National Democratic Party, the Druk National Congress, the Bhutan Gurkha National Liberation Front, the Bhutan Democratic Socialist Party, The Communist Party of Bhutan (Marxist-Leninist- Maoist), and the smaller ones like the People's Forum for Democratic Rights and the Students' Union of Bhutan. All 47 seats were won by the two royalist parties. Clearly, the new system of governance is still evolving

In 2008, THE UNION OF MYANMAR (BURMA) is governed by a military regime. The Head of State is also the Chairman of the State Peace and Development Council (SPDC) and Commander-in-Chief of the Defense Services. The majority of ministerial and cabinet posts are held by military officers, with the exception of Health, Education, Labor, and National Planning and Economic Development. These cabinet posts were held by civilian technocrats Since the announcement of the referendum in February 2008, the Burmese military government stepped up its repression,. The new draft constitution was the product of a fourteen year fourteen National Convention. Criticism of the National Convention was punishable by prison sentences of up to twenty years. Under the new constitution the military would control about twenty-five percent of the seats in parliaments the army chief of staff would exercise absolute power whenever he deemed that the nation faced a national emergency.

Having long ignored the machinations of the military rulers, the elected delegates in the 1990 People's Assembly election formed the National Coalition Government of the Union of Burma (NCGUB), a government-in-exile in the Washington DC suburb of Rockville, Maryland with the mission of restoring democracy. Dr. Sein Win, a first cousin of Aung San Suu Kyi, is the prime minister of the NCGUB since its inception. It comes closest to being a parliament but remains outlawed by the military government.

THE INDIAN PARLIAMENT consists of two houses - the Lok Sabha and the Rajya Sabha. The Lok Sabha is also known as the "House of the People" or the Lower House. Almost all of its members are directly elected by citizens of India. The Lok Sabha has greater powers than Rajya Sabha since it can precede or overrule the upper house in many matters. The Lok Sabha can have up to 552 members as envisaged in the Constitution of India (Article 81). It has a term of five years but may be dissolved earlier by the President of India if so advised by the prime minister. A maximum of 530 members from the States and another twenty members from Union Territories are directly elected by the people on the basis of universal adult suffrage. Every citizen over the age of eighteen years is eligible to vote. There are some reserved seats for members of Scheduled Castes and Scheduled Tribes.

Two members can be nominated by the President of India. The Rajya Sabha is also known as "Council of States" or the Upper House. Its members are indirectly elected by legislative bodies of the States. It has a total of 250 members and the chamber cannot be dissolved. Each MP has a term of six years and elections are held for one-third of the seats after every two years. Twelve members are nominated by the Indian President in recognition of their special knowledge or experience in the fields of literature, science, art or social services.

In THE MALDIVES, a new constitution was introduced in 1988. It replaced the old one created in 1968. Under the new constitution, a unicameral 50-members People's Assembly (Majlis) was to be elected for a five-year term. Two members from each of the provinces (atolls) and from Malé, the capital, were directly elected by the people. The remaining eight were appointed by the president. The head of state, the president of the country was to be elected by the Majlis and confirmed by a national referendum. In March 2006 The Maldivian government undertook to hold the first multi-party election in 2008. Such an election was duly held in October 2008 and Maldivians went to vote in large numbers that the long lines at some polling centers obligated them to stay open for up to twelve hours longer than planned. The incumbent President Maumoon Abdul Gayoom led the first round poll with forty percent of the landmark vote, but still short of the 50 percent needed to avoid a run-off. Hence, he had to face a run off with second-place finisher Mohamed Nasheed who had secured twenty-five percent of the votes. In the run of poll Nasheed surprised Gayoom by being elected.

NEPAL, under the 1990 Constitution, had a two chamber Parliament (Sensed). The House of Representatives (Pratinidhi Sabha) had 205 members elected for five year term from single-seat constituencies. The House of the States (Rashtriya Sabha) had 60 members, thirty-five elected by the Pratinidhi Sabha, fifteen were representatives of Regional Development Areas and ten were appointed by the king. The Parliament was dissolved by King Gyanendra in 2002, for failing to quell the Maoist insurgency in the country. The subsequent direct rule by the king, too, failed perhaps because India forsook him and took an active part in brokering the peace process by persuading autonomy-minded southerners in the Terai region not to reject or derail the elections for a proposed Constituent Assembly. In April 2008 nearly 65 percent of the country's voters exercised their franchise.

The Maoists, though without an absolute majority, were the clear winners. The monarchy was abolished in June 2008. The deposed king was not exiled, imprisoned, or murdered. As an interim arrangement, he was quietly allowed to shift to the summer palace, which was among the royal residences that were already nationalized. The Maoists also moderated the hard-line communist rhetoric of old. Another South Asian country is evolving towards its own form of democratic governance.

PAKISTAN'S 1973 Constitution created a parliamentary system with the president as head of state and popularly elected prime minister as head of government. However, under the Eighth Amendment to the constitution (1988) the country acquired a semi-presidential system. Pakistan has a bicameral legislature that consists of the Senate (upper house) and the National Assembly (lower house). The President, the Senate and National Assembly make up the Majlis-i-Shoora (Council of Advisors). The country's president has the authority to dissolve (and thereby trigger new elections for) the National Assembly but not for the Senate. The political process was revived in February 2008. The major political parties reasserted their legitimacy at the polls by decisively defeating the military-backed party. In August 2008, the discredited for military dictator, President Musharraf resigned from office.

SRI LANKA acquired a presidential system of government under a new constitution introduced in 1978. The country has a 225-member unicameral legislature elected for a six year term by a combination of universal suffrage and proportional representation. A total of 196 members are elected from twenty-five multi-member Electoral Districts. The remaining twenty-nine are from the National List consisting of political parties and independent groups in proportion to their share of the national vote. The president has the power to summon, suspend, or end a legislative session and to dissolve Parliament.

Appendix III

Significant Economic Entities and Terms

Asian Development Bank (ADB)

Established in 1966, the bank is owned by 63 member countries, most of whom are from within the region. Headquartered in Manila, the Philippines, the ADB has a prescribed capital of $23 billion. Japan and the United States are the largest stock-holders in the bank, each owning sixteen percent of the shares. The overarching goal of the Bank was to reduce poverty in the Asia and Pacific region by providing loans, grants, and technical assistance. Accordingly, all South Asian countries have benefited from the loans from this multilateral development finance institution. The bank has offices in most of the borrowing countries in the Asia and Pacific region as well as in Frankfurt, Tokyo, and Washington, DC. As the focus of ADB is the reduction of poverty, it emphasizes the promotion of pro-poor, sustainable economic growth, social development, and good governance. While doing so, the bank also concentrates on the protection of the environment, promotion of gender equality, the development of the private sector in member countries, and on regional cooperation. During the past few years disaster relief has become an unexpectedly major part of the bank's activities. In 2006, it was a bird flu epidemic, in 2005, an earthquake in the Indo-Pakistan region, and the Tsunami in 2004. In the same vein the bank has paid special attention to a country ravaged by thirty years of disaster: Afghanistan. It provided up to $500 million in highly concessional loans and grants over the first three years of the Afghanistan Interim Administration.

Exclusive Economic Zone (EEZ)

A wide belt of sea and seabed adjacent to the national boundaries where the littoral state claims preferential fishing rights and control over the exploitation of mineral and other natural resources. Most South Asian states, like many others across the world, claim 200 nautical miles. The overlap of boundaries with neighboring states sometimes prevents the EEZs to be claimed to the full limit.

Food and Agriculture Organization (FAO)

A United Nations specialized agency established in 1945 to raise living standards and increase the availability of agricultural products.

GROSS DOMESTIC PRODUCT (GDP)

It is a measurement of the value of domestic goods and services produced by an economy over a period of one year. Only output values of goods for final consumption and investment are calculated because the values of primary and intermediate production are assumed to be included in final prices. GDP is sometimes aggregated and shown at market prices, thereby implying that indirect taxes and subsidies are included; when these have been eliminated, the result is GDP at factor cost. The word gross indicates that deductions for depreciation of physical assets have not been made.

Gross National Product (GNP)

It is the computation of GDP plus net income or loss from transactions with other countries. It can be calculated at market prices, which include indirect taxes and subsidies. Because indirect taxes and subsidies are only transfer payments, GNP is often calculated at factor cost by removing indirect taxes and subsidies.

International Monetary Fund (IMF)

Established along with the World Bank in 1945, the IMF is a specialized agency affiliated with the UN. The IMF is responsible for stabilizing international exchange rates and loans to its member countries, when they encounter difficulty in managing their balance of payments. The loans may carry oppressive conditions requiring significant internal economic adjustments by the recipient nations, especially those in the developing world.

London Club

An informal group of commercial banks that collectively negotiate the rescheduling of debt with a particular country. The group has two committees, an economics committee that develops economic data projections and a self-explanatory negotiating committee. Committee members are usually drawn from the five principal banks that hold the largest amounts of a particular country's debt.

Paris Club

Formed in October 1962, it is the informal name of a consortium of creditor countries (Belgium, Britain, Canada, France, Germany, Italy, Japan, the Netherlands, Sweden, Switzerland, and the United States) that have made loans or guaranteed export credits to developing nations. The organization has no formal or institutional existence. Its secretariat is run by the French treasury. The group meets in Paris to discuss the borrower's ability to repay debts. Accordingly, it works closely with the International Monetary Fund to which all of its members, except Switzerland, belong. The club also maintains close ties with the World Bank and the United Nations Conference on Trade and Development (UNCTAD). The Paris Club is also known as the Group of Ten (G-10).

United States Export-Import Bank (Eximbank)

An independent corporate agency of the U.S. Government. It was founded in 1934 to stimulate foreign trade during the Great Depression. The Eximbank facilitates export financing of American goods and services by neutralizing the effect of export credit subsidies given by other governments and by absorbing reasonable credit risks that are beyond the reach of the private sector.

World Bank

The informal name used for four affiliated international institutions: the International Bank for Reconstruction and Development (IBRD), the International Development Association (IDA), the International Finance Corporation (IFC), and the Multilateral Investment Guarantee Agency (MIGA). The IBRD, launched in 1945, primarily provides loans at market-related rates of interest to developing countries. The IDA, a separate loan fund but administered by the staff of the IBRD, was set up in 1960 to furnish credits to the poorest of countries on much easier terms than the conventional IBRD loans. The IFC, founded in 1956, supplements the activities of the IBRD through loans and assistance intended to encourage the growth of productive private enterprises in the lesser developed countries. The president and certain officers of the IBRD hold similar positions in the IFC. MIGA, established in 1988, provides insurance for private foreign investments in developing countries against various noncommercial risks. All four institutions are owned by the governments that subscribe capital to the World Bank group. To participate in the World Bank group, member states must first belong to the International Monetary Fund.

Glossary

AFGHANI: Afghanistan's monetary unit.

AMIR: Former title of rulers (kings) of Afghanistan

BANGLA: Official language of Bangladesh; often referred to as Bengali before 1971 in United Pakistan. In India the language is known as Bengali.

CALIPHATE: (Arabic, "Khalifa") Political leadership of the Muslim community based on the concept that the head of state (caliph) is the successor to the Prophet Mohammed's political authority. The caliphate is not a nationalistic state or a state just for Muslims. Citizenship in Islam is based on someone permanently living within the territories of the Islamic State regardless of their ethnicity. According to Sunnis the Caliph should be elected by Muslims, whereas, Shias accept only an imam who is a direct descendent from the family of the prophet ("Ahl al-Bayt").

CRORE: A unit of measure (1crore=10 million).

DEVANAGARI: (Literally, "The script of the city of the gods.") It is the script used in the written forms of Hindi, Marathi, Nepali, Sanskrit, and in some forms of Konkani. A number of other Indian scripts are closely related. Tamil is a notable exception, though like most dynamic languages it too has incorporated some of the script from Devanagari.

DISTRICT: The major administrative subdivision in British India.

DZONG: Bhutanese combined administrative and religious complex; a fortified monastery and often the seat of government for the local jurisdiction.

EAST BENGAL. East or East Wing of Pakistan. (15 August 1947- 16 December 1971): The region seceded in 1971 to become Bangladesh.

EELAM: Also called Ilankai. It is the Tamil name for the island of Sri Lanka.

HADITH: (Arabic, "Tradition"): The tradition codified and based on the precedent of the Prophet Muhammad's actions and sayings that serve as one of the sources of Islamic law.

IMAM: Generally means the leader of congregational prayers, implying no ordination or special spiritual powers beyond sufficient education to carry out this function. The word is also used by most Sunnis to mean the leader of the Islamic community. Among Shia Muslims, it indicates a descendant of the House of Ali and is considered as God's designated repository of the spiritual authority inherent in that line. The identity of this individual and the means of ascertaining his identity have been the major issues causing divisions among the Shias.

JIHAD: The struggle to establish the law of God on earth, often misinterpreted to simply mean as "holy war."

LAKH: A unit of measure equal to 100,000.

MUHAJIR: Immigrant or descendant of immigrants from India who left for Pakistan after partition in 1947. Such immigrants were called Biharis in East Pakistan (Bangladesh). The concept has great religious and cultural significance in Islam as the Prophet Mohammed was himself a muhajir when he fled from Mecca to Medina in AD 632.

MUJAHIDEEN (SING. MUJAHID). Warriors for jihad (*see above*). During 1979-96 it was commonly used to denote Afghan freedom fighters.

NGULTRUM: Bhutan's unit of currency adopted in 1974. Large ngultrum amounts are counted using the Sanskrit terms, lakh (100,000) and crore (10 million). The term is derived from the Dzongkha, ngul, meaning silver. In 1957, Bhutan followed India by decimalizing its currency.

PAKHTUNS: The term used for speakers of Pakhtu or Pashtu, who are frequently called Pathans or Pashtuns.

PAKHTUNWALI: Tenets of the Pakhtun code of honor.

RUPEE (Re; plural: Rs): The basic unit of currency consisting of 100 paise (sing. Paisa) used in most countries of the Indian subcontinent. The Nepalese rupee is linked to its Indian counterpart and is fully convertible though restrictions were imposed during the 1989-90 trade and transit dispute between the two countries. The Mauritian (MauR) and the Seychelle rupee (SRe) contain 100 cents instead of paise and the rufiyaa (Rf), of the Maldives consists of 100 laari.

SHARIA: Islamic law. The law is based on the Holy Quran and the Sunna (Arabic, "custom") and its interpretations by early leading Muslim jurists. There are four major Sunni schools (of which the Hanafi is dominant one in Pakistan) and one main Shia school (Jafariya).

SHIA: Also called Shiite. The term is derived from *Shiat Ali* (the Party of Ali). It is the smaller of the two great divisions of Islam. An estimated fifteen percent of the global Muslim population is Shia. India, Iran and Pakistan are home to most of the Shias on the planet. Shias support claims of Imam Ali and his descendents as the holders of the caliphate. Most Shias revere twelve imams, the last of whom is believed to be hidden from view.

SINHALAS: The largest ethnic group in Sri Lanka. It is predominantly distinguished by language from other communities on the island. In 1981, the Sinhalese constituted about 74 percent of the country's population. Over 90 percent of them are Theravada Buddhists. Their ancestors probably migrated from northern India around 500 B.C.

SUFI: The etymology of the term is unclear. Generally, the term is considered to be derived the Arabic word for wool, *suf*. Some Greco-Roman scholars trace it to be a derivation of Sophie, the universal divine spark that embodies wisdom. The Arabic etymology is more widely accepted because most sufis wore a plain woolen robe, as a symbol of dedicating oneself to a life of mysticism. Sufis seeking a mystical union with God were condemned by some Sunni legal schools.

SUNNI: The term has its origins in *sunna* meaning "custom," thereby conveying both orthodoxy and accepted tradition. Sunnis form the larger (about 85 percent) of the two great divisions of Islam. Sunnis supported the traditional method of election to the caliphate and accepted the Umayyad line. On this issue, the Sunnis split from the Shias in the great schism within Islam.

TAKA: Bangladesh's unit of currency adopted in 1971. It is supposedly derived from *tonka*, the Iranian coinage used during the Delhi

Sultanate. There are a number of alternative explanations as well. One taka consists of hundred paise.

THERAVADA BUDDHISM: Literally, the Buddhism that is "the way" or the "doctrine of the elders." The two predominantly Buddhist countries in South Asia, Sri Lanka and Burma (Myanmar), follow the Theravada school of Buddhism. This tradition, also known as *Hinayana* (Lesser Vehicle), preserves the clear understanding that the Buddha was a man who achieved enlightenment. Some of his accomplished followers became monks and further propagated his teachings. This is in contrast to the *Mahayana* (greater vehicle) Buddhism, which frequently projected the Buddha as a superhuman being capable of performing miracles. In addition, the *Mahayana* school is filled with a pantheon of enlightened figures (bodhisattvas) who help others achieve enlightenment. Unlike *Mahayana*, Theravada Buddhism has no central religious authority.

ULAMA: A man trained in Islamic theology.

ZAKAT: Islamic system of social welfare based on an alms tax of 2.5 percent on wealth held for more than a year. The Holy Quran states that this sum should be given to the poor, the needy, workers who collect Zakat, new converts to Islam, to free the enslaved, to those burdened by sudden expenses, and to traveling foreigners.

Index

9/11, 21, 29, 30, 38, 45, 53, 77, 95, 109, 115, 125, 138, 141, 146, 152, 156, 158, 161, 163, 172, 192, 194, 196, 199, 209, 220, 223, 248, 259, 260, 265, 267, 274
11 September 2001, *see* 9/11

Acheson-Lilienthal Report, 117
Adam, William, 19
Afghan Physicians Association of America (APAA), 88
Afghanistan-U.S. Relations, 19
Aids/HIV in South Asia, 23
Al-Qaeda, 22, 27, 44, 45, 109, 146, 191, 195, 223, 248, 249, 250, 267, 278, 283
Al-Wahhab, Mohammad ibn Abd, 29
Al-Zawahiri, Ayman, 28, 109
Ambedkar, Bhim Rao, 30
American Association of Physicians of Indian Origin (AAPI), 88
Amin, Hafizullah, 30, 223
Anand, Gujarat, 91, 150
Anti-Soviet Resistance Groups of Afghanistan, 31
Arab-Afghans, 28, 33
Asian-American Hotel Owners Association (AAHOA), 34, 35
Association of Physicians of Pakistani Descent in North America (APPNA), 88
Atoms for Peace Program, 81, 118
Australia Group (AG), 76

Bagram, 36, 77
Bains, Didar Singh, 36
Ballistic Missile Defense (BMD), 275
Baltimore Clipper, 37
Bamiyan Buddhas, 247
Bangalore, 55, 56, 91, 126, 224, 230, 244
Bangladesh Medical Association of North America (BMANA), 88
Bangladesh-U.S. Relations, 37
Beg, General Mirza Aslam, 41
Besant, Annie, 165, 252
Bhattarai, Baburam, 38, 61, 204
Bhopal Gas Leak, 39
Bhutto, Benazir, 40, 149, 173, 188, 226, 241, 247, 249, 251, 259, 284
Bhutto, Zulfikar Ali, 40, 42, 59, 91, 129, 134, 143, 144, 149, 194, 216, 233, 284, 287
Biden, Joseph, 196, 266, 286
Bin Laden, Osama, 21, 34, 44
Birendra, King, 60, 178
Bombing of U.S. Embassies in Tanzania and Kenya, 45
Bonn Agreement, 45, 46, 138, 151
Borlaug, Norman Ernest, 46
Bose, Amar Gopal, 46
Bowles, Chester, 47, 90, 255
Brahmo Somaj, 19, 72
British Raj, 48, 254
Brown Amendment, 205
Burma (Myanmar)-U.S. Relations, 48
Burmese Medical Association of North America (BMANA), 88
Burton, Danny Lee (Dan), 51
Bush, George Herbert Walker, 52, 99, 140, 141, 195, 205, 212

Bush, George Walker, 22, 26, 51, 52, 61, 67, 119, 120, 121, 125, 149, 167, 190, 196, 199, 220, 232, 234, 266, 267, 268, 275, 286
Business Process Outsourcing (BPO) and Information Technology (IT) in India, 54

California's Yuba City and Imperial Valley, 113
Carter, James (Jimmy) Earl, 21, 39, 59, 140, 180, 195, 199, 204, 219
Carter, Lillian, 167, 199
Casinos in South Asia, 61
Center for Afghanistan Studies (CAS), University of Nebraska at Omaha, 62, 161
Central Treaty Organization (CENTO), 63, 91, 194, 259
Cheney, Vice President Richard, 139
China, 15, 17, 32, 34, 37, 43, 47, 48, 49, 51, 52, 64, 76, 79, 81, 90, 91, 96, 112, 123, 124, 125, 134, 148, 166, 171, 178, 184, 185, 191, 193, 203, 212, 213, 219, 232, 234, 238, 250, 263, 264, 315, 326, 327, 328, 329, 330
China-Burma-India Theatre of Operations (CBI), 64
Choudhary, Chief Justice Iftikhar Muhammad, Pakistan, 228, 286
Clinton, Hillary Rodham, 186
Clinton, William Jefferson, 27, 38, 53, 87, 96, 124, 125, 130, 141, 165, 205, 220, 257, 275
Comprehensive Test Ban Treaty (CTBT), 275
Cooke, Hope, 67
Coomaraswamy, Ananda, 68
Cordovez, Diego, UN Special Representative, 103
Cornwallis, Lord Charles, 69
Correa, Charles, 70
Cotton, 70
Cray XMP-14 Super Computer, 103

Dabhol, 85, 87
Dall, Charles, 72
Daud, Sardar Muhammad, 31, 33, 72, 92, 163, 198, 201, 208, 259, 282, 283
Dauletabad Field, 187
Dayal, Lala Har, 109
Defense Related U.S. Export Controls, 74
Dostum, Abdul Rashid, 36, 77, 108, 109, 163, 176, 208
Dot Busters, 78
Dow Chemical, 40
Dulles, John Foster, 65, 79, 81, 122, 166, 183, 235
Durand Line, 20, 197, 198

Eisenhower, Dwight David, 20, 53, 73, 79, 81, 118, 122, 139, 183, 282
Eliot, Thomas Stearns, 81
Ellis and Angel Islands, 82
Emerson, Ralph Waldo, 82, 253
Energy Overview of South Asia, 83
Enron Power Plant, 85
Ensminger, Dr. Douglas N., 90
Ethnic Medical Associations in the United States, 88

F-16 Fighter Planes, 66, 205, 266
Federally Administered Tribal Areas (FATA), 172, 195, 251
Ford Foundation, 46, 90, 104, 117, 213, 216
Ford, Gerald Rudolph, 59, 91
Fulbright Program, 92

Galbraith, John Kenneth, 96, 139, 184

Gandhi, Indira Priyadarshini, née Nehru, 59, 60, 92, 97, 99, 102, 134, 148, 176, 178, 183, 203, 210, 211, 241
Gandhi, Mohandas Karamchand, 99, 100, 102, 121, 131, 147, 177, 186, 198, 220, 221, 231, 242, 253, 254
Gandhi, Rajiv, 102, 124, 178, 210, 211, 232
Gandhji and the Jewish Question, 100
Geneva Accords, 103
Grameen Bank, 279, 320
Green Revolution, 46, 104, 105, 124, 135, 203, 268
Guantanamo Bay, Cuba, 160
Gunboat Diplomacy, 124, 149, 183

Hammarskjöld, Dag, 270
Harlan, Josiah, 107
Hart-Cellar Act (1965), 113, 265
Harvard University, 19, 96, 117, 217, 224, 240, 243, 245, 297, 298, 306, 324
Hekmatyar, Gulbuddin, 32, 33, 108, 109, 249
Helmand Valley Development Project, 20
Hindustan Ghadr Party, 109, 113
Hyde, Henry J., U.S.-India Atomic Energy Act of 2006, 119

Ice, 111, 276
Immigration from South Asia, 111
Indian American Forum for Political Education (IAFPE), 115, 116
Indian Institutes of Management (IIM), 116, 117
Indian Institutes of Technology (IIT), 117
Indo-U.S. Nuclear Cooperation, 117
Indo-U.S. Relations, 122
Indus Waters Treaty, 128
International Traffic in Arms Regulations (ITAR), 74
Inter-Services Intelligence (ISI), 43, 128, 142, 156, 157, 188, 247

Jammu & Kashmir Issue in U.S. Policy, 53, 67, 125, 130, 171
Jinnah, Mohammed Ali, 42, 131
Johnson, Lyndon Baines, 133, 140, 169, 203
Jones, Norah, 135, 226
Joshi, Anandibai, 135
Judson, Adoniran, 136

Kahn, Louis Isadore, 137
Kansi, Mir Aimal, 137
Karen and Kachin Christians, 136
Kargil War (1999), 227, 275
Karzai, Hamid, 22, 78, 138, 206, 209, 267, 284
Kennedy, John Fitzgerald, 47, 133, 139, 183, 184, 199, 217, 233
Khalilzad, Zalmay, 140, 187
Khan, Abdul Quadeer, 141
Khan, Akhtar Rahman, 142
Khan, Yahya, 148, 183
Khan, Habibullah, 142
Khan, Liaquat Ali, 143
Khan, Mohammed Ayub, 133, 140, 142, 143, 174, 183, 194, 217, 233
Khan, Gulam Ishaq, 41, 226
Khartoum, Sudan, 27, 44
Khobar Barracks Bombing, 28
Khorana, Hargobind, 144
Khost, 145
Khyber Pass, 146
King, Martin Luther, Jr, 102, 147
Kipling, Rudyard, 107
Kissinger, Henry Alfred, born Heinz Alfred, 91, 92, 147, 233
Krishnamurti, Jiddu, 252
Kurien, Varghese, 150

Lahore University of Management Science (LUMS), 151
Ledo Road (later called the Stilwell Road), 48

Liberation Tigers of Tamil Eelam (LTTE), 236, 261, 267, 331
Loya Jirga, 138, 151, 223, 284
Luce-Celler Bill (1946), 221, 231, 265

Madrassas, 152, 250
Maktab al Khadamat (MAK, Office of Service), 44
Maldives-U.S. Relations, 161
Masih, Iqbal, 162
Massachusetts Institute of Technology (MIT), 47, 70, 117, 228, 230, 239
Massoud, Ahmad Shah, 33, 162, 238
Matteo, 163
Mayo, Katherine, 164, 221, 245
Mazar-e-Sharif, 77
Mazari, Abdul Ali, 32, 164
Meena, Keshwar Kamal, 32
Mehta, Ajai Singh, 164
Mehta, Zubin, 165
Menon, V. K. Krishna, 165
Midnight's Children (book), 214
Missile Technology Control Regime (MTCR), 76
Missionaries, 136, 166, 271
Mohammed, Khalid Shaikh, 278
Monsanto, 71
Montagu, Edwin, the Secretary of State for India, 11
Moran, Father Marshal, 168
Mother India (book), 164, 221, 245, 293
Moynihan, Daniel Patrick, 168, 184, 261
Mujahideen (Arabic Freedom Fighters), 31, 32, 33, 34, 44, 74, 103, 129, 138, 140, 142, 145, 146, 162, 169, 188, 238, 246, 288
Mules, 170
Musharraf, Pervez, 41, 67, 142, 158, 171, 195, 227, 234, 248, 250, 284, 285
Mutual Defense Agreement (MDA), 174

Najibullah, Mohammed, 77, 103, 138, 164, 175, 202, 208
Namgyal, Palden Thondup, Chogyal of Sikkim, 68
Nanautawi, Maulana Muhammad Qasim, Deoband, 154
Narain, Jaiprakash, 176
National League for Democracy (NLD), Burma, 49, 241
Nehru, Jawaharlal, 38, 79, 90, 94, 97, 123, 124, 128, 134, 139, 140, 143, 166, 176, 184, 198, 214, 254, 255, 261
Neo-Buddhists, 30
Nepal Civil War, 178
Nepal-U.S. Relations, 180
NGOs in Bangladesh, 182
Nixon, Richard Milhous, 91, 98, 135, 148, 168, 181, 183, 233
Nonalignment and Non-Aligned Movement (NAM), 178, 184, 219
Nuclear Non-Proliferation Treaty (NPT), 66, 76, 122, 185
Nuclear Proliferation Prevention Act (Glenn Amendment), 124
Nuclear Suppliers Group (NSG), 75

Obama, Barack Hussein, 186
Oil and Gas Pipelines, 187
Ojhri Camp Explosion, 188
Olcott, Colonel Henry, 236
Operation Enduring Freedom, 161, 195, 206, 250
Opium Production in South Asia, 189

Padma Vibushan, 97, 144
Pakistan-U.S. Relations, 194
Pandit, Vijayalaxmi, 90, 198
Paramhansa, Swami Ramakrishna, 244
Pashtunistan (or Pakhtunistan) Issue, 73, 196, 282

Peace Corps, 60, 167, 181, 199, 200
Pentagon, 7, 21, 29, 45, 196, 269, 270
People's Democratic Party of Afghanistan (PDPA), 201
PL 480 Food Aid, 124, 134, 169, 202, 219
Pokhran, 53
Poppy for Medicine Project, 192
Powell, Colin, 38, 53
Prachanda, *Nom de Guerre* used by Pushpa Kamal Dahal, 39, 60, 180, 203
Pressler Amendment, 195, 205
Provincial Reconstruction Teams (Afghanistan), 206

Qureshi, Moeenuddin Ahmed, 207
Qutb, Sayyid, 29

Rabbani, Burhanuddin, 32, 33, 74, 77, 108, 109, 164, 208, 249
Rai, Lala Lajpat, 209
Rao, P.V. Narasimha, 66, 209, 232
Rapti Valley Multi Purpose Project, 211
Reagan, Ronald Wilson, 98, 102, 124, 140, 146, 211, 245
Revolutionary Association of the Women of Afghanistan (RAWA), 32
ice, Condoleezza (Condi), 51, 53, 125, 141, 212
ockefeller Foundation, 46, 104, 213
oosevelt, Eleanor, 198, 214
oosevelt, Franklin Delano, 37, 96, 122, 213, 254
oy, Raja Rammohun, 19, 271
ushdie, Salman, 214

abu, 216
alam, Abdus, 216
Salinity Control and Reclamation Programme (SCARP), 217
Sanctions as a Stratagem in U.S. Foreign Policy, 217
Sanger, Margaret, 220
Saudi Arabia, 27, 29, 32, 34, 44, 142, 153, 159, 169, 173, 222, 227, 247, 252
Saund, Dalip Singh, 221
Saur Revolution, 31, 77, 222
Sayyaf, Abdul Rasool, 28, 33, 222
Scudder, John, 224
Sen, Amartya Kumar, 224
Sen, Keshub Chandra, 72
Shankar, Ravi, 135, 225, 226
Sharif, Mian Nawaz, 67, 171, 172, 173, 188, 226, 286
Shastri, Lal Bahadur, 97
Silicon Valley, 127, 228, 229
Simla Agreement, 40
Singh, Hajom Kissor, 72, 272
Singh, Jagjit (J. J.), 231
Singh, Jaswant-Strobe Talbott Talks, 53, 66, 125, 212
Singh, Manmohan, 53, 66, 119, 231
Sino-Pakistan-American Connection, 232
South East Asia Treaty Organization (SEATO), 91, 194, 234, 259
Spelling Bee Contests, 234
Sri Lanka Medical Association of America (SLAMA), 88
Sri Lanka-U.S. Relations, 235
Star Spangled Banner and India, 237
Stars and Stripes, 237
State Law and Order Restoration Council (SLORC), Burma, 49, 241, 242
Stinger Missile, 141, 237
Stokes, Samuel Evans Jr., 238
Stone, Edward Durrell, 239, 287
SubbaRow, Yella Pragada, 240
Subrahmanyan, Chandrasekhar, 240
Surat, 9, 237
Suu Kyi, Aung San, 49, 102, 241

Swami Vivekananda, 243

Tagore, Rabindranath, 224, 245
Tahir-Kheli, Shirin Raziuddin, 245
Talbott, Strobe-Jaswant Singh Talks, 53, 66, 125, 212
Taliban, 21, 22, 28, 29, 36, 45, 62, 77, 109, 123, 128, 138, 141, 146, 152, 153, 157, 158, 163, 164, 170, 172, 176, 187, 190, 196, 208, 223, 246, 247, 248, 249, 250, 251, 267, 273, 283
Taraki, Nur Mohammed, 201
Tarapore Nuclear Reactor, 59
Tata, Jamsetji Nusserwanji, 244, 249
Terrorism, the United States, and South Asia, 250
The Dalai Lama, 102, 180, 262
The Indus Entrepreneur (TiE), 230
The Wassenaar Arrangement, 75
Theosophical Society and Theosophists, 252
Thoreau, Henry David, 100, 253, 276
Truman, Harry S., 143, 198, 231, 254
Tsunami 2004, 256
Tuttle, Richard D., 61
Twain, Mark, 257

U. Thant, Maha Thray Sithu, 270
U.S. Central Intelligence Agency (CIA), 27, 49, 90, 91, 109, 129, 137, 138, 146, 152, 167, 171, 181, 259, 260, 261, 262, 263, 283
U.S. Covert Operations in South Asia, 259
U.S. Immigration Laws, 264
U.S. Military Aid in South Asia After 9/11, 265
U.S. Munitions List (USML), 74
U.S.-India Agricultural Knowledge Initiative on Agriculture, 268
U.S.S. Cole, American Warship, 45
U-2 Incident, 63, 233, 259
Union Carbide Corporation, 39
Unitarianism, 72, 271, 272
United States Education Foundation in India (USEFI), 94
United States Educational Foundation in Pakistan (USEFP), 95
United States Military Aid, Categories, 269
Unocal, 50, 62, 141, 187, 248, 272, 273

Vajpayee, Atal Bihari, 17, 66, 274
Vietnam War, 91, 146, 271

Wadhwa, Rakesh, 61
Walden Pond, 276
Watumull Foundation, 276
Whitman, Walt(er), 276
Wilson, Congressman Charles (Charlie), 146
Wilson's (President Woodrow) Fourteen Points Speech, 10
World Trade Center, New York City, 7, 21, 28, 29, 44, 45, 138, 278

Y2K Problem, 280
Yale, Elihu, 10, 278
Youssef, Ramzi, 138, 278
Yunus, Muhammad, 279

Zahir Shah, Mohammed, 73, 138, 139, 140, 282
Zardari, Asif Ali Khan, 41, 173, 174, 227, 284
Zia ul-Haq, Mohammed, 41, 129, 142, 146, 149, 152, 157, 158, 189, 226, 287